# SERIES ON

# ISSUES IN
## SECOND LANGUAGE
## RESEARCH

under the editorship of

## Stephen D. Krashen and Robin C. Scarcella

*ISSUES IN SECOND LANGUAGE RESEARCH* is a series of volumes dealing with empirical issues in second language acquisition research. Each volume gathers significant papers dealing with questions and hypotheses in areas central to second language theory and practice. Papers will be selected from the previously published professional literature as well as from current sources.

## OTHER BOOKS IN THIS SERIES

# SOCIOLINGUISTICS AND LANGUAGE ACQUISITION

**Nessa Wolfson**
University of Pennsylvania

**Elliot Judd**
University of Illinois

EDITORS

**NEWBURY HOUSE PUBLISHERS, Cambridge**
A division of Harper & Row, Publishers, Inc.
New York, Philadelphia, San Francisco, Washington
London, Mexico City, São Paulo, Singapore, Sydney

1983

Library of Congress Cataloging in Publication Data

Main entry under title:

Sociolinguistics and language acquisition.

(Issues in second language research)
Bibliography: p.
1. Sociolinguistics--Addresses, essays, lectures.
2. Language acquisition--Addresses, essays, lectures.
I. Wolfson, Nessa.  II. Judd, Elliot.  III. Series.
P40.S578    1983        401'.9        82-22538
ISBN 0-88377-269-8

NEWBURY HOUSE PUBLISHERS
A division of Harper & Row, Publishers, Inc.

Language Science
Language Teaching
Language Learning

CAMBRIDGE, MASSACHUSETTS

First printing: November 1983

Printed in the U.S.A.                                                5

TO
HARVEY M. WOLFSON
and
KATHRYN REYEN JUDD


For patience and fortitude

# ACKNOWLEDGMENTS

Permission to reproduce material from the following publication is gratefully acknowledged: Joan Rubin, "How to Tell When Someone is Saying 'No.'" *Topics in Culture Learning,* Volume 4, 1976. East-West Culture Learning Institute, Honolulu, Hawaii.

"Communicative Needs in Foreign Language Learning," by Jack C. Richards reproduced with permission from *English Language Teaching Journal* (April 1983) published by Oxford University Press and the British Council.

# CONTENTS

# FOREWORD

## Evelyn Hatch

Sociolinguistics has always been important to researchers and teachers of
TESOL. Discourse analysis, and in particular speech act analysis, has, however,
only recently become a part of this tradition. Because it is a fairly new research
area, there are many issues which need to be worked through and problems to be
solved.

The first issue to clarify is the unit of analysis, what it is that we are
examining when we talk about speech act and speech event research. Second,
we need to know what the important questions are that can be asked about
language learning and language teaching by researchers in this area. Third, we need
to know more about possible methods of data collection. And, fourth, we need to
work out convincing data analyses.

All these points have been discussed in the literature, but it would not be
true to say that there is unanimous agreement on any of them. The unit of analysis
question may be a good illustration with which to begin. Speech act theorists
have been concerned with identifying the functions of utterances—that is, what we
*do* with language. In the Searle and Austin tradition, there are a limited number of
major functions—commissives (promises to do something), expressives (statements
of feelings), representatives (statements which have verifiable truth value), and
declaratives (statements which change the real world on being uttered—e.g., "I
declare you guilty as charged"). Each of these major speech acts can be subdivided.
For example, commissives may be vows, pledges, promises, agreements, showing
a willingness, obligation, or only a proposal to act; representatives may be
assertions, and the speaker may show that the truth value is sure, probable,
possible, uncertain, or negative. Speakers may be convinced, doubtful, making a
conjecture, or hedging, or they may even disassociate themselves from the truth
value of the statement. An expressive may show one's (dis)approval, valuation,
state of (un)happiness, etc. A directive may be a permission, a recommendation, an
inciting, an invitation, an order, or a command. In some systems (cf. van Ek 1976
and Halliday 1973) this breakdown of major speech acts produces a long list of
language functions. In the van Ek system these are the functions of the threshold
actional-functional syllabus.

A variety of syntactic *forms* can serve one speech act *function*. For example,
a directive can be a question (can we have quiet?), an embedded imperative (would
you please be quiet), an imperative (be quiet!), a hint (sure is noisy in here), etc.,
and the choice of syntactic form will be determined in part by a variety of sociolinguistic factors (e.g., sex, age, status of recipient). On the other side, one syntactic
*form* can have a variety of *functions*. A statement such as "McDonald's just opened"

can serve as an invitation for an Egg McMuffin, an explanation for a traffic jam, or a counterassertion to "McDonald's is closed." The context in which the utterance is made determines the speech act function of the utterance and, along with other sociolinguistic variables, may determine its syntactic form.

In defining speech act functions, theorists have primarily cited single sentences. However, as Hymes (1974) notes, any speech act function may stretch out over several utterances. This makes it difficult for the researcher, who must decide just how large the speech act unit really is. For example, a complaint (an expressive speech act) may be a single utterance statement of disapproval—"I don't like all this noise"—with an expectation that a remedy will be forthcoming. However, the complaint unit may have a beginning, an opening (excuse me, hello, I'm your next door neighbor), the statement of the problem (your stereo is really bothering me, the noise is getting to me), a justification (I'm having trouble sleeping, I have to get up early in the morning), and a suggested remedy (could you turn it down a little, how about considering your neighbors). It may even contain a threat if the remedy isn't followed (if you don't, I'm gonna call the cops), and it usually ends with a closing (thanks a lot, sorry to have bothered you). In a more formal complaint, such as student complaints regarding their perception of teachers and final grades which have to be mediated by some higher authority, the complaint may become a mediated hearing, lasting hours and resembling a total court proceeding. If the researcher has selected the complaint as the area to be researched, how much is to be included in the analysis? Should the unit be a single utterance of disapproval, a short stretch of complaint discourse, or an entire complaint hearing?

Another example may make this three-way distinction clearer. In a classroom, a teacher may give a simple directive, such as "solve problem 32." This would be a directive speech act utterance. On the other hand, it might include the interaction between teacher and students as they negotiate the directive prior to arriving at the solution to the problem. In fact, the total class period may be devoted to defining the task. In this case the directive and its execution (or perhaps only its negotiation of there wasn't time to solve the problem) takes up the entire classroom discourse speech event.

In the literature, we have identified these three levels, for want of better terms, as a *speech act* (single utterance functions), a *small speech event* (a single function with a set structure beyond that of the single utterance), and a *large speech event* (a trial, a conversation, a lecture, etc.). The *small* speech events, then, include such things as arguments, invitations and responses, complaints and the negotiated remedy, apologies and their (non)acceptance, compliments and their (non)acceptance, short narratives, jokes, and requests and responses. These small speech events fit within the *larger* speech event of the conversation (or, in the case of written material, within the text). Since some small speech events, such as service encounters, occur in isolation (that is, they make up the whole exchange), the dividing line between speech events and small speech events is not a very clear one. The line between speech act and the small speech event has also not been clear. Olshtain and Cohen, in this volume, offer the term "speech act set" as a replacement for the term "small speech event." This would leave the term "speech event" for the larger speech event unit of analysis. At first glance, this concern with terminology may seem trivial. But it is important, for it sets the defining lines for the units of our analyses. The size of the unit selected by the researcher will depend on the research goals, the questions being asked.

Many claims have been made about the universality of speech acts and speech events. In line with such claims regarding speech acts, Cook (1981b) showed that students do analyze utterances in terms of their function rather than by form. That is, they could differentiate between the directive and representative function of simple statements. On the other hand, Wolfson (1970) has shown that ESL students have a great deal of difficulty in identifying the intent of ambiguous invitations (let's get together sometime soon), whether they are directives or expressive speech acts with a friendship bonding function.

If you look back through the subdivision of each speech act and consider your ESL students, you can probably think of many examples of failure and success in their interpretation and performance of speech acts. Many of the problems probably have to do with the directness or indirectness of the speech act. Tannen (1978), for example, has remarked that her perception of indirectness in a second language (Greek) was different from that of her native-speaker hosts. While chatting, she mentioned that she associated Greece with grapes and was surprised at not having seen any since she came to Greece. She also mentioned that Americans have a special way of fixing eggs, scrambling them. These utterances, meant as polite conversation topics, were taken as directives by her hosts, and she was faced with scrambled eggs and grapes for breakfast from then on. Unfortunately, neither was one of her favorite dishes.

The strength, directness, clarity, and nonambiguous nature of the form of each of the speech acts may make them more or less transparent for the learner. In terms of markedness theory, the most common, most neutral forms of each speech act should be the easiest for learners to acquire. Johnston (1973) makes an observation that supports this notion. Acquiring French in an immersion situation (working in a camp), Johnston noted that she always had to use the most direct statement to give people information. For example, noticing that the pails were missing from an upstairs bathroom, she had no way of knowing whether this information was important or any way of notifying her superiors except in the most direct way. In English, she would have dropped a hint in some subordinate clause and left it to the listener to decide whether the information was crucial or not. This led to her supervisor asking her why she was telling her such nonsense. The problem for the learner is knowing what is nonsense and, when not knowing, how to drop the information unobtrusively into a conversation in an indirect way.

If learners truly learn only the most unmarked, neutral forms for such functions, we should not be overly surprised at Scarcella's findings that foreign students had very high error percentages in terms of the actual language used in carrying out a variety of idiomatic, stereotyped speech acts. In responses to her

Verbal Routines Test (1979), the ESL students (both beginners and university ESL students) made large numbers of errors on such familiar expressions as "shut up, watch out, hurry up, bless you, happy birthday, come on in, time's up." Their errors included (1) paraphrases ("Who's behind the door? " for "Who's there? " "Be in a hurry to be in class on time" for "Hurry up! "), (2) incompletely learned formulas ("Watch up!" for "Watch out!"), (3) translations ("silence" from "silencio" for "be quiet" or "shut up!" and "congratulations" from "Felicidades!" for "Happy Birthday"), and (4) substitutions ("welcome" for "bless you!") which might be overgeneralization of known common formulas or simple guessing.

It may also be the case that second language learners learn only the most polite forms even though polite forms may not necessarily be the least marked. Learners know they must choose language appropriate to a wide range of socio-linguistic variables. By choosing only the form they judge to be most polite, learners may feel they won't make any great social blunders. However, they may be wrong, for rules for changing speech when addressing speakers of differing status (i.e., age, sex, role, and power) are also likely to differ across languages. This formality may easily be misinterpreted as hostility or "distancing" where that was not the learner's intent. In cases where such politeness may seem offensive, where sociolinguistic rules are imperfectly learned, Ervin-Tripp (1972) suggests the utility of retaining an accent. If mistakes are made, it is, she says, better to be designated as a foreigner than to risk insulting or offending listeners. When foreign students come to this country, the frequency weight of informal, colloquial forms begins to break through this politeness register. When this happens, collocations of extremely polite and friendly, informal forms occur. What could be a more inappropriate combination than Scarcella's (1979) examples of "Hello, my teacher" or "Hi, sir" or Ervin-Tripp's hypothetical example, "How's it going, Your Eminence?"

The intent of all these examples is to show that while speech acts may be universal, the range of ways of expressing each differs from language to language and is sensitive to sociolinguistic variables. While second language learners may have directives, commissives, representatives, expressives, and declaratives which are sensitive to sociolinguistic variables in their first languages, it is unlikely that these speech acts are carried out in the same way in the second language.

In the research on small speech *events,* there is evidence that second language learners have difficulty in working through the negotiation involved in each. For example, asking for information calls for more than a question. A few moments ago, a student wandered down the hall and asked the professor in the next office:

Student:     Excuse me.
Professor:   Mmhmm?
Student:     Can you tell me if there's a telephone in these offices?
Professor:   At the end of the corridor.
Student:     Oh, okay, thank you.

In contrast, children in countries around the world seem to try out their English by asking:

Child: What is your name?
E: Evelyn, What's yours?
Child: What time is it now?
E: Five o'clock. What's your name?
Child: (laughs and retreats to friends)

Negotiation of the exchange is necessary. The negotiation must follow the social rules of the small speech event it if is done appropriately.

Learners have many problems in negotiating small speech events, frequently transferring the social rules of the first language to English. Among many examples, Wolfson (1981) cites some exchanges where direct translation is apparent. For example, two Iranian friends transferred compliments as follows:

S: Your shoes are very nice.
A: It is your eyes which can see them which are nice.

And an Iranian boy said to his mother:

S: It was delicious, Mon. I hope your hands never have pain.
A: I'm glad you like it.

Following Wolfson, students in one of my classes collected compliment responses from foreign students and from native speakers. The task was for students to compliment five native speakers of American English and five foreign students on an article of apparel ("That's a nice NP"). While native speakers most frequently acknowledged the compliment with "thanks," they also followed with a bridge to a new topic (e.g., "I got it at Robinsons. I can't believe how expensive they are"). Japanese students were most likely to deny the positive evaluation (e.g., "Oh, no, it's nothing"), which resulted in the native speaker reinforcing the compliment ("no really, I like it a lot"). The need to reoffer the compliment and the lack of bridge led to uneasy continuation of these small speech events for complimenting.

Yet ESL learners do not always find speech acts/speech events difficult. For example, Cook (1981b) gave students a task of asking directions or requesting the time. Their data did not differ much from that of native speakers. They requested and thanked their informants for the information. The heavy use of modals did make the foreign speech seem more formal and polite than native speech. They also used idiosyncratic expressions such as "Thank you I very gratitude you" or "Be so kind of saying the shortest way to the bus station." Nevertheless, the overall structure of the information-seeking task was appropriately done, and the responses to sex and age differences in informants were similar to those of native speakers.

Let's turn now to the *large speech event* such as informal conversations, interviews, written discourse, or even classroom discourse. Overlaps in conversations are, for example, quite appropriate in some languages such as Farsi but are relatively rare in English. A transfer of this overlap strategy, then, to English brands Farsi speakers as being pushy, aggressive, or inconsiderate. On the other hand, long silences in conversations are not only tolerated but appreciated in many other language groups. Since this is one behavior which my immediate family has transferred from Danish, I find it difficult to be around people who talk all the time (by my perception). Undoubtedly, I am seen (by talkers) as morose, silent, and unfriendly. Most native speakers of English feel uncomfortable and rush in to fill the gap when silences longer than 0.3 second occur. Silences by conversational partners are often interpreted not only as unfriendly but as signals that the quiet person disapproves of what the talker has said. This puts talkers on the defensive, and they begin to repair previous utterances. A transfer of these differences in speech event pause length to the English language classroom can have disastrous results. Teachers frequently note that students from some language groups often "interrupt" in class while others not only do not interrupt but do not respond immediately when called upon. Answers to questions need not be given immediately in conversations in American Indian language groups. Children exhibiting such behavior are labeled "nonresponsive" and/or arrogant. Students who constantly interrupt are also seen as "troublemakers."

Scollon and Scollon (1980) have written about misperceptions of groups which can result from the transfer of first language speech event pause length conventions to English. Some of the differences which they summarized between Athabaskan and English speakers show that Athabaskans find it confusing that English speakers talk so much, ask too many questions, interrupt, and don't give others a chance to talk. They feel that English speakers are always getting excited when they talk, aren't careful when they talk about things or people, and even talk to strangers or people they don't know. They often talk about what's going to happen in the future; they think they can predict the future. On the other hand, English speakers find it confusing that Athabaskans avoid talking and only seem to talk to close acquaintances. They are seen as avoiding direct questions and as slow in taking a turn in talking. They are too direct and inexplicit, and their speech is very flat in tone. They deny planning for the future and never say anything about themselves. These differences in amount of talk, the use of language to plan future events, and the amount of silence or lack of silence desired must lead to much misunderstanding.

Other large speech events have also been investigated. The discourse structure of the classroom clearly differs across language/culture groups. Students bring with them expectations of what a language classroom should be like. This expectation is often at odds with the structure of American language classrooms. A great deal of work has also been done comparing written text in different language groups. Claims and counterclaims regarding students' apparent transfer of first language rhetorical style have been ongoing for years. Thus, even in large speech events, learners are likely to experience difficulty in acquiring the new system.

One could argue that none of this is new, that we have always been concerned with what were called cultural differences. Teachers in TESL training programs have written scores of papers pointing out misperceptions due to such differences, and writers have developed materials for the ESL classroom based on what the writer *thinks* native speakers do at each level. What is different is that the research now has a solid theoretical framework as its base. The research is, as you will see in the following papers, not only theoretically based but also empirical in nature. As you can see from my writing above, we all have our favorite anecdotes to give as examples of whatever speech act or speech event we wish to discuss. But the research shows us how unreliable our perceptions of what we do can be. The researcher insists on native speaker baseline data, data collected in a systematic way. The data from second language learners are then compared with what native speakers actually do, not what we think they do.

The data for this research have been collected in a variety of ways. Most researchers are not satisfied with single methods. Natural data are extremely difficult to obtain given present requirements on prior informed consent for audio recording. So, other techniques have often been devised. The use of questionnaires of various types has been tried as one method. These include multiple-choice questions, such as:

Your professor has made statements with which you disagree. In order to express your disagreement, you would say:
(a)     Sir, what you say is a lie!
(b)     Are you truthful about what you said?
(c)     Interesting, but could you give me the source of those findings?
(d)     (I wouldn't say anything)

Another questionnaire format is the Likert scale, where students must rate how strongly they agree with a given statement (1 being not at all and 5 being very strongly):

As you leave a dinner party, your hostess says: "We must do this again sometime soon.", You should reply: 1 2 3 4 5 "Okay, how about next Friday? "

Completion questions are also frequently used:

A friend always asks to borrow money from you. He hasn't repaid you the $20 he borrowed last week but he has just said: "Oh, I forgot my wallet again. Could you lend me a couple of dollars for lunch? " You decide that now is the time to refuse, so you say:_____.

Such questionnaires allow the researcher to collect a large sample at one sitting. The primary disadvantage of multiple-choice and Likert formats is that the data are judgments of appropriateness of form (recognition of appropriate behavior) rather than production of that behavior. They are not necessarily what the learner *would* say in the given situation. Completion questionnaires give the learner a chance to say what he *thinks* he would (or should) say, again not necessarily what would be said in natural performance data.

The wide variety of role-play methods used in research have served to bridge the gulf between questionnaires and natural data. The first role-play type still allows for a large sample to be drawn, since it can be carried out in a language laboratory. Situations are recorded on audiotape and played for the learner. The learner then responds to the taped voice, and that response is the recorded data. This method yields production rather than recognition data, and the speed factor makes it more likely that the response is a natural one (as compared with a completion questionnaire). A second role-play method is that where students hear a taped situation while viewing pictures or slides of the situation and person to whom they must respond. This procedure allows the researcher to test for differences due to the sex and age of the interlocutor. Taped information without this picture prompting will not work as well in eliciting differences in responses to sociolinguistic variables. Another possibility is the use of puppets as interlocutors. Puppets can portray status characteristics (age, sex, role, etc.) which the experimenter may not possess. The technique reportedly works well with children. Another type of role play is to have the learners read or hear the situation and then respond orally directly to the experimenter. Finally, full role play with or without preparation time has been used. The actors may be all learners or learners and native speakers (depending on the research questions being asked).

Natural data, of course, are somewhat more difficult to obtain, but it's not impossible. Some functions are easy to collect. For example, introductions occur at parties, at first gatherings of groups, and more formally, prior to a speaker's taking over the platform at conferences. They even appear in written form in the beginning of many magazines which give information on their contributors. There are many opportunities for natural data collection across a range of formal to informal situations, and the effects of the sociolinguistic variables of status are easily observed. First language researchers have also been able to study such speech acts/events as directives, question asking, warnings, and problem solving events in the classroom. For example, directives can be collected from children who have been given the job of "being teacher," instructing others on various tasks. Warnings can be elicited by telling children about to use some piece of equipment not to use it because it's broken and then giving them the job of keeping other children from using it. The literature on the acquisition of speech acts by young children abounds with interesting procedures for data elicitation.

In the classroom, tape recorders are everywhere. It's a bit more difficult to use them unobtrusively elsewhere. Logging very short stretches of natural data is possible. Ervin-Tripp (1977), for example, had her students collect directives in a wide variety of natural sitations using a logging technique. It has also worked well, as can be seen on Wolfson's work on compliments, for other speech acts.

Some researchers run tape recorders constantly at home and in their offices. The problem of prior informed consent, however, militates against this practice.

Natural data can be critical in some research—for example, the description of conversational speech events. It may be possible in other cases to use multiple measures. If data collected via questionnaires can be validated by natural data, large samples can also validate small samples of natural data. The more methods used, the better. Hopefully the results will be similar (or differences can be logically explained).

The major questions asked in the research to date are straightforward: Can the units (the structure of the unit, the syntactic forms of utterances in the unit, and the variation in form due to sociolinguistic variables) be described for various languages? Are the units universal (the structure of the unit, the syntactic forms, etc.)? Can performance of learners (both first and second language learners) on these units be described? If so, are there differences in native speaker and second language learner data? If differences occur, how can the differences best be accounted for (e.g., first language transfer/interference, markedness theory, social sensitivity linked with developmental factors)? A whole host of related questions can be asked regarding second language learners (e.g., do different learner types learn best using a small speech event learning strategy, is there an order of acquisition for various functions). However, such questions will have to wait for the future until evidence on the basic questions has been gathered.

While the basic questions are straightforward, the task of answering any of them is not. We have already seen that each of the six speech acts, examined in the light of empirical data, blossoms into a wide range of subdivisions. The syntactic forms used may vary as these subdivisions are softened or hedged, strengthened or aggravated in response to the status of the interlocutors and in response to the setting. The unit, too, may expand from a single utterance to a very large piece of discourse all of which must be systematically described. To do this for a wide variety of languages, then to draw contrasts across languages, to look at developmental data from first and second language learners, and then to account for it all is a monumental task.

The papers in this book address the questions of description of speech acts and speech events using data of native speaker and second language learners as evidence. Together with papers in Larsen-Freeman (1980), which look at large speech events, this book offers the first collection of empirical research in the field. As the research accumulates and as the many methodological problems of data gathering and analysis are solved, teachers and theorists both should learn a great deal more about "how we do things with words."

## REFERENCES

Austin, J. L. 1962. *How to Do Things with Words.* Cambridge, Mass.: Harvard University Press.

Cook, V. 1981a. "Some uses for second language research." Paper presented at New York Academy of Science Conference on Native Language and Foreign Language Acquisition, New York.

Cook, V. 1981b. "Language functions in second language learning and teaching." Paper presented at AILA, Lund, Sweden.

Ervin-Tripp, S. 1972. On sociolinguistic rules: alternation and co-occurrence. In J. Gumperz and D. Hymes (eds.), *Directions in Sociolinguistics*. New York: Holt, Rinehart & Winston.

Ervin-Tripp, S. 1977. "Wait for me, roller skate! " In S. Ervin-Tripp and C. Mitchell-Kernan (eds.) *Child Discourse*. New York: Academic Press.

Halliday, M.A.K. 1970. "Language structure and language function." In J. Lyons (ed.), *New Horizons in Linguistics*. London: Penguin.

Halliday, M.A.K. 1973. *Explorations in the Functions of Language*. London: Edward Arnold.

Hymes, D. 1974. *Foundations in Sociolinguistics*. Philadelphia: University of Pennsylvania Press.

Johnston, M. V. 1973. "Observations on learning French by immersion." Psycholinguistics paper, UCLA. Abstracted in E. Hatch (ed.). *Second Language Acquisition*. Rowley, Mass.: Newbury House.

Larsen-Freeman, D. 1980. *Discourse Analysis in Second Language Research*. Rowley, Mass.: Newbury House.

Scarcella, R. 1979. "Watch up! prefabricated routines in adult second language performance." *Working Papers on Bilingualism*. 19: 79-88. Toronto, OISE.

Scarcella, R. 1979. "On speaking politely in a second language." In C. Yorio, K. Perkins, and J. Schachter (eds.), *On TESOL '79*. Washington, D.C.: TESOL, 275-287.

Scollon, R., and S. Scollon. 1980. Athabaskan-English Interethnic Communication. ms.

Searle, J.R. 1969. *Speech Acts: An Essay in the Philosophy of Language*. Cambridge: Cambridge University Press.

Tannen, D. 1978. "Ethnicity as conversational style." Paper presented at American Anthropological Association, Los Angeles, November.

van Ek, J. 1976. *The Threshold Level for Modern Language Teaching in Schools*. London: Longman.

Wolfson, N. 1979. " 'Let's have lunch together sometime': perceptions of insincerity." Paper presented at TESOL, Boston.

Wolfson, N. 1981. "Compliments in cross-cultural perspective." *TESOL Quarterly,* 15: 2, 117-124.

# PREFACE

*Sociolinguistics and Language Acquisition* is designed to meet a need in two disciplines: sociolinguistics and applied linguistics. In fact, the origins of this book stem from the authors' observations that there was little available scholarship for those interested in applied linguistics from a sociolinguistic perspective. We first met on a plane returning from the 1978 TESOL Convention in Mexico City and began to voice this concern to each other. The following year, at the Boston Convention, we began to talk seriously about planning a colloquium on sociolinguistics and TESOL and started to contact others who might share these interests. The first Colloquium on Sociolinguistics and TESOL was held in San Francisco in 1980. That colloquium provided an opportunity for those of us with similar interests to meet and to listen to papers dealing with sociolinguistics and applied linguistics. We then decided to make the colloquium an annual event and held the second one at TESOL Detroit in 1981 and the third at TESOL Honolulu in 1982. We have every expectation of continuing the colloquium at future TESOL conventions. These colloquia have shown us that many in TESOL and applied linguistics believe that a sociolinguistic perspective can lead to significant insights in investigations of second language acquisition and second language teaching.

Several of the papers in this text—those by Leslie Beebe and Jane Zuengler; Christopher Candlin, Hywel Coleman, and Jill Burton; Christin Carpenter; Richard Day; Lynne D'Amico-Reisner; Robin Scarcella; Richard Schmidt; and Nessa Wolfson—were presentations given at the Detroit Colloquium on Sociolinguistics and TESOL and revised for inclusion in this anthology. Elite Olshtain, Andrew Cohen, Elliot Judd, Teresa Pica, Jack Richards, and Joan Rubin have also delivered papers at and participated in the various TESOL colloquia, but their papers included here have never been presented at these forums. Finally, we asked Evelyn Hatch to author the foreword to the text and Shoshana Blum-Kulka, Joan Manes, and Lisa Huber (a joint author with Lynne D'Amico-Reisner and Nessa Wolfson) to allow us to print their works in this book. Thus, while the Colloquium on Sociolinguistics and TESOL has been the central source for the papers in this collection, it has also served as a catalyst for other pieces of writing on subjects related to sociolinguistics and applied linguistics.

Our aim in this text is twofold. The first is to share with a wider audience some works which discuss the interrelationships between sociolinguistics and second language acquisition and teaching. The papers we have included are quite diverse in the topics studied, the research methods employed, and the findings discussed. However, each author shares our belief that sociolinguistics has an important role to play in second language acquisition and teaching. Second, we see this text as a beginning. We hope that the papers here will spur others to investigate second language acquisition and teaching from a sociolinguistic perspective and continue along the lines that we have started.

We are also aware that sociolinguistics has other contributions to offer to TESOL and applied linguistics—e.g., in the areas of language policy and planning, languages in contact, translations, cross-cultural investigations, and dialectal issues. We felt that our efforts here should be directed at exploring just one area, with the hope that others will pursue some of the topics just mentioned.

In closing, we would like to thank Michael Long for providing valuable comments on two of the papers in this text. We further express our gratitude to Linda Sperry and Marsha Yorinks for their help in compiling the final bibliography. Lastly, we thank our families, colleagues, and students, who have provided us with encouragement, support, and patience when we most needed their help.

ELJ
NW
Chicago, September 1982

# SOCIOLINGUISTICS
## AND
# LANGUAGE ACQUISITION

# I

# PATTERNS AND RULES OF SPEAKING

# INTRODUCTION

## Nessa Wolfson
### University of Pennsylvania

An important aspect of sociolinguistic research is the descriptive analysis of the conventions, patterns, and constraints which together comprise native speakers' knowledge of what constitutes appropriate speech behavior in the speech communities of which they are members. From the point of view of language teaching and learning, it is crucial to recognize that rules for the appropriate conduct of speech vary considerably from one society to another. This means that although second language learners have communicative competence in their native language(s), there is no reason to assume that they will be able to translate this ability into successful interactions with native speakers of the target language community.

The first three articles in this part address the issue of the nonuniversality of rules of speaking. Rubin, in her description of the difficulties involved in recognizing denials and refusals in situations where one is a foreigner, demonstrates that such a seemingly superficial speech act as saying "no" may be extremely difficult for the nonnative speaker to interpret. Forms which appear to be readily translatable from one language to another are found to serve different, and sometimes opposite, functions. In response to an offer, an English speaker may accept with a "thank you," while to French speakers, the equivalent form functions as a polite refusal. Such comparisons of form and function across cultures do not, as Rubin points out, begin to capture the complexity of rules for appropriate usage. The competent speaker needs to know not only the meanings or functions of the various forms but also which ones are appropriate to use in which speech situations. Indeed, if nonnative speakers are to be able to interpret what is said with any accuracy, it is necessary for them to understand the cultural values which underlie speech.

As a result of their ongoing work on apologies, Olshtain and Cohen suggest that speech acts be studied as sets of formulas which perform the same function. Noting that the speech act of apologizing may be performed by the use of any one of several possible formulas, they offer the term speech act set to refer to the entire category. Differential preference for one form over another will, they suggest, be related to such features of the speech setting as the gravity of the offense and the relative status of the participants. Formulas may of course occur in combination with one another. Interest in cross-cultural differences and in discovering what it is that nonnative speakers must know in order to communicate effectively in the target language led Olshtain and Cohen to the empirical study of native speaker norms as a basis of comparison. Since norms as to what behavior calls for an apology differ greatly from one society to another, it is obviously not enough for nonnative speakers to learn the formulas or routines for apologizing in the target language. They must also learn which formulas are appropriate to which situations. In order to discover how and to what extent first language norms interfere with second language performance, Olshtain and Cohen studied not only native responses in both Hebrew and English but also nonnative speaker responses of native Hebrew speakers in English and native English speakers in Hebrew.

In addition, Olshtain and Cohen review a number of studies in which the same basic design was followed as in their own research. That is, subjects were given a series of written situations and asked to respond to them by role playing. The situations are carefully contrived to tease out variables related to severity of the offense being apologized for and the social status of the offended party. Findings reveal considerable regularity in choice of form by native speakers of each group. Deviation from native speaker norms, however, seemed to depend not only on negative transfer but on degree of linguistic proficiency of the nonnative speaker and interestingly enough, on "preconceived notions of the target sociocultural rules relating to the particular speech act." That is, language learners from some cultures seemed to recognize and be willing to adapt to perceived rule differences, while those from others rejected the notion of sociolinguistic relativity and insisted that appropriate speech behavior was not negotiable. The finding that some cultural groups are more prone than others to equate speech behavior with character is interesting in itself, since it touches on the question of whether and to what extent communicative competence can be taught.

With respect to universals, Olshtain and Cohen find that they exist only at a very general functional level while the actual realizations of speech acts are strongly conditioned by culture-specific rules. For this reason, materials developers are advised to base their work on the findings produced by empirical research into sociolinguistic rules.

If Rubin's and Olshtain and Cohen's papers point strongly to the nonuniversality of speech act rules, it is the basic thesis of Blum-Kulka's paper to demonstrate that speech act strategies are not universal. Indeed, it is seen as a serious weakness of earlier work that some scholars claimed to have worked out universals by basing their analyses on their intuitions as native speakers of English. Focusing on the perspective of second language learning, Blum-Kulka points out that the issue of universality is crucial to what is considered to be the task of the language learner. She argues that precisely because there is great variation among languages, second language learners often fail not only to choose an appropriate form but to get their meanings across at all.

Citing the results of a study designed to compare the speech act performance of nonnative speakers (English speakers learning Hebrew) with that of native speakers of both English and Hebrew, Blum-Kulka amply demonstrates her point. Even where languages share request strategies (imperatives, in this case), they are found to have "different illocutionary force potential."

A very interesting conclusion which Blum-Kulka draws from her study is that second language learners "seem to develop an interlanguage of speech act performance" which differs from both first and second language native usage. Transfer of rules from native to target language results in violations of norms of appropriateness. On the basis of the differences found to exist between speech act strategies employed by native speakers of Hebrew and English, Blum-Kulka suggests that a nonuniversalistic approach to the analysis of sociolinguistic behavior is by far more realistic.

Knowledge of appropriate sociolinguistic behavior is crucial to successful interaction, and language learners are in need of as much information of this kind as possible. Even teachers and materials writers who are themselves native speakers of the students' target language are not necessarily able to describe the rules for appropriate speech behavior in their own societies. The problem is a complicated one, since it relates to the ability of participants to be objective about their own and others' behavior. The remaining articles in this part are descriptions of the sociolinguistic behavior of native speakers of English as they engage in a variety of speech events. All the research involved the observation and recording of naturally occurring speech behavior. From the findings reported here, we see that native speaker intuitions, while they are very useful in some respects, may also be seriously misleading.

In their work on dentist-patient communication, Candlin, Coleman, and Burton give evidence of the fact that participants' perceptions of what happens in a speech situation may be quite contrary to what actually does happen. Basing their analysis on 125 hours of observations of dentist-patient consultations, the authors show that dentists and patients have quite different expectations concerning the amounts and topics of the talk each will engage in. In analyzing their findings, they introduce the term discoursal set to refer to the interlocutor's sense of what is "expected and allowable behavior." The fact that dentists and patients have distinct discoursal sets, along with the fact that the dentist is, by virtue of his role, in control of the interaction, often leaves patients with a sense of frustration. Patients feel that they are not given adequate opportunity to express themselves on the topic relevant to the consultation. Since they expect the dentist to listen to their complaints, and dentists display a regular pattern in which they either ignore these or dismiss them as irrelevant, patients are left with doubts as to the effectiveness and appropriateness of the treatment. As Candlin et al. point out, it is of particular interest that patients, frustrated in their attempts to communicate their complaints, perceive themselves as not having been given an equal opportunity to talk at all. Objective analyses of tape-recorded consultations show that contrary to their perceptions of what takes place, patients actually do a considerable amount of talking.

The difference between perception and reality with regard to amount of talk may be seen as one which reaches into many areas of human interaction. Although we are not yet in a position to do more than speculate here, it may well be that much of the frustration and resentment which occurs in interactions between very different sets of interlocutors stems from a similar cause. Family members, for example, who are not given equal opportunity to talk about a specific topic may well perceive themselves as never having an equal opportunity to talk at all, even though an objective view of family interactions might well reveal that the reality was far different from the perception.

The study of dentist-patient interactions brings to light one example of the way adults in our society may, through the authority conferred by their professional role, control what other adults may say. The way in which language is used to exert power over others, especially in medical situations, is a provocative issue and one to which sociolinguistic research has a great deal to contribute. Since these patterns are likely to be rather different from one society to another, it would be useful for nonnative speakers to know what strategies native-speaking patients use in order to "seize" the opportunity to communicate their complaints.

Even in situations where professional status is not an intervening variable, interactions between adults often are a subtle struggle for power. Certainly adult-adult interactions are not always smooth. Indeed, it frequently happens that adults feel the need to communicate complaints or disapproval of one another. In her study of expressions of disapproval, D'Amico-Reisner examines just this phenomenon. Defined by contextual variables, the syntactic forms in which an expression of disapproval (EOD) occurs are a linguistic mechanism by which speakers of middle-class American English manipulate social behavior. To isolate the speech patterns that signal disapproval, naturalistic data were recorded and transcribed according to the function of the speech act in question. After the linguistic options were enumerated, they were analyzed with respect to contextual variables, framing devices, and intrautterance lexicon. This study of disapproval exchanges in naturally occurring speech shows discourse to be a complex, cooperative process between participants of a social interaction. Reflective of the weight of a violation, the way in which the relative status of the participants is defined, and the sociolinguistic setting, the unfolding of a disapproval exchange reveals a great deal about a speaker's rights, obligations, and expectations. It underscores the complexity of communicative competence and the importance of understanding not only the stylistic variation of single moves but the strategies used by speakers in complete exchanges where a message of disapproval is conveyed.

Studies of the ways in which people refuse and deny, apologize, complain, and express disapproval of one another give us insights into patterns of interaction and into the underlying cultural values which are thus expressed. Obviously, however, not all interactions between adults express negative evaluations. Indeed, as both Wolfson and Manes demonstrate in their work on compliments, Americans depend to a large extent on the expression of approval for the creation and maintenance of social relationships. From the point of view of materials developers, teachers, and second language learners themselves, it is useful to know that compliments are highly formulaic in nature. In analyzing a corpus of 686 compliments collected in a wide range of naturally occurring speech settings, it was found that almost all the data fell into a very small number of syntactic and semantic patterns.

As Wolfson points out, compliments as used by middle-class speakers of American English serve a wide variety of functions. They occur in conjunction with and even as substitutes for such other speech acts as thanks, greetings, apologies, and interestingly enough, criticism. Separating out compliments which have to do with appearance from those related to performance or ability, Wolfson shows that the relationship between interlocutors has a good deal to do with the type and topic of the compliment which may be offered. Age and status are important variables, as is sex of addressee.

Since compliments are, by their very nature, reflective of the value system of the speech community, a serious potential for communicative breakdown exists when second language learners are involved in such interactions. For this reason, it is strongly suggested that materials developers and teachers make use of the findings being reported.

With respect to the way in which cultural values are reflected by compliments, Manes gives an account of some of the most commonly expressed of these values. Newness, for example, is almost invariably noticed and commented upon in a complimentary way. The fact that members of our society are regularly given overt approval when they are seen to own something new has interesting implications. Little wonder that ours is a consumer society if newness is valued so highly. The fact that consumer spending is vital to our economy gains new meaning when we realize that we ourselves are constantly engaged in subtly encouraging one another to go out and buy.

As Manes points out, it is not only the compliments themselves but also responses to them which depend on the underlying cultural assumptions of the society for their force. Thus, in attempting to show modesty by downgrading or deflecting a compliment, speakers make use of the value system in interesting ways. Most speakers do not reject a compliment outright except to very close friends or family members. However, a man who is told that he has done an unusually good job will not usually accept all the praise for himself but will indicate that the job was made easy by the fact that he had good tools. Thus, the speaker is able to agree with the compliment while refusing credit for it. Similarly, a woman who is complimented on a new item of clothing may accept the compliment but refuse credit for it by saying that the belonging under consideration was a gift and therefore not the result of her own taste. If we consider that compliments are frequently given about objects which are new, expensive, or tasteful, it is very interesting to see that a favored technique in deflecting compliments is to deny not the value which has been expressed in the compliment, but one which has not. Thus, if the response to a compliment indicates that the addressee bought the object on sale, she is able to accept the compliment but at the same time downgrade the object of it by denying that it possesses another highly valued attribute, that of being costly. If an item is complimented for its beauty, the response can downgrade it by saying it is old, and so on down the line.

The ability to interpret, give, and respond to compliments appropriately in our society is a social skill which can add greatly to the language learner's opportunities to enter into friendly relationships with native speakers and incidentally gain needed practice in using the target language.

While it is true that giving compliments is one of the ways in which middle-class Americans open conversations, nonnative speakers desirous of social interaction with members of the target language speech community will need to know a great deal more if they are to be successful in making friends. One of the most obvious and yet elusive speech acts leading to the forming of social relationships with others is the invitation.

In their study of the way invitations work in middle-class American society, Wolfson, D'Amico-Reisner, and Huber show that such a seemingly simple speech act as that of inviting is open to serious misinterpretations on the part of both native speakers and language learners. Following on earlier work by Wolfson alone, invitations were collected through participant observation of everyday interaction among a great variety of native speakers. The data showed that invitations may be categorized as unambiguous or ambiguous. Unambiguous invitations required that a reference to time and/or mention of a place or activity be given as well as a request for a response. These clearly unambiguous invitations, however, were found to occur in only about one-third of the data, while all the rest contained negotiations. The start of the invitation negotiation is termed by the authors "the lead." This is a question or comment which cues the addressee to the fact that the speaker is interested in entering into a discussion about the possibility of a social commitment. The lead usually contains one of the properties of the unambiguous invitation, leaving the rest to be worked out during the negotiation if both parties are sufficiently interested in pursuing the matter. The lead itself is not, however, an invitation, and it is this which nonnative speakers find so difficult to deal with. Language learners must be shown how to identify leads as being distinct from full invitations, and how to encourage the speaker by entering into the sort of negotiation which has the potential of resulting in a firm social commitment.

Of the eight articles in Part I, then, the first three describe sociolinguistic findings in situations where speech communities using different languages are contrasted with one another. In addition to shedding light on the particular speech act upon which the study was focused, each paper provides strong evidence against a universalistic approach to the study of communicative competence. Having investigated the ways in which rules of speaking contrast from one society to another, these scholars make clear the need for further work to uncover the patterns and rules of different societies. Clearly, if the language teaching profession is to profit from sociolinguistic research, these differences must be recognized.

The five papers which make up the second half of Part I are all reports of sociolinguistic studies which took as their starting point the need to describe a single speech act or event in the context of its use within an English-speaking community. In each case, data were collected through careful observation and recording, and in each case the analysis revealed a strong regularity of pattern at all levels. Whether we examine dentist-patient interactions in which one party is attempting to communicate complaint while the other is dismissive of all such attempts, the ways adults express disapproval to one another or the ways in which they attempt to modify the behavior of interlocutors through the use of compliments, or the delicate and difficult art of negotiating for social commitments, it is apparent that sociolinguistic behavior is highly patterned and strongly reflective of the social structure of the society in which it occurs. Thus we see that the sort of insights we gain into native speaker behavior can greatly enrich our ability to help language learners to achieve the desired goal: communicative competence.

# 1

## HOW TO TELL
## WHEN SOMEONE IS SAYING "NO" REVISITED[1]

**Joan Rubin**
*National Center for Bilingual Research*

One of the more important communicative tasks that confronts a traveler is the recognition of when a speaker has said "no." That is, one needs to be able to recognize that a respondent has refused or denied that which the speaker has demanded, solicited, or offered. Equally, one needs to acquire the appropriate manner in which to respond in the negative when offered, solicited, or demanded something. Granted that it is sometimes difficult to recognize a refusal in one's mother tongue where the answer might be ambiguous or deliberately obscure, nonetheless in many encounters the meaning is clear if one knows how to read or interpret the appropriate signals.

A first task for the visitor abroad is to discover which forms are used to fulfill this function. If we compare form and function across cultures, it soon becomes clear that one form may be used to mean different things in another culture than in one's own. For example, in Turkish "no" is signaled by moving one's head backward while rolling one's eyes upward. However, to an American this movement is close to the signal used for saying "yes." Further, in still other cultures, head shaking may have nothing to do with affirmation or negation. In parts of India, rolling the head slowly from side to side means something like "yes, go on, I'm listening." Thus, as one goes from culture to culture, form and function may not match. A foreigner who wants to communicate appropriately must develop the competence of sending and receiving "no" messages.

In order to understand the meaning of a new set of forms, it takes more than learning the forms that are used for denial or negation. Foreigners must also learn when and to whom they must use the proper form. That is to say, one must learn when and to whom it is appropriate to use a particular form which means "no."

For example, how do employees refuse a request from their employer? This may well be different from saying "no" to a peer. It will be important as well to understand what the appropriate conditions for saying "no" are. Speakers may be insulting the foreigner deliberately by the form of "no" they use. These conditions must be learned along with the form for "no," or important messages may be missed.

However, not only the appropriate form and setting must be learned but also the underlying values of a culture will alter an interpretation of what is meant by a particular form even if used in the right setting. We will find that deep-seated cultural values will affect the proper interpretation of a particular form. Without knowledge of the central values, the traveler may never understand properly what message the speaker is really trying to convey. Each of us carries around certain central values which underlie our behavior. These might be values such as being hospitable, being respectful, "time is money," or humans as mechanistic beings.

Finally, individuals tend to have idiosyncratic ways of sending and receiving "no." One of my students wrote a paper once on how she knew what was the most auspicious time to ask her father for something so as to avoid his saying no and thus more easily gain the favor she was asking for.

We can all recount tales of misunderstanding while residing in a foreign culture. Here are a couple of my own: (1) While living abroad, I invited people to parties or dinner at my house. Although I requested an RSVP, I never got any. As a result, it was necessary to prepare a large amount of food in case they all came. I was annoyed that I hadn't understood the cues for negation. (2) On several occasions, I found that I couldn't interpret the servants' ways of saying no. (3) In the United States, negotiations with North Vietnam were often misinterpreted. The President often said: "I'll talk peace *anywhere, anytime*." I think that one meaning which can be attributed to this sentence is "no I won't." The reason for this interpretation is that in most United States areas, when a person says "drop in any time," this is not an invitation. Rather, if one really wanted to extend an invitation, one would need to specify when and where to meet. By saying "anywhere, anytime" without being more specific, the President made his willingness to negotiate seem dubious. (For a fuller discussion of the American approach to invitations, see Wolson 1979; Wolfson, D'Amico-Reisner, and Huber, this volume.)

This paper will provide evidence for one of the claims of the field of socio-linguistics which is concerned with understanding the speech act by looking at speech variation and social structure and rules. The claim is made that the interpretation of the speech act requires understanding it as a totality. Further, it is claimed that it won't do to merely look at the form-function relation inherent in any speech act in order to be able to interpret the message for use of a particular form. One must also look for the underlying values inherent in the speech act. All of this kind of know-ledge comprises what is meant by the term "communicative competence," i.e., the ability to interpret the full meaning of a message and the ability to formulate such messages properly.

Looked at in this deeper way, the teaching of language would greatly benefit by providing the student with this kind of information about the culture and the proper use of the language. Language teaching often stops short in describing form-function relationships. At best, it gives clues as to the social parameters involved. Only rarely are students given information about the underlying values of a speech act. Part of the reason this is not taught is that teaching materials are not organized in this manner and the details of a value system are more difficult to discern than either form-function relations or the social parameters of the speech act. However, if students are to use a language effectively, it is essential that we provide them with this sort of information.

This paper will exemplify what the three levels of understanding a speech act look like for one kind of speech act, namely, negation. It will illustrate how all three are needed in the interpretation of the message of negation.

## FORM-FUNCTION RELATIONS

It's not hard to find examples of similar ways of expressing "no" relations across several cultures. These are worth listing:

1. Be silent, hesitate, show a lack of enthusiasm. In many cultures in the world, being silent is a way of refusing an offer or an invitation or of giving an answer.
   - When asked whether you liked a movie or a dress, be silent.
   - If you receive a written invitation, don't answer.

The big problem for a foreigner is that silence may mean many other things. Among the Western Apache, as Basso (1972) has shown, silence is used in "social situations in which participants perceive their relationship vis-à-vis one another to be ambiguous and/or unpredictable." Basso argues that "silence is defined as appropriate with respect to a specific individual or individuals."

2. Offer an alternative. In some cases in order not to offend or to direct the conversation away from the request, the addressee may divert attention by suggesting an alternative.
   - How do you like this book?
     It's good but I prefer—
   - What time should we meet? Around 5?
     How about 4:30?
     Let's make it 5.
   - Mary can you help with the cooking?
     Susan can do it better.
3. Postponement (delaying answers). Often in response to a request to perform something or to an invitation, "no" is indicated by postponement.
   - Can you come over this evening?
     Not today, next time, I'll let you know.
   - I think it's a great idea but I don't have time at the moment.
   - Say "yes" late (i.e., let the host know so late, it's impossible for them to act).
   - We're very busy now but we'll get someone on it as soon as possible.
   - We'll take the matter under advisement.
   - Sylvia, can you do this?
     Mañana (note that this is translated as tomorrow but its real meaning in this situation is a subtle negation).
   - We aren't ready for your service yet.

4. Put the blame on a third party or something over which you have no control.
   - My husband doesn't want me to, or I'll have to ask my husband.
   - We'll put it up to the committee but I can't promise anything.
   - I can't drink because I have a bad liver.
   - My budget doesn't permit me to go.
   - It's too expensive.
   - Tell Arthur Murray dance studio salespersons while talking on the telephone: "I'm sorry I only have one leg" (even when the speaker has two legs but wants to avoid a sales pitch).

5. Avoidance. One way to answer a question or an offer is to avoid responding directly.
   - If a boy comes to visit a girl, don't be at home to him.
   - If offered food you don't like, say "I like X more."
   - How do you like my dress?
     It's interesting (i.e., the addressee doesn't like it; interesting is a nondescript word with no real meaning here).

6. General acceptance of an offer but giving no details.
   - In the United States, "drop in any time" is generally not taken as an invitation.
   - In Arabic-speaking countries, the following is a negation:
     Let's have a picnic next Saturday?
     Imshaallah (God willing), (equivalent to "no").
     But Imshaalah plus time and details (equivalent to "yes").
   - In Taiwan: I'll come but . . . (equal to "no").

7. Divert and distract the addressee.
   - In Hawaiian culture when a leader at a meeting begins to be too bossy, he may find two kinds of refusal of his orders:
     Silence and a lack of enthusiasm (a hostile response)
     Playful questions and misbehavior (breaks up tension)
   - In the United States, diverting a question is done by questioning the question.
   - How old are you?
     Why do you ask? How old do you think? (Weiser 1975).
   - Address the speech act but not the content.
     Please close the door.
     Why?

8. General acceptance with excuses.
   - It's a good idea but . . .

9. Say what's offered is inappropriate.
   - It's not quite suitable.
   - It isn't good management practice.
   - It's ahead of its time.

Many of these nine approaches to saying "no" are found in every culture. A foreigner has trouble when the relation between form and meaning is not the same in two different cultures. For example:

1. Silence may mean "no" in one culture but "maybe" in another. In the United States if you don't receive an answer to an inquiry, it means "no." However, in Britain it means "maybe" or "I'll write later when I have something to say." Among the Western Apache, silence is used when meeting strangers, during the initial stages of courting, when children come home, when being cussed out, and when one is with people who are sad. Basso (1972) notes that "keeping silent among the Western Apache is a response to uncertainty and unpredictability in social relations" (p. 83).

2. Verbal cues may give one message but nonverbal cues another. An example is that of a Toradjan in Indonesia who worked as a laborer in a school headed by a British principal. The laborer always said "yes" but let her know by his body position that he didn't intend to do it.

3. Societies differ in how food is offered and accepted and rejected:

- In the United States, a hostess will offer more food usually only <u>once</u>.
  Have some more.
  No, thanks, I'm really full.
  O.K.
- In parts of the Arab world and many other parts of the world one mustn't accept food the first or second time it is offered; however, refusal the third time is definitive.

| *Host* | *Guest* |
| --- | --- |
| Have some. | I'm full. |
| I know you're full but have some more for X's sake. | As much as I like X, I do have to refuse. |
| For my sake, have some. I cooked the food. | For your sake, I'll take some (may then leave it on the plate). |

An anecdote was recounted by an Arab speaker's first encounter with some Americans. On his first visit to an American home, he was served some delicious sandwiches. When the hostess came to offer seconds, he refused. Much to his chagrin, the hostess didn't repeat the offer. Thus the Arab sat there, confronted by some lovely sandwiches which he couldn't eat.

4. In France, when offered something, the best refusal is "merci." The translation of this word is "thanks" but it means "no, thanks." in the United States "thanks" means "yes, thanks."

5. Jakobson (1972) showed that head movements for "yes" and "no" differ from culture to culture.

6. Saying "no" is also related to the variety of language used by the respondent: In some Arab groups, when you are invited to a feast; if the addressee responds in collquial Arabic and says "yes, sure I'll come," the speaker knows that the person will come. However, if the speaker responds using some classical Arabic, his/her response means "no."

7. In Japan and Korea, a question is more polite when phrased negatively:

- "Wouldn't you like some more tea?" An American would normally respond: "yes" meaning: Yes, I would like some more tea, but a Japanese or Korean would say: "No" meaning: It is not the case that I would not like more tea.

One of the more interesting observations about "no" is that sometimes "no" may mean "maybe" given the right time and circumstances. This is a quite important function in boy-girl relations and in politics. An example of this function is shown by the following sex-biased joke:

What's the difference between a lady and a diplomat?
When a diplomat says "yes," he means "maybe."
When a diplomat says "maybe," he means "no."
When a diplomat says "no," he's not a diplomat.

When a lady says "no," she means "maybe."
When a lady says "maybe," she means "yes."
When a lady says "yes," she's no lady! ! !

It becomes important to know when a "no" is negotiable. Members in their own society need to know when a "no" is negotiable. Children, employees, and diplomats most often need to learn this quickly.

## SOCIAL PARAMETERS OF SAYING "NO"

All these examples lead us to be careful not to assume that similar forms have the same function cross-culturally. We also know that we shouldn't assume that the task is one of merely finding the proper form to express a function. The form-function relationship is just the tip of the iceberg. We also need to consider how the performance of the speech act is related to social structure (that is, how you should address superiors, equals, and respected persons and how this relates to your own status). In some cultures, children can be more direct than in others. In addition, we need to consider how the speech act is related to a whole set of values attached to these behaviors.

Some of the social features can be spelled out. For example, in many societies, how you say "no" is more important than the answer itself. It is more important to maintain proper social relations than to be definitive.

Some examples which are related to social structure features are:

- In Korea, when old men offer younger men food, the younger ones may not refuse.
- In the Marshall Islands, one is not permitted to say "no" to a chief's son.
- In Poland, the older a person is, the harder it is to refuse.
- In Taiwan, the closer a relative is, the easier it is to say "no."

In many societies a higher value is placed on maintaining social relations than on getting an answer. For example, in the Philippines, one tries to avoid the embarrassing situation where someone can say "no" directly to you. Instead you send out "feelers." For example, if you want to be invited to a party, you might say to a person who you know is giving a party: "I hear that you are a good cook/have a nice place." The addressee may refuse by saying: "It's only for extended family." Or, if you want to get a job for some relative, you may send out a feeler (so as not to be faced with a refusal). An example of this kind of transaction is:

- By the way, I hear you have a job to fill. I have a nephew who is hard-working and who lives not too far away.
  If yes, discuss his merits for the job.
  If no, shift responsibility to a third party by saying, "There's a committee deciding it."
- If employees want raises in salaries, they may send out a feeler by telling a sob story telling how much in need of money they are. Boss can refuse by saying how bad sales are going or how tight the budget is this year.

In Taiwan, where there seems to be a similar effort to maintain social relations and to avoid embarrassing situations, to get a job one would go through an intermediary. Likewise, to find a marriage partner, Taiwanese would go through a broker. The broker (usually a friend) would arrange a gathering of the three sides by going to a show or preparing a meal. The girl can indicate her interest or lack thereof by whether she will sit by the boy or not.

15

In the Arab world, it is common to use a go-between to get a job, arrange a marriage, or get into a private school so that a direct refusal is prevented. However, unlike the Philippines, in arranging a job for a relative, one may tell the employer that there is a candidate who is worthless but who will shine under the tutelage of the employer.

On occasion in maintaining good social relations, one may not say no; yet if one cannot fully comply, one should do something to indicate good will. For example, in Taiwan and the Trust Territory, invitees to a party, funeral, or wedding must show they are a part of the community by attending. However, if this is impossible, they should either show up, if only for a few minutes, or send a representative, friend, or child.

In some cases, social relations may be such that people understand the interchange only if they know both the question and the answer. For example, in Taiwan if food is offered and the guest refuses and if food is not offered again, he/she may feel that the host/hostess is stingy. The whole speech act consists of a series of questions and answers. In India, if people are offered food once and refuse and if no second offer is made, they may recognize that the first offer was just a formality. In Indonesia, if people ask a wrong question (i.e., one that shouldn't be asked), they may get a strange answer. For example, if a girl is asked by her sister-in-law whether she has a boyfriend, she will deny it because she is embarrassed to admit having one.

Recognizing a "no" not only depends on finding the proper form-function relationship, it depends as well on the setting and social structure which dictates how and when "no" may be said. Interpretation of a negative is also related to underlying values in a society. In many cases, the problem is not one of truth and forthrightness; rather it is one of how people like to be treated and talked to.

## VALUES

In addition to knowing the form-function relation and the social constraints on how to say "no," these are some basic values of how to behave in a society. That is, basic to any social communication are the underlying values which participants in a communicative act hold. It is important to have an understanding of how a society approaches social interaction in order to send and interpret messages properly. Given this understanding, we can predict where communication can break down when the goals of two individuals belonging to different value systems come into conflict.

In many cultures, saving one's own and/or another's face is high on the list of values in social interaction. This seems less important in American and European cultures. Here are a couple of examples where these values come into conflict and result in misinterpretation and judgments regarding the interlocutor.

1. Richard Applegate (1975) notes that Americans are very concerned with getting exact information about such matters as times, places, and routes. Hence, when an American is asked for directions he/she tries to share this information or if uncertain, he/she will admit

to this and then venture a guess. In other cultures the focus may not be on the passing of accurate information but rather on maintaining social relations. For example, in Vietnam, if someone a few steps higher asks for information from a peasant, such as: "Is this the way to the station?" the usual response is *do phai* "That must be." The reason for this response, which may not be at all acceptable, is that the peasant wants to avoid contradicting a superior person or doesn't wish to make him/her appear ignorant. If the American assumes the accuracy of the response, he/she may very well be led astray and may become angry and frustrated. For the American, the Vietnamese response seems evasive and the individual judged as irresponsible or even deceitful. Certainly, given the American emphasis on "time is money" the peasant has caused the American considerable loss. On the other hand, the Vietnamese may be puzzled by the American's anger. The Vietnamese peasant feels comfortable because he/she has provided a socially responsible answer. If the American wanted to find out information, he/she as a superior should seek out an intermediary so that the addressee needn't put anyone in an embarrassing situation.

2. Elinor Ochs Keenan (1976) offers a different example of how knowing cultural values is essential in sending and interpreting messages. She reports that in Madagascar, in a small village which speaks Malagasy, *new* information is considered a rare commodity. Hence, when a speaker asks for information about some future event such as: "When is the turning of ancestral bones to take place?" the response will not be very precise. It will be something like: "I'm not certain" or "In a bit" or "Around September." The reason for this imprecision is that speakers do not wish to commit themselves publicly to a precise date until certain the event will take place. Otherwise, he/she will be guilty of premature or faulty judgment. Natives of this village understand this response as being related to the value of saving one's own face. Americans would be more likely to judge the response as uncooperative or unfriendly.

The problem is that a speaker may know the form-function relation and use it correctly, but underlying values may require a different kind of answer.

## CONCLUSION

A great deal of knowledge is required to send or receive a message of "no." The acquisition of communicative competence requires all three levels of knowledge. First, a person from another culture must find the appropriate form-function relation. Next, one needs to learn which social parameters enter into the speech act. Finally, it is essential to get a grasp on the underlying values in a society.

Saying "no" is not simply finding the proper form-function relation. Rather, that is only the tip of the iceberg, and visitors to an unfamiliar country need to probe more deeply if they are to express themselves adequately and interpret messages sent by a native.

## NOTE

1. This is a revised paper of the same article which appeared in *Topics in Culture Learning,* August 1976. I am indebted to a number of people for the examples found here. I especially want to thank Steven Boggs, Greg Trifonovitch, and David Wu for their helpful examples. Thanks too to Jerry Boucher and Merle Stetser for their comments on the earlier version of this paper.

# 2

## *APOLOGY: A SPEECH-ACT SET*

Elite Olshtain
*Tel Aviv University*

Andrew D. Cohen
*Hebrew University of Jerusalem*

Recent interest and research directed toward sociolinguistics and ethnographic studies have heightened the ESL/EFL methodologist's awareness of the need to incorporate such a focus in TESOL planning. The shift from grammatical to communicative competence in language learning has further reinforced that need. A growing number of textbook writers, curriculum designers, teacher trainers, and language teachers have been eagerly awaiting the latest results of sociolinguistic research.

Although the importance of communicative competence in TESOL is fully recognized, research on the specific components that make up such competence is still limited. If the learner of a new language is to acquire the rules for appropriate use of the linguistic forms in that language, we need to know more about those rules. The study of speech acts can provide us with better understanding and new insights into the interdependence of linguistic forms and sociocultural context.

The objective of this paper is to relate theoretical descriptions of speech acts to empirical studies involving data collected from language users. We will focus on the act of apologizing, which will be referred to as a "speech-act set." Our discussion will relate to a group of studies conducted by ourselves and by our students. Certain research issues which have been underscored by these studies will be discussed, and recommendations for the application of such research to TESOL will be presented.

## THE SPEECH-ACT SET

Since Hymes (1964) introduced the notion of communicative competence encompassing both the speaker's knowledge of the linguistic rules as well as the sociocultural rules for appropriate use, there has been an increasing interest in empirical research in the area and in practical applications of such sociolinguistic studies. Perhaps the most important realization of language teaching methodologists has been the fact that effective communication involves the processing of social as well as linguistic knowledge.

The development of speech-act theory (Austin 1962; Searle 1969, 1975, 1976; Sinclair and Coulthard 1975) has given us a better understanding of what a speaker needs to know in order to perform effectively and appropriately in the act of communicating. Speech-act theory has also stimulated research focusing on speech events and speech acts, the results of which have made us more aware of the interplay of situational, sociolinguistic, and linguistic types of knowledge.

The distinction proposed by Hymes (1972) among speech situation, speech event, and speech act provides the sociolinguistic researcher with a framework for studying communicative competence. This framework provides a hierarchy which places the *speech situation* at the top, having the broadest scope; *speech events* come second since they take place within the speech situation; and *speech acts,* which have the narrowest scope of the three, come at the bottom of the ladder. According to this hierarchy one finds many *speech situations* within a *speech community*—e.g., meals, parties, auctions, and conferences, which in themselves are not governed by consistent rules. *Speech events,* on the other hand, are restricted to activities that are directly governed by rules of speech—e.g., lectures, introductions, advertising, and two or more party conversations. *Speech acts* are the minimal terms on the scale and refer to the acts we perform when we speak: giving reports, giving advice, agreeing, complaining, apologizing. *Speech acts* are thus defined in terms of discourse functions.

Although a speech act can occur within various speech events (one can apologize as part of a two-party conversation or as part of a lecture), they are triggered by specific behavior or discourse situations that need to be defined beyond one sociocultural context as well as within each such context. It may be that a person would need to apologize when hurting another person unintentionally—no matter where the situation occurred. Yet different degrees of severity in the action or different circumstances related to the behavior may call for different types of apologies and different intensities of such apologies in different cultures. We need to focus our descriptions of speech acts on non-language-specific and language-specific features as well as on situation-specific information.

Austin (1962) drew our attention to the fact that many speech acts in English are closely related to the verbs that carry the semantic meaning implied in the speech act—for instance, "to request," "to complain," "to suggest." On the basis of Austin's notion of a performative act these verbs are referred to as performative verbs; they "name" the act which is being performed. Yet, as Searle (1976) has pointed out, these verbs are not really markers of the force of speech acts. A variety of verbs, although differing in semantic meaning, may be useful in bringing about the realization of the same speech function. In fact, only in very formal speech events would one prefer to use expressions like "I request . . . " or "I apologize . . . " as opposed to expressions like "Please give me . . . " or "I'm sorry." Moreover, as Searle (1975) points out, some speech acts are indirect—in other words, one speech act is brought about indirectly by performing another one. Thus a statement like "the food smells delicious" may in one instance serve as an expression of the speaker's hope that dinner will soon be ready, and in another as just a compliment for the hostess.

In this paper we would like to suggest a slight expansion of the notion "speech act" so as to clarify the relation between a discourse situation and the specific utterances that can qualify for certain speech functions. Since we intend to focus on apology, we will be concerned with the discourse situations which usually call for apologies and with the semantic formulas that would be appropriate for natives in such situations, in English and in other languages.

The act of apologizing is called for when there is some behavior which has violated social norms. When an action or utterance (or the lack of either one) has resulted in the fact that one or more persons perceive themselves as offended, the culpable person(s) needs to apologize. We are dealing here, therefore, with two parties: an apologizer and a recipient. However, only if the person who caused the infraction perceives him/herself as an apologizer do we get the act of apologizing. The act of apologizing requires an action or an utterance which is intended to "set things right." Whether a specific discourse situation calls for an apology and whether a certain utterance qualifies as such an apology will depend on both linguistic and sociocultural norms.

In our effort to study apologies, we soon realized that the literature did not provide us with a good working definition of the notion "speech act." The difficulty of defining the term "speech act" is discussed by Schmidt and Richards (1980). They point out the key problem, namely, the fact that a speech act cannot be equated to a sentence, an utterance, or a turn since it is in essence an act and not only a unit of speech. According to Schmidt and Richards, Searle's (1976) classification of speech acts is still the best taxonomy available. According to this taxonomy, apologizing is an "expressive" act[1] along with other speech acts such as "thanking," "congratulating," and "offering condolences." Searle's taxonomy gives us, at best, a useful classification of speech acts but still leaves us without an operational definition of what a speech act actually is.

On the basis of our work on apologies, we would like to suggest that sociolinguistic research dealing with speech acts concern itself more with the internal composition of a speech act. We know that a speech act can be performed in a number of different ways—i.e., by using the relevant performative verb, by using a direct act, or by using an indirect one. We have not yet been concerned sufficiently, however, with all the potential types of sentences or utterances that together create a set of parameters belonging to any particular speech act.

Fraser (1980) describes "semantic formulas" used in executing the act of apologizing. Each semantic formula consists of a word, phrase, or sentence which meets a particular semantic criterion or strategy, and any one or more of these can be used to perform the act in question. We would like to suggest that our goal be the description of the maximal potential set of semantic formulas for each act. Therefore, a "speech act set" would consist of the major semantic formulas, any one of which could suffice as an "emic" minimal element to represent the particular speech act. A combination of some of the formulas or all of them is also possible. Research will have to concern itself with the reasons why sometimes speakers prefer one formula and at other times another. This differential preference will need to be examined as it relates to the particular discourse situation within which the speech act is performed.

Apology then has a *speech act set* which will consist of a number of semantic formulas. The question now arises as to how we can arrive at the description of the complete speech-act set. We must first accept the fact that this is an idealized goal which requires considerable research of an ethnographic and sociolinguistic nature. The long-range aim can be defined as the quest for the semantic formulas which are non-language-specific, or in other words, *universal* in nature. The realization of such formulas might, however, be language-specific. Thus it may be reasonable to expect all apology acts to contain some form of an "expression of responsibility" on the part of the apologizer who has caused some infraction. Yet the specific sociocultural situations in which native speakers will produce this expression of responsibility may vary significantly from language to language. Furthermore, the speech-act set, as well as any one formula within it, can be situation-specific. In addition, semantic formulas can be expressed through direct or indirect utternaces. It is therefore necessary to apply the notion of *indirect speech,* as initially developed by Searle (1975) and further studied by others (Brown and Levinson 1978, Labov and Fanshel 1977, Shoshana Blum-Kulka 1982), to the semantic formulas within the speech act. The application of such an approach will become clearer in the subsequent discussion of the apology speech act set.

## APOLOGIES

In describing the apology speech act set, we are assuming that there are two participants—one perceiving him/herself as deserving an apology and the second perceived by the first as having the responsibility for causing the offense. The second participant, therefore, needs to apologize yet may not perceive him/herself as responsible for the offense and may therefore choose to accept or deny it. With regard to the interaction between the recipient and the apologizer, we can describe the apology speech act set from a number of different points of view:

1. The recipient's expectations based on his/her perception of the degree of severity of the offense
2. The offender's apology based on his/her perception of the degree of severity of the offense
3. The offender's apology based on the extent of reprimanding expected from the recipient
4. The interactive nature of both the initial apology and the recipient's response
5. The social status of the two participants
6. The way the tone of voice may function to convey meaning

The first five points of view are usually integral aspects of the discourse situation within which the apology occurs, and they will be discussed with regard to how they affect the choice of *semantic formulas* within each apology speech-act set. (Tone of voice is mentioned in passing below in relation to the judged acceptability of an apology.) The discussion will focus on two dimensions: (1) the severity of the offense and (2) the status of the recipient. Thus a more serious offense might bring about an expression of apology like "I'm terribly sorry" (high intensity) as opposed to "I'm sorry" (low intensity). Similarly, one may offer an apology of higher intensity to a recipient of a higher status. In the Cohen and Olshtain (1981) study which will be described below, special situations were chosen in order to allow for varying degrees of intensity.

In discussing the semantic formulas of the apology speech-act set, we need to distinguish between the case in which the offender perceived the need to apologize as opposed to the case where he/she denies all responsibility. When the offender is positively inclined to apologize, five potential semantic formulas seem to emerge:[2]

1. An expression of an apology
2. An explanation or account of the situation
3. An acknowledgment of responsibility
4. An offer of repair
5. A promise of forbearance

In most cases just one of the formulas is sufficient in order to perform an apology, but often two or three are combined together and thus create higher intensity of apology.

"An expression of apology," the first formula in our set, consists of a number of subformulas:

a. An expression of regret, e.g., "I'm sorry."
b. An offer of apology, e.g., "I apologize."
c. A request for forgiveness, e.g., "Excuse me." "Please forgive me." or "Pardon me."

In all these subformulas the apology is direct and one of the apology verbs is used: "apologize," "be sorry," "forgive," "excuse," and "pardon." It may very well be that the major semantic formulas in a speech-act set are non-language-specific and that each language has a direct expression of apology using one or more of the "apology" verbs. The number of subformulas and their appropriateness to certain discourse situations would vary, however, from language to language. Moreover, which of the subformulas is most common in any language may be specific to that language. In English it seems that the first subformula, an expression of regret, is most common.

The second formula is "an explanation or account of the situation" which indirectly brought about the offense and is offered either in addition to or in lieu of the expression of an apology. Thus a person late for a meeting might explain "The bus was delayed." We might hypothesize that the semantic formula as such is non-language-specific, while its appropriateness to certain discourse situations may be language-specific.

2. The third formula is "an acknowledgment of responsibility" and is non-language-specific. This formula will be chosen by the speaker/offender only when he/she recognizes responsibility for the offense. There are four subformulas in this case, and they can be described as follows:

- a. Accepting the blame, e.g., "It is my fault."
- b. Expressing self-deficiency, e.g., "I was confused." "I wasn't thinking." or "I didn't see you."
- c. Recognizing the other person as deserving apology, e.g., "You are right!"
- d. Expressing lack of intent, e.g., "I didn't mean to."

Among these four subformulas we see that only the first one is a direct acknowledgment of responsibility while the other three are indirect expressions of responsibility.

4, 5. The last two semantic formulas in the above set are situation-specific. An offer of repair would be relevant only if physical injury or other damage has resulted (e.g., "I'll pay for the broken vase" or "I'll help you get up"), while a promise of forbearance relates to a case where the offender could have avoided the offense but did not do so, perhaps repeatedly; e.g., when someone has forgotten a meeting with a friend more than once, the person might want to say something like "It won't happen again." These two semantic formulas can therefore occur only if the specific discourse situation calls for such formulas.

We have so far discussed the case where the offender recognizes the need to apologize. We will now consider the case where the need to apologize is rejected. One possible case is where the offender does not react at all. When there *is* a verbal reaction, it can be:

1. A denial of the need to apologize, e.g., "there was no need for you to get insulted."
2. A denial of responsibility
   a. Not accepting the blame, e.g., "It wasn't my fault."
   b. Blaming the other participant for bringing the offense upon him/herself, e.g., "It's your own fault."

The above description of the semantic formulas comprising the apology speech act set will serve as a framework for discussing the various studies that we and our students at Hebrew University, Tel Aviv University, and UCLA have carried out.

## ISSUES IN STUDYING NONNATIVE SPEAKERS' SPEECH ACTS

The studies that will be discussed in this paper were motivated by a number of issues that have emerged out of the need to describe communicative competence. The following are some of the leading issues:

1. What kind of proficiency does the nonnative speaker need to have, in addition to linguistic proficiency, in order to accomplish the act of communicating successfully?

2. Can we describe the typical preferences that native speakers of a language manifest as they select semantic formulas for performing a certain speech act?

3. Can we develop measures for use in cross-cultural comparison of native-speaker preferences in selecting semantic formulas for certain speech-act sets?

4. Do we find evidence for language-universal components of speech-act sets?

Given our research interest in the act of apologizing in both first and second language, we saw the need to collect empirical data on the way in which apologies are performed in each of the languages with which we worked. In other words, we felt it necessary to set up native-speaker norms before we could study the difficulties faced by nonnative speakers.

As Manes and Wolfson (1981) state in their paper on the compliment formula, the best approach to collecting data about speech acts is the ethnographic approach—i.e., the collection of spontaneous speech in natural settings. From our perspective, however, there are disadvantages to collecting data in this way. Collecting a corpus of naturally occurring speech behavior takes considerable time. In addition, some speech acts, like apologies, occur less frequently and are more situation-dependent than others. Furthermore, we wanted to determine the selection and realization of semantic formulas in given discourse situations in order to produce archetypal sets for each given situation in each language.[3] We therefore decided to set up a number of fixed discourse situations to use as a constant element in a series of studies (Cohen and Olshtain 1981).

In order to establish what the nonnative speaker needs to know in order to communicate successfully, we must have a description of the apology speech-act set in the target language and in the native language. We can then analyze nonnative performance data in terms of negative transfer, avoidance of negative transfer, and lack of linguistic or sociocultural proficiency. This was the approach followed in Cohen and Olshtain (1981). Another way of evaluating successful communication by nonnative speakers is to have their performance evaluated and rated by native speakers in terms of its acceptability, an approach followed by Blum-Kulka (1982) and by one of the student studies reported subsequently in this paper. Perhaps a combination of both approaches would be most revealing.

Another issue is the extent to which nonnative speakers' lack of linguistic proficiency is or may be the cause for deviation from native-speaker norms. Nonnative speakers may choose different communication strategies in order to overcome their perceived lack of proficiency: they may either be very concise and tend to use the most general semantic formulas, or they may choose to elaborate and "say too much" in order to express their need to apologize. Thus, often the lack of appropriateness is a direct result of the lack of linguistic and not necessarily sociocultural proficiency. Moreover even with regard to non-language-specific semantic formulas, the nonnative speaker may resort to the strategy of avoidance due to lack of linguistic proficiency. This can only be studied by comparing L1 norms with L2 norms.

Another issue in nonnative speakers' performance is their preconceived notions of the target sociocultural rules relating to the particular speech act.

Jordens and Kellerman (1981) studied the learner's perception of how distant the target language is from the native language, the learner's perception of markedness which is transferable to the new language, and how these perceptions affect learning strategies. In our studies we felt that it would be important to focus on the learner's perception of the speech act in terms of language specificity or language universality. In the case of apologies, for instance, if the learner's perception is that "one apologizes profusely or not very frequently" in the target language, the tendency might be to increase or lower the degree of apology, respectively. On the other hand, if the learner perceives the speech act as universal in nature, the tendency might be to transfer apology behavior directly from L1. This aspect was studied to some extent in the Olshtain (1981) study.

Finally, we come to the issue of establishing universal features of speech-act sets. Once we have established archetypal sets within a number of languages, we could conduct cross-cultural comparison of these speech acts. Such comparisons would render a list of components having universal features, at least with respect to the languages in question. As we continue to do such cross-cultural studies, a more complete picture will emerge.

## REVIEW OF APOLOGY STUDIES

### The Cohen and Olshtain Hebrew University Study

Our first apology study involved eight apology situations selected to assess cultural competence. We were looking for language behavior in apologizing that reflected negative transfer from native language, an avoidance of negative transfer, or lack of grammatical proficiency. Four of the situations were especially set up to elicit different degrees of intensity of regret (e.g., "sorry" vs. "I'm really sorry")—hitting a car; and bumping into a lady (1) hurting her, (2) just shaking her up, and (3) because she was in the way. The remaining four situations were meant to assess the effect of status of the addressee on the formality of the apology—insulting someone at a meeting, forgetting a meeting with (1) a boss, (2) a friend, and (3) your son.

The situations were randomly ordered and responses elicited without an intended reply from the addressee. The respondents read the situation to themselves, and then the investigator role-played the person doing the apologizing.

The subjects were 44 college students around 20 years of age. Twelve were native English speakers (E1), who provided data on how English speakers apologize in their native language. The remaining 32 were native Hebrew speakers, 12 of whom provided Hebrew (H1) responses and 20 of whom provided English-as-a-foreign-language (E2) responses.

We found situations in which E2 deviations from the cultural patterns of E1 appeared to be a result of negative transfer from H1 patterns since the deviant patterns were similar to those present in H1 responses. For example, E2 speakers did not express an apology as much as E1 speakers in insulting someone at a meeting and in forgetting to take their son shopping. Nor did E2 speakers offer repair as frequently as E1 speakers in forgetting a meeting with their boss and in forgetting to take their son shopping.

There were also situations in which E2 responses were more like E1 than H1 responses. It may have been that in these situations E2 speakers were successful at avoiding negative transfer of sociocultural patterns operating in their native language. For example, E2 speakers expressed an apology frequently in bumping into a lady because she was in the way, as E1 speakers did but unlike H1 speakers. Also, E2 speakers acknowledged responsibility like E1 speakers, in forgetting a meeting with the boss and in insulting someone at a meeting.

We did find certain situations where E2 responses seemed to indicate a deficiency in linguistic proficiency—situations where E1 and H1 responses were similar and more complete. In other words, there were situations in which E2 respondents may not have been proficient enough in English to readily include the expected semantic formula in their responses in the testing situation. For instance, E2 speakers were less likely than E1 or H1 speakers to offer repair in backing into someone else's car and in bumping into a lady, hurting her. Likewise, E2 respondents were less likely to acknowledge responsibility in the situation of bumping into a lady, shaking her up a bit.

We also found that E2 responses did not always reflect the appropriate intensity of regret (e.g., "I'm *very* sorry."). For example, in the situations of forgetting to get together with a friend and bumping into a lady, hurting her, E2 respondents did not intensify their regret as much as E1 respondents. This deviation may well have been the result of native-language transfer, since intensity in Hebrew can be signaled by an interjection. With respect to stylistic behavior, we found only negligible deviation for both E2 and E1 respondents.

There was a numerical component to this study—i.e., the generating of a rating scale. This component will be referred to under Applications below.

Finally, this study provided a set of data from which it would be possible to derive an archetypal apology for each of the apology situations. Table 1 suggests what such apologies might look like. Their semantic formulas are labeled, using the formulas that we had developed for that study.

## A Hebrew University Study of Apology Based on Dramatic Role Play by Pairs of Hebrew-Speaking Children

Ilana Yaacov, a student of Cohen's at the Hebrew University, did an apology study using as native-speaker respondents Israeli elementary students (grades 2 and 4) participating in a drama class. The focus of this study was on the degree of apology that a child would use in response to the severity of the offending action. Two children were given the task of role playing the two participants in each apology situation (same sex and cross sex). The following is a typical situation from this study:

Two girls are participants in an apology situation in which the recipient owns a beautiful dress she received for her birthday, which the offender borrowed for a special occasion. The dress got damaged in the process. The girls act out the same situation three times, but each time a

26

**Table 1**    Archetypal Apologies by Situation

*Insulting someone at a meeting*
    I'm very sorry. (APOL) I really didn't mean it as a personal insult. (RESP)

*Forgetting a meeting with your boss*
    I'm sorry. (APOL) I completely forgot about it. (RESP) Is it possible for me to make another appointment? Can we meet now? (REPR) This won't happen again, I promise. (FORB)

*Forgetting a meeting with a friend*
    I forgot all about our meeting. It slipped my mind. (RESP) I'm sorry. (APOL) We can arrange another time shortly. (REPR)

*Forgetting to take your son shopping*
    Ah, sweetie. Mommy didn't mean to forget. (RESP) I'm sorry. (APOL) I promise to make it up to you as soon as I get home today. (REPR) It won't happen again. (FORB)

*Backing into a car*
    I'm very sorry, sir. (APOL) I didn't mean to. The fault is totally mine. (RESP) I'll take care of it. (REPR)

*Bumping lady, spilling packages and hurting her*
    I'm really sorry. (APOL) I didn't see you. (RESP) Are you O.K.? Can I help you? Let me help you pick everything up. (REPR)

*Bumping lady, shaking her up*
    I'm sorry. (APOL) I didn't mean to bump into you. (RESP) Let me help you pick up these things. (REPR)

*Bumping lady because she is in the way*
    I'm sorry for knocking into you (APOL), but you were in my way.

KEY:    APOL — expression of an apology
        RESP — acknowledgment of responsibility
        REPR — offer of repair
        FORB — promise of forbearance

different degree of severity of damage is assumed: (1) the dress is dirty, (2) the dress is torn, (3) the dress is lost.

This study found the following: when apologizing at the lowest level of severity, the offender mostly used the semantic formula "an expression of an apology" and a subformula of "acknowledgment of responsibility"—expressing lack of intent. At the two higher degrees of severity, offenders used the formula "offer of repair." Perhaps the most striking finding in this study was that the children tended to "deny responsibility" when apologizing at the highest degree of severity, since they expected strong reaction from the recipient. Although in this case the subjects were young children, this finding would suggest that we need to study the relationship at various age levels between the type of apology selected and the extent of reprimand expected from the recipient.

### The Olshtain Study of Adult Learners of Hebrew

This study focused on speakers of Russian and English learning Hebrew in Israel. The eight original apology situations that had been used in the Cohen and Olshtain (1981) study were once again utilized for data collection in this study.

Furthermore, the native-speaker response norms for apologies by discourse situations as developed in the earlier study served as the basis for both cross-cultural comparison and evaluation of the nonnative speakers' production in Hebrew.

The group of 12 English speakers from the earlier study represented the English native norm and the group of 12 Hebrew speakers represented the Hebrew norm. For the Olshtain (1981) study a group of 12 Russian speakers were given the same situations in order to collect data on Russian and thus arrive at a norm in Russian. In addition, a group of 13 speakers of English and 14 speakers of Russian, all learning Hebrew at about the same level of proficiency (intermediate to advanced) were asked to react to the eight situations in Hebrew. They were given cards with the situation written out both in Hebrew and in their native language, and then the investigator acted out the initial statement by the recipient of the offense to which the subjects had to react in Hebrew. The subjects were mostly in the 20 to 30 age group, with a small number of Russian speakers slightly older. They had all been living in Israel from 6 months to 2 years. Their Hebrew was approximately at the same level since some of them had had Hebrew before they had arrived in Israel. There was an equal number of men and women.

The study first dealt comparatively with the norms for apologizing in each of the three languages. The conclusions drawn from this part of the study established that the major semantic formulas were "universal," at least with respect to the three languages studied. The average frequency of all semantic formulas except "offer of repair" was higher for English (L1) and Russian (L1) than for Hebrew (L1). The study found that the highest degree of apology overall was in English, somewhat lower in Russian, and the lowest in Hebrew. The comparison could be described as follows:

English > Russian > Hebrew

On the other hand, the formula "offer of repair" stood out as fairly high in Hebrew, though still slightly lower than in English, but considerably higher than in Russian. On the basis of this cross-cultural comparison one might expect that the learner of Hebrew who is sensitive to overall differences will apologize less in Hebrew than in the native language.

In addition to the data collection carried out as part of this study, the subjects were also interviewed in order to establish their overall perception of apology as language-specific or language-universal. It was found that English speakers tended to perceive spoken Hebrew as calling for fewer apology acts and therefore maintained that one needed to apologize less in Hebrew. The speakers of Russian, on the other hand, had a much more universal perception, claiming that people need to apologize according to their feelings of responsibility regardless of the language which they happen to be speaking.

We found that speakers of English in fact did tend to apologize considerably less in Hebrew (H2) than they did in English, consistent with their perceptions about H2, while speakers of Russian apologized more in H2 than in their native language, again consistent with *their* perceptions about H2.

The Olshtain (1981) study seems to point to the fact that attitudes and preconceived notions about the target language and the universality of the speech act may play a significant role in the performance of adult learners. Moreover, it raises the question of the relationship among the semantic formulas within the speech-act set, a relationship that may produce differences in cross-cultural comparison.

## The UCLA Studies

Four graduate students in the TESL Program at the University of California, Los Angeles (UCLA) did apology studies under Cohen's supervision. A brief description of some of the salient features of these projects is presented below. The studies are valuable both for the methodological decisions taken and for some of the more striking findings that warrant scrutiny despite the small sample sizes.

*The Ford Study—Apologies in English and Spanish*    In this study (Ford, 1981) there were eight apology situations, five of which were in the Cohen and Olshtain study. This time there were also three situations that did not call for apologies (two request situations and one in which the subject was apologized to). The investigator reported doing this in order to keep the subjects' attention and to make them think carefully before each response.

The subjects were three native English speakers who served as E1 respondents and three Spanish-speaking Latin Americans who served as both S1 and E2 respondents. The investigator also used two of the E1 respondents plus another E1 speaker to be raters of the acceptability of E2 apologies on a three-point scale.

In analyzing her data, Ford saw the need to make "excuse" a separate semantic formula, rather than a subformula of "expression of apology." She also formed a semantic formula called "intention"—i.e., a statement that the act was unintentional.[4]

Ford's major finding was that the Spanish speakers, in both S1 and E2 responses, expressed an apology twice as often as did E1 speakers. This finding is consistent with a common belief that Latin Americans are more polite than Americans in certain ritualized interaction situations.

Ford's use of raters to determine the acceptability of apology not only provided information as to which speakers and situations produced the most and the least acceptable apologies. The raters also provided explanations as to why they rated responses as they did. For example, "tone of delivery" was considered important. One subject was rated down in two situations for not sounding regretful enough. Another factor was inappropriate word choice. In one case, the word was not stylistically appropriate in that the respondent used the slightly disrespectful word "lady" in "I'm sorry, lady. I didn't see you." In another case, the word reflected an inaccurate word choice—"guess" instead of "hope," in "I guess I didn't hurt you."

*The Castello, Kim, and Wu Studies—Apologies in English, Spanish, Korean and Chinese*    Three apology studies were conducted as a team effort. Each investigator used the same eight situations, which were fashioned for the most part after Cohen and Olshtain (1981). The situations were designed to tap intensity of regret and stylistic formality. The situations included coughing in the middle of a sentence, missing a meeting with a professor, missing lunch with a friend, not having data ready for a professor, bumping into another student's tray, picking up the wrong umbrella from a man/from a woman, and damaging a friend's bike. In this study, the informants were *not* told to apologize but simply to react—i.e., "How would you react? What would you say, if anything?" This allowed for a non-apologetic response.

In the English-Spanish study (Castello, 1981) there was a native English (E1) respondent and a native Spanish speaker, who provided both S1 and E2 responses. In the English-Korean study (Kim 1981), there was also a native English (E1) respondent and a native Korean speaker (providing K1 and E2 responses). In the English-Chinese study (Wu 1981), there were three native English (E1) respondents and three native Chinese speakers (providing C1 and E2 responses).

The three investigators included in their data analysis a semantic formula called "offer of explanation,"[5] and found that all the E2 responses included an explanation of the situation, whereas this was generally not the case in native-language (E1, S1, K1, or C1) responses. Thus, sometimes nonnatives are deviant for saying too much, not just for saying too little. For example, in the situation of taking the wrong umbrella, the E1 respondents usually refrained from offering an explanation. They just said something like "Right you are. So sorry. There you go," while a Chinese E2 respondent said, "Oh, excuse me. I didn't want to take away your umbrella. Uh . . . if I wanted to take your umbrella away, I should take away my umbrella also. But my umbrella is still in the place."

Whereas we (Cohen and Olshtain 1981) found that Hebrew E2 respondents did not intensify their expressions of regret as much as E1 respondents, Wu found Chinese respondents intensified regret far more than E1 respondents, in both E2 and C1 responses. The E1 respondents used three times more low-intensity regret ("I'm sorry") than high-intensity regret ("I'm very sorry"). The E2 responses reflected almost twice as much high-intensity as low-intensity regretting, and C1 responses more than three times more high-intensity regretting. Thus, while Hebrew E2 speakers may appear somewhat rude to native English speakers when expressing regret, Chinese E2 speakers may appear overly polite, even obsequious.

To get a feeling for apologies across languages, we will look at responses across languages in one situation in this set of studies, that of a student's not having data ready to show a professor. This situation was meant to collect data on the issue of apologizing to someone at a higher status level.

*Situation*

You are a student doing independent study. You had promised your professor that you would have your data ready by a certain date. The date arrives and you don't have it ready. (You had too much work in all of your other classes and just got behind.)

*Responses:*

*English E1:* I'm sorry but I don't have my data ready yet. I've been really busy with my other classes. I just haven't been able to get everything done that I promised to do for you. But I promise to get it in as soon as possible. I'm working hard on it now.

*Spanish E2:* I'm sorry. I have not yet obtained all your data. I will need a few more days. You
   know, I've had so much work with the other assignments these days.
*Korean E2:* I'm terribly sorry, sir. I can't prepare data. I have many things to do. Within ten
   days, I try to report it to you. Sorry.
*Chinese E2:* I'm so sorry I didn't finish you give me the task, because this week I have a heavy
   task.

These are not intended to be archetypal nonnative responses. As is evident even
from this small sampling, the utterances are from nonnatives at varying levels
of linguistic proficiency.

## METHODOLOGICAL ISSUES AT LARGE

Conducting research on speech-acts sets has brought up a number of methodological
issues which have yet to be mentioned in this paper. These issues relate to three
broad areas—design of the study, data-collection procedures, and data analysis.

### Study Design

We have already made an effort to look at the effects of the status of the person
receiving the apology upon the formality of the apology (e.g., student to professor
or employee to boss). We have also looked at the intensity of apology according
to the perceived severity of the offense. We have not dealt with the sex of the
apologizer and the recipient in any systematic way. A set of three UCLA/TESL
M.A. studies of complaints by native speakers of English (Schaefer 1982), Spanish
(Giddens 1981), and Japanese (Inoue 1982), respectively, have dealt systematically
with the sex of respondent and addressee. Twenty males and 20 females have
served as respondents in each study, and the sex of the addressee for each situation
is alternated for two male/female subgroups of 10 respondents. This procedure has
produced striking results, particularly in certain situations (e.g., Spanish speakers
complaining to same/opposite sex about their smoking in a nonsmoking section
on an airplane; Giddens 1981).

Another design issue is how to avoid getting response sets from the respondents. Even though we presented the situations in a different random order to each
of our students in the Cohen and Olshtain (1981) study, the students still were
into a mind set that what they had to do was to apologize. Hence, there could have
been a carry-over effect from one response to another. In her study, Ford (1981)
added a few distractor situations to offset this. Castello (1981), Kim (1981), and
Wu (1981) refrained from instructing students to apologize, and thus left the students more to their own devices. The former approach of having distractor
situations lengthens the elicitation session. The latter approach of not stipulating
that apologies are called for may not produce a desired quantity of apologies.

Another design issue involves care in devising situations. In the Cohen and
Olshtain (1981) study, there were three responses delivered over the phone, all
regarding forgetting an encounter. We did not consider the fact that the medium
of the telephone may well influence the respondent's output. Perhaps the

respondent is purposely more terse or even more deferential. Furthermore, the nonnative may have more difficulty in communicating over the phone, since the nonlinguistic cues are absent.

## Data Collection

From comments that Ford's and Castello's respondents made, it was clear that there was confusion over the fullness of response desired. The respondents indicated that it was only polite to give a brief apology and then wait for the other person to respond. Perhaps the instructions for one-response elicitations need to point out that the respondents are to give as complete a response as they would if they were interacting conversationally over the matter.

Another issue that has come up concerns the language that the instructions are given in. In Cohen and Olshtain (1981) instructions and descriptions of the situations were always given exclusively in the native language of the respondent. It has been pointed out to us that providing the instructions in the target language for the task (or bilingually) may enhance the responses.

## Data Analysis

We have focused attention on the presence and absence of semantic formulas in native- and second-language apologies, but we have not dealt with the issue of their ordering. The set of complaint studies mentioned above has looked carefully at this issue, and this appears to be a fruitful area for investigation. In other words, it may be that two languages use the same semantic formulas for a given situation or set of situations but order these formulas differently. In the case of complaints, the main issue is whether a respondent states the actual complaint before or after justifying the need to complain.

Another issue in data analysis which we have not dealt with in apology studies but which has been analyzed in the complaint studies concerns "valuation." Valuation refers to utterances which make a judgment about what is being said—i.e., reflecting feelings toward the addressee or toward the situation. In the complaint studies, the investigators have found that valuation is usually embedded in one of the other semantic formulas. In other words, a respondent can give a justification, like "I've had to wait an hour for this cold pizza," or can give it with valuation added, "I've had to wait a whole hour just for this lousy, cold pizza."

## APPLICATIONS

### Teaching a New Language—Designing the Syllabus and Writing Textbooks

Emphasis on the communicative function of language has raised at least two important issues relating to syllabus design and materials construction:

1. If communicative competence is the ultimate goal in the second and foreign language courses, how do we define such competence in useful, operational goals?
2. How do we translate communicative competence into "teaching chunks" that can serve as the elements of the syllabus or the textbook in the new language?

The notionally based syllabus, as first suggested by Wilkins (Bibliography, 1976) and later discussed in many papers and presentations (see, in the Bibliography, Campbell, Rutherford, Finocchiaro, and Widdowson in Blatchford and Schachter 1978; Crandall and Grognet 1979), is an attempt to incorporate sociocultural competence, as one aspect of communicative competence, into the teaching syllabus.

Sociocultural competence, in the framework of our study, refers to the speakers' ability to determine the pragmatic appropriateness of a particular speech act in a given context. At the production level, it involves the selection of one of several grammatically acceptable forms according to the perceived degree of formality of the situation and of the available forms. Therefore, communicative competence needs to be translated into the choices and preferences which the learner will have to be able to make in order to perform speech acts in the new language.

As discussed earlier in this paper, in order to evaluate the knowledge of a nonnative speaker or to plan the content of a teaching program, we must have a description of the speech-act sets in the target language. We can then make didactic decisions related to teaching. As an example of such decision making, let us consider the case of the apology speech-act set.

At the present stage of analysis we know what major semantic formulas make up the English apology speech-act set. For the purpose of syllabus design we will assume that the learner needs to know how to apologize in a variety of interactive discourse situations in the target language. However, which of these are the most likely to be encountered by a specific group of learners will have to be considered separately in each case. As a result of such considerations, syllabus designers need to come up with a list.

Once we have developed a tentative list of apology situations relevant for a particular group of learners, we need to decide which of these are suitable for the early part of the course of study and which should be left for a later stage. Such sequencing decisions will depend mostly on the immediate needs of the learners, but course designers will also have to take into account the "spiral" reintroduction of the apology speech act throughout the entire course of study.

The next step in the syllabus design process will be to decide which and how many semantic formulas should be introduced at each point in the syllabus or textbook, in accordance with the situations which have been selected. Such decisions can be made only when good descriptions of speech-act sets are available for both L1 and L2. In order to lead the learners to an ultimate level at which they will make their own choices, we need to expose them to the patterns used most commonly by native speakers of the L2. Sociolinguistic research has already been of great help in this respect. Manes and Wolfson (1981) emphasize the relative "lack of originality" expressed by native speakers in English compliments. They point to the striking repetitiveness of linguistic forms in English compliments. From our own studies concerning apologies we can further reinforce this point; within each of the five major semantic formulas of the apology speech act set, there is relatively little variation. The form "I am sorry" is by far the most widespread expression of apology.

It seems logical to us to incorporate the most commonly used linguistic forms that represent the major semantic formulas of a speech-act set in the initial part of the course of study, while the various subformulas can be introduced gradually as part of the spiraling organization of the syllabus. Furthermore, considerations as to intensification of the speech act need to be incorporated in the teaching materials. As reported above, our findings (Cohen and Olshtain 1981, Olshtain 1981) showed that at times nonnative speakers avoid intensification when they are not confident of the appropriate linguistic form, while at other times they overelaborate their speech acts hoping to create intensification (as in the UCLA studies noted above). We would therefore suggest including in the teaching materials situations which call for intensification of the speech act.

Many modern language textbooks, especially those which have appeared in the last 5 or 6 years, have attempted to incorporate sociocultural information as an integral part of language functions. They have often suffered, however, from lack of theoretical descriptions and research evidence on which to base their selections. Some of these materials allot considerable attention to the use of performative verbs in realizing the speech act, when we know that in fact the use of such verbs in native speech is usually limited to very formal situations. It is necessary, therefore, for textbooks and teaching syllabuses to reflect the constantly widening scope of sociocultural research related to speech acts.

## Testing

It was out of a desire to design a test of truly functional language ability that we initially undertook the task of investigating apologies in English, Hebrew, and EFL. Clearly, the research effort has expanded well beyond that initial interest. As we have seen, there are pressing needs for information on speech act sets for teaching and for textbook writing. There still remains, however, the task of producing a test of sociocultural competence.

The Cohen and Olshtain (1981) study introduced a rating scale in which nonnative respondents were given a point for using a semantic formula or for intensifying an expression of regret in situations where our findings showed that their language group as a whole underused this formula in comparison with native speakers.

This rating scale was plagued by the problem of establishing clear-cut criteria for determining *deviant* utterances and for subsequently deciding *which* semantic formulas to give credit for. We have learned that it is hard enough to establish the patterns of use of semantic formulas for a given speech-act set like apology among *native* speakers, let alone among nonnatives. We have seen that the nature of the situation, the age and status of the respondent, and a number of other factors can play a role. The problem is that as more variables are introduced into test construction, the amount of testing time called for increases dramatically.

Even given these constraints, we have the sense that a testing instrument which can rate nonnative speakers according to specific semantic formulas within speech-act sets has the potential of being more informative and possibly more valid than those which rely exclusively on global ratings. We envision at some point in the future a sociocultural assessment instrument based on a bundle of speech-act sets (e.g., apologies, complaints, refusals) in which each speech-act set has been subjected to careful empirical investigation. In this way the test will ideally assess nonnatives' sociocultural competence in relation to what natives *actually* do in given situations rather than what they are thought to do.

We recognize that empirical research on speech-act sets is still in its early stages. We envision that a number of such studies will be conducted in the future. We welcome them, and look forward to learning from their findings.

## NOTES

1. As distinguished from representatives (e.g., stating), directives (e.g., requesting), commissives (e.g., promising), and declaratives (e.g., excommunicating).

2. This is a revised version of the set of semantic formulas presented in Cohen and Olshtain (1981), based on some of the results from later studies.

3. We envisioned an archetypal speech-act set to include the following for a given discourse situation: the selection and ordering of semantic formulas, and their most prevalent syntactic and semantic realizations (i.e., what the given utterances would actually look like).

4. At the same time that Ford was making these modifications in the original set of semantic formulas and subformulas, Olshtain (1981) was coming up with a similar classification. These were incorporated in the apology speech-act set as presented above.

5. Like our semantic formula 2 above.

# 3

## INTERPRETING AND PERFORMING SPEECH ACTS IN A SECOND LANGUAGE—A CROSS-CULTURAL STUDY OF HEBREW AND ENGLISH[1]

Shoshana Blum-Kulka
*The Centre for Applied Linguistics*
*The Hebrew University, Jerusalem*

A: Do you want to come in?

B: No thanks, really I can't.

A. Oh, come on. You've been to church, have a reward. Have some coffee.

B: No, look ( . . . ) You're a doll, but I got this wife now.

A: I beg your pardon.

B: But thanks, anyway.

(John Updike, *Rabbit Run,* p. 223)

For a native speaker of English, the above conversation is rich in implications, though the meanings negotiated between the two speakers are never expressed directly. This reader somehow knows that the woman's (A) invitation must have implied for the man (B) something else besides coffee, and it is this other, implied invitation that he declines by mentioning his wife. The woman's next line—"I beg your pardon"—might be understood in a number of ways. She might be showing indignation or being—presumably—misinterpreted. She might be apologizing for having made her offer. She might be simply signaling noncomprehension.[2] Will this dialogue retain all its meanings in any other language besides American English? Would it be understood in the same way by a nonnative speaker of English? To answer these questions we have to be able to analyze the kinds of linguistic and nonlinguistic information needed for the interpretation of the speech acts performed in the above dialogue. Such an analysis would show that though the first four lines in the dialogue can be interpreted on the basis of general conversational rules of the type proposed by Grice (1975), the function of the phrase "I beg your pardon" in the context depends on its linguistic meaning potential in American English. As a result, this last phrase might lose its double meaning in translation and might be misinterpreted by a nonnative speaker of English.

Speech acts constitute an aspect of language use which is often highly complex in the mapping of form and meaning. Linguistic, social, and pragmatic knowledge must be present for success. Though certain basic phenomena of speech-act performance, such as indirectness in discourse, might be based on universal principles (Brown and Levinson 1978), their manifestations may vary systematically from language to language. As a result, second language learners might fail to realize speech acts (especially indirect speech acts) in the target language in terms of both communicative effectiveness and social appropriateness.

The nature of cross-linguistic variation in speech act patterns is investigated in the paper through the examination of social control acts (such as directives) in Hebrew and English. The difficulties inherent in the acquisition of the knowledge required for success communication in a second language are demonstrated by the interlanguage speech-act performance produced by learners of Hebrew as a second language.

## THE CLAIM FOR UNIVERSALITY

How universal are the rules that govern speech-act interpretation and performance?

In discussing indirect speech forms, Searle (1975, p. 76) points out that by recognizing the fact that certain standard forms in each language might acquire *conventional* uses as indirect acts, i.e., might be used idiomatically as polite forms of requests, we can explain why there are differences in indirect speech forms from one language to another. He claims that "the mechanisms are not peculiar to this language or that, but at the same time the standard forms from one language will not always maintain their indirect speech-act potential when translated from one language in another" (Searle 1975, p. 76). I would like to argue that the first part of this claim is correct only if "mechanisms" are defined in the most general terms and that the second part is true only if "translation" is understood as "literal" or "formal" translation.

The "mechanisms" in Searle's theory are described as being of a general nature, having to do with the theory of speech acts. "Each type of illocutionary act has a set of conditions that are necessary for the successful and felicitous performance of the act" (Searle 1965, p. 71), the principles of cooperative conversation, and shared background information. Searle's "set of conditions" are labeled "pragmatic preconditions" by Labov and Fanshel (1977), who specify the preconditions that must obtain even for a direct form such as an imperative to count as a valid request: the hearer must believe that the speaker believes that there is a *need* for the action and the request, that the hearer has the *ability* and *obligation* to carry it out, and that the speaker has the *right* to tell the hearer to do so. By applying this rule in context, we should be able to distinguish between imperatives that are valid requests and those that are not. Labov and Fanshel's rule of request is defined in purely *pragmatic* terms; hence the rule should apply to any language that has imperative forms.

It follows that a second language learner who has acquired the use of imperative forms in the target language should have no difficulty in distinguishing between valid and nonvalid requests or in performing directives by the use of imperatives. As we look at other ways of performing requests, this clear division between "pragmatic" and "linguistic" factors becomes much more complex.

It becomes evident either that some of the proposed pragmatic rules, at least for indirect requests, do not hold across languages or that we need to specify a new rule to account for a mechanism for making requests that has no equivalent in another language. For example, Searle's propositional-content-condition for directives states that "the sentence predicates a future act A of H (hearer)." In English, speakers can make a request by asking someone whether this condition obtains ["will, (would) you do it"]. In Hebrew, a question that predicates the future act of the hearer is considered conventionally a request for information, *not* for action. (Ta'ase zot? → will you do it?). On the other hand, one standard way for making a request in Hebrew is to ask about the general possibility of obtaining something. (Efšar leqabel et . . . is it possible to get . . . ).[3] The last example suggests that the argument presented by speech-act theoreticians is not as divorced from linguistic considerations as it seems to be.

A similar line of argument is presented by Green (1975) in discussing the possible universality of the "conversational postulates" proposed by Gordon and Lakoff (1975). Green (1975, p. 138) reports that her findings contradict Gordon and Lakoff's claim that their postulates hold for all languages. For example, four out of the five languages she checked did not have the postulate which would permit one to ask people to do something by asking them if they expect to do it in the future.

From a second language acquisition perspective, the issue of "universality" is a crucial one; if it were true, as Searle claims, that "the mechanisms" for indirect speech acts are not language-specific or that the "conversational postulates" proposed by Gordon and Lakoff hold for all languages, the task of acquiring a second language would not involve a process of learning "how to mean" in another language. This line of reasoning has been followed, for example, by Fraser (1978). Fraser argues that second language learners do not have to learn "how to code their intentions" in the target language. Once they acquire the linguistic means necessary for realizing their speech acts, they only have to learn the social-appropriateness rules that specify how to choose among available forms in any given context. Contrary to such claims, I would like to argue that the nature of the interdependence among pragmatic, linguistic, and social factors that determine speech-act realization varies from one language to another, and that as a result, second language learners often fail to realize their speech acts in the target language both in terms of *effectiveness* (getting their meaning across) and in terms of social appropriateness.

The evidence to support my position comes from data obtained in an empirical study designed to compare the speech-act performance of second language learners (native speakers of Canadian English, learning Hebrew) with that of native speakers of both Hebrew and English.[4] The evidence will be presented in two parts; the first presents an analysis of the speech-act forms used by native speakers from a Hebrew-English cross-cultural point of view; the second analyzes the effectiveness and appropriateness of the forms used by the learners of Hebrew from the point of view of native speakers. Strategies, Procedures, and Linguistic Realization: Are the conventional procedures for realizing a certain speech act shared across languages?

Fraser (1978) has recently claimed that the strategies for performing illocutionary acts are essentially the same across languages. Fraser uses the term "strategy" to refer to "the particular choice of sentential form and meaning which the speaker employs in order to perform the intended act" (Fraser 1978, p. 12). I will try to show that the similarity is illusory and tends to disappear on close analysis.

In comparing strategies across languages, we should try to distinguish between the procedure by which the speech act is performed and the specific linguistic realization this procedure takes. By moving from "procedure" to "linguistic realization" we are moving from pragmatic and social considerations to linguistic ones. These "procedures" have a higher potential as candidates for "universality" than the specific linguistic forms they take. Consider the following:

1.         Hebrew                English

Ata yaxol lehalvot li et hakesef? →   Could you lend me the money?
(Can you lend me the money?)[5] →   Can you lend me the money?

In this case the procedure is shared across languages: in both Hebrew and English, one can make a valid request by appealing to the hearer's ability to do the act. Another property of the strategy that is shared across both languages is that in both it has the same "primary" and "secondary" illocutionary force (to use Searle's terms), so that the following conversation could have just as well taken place in Hebrew, with exactly the same perlocutions.

2. Child:   Can you fix the needle?
   Adult:   I'm busy.
   Child:   I just wanted to know if you can fix it.
                    (McTear 1973)

Translated into French, German, or Spanish, the utterances in the above dialogue would probably maintain their illocutionary force, since each of these languages has an equivalent strategy:

3. Could you (please)/Konnen sie (bitte)/Pouvez vous (s'il vous plait)/Podria usted (por favor)/Ata yaxol (bvakaša)

On the other hand, the following strategy in Hebrew will not maintain the illocutionary force when translated (literally) into English:

| Hebrew | | English |
|--------|---|---------|
| 4. Ata muxan la'asot zot?<br>(Are you ready or prepared to do it?) | ≠ | Will you . . .<br>Would you . . .<br>Are you willing . . . |

This case raises the problem of where to draw the line when we talk about "shared" and "nonshared" speech-act properties across languages. On the one hand, one could argue that in Example 4—in both Hebrew and English—some reference is made to the hearers' "willingness" to do the act (the strategy questions a hearer-based sincerity condition), and hence the various forms in the two languages are based on the same procedure.

On the other hand, one could also argue that asking about the hearers' "readiness"[6] to do the act is not the same as appealing to their willingness, and hence we should consider "muxan" questions as a language-specific strategy.

I tend to believe that in this case the procedure underlying the strategy is shared across languages (see Table 1). This conclusion is supported by two points from the empirical study: when asked to translate a dialogue that contained the sentence (in Hebrew) "are you ready to go to the store?" native speakers of English used phrases such as "would you like to go to the store?" or "would you go to the store?" Furthermore, in completing the missing sentence from a dialogue by a request form, native speakers of Hebrew used "are you ready?" questions, and native speakers of English (on the English version of the same test) used "would you?" questions.

From a translation point of view, one can say that Hebrew "are you ready?" and English "would you?" are functionally, not formally, equivalent. This example still fits with the explanation given by Searle (1975) to account for differences between languages in speech-act forms: each language has chosen a different idiomatic way by which to realize an underlying similar mechanism.

From a second language learner's point of view, though, the difference in the linguistic realization of this strategy (between Hebrew and English) can have serious consequences; learners' attempts to formulate a "willingness" question in Hebrew by using the verb "roce" ("want"—probably echoing the English "would like to") results in a phrase that fails to carry the illocutionary force of a request. Thus the phrase "do you want to notify the teachers" (ata roce lehodia lamorim) used by learners is not equivalent to "are you ready to notify the teachers" (ata muxan lehodia lamorim") used by native speakers (see Appendix D9).

The following examples further illustrate how variations from language to language in the linguistic realization of a similar procedure might affect its potential illocutionary force.

| 5. | English | | Hebrew |
|----|---------|---|--------|
| | I want you to go | ⟶ | ani roçe šetelex<br>(I want that you'll go) |
| | I would like you to go | ≠ | hayiti roçe šetelex<br>(I would like that you'll go) |

6.　　English　　　　　　　　　　　Hebrew

Why don't you do it?　———→　a. lama ata lo ose zot?
　　　　　　　　　　　　　　　　　(Why are not you doing it)
　　　　　　　　　　　　　　　　b. lama šolo ta'ase zot?
　　　　　　　　　　　　　　　　　(Why (that not) will you do it)
Why not do it?　　　　　　≠　　a. lama lo la'asot zot?
　　　　　　　　　　　　　　　　　(Why not do it)
　　　　　　　　　　　　　　　　b. lama šelo na'ase zot?
　　　　　　　　　　　　　　　　　(Why don't we do it)

In Example 5 both English forms are standard indirect forms of requests, the difference between them being probably one of degree of directness (expressed as politeness). In Hebrew, on the other hand, only the formal equivalent to "I want you to" clearly carries the illocutionary force of a request.

The Hebrew phrase equivalent to "I would like to" is commonly used to describe a hypothetical situation (hayiti roce lalexet aval ani lo yaxol/—I would like to go but I can't). The form is not a standard, idiomatic request form, though it can be used as a politeness marker in requests. A sentence like "I would like you to go now" in Hebrew is hence more ambiguous out of context than in English. The exact status of forms like "would you" or "could you"[7] (as opposed to "will you" or "can you") is also linked to problems of social appropriateness: it may well be the case that these forms are depleted of their force as requests in Hebrew because of a general social norm that allows for more directness in communication than in English, and by this norm "would you" or "could you" might not be considered direct enough—in some contexts—to count as requests. Phrases like "I would like you to leave me alone" ("Hayiti roca seta'azov oti bimnuza") appeared in the data in the responses of learners alone (see Appendix, D8, and Table 2, D8). None of the native speakers of Hebrew used this form for making a request. This difference in usage suggests that the learners transferred the forms from English, without realizing the depletion in illocutionary force that occurred through translation.

Example 6 shows how a stylistic variation can affect illocutionary force potential. Questioning the reason for not doing can serve both in English and in Hebrew as an indirect strategy for requests, as long as the resulting sentence refers directly to the hearer (why don't you . . . ). On the other hand, making a request by way of a general suggestion ("why not do it") will *not* usually have the force of a request in Hebrew unless it is marked by a colloquial "še" (literally "that") form. Thus the difference between "lama lo" and "lama šelo" in Hebrew is not only one of register (the latter being the more colloquial) but mainly one of illocutionary force potential.

This strategy was used in the text in telling a child to get a haircut (D6, Appendix):

7. lama ata lo mistaper?!
   Why don't you get a haircut?!

7a. lama lo lehistaper?
   Why not get a haircut?

7b. (Why (that) don't you get a haircut)
   Lama šelo tistaper?

Example 7 was used by native speakers of English on the English version of the test and by learners in Hebrew. Though native speakers of Hebrew did not use Example 7, a group of 10 native speaker informants agreed that this form *can* be interpreted as a request. This interpretation does not hold for Example 7a; if parents utter Example 7a instead of Example 7 or 7c, they shouldn't be surprised if their suggestion fails to result in action on the part of the child. Though Example 7a might not be effective enough in a home situation in either English or Hebrew, it is not hard to imagine other situations in which in English—but not in Hebrew—the phrase does carry the force of a directive. Thus, for example, if one member of the board tells another at the entrance to the board meeting "why not get a jacket," the suggestion will probably be followed by action. Typically Example 7a was used by learners alone and Example 7c by native speakers of Hebrew alone. In all the examples analyzed so far, the differences between Hebrew and English can be attributed to differences in linguistic realization (Examples 4 and 6) and social-appropriateness norms (Example 5). Example 8 does not fall into this category:

8.     Hebrew                          English

   efšar leqabel et . . . ?            May I have . . .
   (Is it possible to get)             Can I have . . .
                                       Would it be possible . . .

In some contexts, this Hebrew form can be functionally equivalent to English "permission directives" of the type "can I" or "may I" get X.[8] For example, it is standard procedure in Hebrew to address an operator or secretary on the telephone by "is it possible to speak to X" or "is it possible to get X." In the same situation, the English "can I speak to X" has the same function. This particular function or equivalence is also apparent from native speakers' completion of the following dialogue:

9.  D1.  *At the restaurant*
    Dan:  What would you like to eat?
    Ruth:  I don't know, let's have a look at the menu.
    Dan (to the waiter):  Waiter_____?

Native speakers of Hebrew formulated the request in this case (on the Hebrew version) by "is it possible to get the menu," and native speakers of English (in English) used "could we see the menu." But this apparent functional equivalence was not clear at all to the learners. Learners generally tended to avoid "efšar" in requests altogether and used them mainly in contexts where the question could be interpreted literally. ("would it be possible to get a discount," D7, Appendix, and Table 2). This suggests that at least for the learners, the strategy is conceived as Hebrew-language-specific, nonequivalent to any strategy familiar from the mother tongue.

Indirect requests can be considered as evidence for the claim that the mechanisms for realizing an act might be language-specific. Though in the contexts where it is used the form in Hebrew has to fulfill the pragmatic preconditions necessary for any request form to count as a valid request, the way by which the request is realized is *not* a consequence of the speech-act rule contained in the conditions. The point is that the speech-act rule mechanisms described by Searle (1975), as well as Labov and Fanshel's rule for indirect request (1977, p. 82), show a systematic relationship between the preconditions and the actual sentences used as directives. An example like the Hebrew "permission directive" does not fit, as far as I can see, into this kind of generalization—since it does not refer to or concern any of Searle's four preconditions, nor is it "covered" by Labov and Fanshel's rule of indirect request. It could be that the problem lies not with the conditions but with the generalizations; while in specifying the pragmatic preconditions we are dealing with extralinguistic factors, any generalization of the kind "S can make an indirect directive by stating that the sincerity condition obtains" (Searle 1979, p. 45) refers to actual linguistic data and as such is subject to variation from one language to another.

The comparison of English and Hebrew directive types discussed in this section is summarized in Table 1. The analysis yields the following general cases:

1. Conventional, shared procedures for the performance of direct and indirect directives that have similar linguistic realization in Hebrew and English (for example, types 1 and 3 in Table 1)

2. Similar procedures with different linguistic realization in each language (for example, types 2 and 4 in Table 1)

3. Language-specific conventional procedures (for example, type 5 in Table 1)

## POTENTIAL ILLOCUTIONARY FORCE AND RULES OF SOCIAL APPROPRIATENESS

For any two speech-act strategies—listed in Table 1—to be considered equivalent or at least similar across languages, they have to share a similar potential illocutionary force relative to the contexts in which they are conventionally used. Both the differences between languages in the devices available for modulating any given speech act and the social-appropriateness rules that govern the choice of forms in context might affect the force potential of the forms. Since both modulating devices and social-appropriateness rules might be language- and culture-specific, it follows that even seemingly similar strategies in two languages might differ in illocutionary force potential.

One modulating device is mitigation. Mitigation is defined by Fraser (1978, p. 22) as "the intentional softening or easing of the force of the message—a modulation of the basic message intended by the speaker." The linguistic means available for mitigating an act or for aggravating it (modulating it in the opposite way) can be language-specific. For example, Hebrew has no syntactic equivalent to English "tag questions" that are often used to mitigate requests ("You'll do it,

**Table 1**   Some Directive types in Hebrew and English (potential force)[a]

| Directive type[b] | Conventional procedure | | Linguistic realization | |
|---|---|---|---|---|
| | Hebrew | English | Hebrew | English |
| 1. Imperatives | Stating a future act of hearer | Same | Ta'ase[c] zot! (do it) | Do it |
| 2. Question directive | Asking about a future act of hearer | Same | (will you do it) $\neq$ | Will you do it?[e] |
| 3. Ability question | Appealing to hearers' ability to do the act | Same | Ata yaxol la'asot zot? (can you) | Can you/Could you do it? |
| 4. Willingness questions[g] | Appealing to hearers' intention to do the act | Appealing to hearers' willingness to do the act | Ata muxan la'asot zot? (can you) | Will you . . . ? Are you willing . . . ? Would you . . . ? |
| 5. Permission directives[g] | Asking about the possibility of receiving $x$ | ? | Efšar leqabel? (Is it possible to get) | |
| 6. Desire statements | Asserting speakers' willingness | | Ani roça šeta'ase (I want that you) | I want you to . . . |
| 7. Obligation statements | Appealing to hearers' obligation to do the act | Same | Ata çarix La'asot zot (You have to do it) | You have to . . . You should . . .[h] |
| 8. "Why not" questions | Questioning the reason for the act | Same | lama ata lo . . . ? (Why don't you) | Why don't you . . . ? |
| | | | lama šelo . . . ? (Why not?) | Why not? |

a. All forms listed have the potential illocutionary force of directives [fulfill Searle's (1975) essential condition: can *count as* directives]. The table does not specify the pragmatic conditions that might affect this illocutionary force. Also, the list does not attempt to be exhaustive—the forms listed in Hebrew are those that appeared in the data.

b. Except 5, all categories mentioned have been previously discussed in speech-act literature (Searle 1975, Ervin-Tripp 1977, Labov and Fanshel 1977, Fraser 1975). The present taxonomy is meant to highlight some similarities and differences between English and Hebrew.

c. In spoken Hebrew imperatives are realized morphologically either by an imperative verb form or by a second person future verb form.

d. In Hebrew, "please" as a politeness marker in requests has to come at the end of the utterance. In initial position it weakens its illocutionary force.

e. Since Hebrew has no equivalent to the English modal "will," the linguistic realizations are

44

**Table 1** *continued*

| Aggravation device | | Mitigation device | | Politeness markers | |
| --- | --- | --- | --- | --- | --- |
| *Hebrew* | *English* | *Hebrew* | *English* | *Hebrew* | *English* |
| | | | | + bvakaša (please) | Same[d] |
| + Ulay (perhaps) | | + tag (tov) (O.K.) | ≠ tag questions | + please | Same |
| | | + Ulay (perhaps)[f] | ≠ tag questions | + please | Same |
| | | + Ulay (perhaps) (initial) | ≠ tag questions | + please | Same |
| | | + Ulay (perhaps) (initial) | | + please | ? |
| | | | | ? | |

nonequivalent. "Will" refers in row 2 to "future" and in row 4 ("willingness") to "volition." (See Labov and Fanshel 1977, p. 85, for a discussion of this ambiguity in English.)

f. Notice that both "ability" and "willingness" questions can be accounted for (in procedure) by references to Searle's "preparatory condition" (Searle 1975, p. 72). It was felt that the difference in linguistic realization (in Hebrew) warranted a separation into two distinct directive types.

g. Both procedure and linguistic realization in this case are Hebrew-language-specific. Being realized by the syntactically impersonal form (efšar + infinitive), this request form in Hebrew does not mention the actor and refers to the beneficiary only implicitly (Leqabel—receive). In translation, it's functionally equivalent to English permission directives.

h. There is no direct equivalent in Hebrew to the modal "should."

won't you?"). On the other hand, one can aggravate a request in Hebrew by putting the stress on an initial "ulay" (perhaps) "*Perhaps* you'll stop?!").

Thus on a scale of directness, an "ulay" form in Hebrew can figure higher than the imperative. Consider the following:

10.  Hebrew                                    English

aggravating:  ta'azov oti bimnuza!    ⟶    Leave me alone!
              (Leave me alone)
              ulay ta'azov oti         ≠    *Perhaps* you could leave me alone?!
              bimnuza?!
              (Perhaps you'll leave
              me alone)!

In the most general terms, Hebrew social norms allow for more directness than English ones (at least American English). As Levenston (1968, 1971) has noted, speech-act patterns that are perfectly acceptable socially in Hebrew might not be acceptable at all in English, and vice versa. Thus, it is accepted procedure in Hebrew, at least in semiformal situations, such as around a conference table, to disagree by telling the other directly that he is wrong (ata to'e—literally you're wrong) or by denying the facts ('Io naxon—not true), while English speakers under the same circumstances feel a need to soften the act by: "I may be wrong but . . .", or "Are you sure . . ."? etc. Though the Hebrew direct patterns are linguistically possible in English under the same circumstances, they probably will not be considered socially acceptable.[9] Another example is Japanese speech-act norms compared with American ones. Americans don't seem to mind being commanded to drink Coca-Cola ("Drink Coca-Cola!") or being instructed how to use their money ("Buy now, Pay later!") or with whom to pray ("Pray Together, Stay Together!").[10] As Higa (1971) remarks, such a free use of direct impera-tives in advertisements is unthinkable in a Japanese social context. A study of Japanese and American newspapers and magazines showed (Higa 1971) that 70 percent of the Japanese advertisements used some kind of indirect pattern, while 62 percent of the American advertisements used indirect imperative forms.

A form's degree of directness, relative to culture-specific social norms, affects its illocutionary force potential. As a result, even a "direct" strategy of request, such as imperatives, does not really share the same force potential in Hebrew and English. This point can be shown by examining the completions of English and Hebrew native speakers to two of the dialogues in the Appendix.

11.  D2          *Driver and the policeman*
     Policeman:  Is that your car there?
     Driver:     Yes. I left it there only for a few minutes.
     Policeman:  _____
     Driver:     O.K.  O.K.  I'm sorry. I'll move at once.[11]

The incident depicted by this dialogue was believed to be governed by specif-ic, culture-bound social norms. Israeli policemen are known to be notoriously direct (and impolite), while their North American (at least Canadian) counterparts in a situation similar to the one evoked in the dialogue would be much less direct. This difference in social norms is reflected in the responses; the majority of native speakers of Hebrew used imperatives, while native speakers of Canadian English used hint statements like "it's a no stopping zone." (D2, Table 2)

On the other hand, the situation depicted in D8 (girl trying to get rid of stranger on the street, Appendix) was believed to be governed by cross-culturally shared norms. As expected, both native speakers of English and native speakers of Hebrew used some kind of direct strategy. But while the directness in English was achieved mainly by lexical means ("get lost" being a "soft" expression compared with some other responses), the Hebrew responses were divided between equivalent imperatives ("Leave me alone") and the language-specific aggravated imperatives (Perhaps you'll leave me alone).

These examples show that a similar strategy of request (imperatives) is considered by native speakers of Hebrew and English as having a different illocutionary force potential. For native speakers of Hebrew the use of the imperatives was judged to be both appropriate and effective in one context (D2) but not effective enough (for some) in another (D8).

From the English native speakers' point of view, the use of imperatives was judged to be socially inappropriate in one context (D2) and both appropriate and effective in another (D8). As will be shown in the following section, such differences in the relative status and potential force of even similar strategies across languages can lead to both inappropriate and ineffective speech-act realization on the part of second language learners.

## THE PROBLEMS INVOLVED IN REALIZING SPEECH ACTS APPROPRIATELY AND EFFECTIVELY IN A SECOND LANGUAGE

The learners in this study, as mentioned above, were all native speakers of English, studying Hebrew at York University in Toronto (see footnote 4). All the learners have spent some time in Israel (between a month to a year) and were familiar to some extent with the register of spoken Hebrew. The discussion that follows is based on a comparison of learners' responses on the discourse completion test (see Appendix) with those of native speakers of Hebrew on the same test, and with those of native speakers of English on the English version of this test. The results discussed here are summarized in Table 2.

The main conclusion that seems to emerge from the data is that second language learners seem to develop an *interlanguage* of speech-act performance, which differs from both first and second language native usage.[12] The interlanguage of speech-act performance is manifested in the following ways: (1) usages similar to those of native speakers in all ways, (2) usages that differ from those of native speakers on a scale of directness (violating social-appropriateness norms), (3) usages that differ from those of native speakers in linguistic realization and/or procedures (possibly causing an unintended shift in illocutionary force). These similarities and differences can be, in part, explained by viewing the rules that govern speech-act performance and interpretation across languages as ranging on a

**Table 2** Use of Directive Types in 8 Items[a] (Typical Responses)[b]

| | | Hebrew | | English |
|---|---|---|---|---|
| | | Native Speakers (32) | Learners (19) | Native Speakers (10) |
| 1. | D3 | Ata yaxol . . . (69%)[c] (Can you lend me . . . ) | Same (42%) | Could you lend it to me? (7) |
| 2. | D9 | Ata muxan . . . (63%) (Are you ready to notify?) | (1) Same (21%) (2) Ata roçe . . . (16%) (Do you want to . . . ?) | Would you call them (7) |
| 3. | D10 | Ulay tixtov . . . (75%) (Maybe you'll write . . . ) | Same (37%) | Why don't you write to grandma? (8) |
| 4. | D17 | Ulay ata telex . . . (69%) (Maybe you'll go?) | (1) Same (42%) (2) Ata yaxol . . . (32%) (Can you go?) | Could you go? (6) |
| 5. | D7 | Efšar leqabel . . . (56%) (Is it possible to get a discount?) | (1) Same (42%)[d] (2) At yexola latet . . . (32%) (Can you give me . . . ) | Would it be possible to get a discount? (3) |
| 6. | D1 | Efšar leqabel . . . (69%) (Is it possible to get the menu?) | (1) Same (26%) (2) Tavi . . . (37%) (Bring me the menu) | Can we see the menu please? (4) Could we have the menu please? (6) |
| 7. | D8 | Ta'azov oti bimnuxa (66%) (leave me alone) | (1) Same (31%) (2) "I am not interested" (63%)[e] | Get lost (7) |
| 8. | D2 | Taziz et hamxonit (78%) | (1) Same (49%) | It's a no stopping zone (6) |

a. The responses presented in Table 2 are: (1) the most frequent responses of native speakers, (2) the most frequent responses for learners, and (3) forms of special interest used by learners.

b. The forms are presented by items because it is believed that the situations depicted by the dialogues on the test *are not equivalent* in their potential range of acceptable directive types. This can be seen by the variation across items in the native speakers' responses.

c. Agreement on choice of directive type among native speakers reached 78 percent (D2) in some cases, while among learners it never exceeded 42 percent.

d. Note that more learners used "is it possible to get" in the context where it can be interpreted literally (D7) than in the context where it is used as a conventional indirect form of request (D1).

e. Included in the 63 percent were all responses that *hinted* at the girls' wish to be left alone.

continuum from the cross-culturally shared, possibly universal rules to the language- and culture-specific ones.[13] Second language learners' performance seems to approximate native usage where the rules are cross-culturally shared and to deviate from native usage where the rules are language- and culture-specific. The above offered explanation accounts, for example, for the similarity between learners' and native speakers' responses in completing the following dialogue (D16, not included in Table 2):

12. A: What do you think of our new boss?
    B: Not very nice.
    C: Not nice? I think he's _____!

This dialogue was constructed on the basis of the observation that when a speaker questions a proposition stated by the previous speaker, he is often signaling disagreement with that proposition. It was assumed that such conversational rules operate according to Grice's maxims (Grice 1975) and are shared cross-culturally. The maxim violated in D16 is that of relevance: answering a statement by questioning it is not relevant unless the speaker is implying disagreement with that statement. It was expected that since this rule is not language- or culture-bound, it will operate in the same way for native and nonnative speakers of the language. The results support this claim. Most native speakers of Hebrew (90 percent, $n = 20$) and most learners (83 percent, $n = 19$) completed the dialogue with an emphatic contradictory statement like "He's great." Native speakers of English had a similar interpretation (8 out of 10). In all three groups, some interpreted A's question as implying disagreement with the strength with which B's statement has been made, as shown by answers such as "he's awful" or "he's a real menace."

If we also understand the notion of a "cross-culturally shared language-specific continuum" as referring to similarities and differences in actual speech-act forms, then this explanation can also account for learners' preference for similar forms (like "could you" questions, see D3 in Table 2) and apparent avoidance of language-specific ones (such as possibility questions, see D6). The fact that we can point to cross-culturally shared rules of speech-act performance suggests that learners face the task of learning a second language equipped with possibly a universal pragmatic competence that will help them in certain aspects involved in interpreting and performing speech acts in the target language. The following results suggest that learners indeed activate a non-language-specific pragmatic competence in attempting to communicate in a second language.

1. Learners' *choice* of speech-act form *varied* across situations. The variation shows that learners were almost as sensitive as native speakers to contextual constraints. (Each learner used at least four request forms as compared with at least six forms used by each of the native speakers.)
2. The *range* of speech-act forms used by learners included both explicit *direct* forms (like imperatives) and conventional *indirect* forms (like "could you" questions.) (see Table 2 for details).

However, cross-culturally shared rules account only in part for speech-act realization in every language. Therefore, it is perhaps not surprising to find that transferring native language pragmatic competence and applying linguistic competence in the second language does not necessarily ensure appropriate and effective speech-act realization in the second language. The results show this last point in two ways:

1. Violation of social-appropriateness norms *and* shifts in illocutionary force
2. Violating social appropriateness in the target language

The nature of the test used in this study allows for an analysis of second language learners' degree of adaptability to target language social-appropriateness norms from two aspects only: (1) conformity to or deviation from acceptability norms and (2) degree of directness in realizing a speech act.

A statistical analysis performed on the data showed that the distribution of learners' responses for each item differed significantly from that of native speakers. In each case, the forms most frequently used by native speakers were not as frequently used by learners and vice versa. High agreement among native speakers on the choice of a specific form in a given context can be considered as an acceptability judgment. Considered this way, the most frequently used form is the most acceptable one. By preferring different forms to the ones agreed on by native speakers, learners thus might violate target language acceptability norms.

The results also reveal a general tendency on the part of the learners to be *less direct* than native speakers in their choice of speech-act form, probably to some extent because of *transfer of social norms*. Thus, for example, the distribution of responses for D2 (see Table 2) shows that most native speakers expect an Israeli policeman to make an explicit, direct demand ("move the car") while learners are divided between those that conform to this expectation and those that expect a less direct strategy. ("You have to move the car" or "The car should be moved.") In asking directions from a stranger on the street (D14, see Appendix), only learners felt a need to follow the "attention getter" (excuse me . . . ) with the polite indirect "could you tell me please." All native speakers of Hebrew (but none of English!) used a direct question. ("Where is the railway station?") In yet another case which was interpreted by native speakers as requiring a high degree of directness (D8), most learners realized their speech-act in Hebrew by using hints ("I'm not interested;" "I don't have time for you") while native speakers of English (in English) did not hesitate to show the same kind of bluntness as native speakers of Hebrew (in Hebrew). ("Get lost." See Table 2.) In this last case, though, learners' "less directness" is probably due to either lack of linguistic means or a reluctance on the part of the learners to express emotions directly in a language over which they do not have full control. These results indicate that second language learners violate norms of social appropriateness in the target language to some extent in predictable ways. It still remains to be shown how such violations might also affect the illocutionary force of learners' utterances, leading to possible breakdown in communication.

As discussed above, "ability questions," (could you, can you) are similar across Hebrew and English in both procedure and linguistic realization. It is therefore not surprising that second language learners of Hebrew acquire this strategy easily and—in some contexts—use it in appropriate and effective ways (for example, in asking for a loan (D3), "could you lend me the money"; see Table 2). But this apparent similarity in form and function across the two languages does not hold for all contexts. This point emerged from considering native speakers' and learners' responses to the following dialogue:

13.   D17   *Husband and wife*
      Diane:   There's a PTA meeting tonight.
      Robert:  Are you going?

Diane:    I'm exhausted _____?
Robert:   When does it start? I can't be there before eight.

As can be seen in Table 2, one of the strategies used by native speakers of English for making the request in this case was "could you" questions. This strategy *was not used* by any of the native speakers of Hebrew. On the other hand, it was quite frequent (42 percent) among the learners. From a second language acquisition point of view, the process operating here is one of overgeneralization: the learner extends the use of ability questions (as requests) to contexts where native speakers prefer a different strategy.

From a speech-act realization point of view, the most important point to note about the use of this form is that in the given context *it does not carry the illocutionary force of a request* in the same way as it does in English. This observation was confirmed by native speakers of Hebrew who suggested that a wife asking her husband "could you go to the meeting" (in Hebrew in the given context) is likely to be interpreted as genuinely seeking information whether he is able to go, only possibly hinting at the implication that she is requesting him to go.

The force of the form in English derives from the conventional use of "can you" questions as requests: this convention does not hold for the given context in Hebrew. It follows that despite their seeming similarity, as claimed above, "can you" questions *do not share the same illocutionary force potential* in Hebrew and English.[14]

For the second language learner, awareness of the potential illocutionary force of any conventional speech-act form is essential for achieving communicative ends in the target language. Since the language-specific contextual constraints on neither cross-culturally shared strategies nor language-specific ones are very clear, learners might fail to get their intentions across using either the former or the latter. We have seen one example of a shift in illocutionary force in the use of a cross-culturally shared strategy (Example 13). A similar shift in meaning was also observed in the use of language-specific strategies. In attempting to formulate a request from a subordinate (D9), some learners used the Hebrew equivalent of "Is it possible to notify the teachers" (see Table 2). As in the case of D17, the strategy fails to carry the illocutionary force of a request in this context in Hebrew. In this example, the shift in illocutionary force might be due to linguistic realization: permission directives of this form in Hebrew are conventionally realized with the verb to "receive" ("is it possible to receive X") and if a verb of action is mentioned at all, it is prefixed by a performative verb ("is it possible to ask you to do X").

Similar shifts might occur as a result of "wrong" lexicalization. Using in the context of D9 (request from a subordinate) the Hebrew equivalent of "Do you want to notify the teachers" (ata roce lehodia lamorim), as some learners did (16 percent), fails to achieve the desired effect. The learners' phrase in Hebrew is probably an attempt to formulate a "would you like to" request in Hebrew. The weakening of the request force is due to the fact that this strategy is conventionally lexicalized in Hebrew by "muxan" (ready—prepared) and not by "roce" (wish/want).

51

The discussion in this section can be summarized as follows:

1. Second language learners seem to realize their speech act in the target language successfully in cases which are governed by cross-culturally shared rules (D16) and in cases where the specific choice of speech-act strategy is also cross-culturally shared (D3).
2. Second language learners seem to violate social-appropriateness norms in the target language in ways that indicate a transfer of social norms from the native language.
3. Second language learners might fail to realize their speech acts effectively by either extending or overgeneralizing the potential illocutionary force of shared and nonshared strategies to inappropriate contexts (D9 and D17) or by failing to follow target language conventions of usage in the realization of language-specific strategies (D9).

## SUMMARY AND CONCLUSION

The two basic claims argued in this paper are:

1. Languages might differ in the procedures, linguistic realization, and potential illocutionary force of indirect speech-act strategies for (at least) requests.
2. As a result, second language learners might fail to realize their speech act in the target language in terms of both social appropriateness and effectiveness.

The evidence for the first claim came from data obtained from native speakers of Hebrew and English and for the second from data obtained from learners of Hebrew as a second language.

From a speech-act theory point of view, the results suggest that the differences between English and Hebrew strategies for requests justify a "nonuniversalistic" approach to the analysis of speech-act forms across languages. This does not mean that there are no universal or at least cross-culturally shared properties of speech-act realization. It does mean, though, that further comparisons between languages on these lines will have to account for the complex nature of the interdependence among pragmatic considerations, linguistic meaning, and social rules of usage that govern speech-act realization in any particular language. The issue of speech-act "universality" is far from being resolved by the findings reported here. Nevertheless, the analysis of some request forms in Hebrew and English presented suggests that the way in which the interrelationship among pragmatic, linguistic, and social factors is manifested in language varies considerably from one language and culture to another.

From a second language learning perspective, the results suggest that certain aspects of speech-act realization rules are, in fact, transferred to the task of learning a second language but that this transfer is not sufficient to ensure successful communication. Native speakers know as part of their communicative competence that they can realize speech acts in the native language both directly and indirectly and that there are certain pragmatic and social rules which dictate the choice of speech-act form in various contexts. They also know the linguistic means available for mitigating or aggravating any speech act and are hence able to modulate the forms if they do not achieve the desired perlocution. Faced with the task of learning a second language, speakers expect to find equivalent linguistic means and social rules in the target language. Once they acquire a certain level of linguistic competence, they will also, presumably, try to activate their pragmatic competence in achieving their communicative ends. At this point, they might easily fail.

Misunderstandings and violations of social norms are bound to appear because only the basic properties of speech acts (like direct versus indirect ways) are shared across languages; the actual ways by which these properties are realized might differ in every respect. It follows that as long as we do not know more about the ways in which speech acts are realized in any particular language, learners will continue to be puzzled by the difficulties encountered in attempting to convey intentions in a language other than their own.

## APPENDIX

### Discourse Completion—Test B*
### (English Version)

D1.  *At the restaurant*
   Dan: What would you like to eat?
   Ruth: I don't know, let's have a look at the menu.
   Dan (to the waiter): Waiter _____?

D2.  *Driver and the policeman*
   Policeman: Is that you car there?
   Driver: Yes. I left it there only for a few minutes.
   Policeman: _____!
   Driver: O.K. O.K. I'm sorry. I'll move at once.

D3.  *Among friends*
   Dan: Ron. I found a great apartment but I have a problem. I have to pay the landlady
       a $500 deposit by tonight.
   Ron: And you haven't got it?
   Dan: No. I'll get my salary only next week.
   _____?

   Ron: Sorry, no. I'm out of money right now.

D6.  *Mother and son*
   Peter: Mum, where is the hairbrush?
   Mother: In the bathroom, of course. Peter, your hair is down to your knees.
   _____?

   Peter: I don't want a haircut!

D7.  *At a second hand dress shop*
   How much is that dress?
   $50
   That's expensive. _____?
   Sorry, all our prices are fixed.

D8.  *In the street*
   Boy: What's the time, please;
   Girl: Three thirty.

Boy: You're nice, say, what's your name?
Girl: It's none of your business.
Boy: How about having a drink with me?
Girl: No!
Boy: What about tomorrow?
Girl: Listen, _____! ! !

D9. *A teachers meeting*
Teacher: Where's the next meeting?
Principal: Next Wednesday at 8:00. We'll have to notify the people who aren't here
    tonight. Richard, _____?
Richard: O.K. I'll do it.

D10. *Mother and son*
Peter: Mum, I'm bored.
Mum: Don't you have any homework?
Peter: No, we are going on a trip tomorrow.
Mother: I have got an idea. _____?
    You know Grandma would be delighted to get a letter from you.

D16. *At the office*
Sandra: What do you think of our new boss?
Sharon: Not very nice.
Sandra: Not nice? I think he's _____.

D17. *Husband and wife*
Diane: There's a PTA meeting tonight.
Robert: Are you going?
Diane: I'm exhausted, _____?
Robert: When does it start? I can't be there before eight.

* The items presented are only those discussed in the paper.

## NOTES

1. I am indebted to Patrick Allen, Ellen Bialystock, Michael Canale, Gila Hanna, Michael Szamosi, Merril Swain, and Jessica Wirth for very helpful comments on earlier drafts of this paper. I would also like to express my gratitude to Galia Hatav for giving me access to her students at York University and for her help in conducting the study.

2. Updike actually confirms the first interpretation and offers the reader a new kind of ambiguity. The woman slams the door in the man's face, and the hero is puzzled: "Was she mad because he had turned down a proposition or because he had shown that he had thought she had made one?" (Updike 1960, p. 224).

3. The nearest equivalent in English to this form would be "would it be possible" used as a request form. The claim that the mechanism manifested in the case of Hebrew is language-specific is supported by the fact that Hebrew "possibility questions" are a very common conventional request strategy, while the English equivalent is not. This means that an English "would it be possible to get X" is more likely to be interpreted literally than the same question in Hebrew. (The English example has been pointed out to me by Chaim Robin, personal communication).

4. The subjects in the initial study were: (1) 19 adult learners of Hebrew, all studying at York University in Toronto; (2) 32 adult native speakers, all students at the Hebrew University; (3) 10 native speakers of English, all graduate students at the Modern Language Centre at the Ontario Institute for Education, in Toronto. The instruments were: (1) a

discourse translation test, administered to learners only. This test contained short dialogues learners had to translate into English. The purpose of the test was to establish the proficiency level of subjects and ensure their familiarity with the register of spoken Hebrew. (2) A discourse-completion test administered to learners and native speakers (see Appendix). This test required the completion of a blank in a given dialogue. An English version of the test was administered to the native speakers of English (see Appendix for this version). (3) Role-playing tasks presented to learners and native speakers. The discourse-completion test was administered to all subjects in writing. To prevent reading difficulties, the dialogues in this test were recorded (using neutral intonation) and subjects listened to the tape before completing each item. The data obtained from the translation test confirmed the learners' familiarity with the register of spoken Hebrew and subsequently were not analyzed further. In the data obtained from the role-playing tasks, native speakers' performance differed from that of learners to a degree that invalidated any comparisons. The results referred to here are based on a comparative analysis of the data obtained by the discourse-completion tests. Data obtained by subsequent testing of another group of 45 learners of Hebrew brought further evidence to the findings reported on here. For the analysis of all the results, see Blum-Kulka 1980.

5. The translations in all the examples are more or less literal. →signals functional equivalence between the two forms. ≠ signals nonequivalence functionally.

6. "Muxan" in Hebrew literally means "ready" or "prepared" as in "ata muxan labxina"? → Are you prepared for the exam?

7. Hebrew does not have a verbal group of modal auxiliaries comparable with English. For further discussion of modals in English and Hebrew from a linguistic point of view, see Levenston (1970, pp. 108-127).

8. The label "permission directives" is borrowed from Ervin-Tripp (1977).

9. Note that the English phrase *"Perhaps* you could leave me alone" is a pseudo-polite, ironic variation of the direct command. (I am indebted to Patrick Allen for the English example.)

10. The latest version I heard in Canada this winter: "Ski together, stay together."

11. The "clumsiness" of this dialogue in English is further evidence for the differences between the two cultures in social norms; for one thing, the driver speaks much more than he would probably in English.

12. I am using the term "interlanguage" in its meaning in second language acquisition studies. For the original conceptualization of the term, see Selinker (1972).

13. See Blum-Kulka 1978 (in press) for a discussion of the relevance of this approach to the study of translation.

14. The point is further illustrated by the following story. An Israeli-born linguist who has been living in the United States for several years told me that she often has difficulties in making her intentions clear to the Israeli teachers she is in charge of at a Modern Hebrew department at an American university. Her specific example was asking a teacher (in Hebrew) "could you get the test ready by Friday" and the teacher replying "I'll try." Obviously, the teacher failed to interpret the question as the directive it was meant to be. The communicational mixups between the Israeli speakers involved probably stem from the fact that one of the speakers applied to her first language (Hebrew) speech-act realization rules borrowed from her second language (English). For her listeners this is masked by her otherwise perfect Israeli Hebrew.

# 4

## DENTIST-PATIENT COMMUNICATION: COMMUNICATING COMPLAINT

**Christopher Candlin, Hywel Coleman, and Jill Burton**
*Department of Linguistics and Modern English Language,
University of Lancaster*

Drawing upon a larger study of dentist-patient communication (Candlin, Burton, and Coleman 1980) we focus in this paper upon how patients communicate complaints and the ways dentists respond. We chose this aspect of the communication between dentists and patients for three main reasons:

1. The exchange of accurate information is of obvious medical importance.
2. It appears that dentists and patients may have contradictory impressions of the role that patients' descriptions of complaint should play in this exchange.
3. Attending or not attending to patients' complaints may be a means of determining dentists' professional "styles" in consultations.

The first section of the paper, after briefly underlining the first item above, examines in more detail the notion of contradiction suggested by (2). The remaining sections of the paper characterize the various settings in which dentist-patient communication takes place and look in detail at the nature of patient complaints in a variety of consultations, thereby illustrating, and incidentally confirming, the assumption in (3) above.

### THE EXCHANGE OF INFORMATION

Why, indeed, study dentist-patient communication at all? The question appears to be paradoxical, if not amusing. Popularly, after all, little communication, certainly not of the verbal kind, is held to take place in dentists' surgeries and in the wards of dental hospitals. Patients, in most patients' experience, are there to be acted upon and not to engage in talk. If this is indeed so, then of course, as Shuy (1973) points out in his work on doctor-patient interaction, such apparently one-sided communication would be no less worthy of study, since, like him, one might well presume that benefits to both participants would accrue and better medicine would be done if both parties engaged in relevant talk.

Recent research in the communication between doctor and patient has revealed shocking evidence of what happens when a field ignores function at the expense of technology. Although 95% of the potential success of medical treatment depends on obtaining accurate information from the medical history interview, little or no attention is given in medical schools to the training of physicians in interviewing techniques or the language and culture of patients from different socioeconomic, racial or ethnic backgrounds.

(Shuy 1973, p. 325)

Comparable work on doctor-patient communication carried out in British hospitals, emphasizing problems of cross-cultural understanding, has been reported at length in Candlin, Bruton, and Leather (1974, 1976, 1978) and in Candlin, Leather, and Bruton (1976) and would certainly bear out Shuy's United States' experience. Both studies show clearly that the availability of accurate information is crucial for effective medical treatment. We have assumed that the provision of such information is no less important for dental treatment. The implication of what has been said so far is that both patients and dentists are party to the nonprovision of information in the consultation. Certainly, dentists who participated in the study from which material for this paper was drawn frequently claimed that in the majority of cases diagnosis of patients' complaints could be made by simple visual examination. Only exceptionally did dentists feel that they had to supplement a visual examination with patient interrogation. When questions were asked by dentists, they were held to be "ceremonial" rather than "functional" and as such not relevant to the activities of examination, diagnosis, and treatment. Furthermore, and as an aside to be examined in detail in later sections of this paper, there is an unstated corollary to this dentist view, namely, that any information that *was* supplied by patients was in most cases likely not to be acknowledged as relevant. Now, in making this statement, we are aware that it can be argued that observers who are not themselves dentists are incapable of making any objective assessment of the validity of such an evaluation of the function of questions. All that one can do in response to this, and we have done, is to assess dentists' own views on the validity of the explanation offered in any given case. This can be supported by a discovery of the extent to which patients feel the need to describe their symptoms to their dentists. If one does pursue this line, there is some evidence (Fitton and Acheson 1979) that patients do have expectations that they will be asked to describe their symptoms or at the very least feel the need to describe them. Fitton and Acheson go on to make the tangential but important observation that to the extent that such expectations are frustrated, patients will be disappointed and dissatisfied, states, they observe, that may discourage effective communication.

We have then a scene in which it appears that communication is important, both for effective treatment and for patient satisfaction, yet one in which one party, namely, the dentist, feels that communication with patients is either unimportant or at best "ceremonial" and in which the other party, the patient, desirous of communication, frequently perceives its absence and is accordingly not only dissatisfied but inhibited from communicating and breaking the mold.

We have been referring obliquely so far to "assumptions" and "perceptions" by the coparticipants; interestingly, it appears that such assumptions and such perceptions may be more addressed in the abstract than enacted in the real. For the data in our original study amply document that patients and dentists do in fact do a good deal of talking during consultations. Patients are frequently involved in discussion of their treatment or in more general conversation. What is more, despite, as we say, a generally held assumption of patients that they had little opportunity for speech, there were many opportunities for them to take a turn at talking which, however, were not taken up. To isolate another facet of this general theme of disparity between perception and reality, we can evidence cases where patients complain that dentists do not explain treatment to them while the transcripts amply demonstrate the contrary to be the case. If dentists do explain, why do patients fail to recognize the explanation? Yet a further example of this disparity: why is it that patients declare that they are often unable to respond to questions directed to them by dentists when the data evidence that, in many cases, they do in fact respond?

From these remarks it becomes at least clear that if we are to understand more fully the matter of exchange of information in dentist-patient communication, especially in the crucial area of communication of complaint, we shall have to examine in more detail this disparity between what is perceived by coparticipants to be the case and what seems to the analyst from the data to be the case.

## RELATIONSHIPS BETWEEN PERCEIVED AND ACTUAL LANGUAGE USE

The literature of social psychology contains numerous instances in which self-report data have been shown to be an unreliable guide to actual performance, and in which subjects' perceptions of phenomena in the immediate environment differ significantly from the reality of these phenomena as revealed in analyzed data. It appears also to be the case that the failure, as it were, of the perceived to coincide with the actual is especially likely to occur when the phenomena or behavior in question are associated with a variable which has high positive or high negative affective value in the community of which the subject is a member. As examples we may adduce here the work of Lambert et al. (1960, 1972), where it was shown that French-speaking Canadians allow greater positive value to the English language and to speakers of English than to their own language or to those who speak it. Again, Coleman (1984) found that Indonesians, working in an isolated community centered on a mining operation in which expatriates maintained a particularly high profile, claimed to use English in 67 percent of their spoken contacts at work with expatriate colleagues. Yet in a similar community a few miles away, in which the "visibility" of expatriates was considerably less, Indonesians claimed to use English in only 42 percent of their relationships with expatriates at work. Furthermore, in the former of the two mining communities, expatriates claimed that in their spoken contacts with Indonesians at work, they used Bahasa Indonesia ten times more frequently than their Indonesian colleagues did when speaking to them. These brief examples from an extensive literature will perhaps suffice to indicate that, at least in terms of language use, perceptions and actuality do not accord. As we say, of course, this is only a particular instance of a more general sociopsychological phenomenon, documented inter alia by Shaver (1977) and Aronson (1965).

## DISCOURSAL SETS AND ACTIVITY TYPES

To make such general observations of disparity, of course, is to offer no kind of hypothesis as to why such disparities might exist. In this discussion we wish to offer such a hypothesis, focusing first, as an example, on that factor most often addressed as a cause of concern by patients, namely, the matter of the allocation of time at talking between the coparticipants. Our argument begins from the assertion that one of the operating principles which speakers expect to find functioning in dyadic encounters is that of an approximately equal distribution of talk between coparticipants, or at most a discrepancy of some 60:40 percent. On the basis of precise statistical evidence from consultations, it is clear that in dentist-patient encounters there is not such an equitable distribution of talk, and what is more, the distribution breaches the 60:40 tolerance already referred to. We are forced to conclude that there is a different operating principle at work in the dentist-patient encounter than that pertaining to the "normal" dyadic conversation. We also assert that associated with such operating principles are what we will call "discoursal sets," that is, an awareness by the coparticipants of what is expected and allowable behavior in an encounter. Within such a discoursal set is a particular behavior relating to the distribution of turns at talking.

It is our primary hypothesis, offered as an explanation of a particular kind for the disparity noted above, that patients and dentists bring to the consultation distinct discoursal sets, instanced here by different awarenesses of appropriate distribution of talk. On this hypothesis, patients believe, from their experience of nonconsultation talk, that there should be a rough parity of turns at talking. Since maintaining such a parity is not one of the operating principles of the consultation as an encounter, it is not surprising that patients perceive that disparity appropriate to the consultation, even if the disparity is of a minor kind, as a gross infringement on their participatory rights in that encounter. That is, even though patients do actually enjoy some opportunity to speak, their *perception* may be that they are being granted no opportunity whatsoever, or only an extremely limited one, simply because their discoursal set from the nonconsultation world is, in their view, not being honored. We referred above to other examples of this kind of disparity of the perceived and the actual, a disparity which we relate here to one of alternative and competing discoursal sets. One such is where, in our data, patients respond to dentists' questions *as though* these questions were "conversational," when in fact the dentist simply required information about the patient's medical history or present condition. As a consequence of this disparity, an inquiry, which in the context of the discoursal set evoked by the dental consultation requires a purely factual reply, may be treated as a conversational cue, as in the following example:

1.  Consultation 25:1

D ye that's tha' that's your problem I'm going to look at that in just a moment but I need to find a little bit more about you in general

{ P  { yes
  D  { first of all you know um let me see wha w what's your

{ P                                                        { yes
  D  health like in general you look a good healthy { person

{ P  I have been until three months ago and I got
  D  to me I

{ P  bronchitis and I've never had it in my life { and it
  D                                              { yeah

P. took me three it's taken me three months to get over it which still left me with bronchial catarrh

{ P  and { I am a healthy person        { I can't understand
  D        { you          you look { healthy you eh ye e

{ P      why { this  I couldn't get over this attack
  D  yes        { yes

{ P  { bronchitis it's that nasty { virus   do you remember
  D  { yes eh                     { yes   yes                yes

{ P  { everyone had it
  D  { yes I remember so that' so you've had bronchitis

D have you had anything in the past like rheumatic fever or diabetes

{ P  no I've never had bronchitis in my { life
  D                                      { no nothing at all

{ =  overlapping utterances

We have suggested, then, that patients frequently take with them, to their dental consultations, discoursal sets (with associated operating principles) which are inappropriate as regards both the quantity (distribution of turns at talking among coparticipants) and the quality (interpretation, here, of the pragmatic value of questions) of the discourse. Levinson (1979) has developed an argument for the notion of activity types which may be illuminating here. Activity types, for Levinson, refer to a fuzzy category, the members of which are goal-defined, socially constituted, and bounded events which place constraints on participants, on settings, and in particular on allowable contributions from the coparticipants in the event.

Types of activity, social episodes, if one prefers, play a central role in language usage. They do this in two ways especially. On the one hand they constrain what will count as an allowable contribution to each activity, and on the other hand they help to determine how what one says will be "taken"—that is, what kinds of inferences will be made from what is said."

(Levinson 1979, p. 393)

Now it is not difficult to see the dentist-patient consultation as a very clearly defined activity type, with easily identifiable participants, settings, and goals. It should not be too difficult for us (as third-party observers) to identify also the constraints on allowable contributions in this activity. However, and significantly, Levinson acknowledges that the task of identifying the activity one is involved in may not be so simple for the participants themselves.

A final issue that arises . . . can be a very real interactional problem that faces conversationalists: How does one ascertain *which* activity one is in at any one point in an on-going inter-action. Sometimes the gross facts of physical setting, time, co-present personnel, etc. are insufficient to determine the activity. . . . A good locus for the study of such activity-identifying process is where misunderstandings arise due to different cultural or sub-cultural origins of participants.
(Levinson 1979, p. 395, note 7)

We are proposing that while the "gross facts of physical setting" and so on are sufficient for patients to determine which activity they are involved in, nevertheless (perhaps because this type of activity is experienced very infrequently) patients can encounter difficulty in identifying and employing appropriate communication strategies and in making contributions which are always and only allowable ones. It is this, we believe, which underlies the perceptions which patients report of not being allowed an opportunity of contributing to the talk which takes place during the consultations.

We have so far focused our attention on the disparity between the patients' overriding impression of not being able to talk and exchange information in the consultation and the demonstration in our data that both patients (and their dentists) do in fact do a lot of talking during consultations. We hypothesized that this disparity could be explained both by general reference to sociopsychological research and by specific reference to the concept of discoursal sets holding within particular activity types for coparticipants, at particular moments of time. Within these discoursal sets we suggested the existence of certain operating principles which related to matters such as the distribution of turns at talking and the pragmatic interpretation of speech acts, such as questions.

In the remaining sections of this paper we shall examine in some detail a development of this hypothesis, namely, that it may be that the patients' perceived lack of opportunity to talk is not so much related to the total amount of *actual* talk which occurs during the consultation as to the amount of talk which is perceived by patients as *relevant* to their condition. That is, the operating principle of distribution relates rather to the talking associated with the symptoms that patients feel they are suffering from. Accordingly, apparent disregard or rejection by the dentist of the patient's self-diagnosis may constitute, for the patient, the very considerable infringement of discoursal rules referred to above. Symptom-relevant talk achieves greater prominence for patients to the extent that talk concerned with other matters fades into insignificance in their perception. It is in this way, it is argued, that the dentist's dismissive response to the patient's admittedly naive self-diagnosis contributes to the patient's perception that the dentist says nothing to him during the consultation and that, accordingly, treatment will be inappropriate and ineffective and, more than that, is not something in which patients themselves can be expected to play any helping part.

## CONTEXTS AND CATEGORIES OF CONSULTATION

During the data-collecting stage of the project 125 dentist-patient consultations were observed, of which 66 were recorded. These consultations involved 12 fully qualified dentists, 7 student dentists, and approximately 120 different patients (some of whom were observed on more than one occasion). All these observations were made in Lancashire and Merseyside in the northwest of England.

### Contexts

The environments in which these consultations took place could be classified into three readily identifiable types:

1. Hospital examinations departments
2. Hospital treatment departments
3. General practice (both private and National Health Service practices)

The first of these contexts of consultation, the hospital examinations department, is characterized by a rapid turnover of patients who present themselves for treatment or who, in a very few cases, are referred by their own dentists. The average duration of examinations department consultations is 5 minutes. From the examinations department, patients are directed to the appropriate hospital treatment department. Hospital treatment departments, the second environment in which consultations were observed, are characterized by the presence of student dentists and, to some extent, by patients who are making repeat visits for further stages of a continuing treatment program. Consultations in this environment tend to be leisurely: the average duration of contact between student dentist and patient is 53 minutes, whilst that between qualified dentist and patient is 12½ minutes. The third environment in which consultations were observed, general practice, is populated largely by a group of patients who are well known to their dentists and who make repeat visits in a continuing program of treatment. The average duration of dentist-patient contact in general practice is 12 minutes, although this ranges from 9 minutes in National Health Service practices to 26½ minutes in private practice.

### Categories

Examination of the data suggested that it would be useful to classify dentist-patient consultations into four categories:

1. Patient-initiated consultations
2. Third-party-initiated consultations
3. Dentist-initiated checkup consultations
4. Dentist-initiated continuing treatment consultations

*Category 1*　　Patient-initiated consultations occur when patients attend for examination without having been instructed by their dentists to do so. The patient and the dentist may be unknown to each other, which is generally the case when consultations of this type take place in hospital examinations departments; or the patient and dentist may already know each other well, which happens occasionally when patient initiated consultations take place in general practice. In all cases, however, patient-initiated consultations may be distinguished from other categories by the fact that, when the consultation commences, the situation is that *patient knows all; dentist knows nothing.* That is to say, only the patient knows why the consultation is taking place—what induced him or her to visit the dentist—even in those relatively rare cases in which the dentist already knows something of the initiating patient's medical history.

*Category 2*　　Third-party-initiated consultations occur when patients are referred by their own dentists to a dental hospital or when patients are referred from one hospital department to another. Consultations of this type generally occur at a very early stage in the treatment administered to the patient and, almost without exception, take place after the referring dentist has made a preliminary examination of the patient. Thus, from the patients' point of view, a third-party-initiated consultation differs little from a patient-initiated consultation in that patients still "know all," or nearly all, about their reasons for attending, since the matter which led them to initiate the original consultation with their own dentist remains unresolved. (They might, however, be somewhat more concerned in a third-party-initiated consultation, as the referring dentist has obviously been unable to deal with the problem unaided.) In a third-party-initiated consultation, however, dentists are in a slightly more advantageous situation than in a patient-initiated consultation. This is because at the very least the referral note from the referring dentist delineates the nature of the problem and may even recommend that a particular type of clinical test be performed. The referral note is read either before the dentist meets the patient or at the very commencement of the consultation, usually before the patient has an opportunity to speak. The situation in third-party-initiated consultations, then, is that *patient knows nearly all; dentist knows next to nothing.*

*Category 3*　　Dentist-initiated checkup consultations typically occur when patients attend for examination in response to their dentists' recommendation. The checkup may be to ensure that an earlier course of treatment has achieved its objectives or may simply be a routine six-monthly examination. However, the patient may have developed new symptoms during the intervening 6-month period between the previous consultation and the present one. In this case, the patient is in a situation somewhat similar to that which is experienced in a patient-initiated consultation, as the patient alone is in possession of knowledge concerning any new symptoms. On the other hand, the dentist may have some prior suspicions as to what the examination will reveal. The situation in dentist-initiated checkup consultations, therefore, is that *patient knows something; dentist knows something.*

*Category 4*    The fourth type of consultation, dentist-initiated continuing treatment, takes place when the patient attends for the next stage in a treatment program which demands a minimum of two consultations and which may extend over a considerable period of time. Typically, patients return once a week for a further stage of treatment. The urgency which originally prompted them to initiate a consultation is no longer experienced. That is to say, patients are probably not experiencing any discomfort; they attend for treatment because they have an appointment not because they seek relief for pain. Furthermore, the patient in this type of consultation frequently has a very unclear idea of exactly what treatment is to be administered. Dentists, on the other hand, know precisely what treatment is to be given to the patient: the consultation holds no surprises for them. The situation in dentist-initiated continuing treatment consultations, then, is that *patient knows next to nothing; dentist knows all.*

## Summary

The distribution by context (environment) and category (type) of the 66 dentist-patient consultations which were recorded during the survey is shown in Table 1. The majority of consultations which occur in the context of a hospital examinations department can be categorized as patient-initiated, in which patient knows all and dentist knows nothing. At the other end of the continuum, the majority of consultations which take place in the environment of a general practice are of dentist-initiated continuing treatment type, in which dentist knows all and patient knows next to nothing. A chi-square test applied to this table suggests strong evidence of an association between the category of consultation and the context in which the consultation takes place.

**Table 1**    Distribution of 66 Recorded Dentist-Patient Consultations by Context and Category

| Context of consultation | Category of consultation | | | | |
| | Patient-initiated | Third-party initiated | Dentist-initiated checkup | Dentist-initiated continuing treatment | Total |
| --- | --- | --- | --- | --- | --- |
| Hospital examinations department | 18 | 1 | 0 | 2 | 21 |
| Hospital treatment department | 1 | 6 | 2 | 6 | 15 |
| General practice | 2 | 0 | 5 | 23 | 30 |
| Total | 21 | 7 | 7 | 31 | 66 |

An attempt is made in Figure 1 to represent in diagrammatic form the relative extent of (1) the patient's knowledge of why the consultation is taking place, and (2) the dentist's knowledge of why the consultation is taking place, at the moment when the consultation commences.

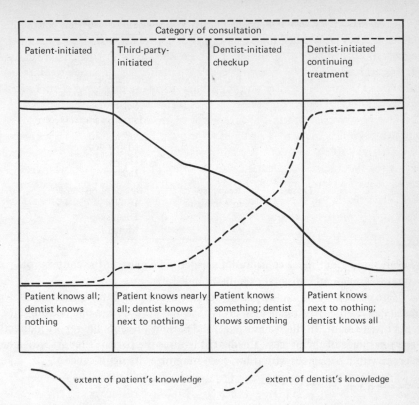

| Category of consultation | | | |
|---|---|---|---|
| Patient-initiated | Third-party-initiated | Dentist-initiated checkup | Dentist-initiated continuing treatment |
| | | | |
| Patient knows all; dentist knows nothing | Patient knows nearly all; dentist knows next to nothing | Patient knows something; dentist knows something | Patient knows next to nothing; dentist knows all |

⌒ extent of patient's knowledge  ⌒ extent of dentist's knowledge

**FIGURE 1**  Diagrammatic Representation of Relative Extent of Patient's and Dentist's Knowledge, at Commencement of Consultation, of Why Consultation Is Taking Place

## STAGES IN THE PRESENTATION OF COMPLAINTS

The process by which a patient presents his or her complaint to the dentist has, maximally, three stages. Associated with each of these stages are certain variables concerning the occurrence of that stage or the manner in which it is conducted. These stages and the variables associated with them are summarized in Table 2. In the remainder of this paper, the process of patient presentation or reporting of complaint is discussed as it occurs in patient-initiated consultations and dentist-initiated continuing treatment consultations. These two categories not only provide particularly clear contrasts in development but are also the most commonly occurring of the four different categories.

## PATIENT COMPLAINT IN PATIENT-INITIATED CONSULTATIONS

The data which follow are taken from two patient-initiated consultations in the context of general practice. The pattern revealed in these consultations recurs,

**Table 2** Summary of Stages in Patient's Presentation of Complaint

| Stage | Performer | Event | Variable |
|---|---|---|---|
| A | Dentist | Cue | Occurrence of cue |
| B | Patient | Presentation of complaint | Occurrence: In response to cue Seized Manner of presentation: Concise Elaborated Direct Indirect |
| C | Dentist | Response to complaint | Manner of response: Ignore Dismiss Minimize |

however, throughout those consultations which take place in the contexts of hospital treatment and hospital examination departments.

The process by which the patient reports a complaint to the dentist involves three stages. In the first, the dentist gives patients one cue, and one cue only, for a report to be made. In the second stage, the patient presents the report indirectly. In the final stage of the process, the dentist ignores the patient's report altogether, disagrees with it, or agrees with it but then minimizes its significance.

## First Case Study

This process can be illustrated by the following consultation involving a merchant seaman who is treated by a dentist whom he has never met before.

2.　　　Consultation 7:3
D　　alright
P　　yep
*D　　you're having trouble are you
{ *P　　yeah the back one ⌠ I had a filling I had a filling in
  D　　　　　　　　　　⌡ which side
{ P　　but it all came out ⌠ and it started to er ( )
  D　　　　　　　　　　　⌡ oh I see　　　　　　just you
D　　rest your head
[8 seconds]
D　　when did it happen
{ P　　when did it start breaking ⌠ up
  D　　　　　　　　　　　　　　⌡ mm mm
P　　well 'bout the last couple of week
D　　is it keeping you awake at night
P　　well it has the last two nights
{ P　　　　　　　　　　　　　mm hm
  D　　now is it eh left side bottom　the very back one
*D　　mm you've got two that are quite bad there
{ P　　　　　　　　　　　　　　　　　　　　　no
  D　　this one further forward's not hurting you　no

66

D     no pain when I touch that just open fairly wide there's pain on that one I'm afraid
          that that's rather a bad tooth to say the least you've got one at the top that's pretty
          bad too but if your pain started on the lower and at the back well we'll remove
          that for you today

{ P     yeah ⌜okay yep
{ D          ⌞okay

The first stage, in which the dentist gives the patient a cue to report his complaint,
is illustrated in this example by the dentist's "you're having trouble are you."

The second stage, in which patients present their complaints, is represented
by "the back one I had a filling I had a filling in but it all came out and it started
to er ( )." Here, the patient describes an event which took place in the recent
past (the break up of his filling) which he believes to be the cause of the problem
which he is presently experiencing (pain). However, pain itself is not mentioned by
the patient; we never discover what "it started to er" do. The patient's report,
then, is made indirectly without straightforward reference to the pain which has
caused him to initiate the consultation. The report is relatively elaborated.

The third stage of the reporting process, in which dentists respond to
patients' report, is represented by "mm you've got two that are quite bad there."
At no point during the consultation does the dentist refer to the patient's diagnosis
that one of his fillings started to "break up" and "come out." In other words, the
dentist ignores the patient's analysis of the problem; the patient never learns
whether he is correct or not in attributing the pain to a crumbling filling.

The following extract is taken from the same consultation.

3.         Consultation 7:3
    D     your teeth heal up pretty well so I mean you haven't had excessive bleeding from
         an extraction you would have

{ P                     ⌜oh  no   no
{ D     remembered that if ⌞(it had)    ( )
    D     you heal pretty quickly
    [17 seconds]
  *P     is it possible that you could also clean them a bit
  *D     erm
    [9 seconds]
  *D     how long are you here
    P     er I'm sailing tonight
    [4 seconds]
  *D     well really what you need is some of these other teeth to be filled and a scale and
         polish your scaling alright you might have a bit of stain your stain's not that bad
         the urgent thing that really needs doing the more pressing thing is filling in this and
         possibly if you're lucky a filling in that top one to save it you know you need
         another full dental appointment to do that

It was suggested above that the first stage of the process of complaint
involves the dentist giving the patient a cue. The cue will not be repeated (unless
the dentist fails to understand the patient's report or the patient fails to perceive
the cue as such). But even if patients believe that they have more than one

complaint, they will be *granted* an opportunity to report on only one of these complaints. Thereafter they must *seize* an opportunity to discuss each of the remaining complaints. The question of seizing opportunities will be discussed in greater detail below, but this patient's "is it possible that you could also clean them a bit," coming unprompted after a 17-second silence, is a typical example of a recurring phenomenon.

The patient's second report is as indirect as his first one, although the method of indirection is different. Rather than tell the dentist that his teeth are dirty, the patient asks the dentist whether it is possible for the latter to clean his teeth a little. That is to say, the patient asks his dentist whether he is capable of administering a certain type of treatment which—although this goes unstated—the patient believes will be appropriate for the condition which the patient believes himself to be suffering from. While the patient's second report, like his first one, is indirect, it is not elaborated. It is in fact typical of reports made during seized, rather than granted, opportunities that they are made briefly and concisely.

The dentist's response to this report is also typical. His immediate response is simply "erm" followed by a 9-second silence. This in turn is followed by a question from the dentist to the patient ("how long are you here"), and the patient's answer is followed by another silence, this time lasting for 4 seconds. At last the dentist presents his own diagnosis ("what you need is some of these other teeth to be filled") and then dismisses the patient's second report as trivial ("a scale and polish your scaling alright you might have a bit of stain your stain's not that bad").

In summary, then, the process by which this patient presents his second complaint—the stain on his teeth—involves only the second and third of the potential three stages, since the dentist's cue or invitation to the patient to present his complaint has already been exhausted at an earlier episode in the consultation. The process therefore commences with the second stage, during which the patient makes his report in an indirect—but concise—way in the form of a highly mitigated question to the dentist about the latter's ability to provide treatment for the complaint. The complaint itself, meanwhile, is not referred to. Finally, at the third stage of the process, the dentist begins by postponing any response at all and then eventually is dismissive and declares the patient's concern to be trivial.

## Second Case Study

It has been argued that the dentist may respond to the patient's reported complaint by ignoring it altogether or by minimizing its significance. The extract which follows is quoted primarily as an illustration of the third way in which dentists typically respond, that is, by openly disagreeing with the patient's self-diagnosis. The consultation takes place in the context of a general practice. The patient is female, in her late forties, and is already well acquainted with the dentist. As she enters the consulting room, she has already begun talking.

4.      Consultation 4:13

```
 *P      (must have something) that was left in and I kept thinking
  P      it would come out come out        because I didn't want
  DSA                                  (   )
  P      a repetition                              I didn't want a
  D                    right come and sit down now
  P      repetition of all that bleeding and rushing to the hospital and restitching and so I
         just thought well I'll keep
  P      persevering                        oh a real old do
  D                    oh you had some er { infection and some
  DSA                                      (excuse me)
  P                                      yes I'm a I'm a real
  D      secondary hemorrhage on it didn't { you
  P      bleeder when the teeth come out always have been and the
  P      health hasn't been too good            and I kept
  D                              no that's right
  P      having   (   )                       well it's still there
 *D                  and what's your trouble now
  P      and it er it  (   )                          yes
 *D                 { there's something brewing there is { there
 *P      I think it's an old tooth or something that didn't come up didn't come out and I
         thought while there's no trouble in the mouth and I've (got) I keep getting ulcers
         in the mouth and I thought while it's quiet and er my chest's better than it's been
         for a while
  P      I'll  (   )    I'll dive in to see you
  D          { is it yeah                   right let's have a
  P                                    mm
  D      look now it's still o-on the same side there
 [6 seconds]
  P                              [chuckles]
 *D      that's a piece of tooth            it's not a whole tooth
  P                                 { I kept hoping it would
  D      by any means it's a piece of { a tooth
  P      come  out              [chuckles]
  D         { that's come along ah          I don't know when
  P               (four years)
  D      they had that out { it's er no it's not one I took out
  P             (   )
  D      for you      I've taken nothing as far back as that
  P      I think it was was it four years this October coming
 [2 seconds]
  P      ah it's about that time since all I had all that trouble
  P      about four years since this October
  D                              yes (   ) yes but
  D      that was nearer the front that was after you'd had teeth
  P                        yes yes this has been I've never been to
  D      out down here
  P      anyone since (   ) I've tried to hope it would work
  P      itself out                                   no
  D              yes well that's not one I took out for you
  P            (   )
  D      it's er it's { one that's been taken out years ago
```

|   |   |   |   |   |
|---|---|---|---|---|
| { P | is it really | [chuckles] | | { ( ) |
| D | | yes | and em | { a little piece has |
| D | come through | | | |

The first stage of the complaint-reporting process in this consultation is somewhat more complicated than the same stage in extract 2. In this consultation the patient does not wait to be invited to present her report; even before entering the consulting room, she has begun to make her report. The patient is typical in that her report is made indirectly, although she is a little unusual (but not unique) in reporting on two different aspects of her complaint. Thus the patient reports, first, that "(must have something) that was left in." That is to say, she reports not on the pain or discomfort which she is suffering but instead on what she assumes to be the cause of the discomfort, the fact that something was "left in." Second, the patient reports on her fears concerning complications experienced during previous dental treatment which led her to delay seeking treatment again. The precise nature of the complaint for which the patient has been delaying seeking treatment is left unspecified. The patient's report is also, clearly, highly elaborated. The dentist follows this introduction by presenting the patient with an invitation to report on her complaint ("and what's your trouble now") which is almost immediately repeated ("there's something brewing there is there"). In this way, the dentist ensures that the consultation proceeds according to the standard procedure despite its rather unconventional introduction.

The patient responds to her dentist's invitation by returning to the first of the two aspects of her complaint in "I think it's an old tooth or something that didn't come up didn't come out." Again, therefore, she reports on the cause of the discomfort which she is suffering—the sudden appearance of a nonerupted tooth—rather than on that discomfort itself.

The particular interest of this consultation lies in the dentist's response to his patient's report. The patient has told him that "it's an old tooth," but in an extraordinarily peremptory manner, which the transcript cannot reveal adequately, the dentist declares, "that's a piece of a tooth . . . it's not a whole tooth by any means it's a piece of a tooth." This, then, is the third technique available for dentists when responding to patients' reports: in addition to ignoring reports or minimizing their significance, the dentist can also openly declare them to be incorrect.

## Summary

We have seen that a pattern occurs in three cases in which patients report their complaints to their dentists (these three cases being taken from two separate consultations). The process commences with an invitation from dentists to patients to present their reports. If patients attempt to initiate the process, however, their initial report will be ignored and the dentist will insist that the process commence with a formal invitation. On the other hand, this invitation will not be repeated at any later point in the consultation, even though patients may perceive that they have more than one complaint which requires the dentist's attention. The only circumstance in which the dentist repeats the invitation is when the patient fails to hear the invitation or properly interpret it. During the next stage, patients make their reports either in response to the dentist's invitation or—if no further invitation is forthcoming—by seizing an opportunity. In both cases, the patient's report is made indirectly. Indirectness may manifest itself by, for example, patients asking if the dentist is able to perform a certain type of treatment (which, presumably, patients consider appropriate for the complaint they have diagnosed themselves as suffering from), or by patients talking about a recent event such as the crumbling of a filling (which, presumably, they believe to have been the cause of the discomfort from which they are suffering), or by patients discussing the fears concerning unpleasant complications which have led them to postpone attending for treatment (which complications, presumably, patients believe might recur if treatment were given for the discomfort from which they are suffering). A report made in response to an invitation from the dentist not only is indirect but is also elaborated; a report made during an opportunity seized by the patient, however, is indirect but concise. Finally, the dentist responds to the patient's report by ignoring it altogether, by flatly declaring it to be incorrect, or by dismissing it as possibly accurate but unimportant. This pattern, though illustrated in only three examples here, appears to occur consistently in patient-initiated consultations in all contexts.

## PATIENT COMPLAINT IN DENTIST-INITIATED CONSULTATIONS

The data of this section are taken from consultations in general practice and in hospital treatment departments, where in fact the majority of dentist-initiated consultations occur. It will be argued that a pattern emerges from the data but that this pattern differs in several ways from that which was revealed during examination of the patient-initiated consultations in the preceding section.

### The Dentist: Opening Techniques

Dentist-initiated consultations represent situations in which the dentist knows everything and the patient knows next to nothing. For the dentist, therefore, the task which is to be performed during the consultation is so self-evident that the patient need not be offered any opportunity to introduce new symptoms. From this viewpoint, the dentist has available three different techniques for opening up consultations of this category:

1. To offer patients no opportunity whatsoever to talk about the state of their dental health
2. To check that the patient understands what treatment is to be given before work actually begins
3. To inquire about the treatment given to the patient in the immediately preceding consultation

These three techniques will be illustrated individually.

*Technique 1*   Many dentist-initiated consultations, of which that quoted in extract 5 is typical, present the patient with no overt opportunity whatsoever to report on any complaints which may have developed since the previous consultation. The patient in this consultation is male, is aged between 40 and 50, and is being treated in a National Health Service practice.

5.          Consultation 4:1
   [patient enters and sits down]
   [dentist, patient and researcher discuss positioning of microphone, ca. 30 seconds]
   [dentist washes hands, hums, and whistles, ca. 26 seconds]
   D     right
   [8 seconds]
   D     right can I have the bite blocks please
   [7 seconds]
   DSA   sorry
   D     have you got the bite blocks bite blocks thank you right now just pop your head
        (back) will you you've got your teeth in have you close together (on your) on your
        back teeth quite relaxed now right together close right together that's it just relax
        and close your lips now that's it that's right bite your teeth together now stay
        together like that quite still that's fine you need opening up a little bit don't you
   P     (yeah)

In this consultation, and in many others like it, the patient enters the consulting room, sits down, and is told to open his mouth ready for work to begin. He is never invited to make any report of any kind about the state of his dental health.

*Technique 2*   In a slightly more "generous" version, the dentist may com-· mence the consultation by confirming with the patient that they both understand what treatment is to be administered. This occurs in the consultation quoted in extract 6, which occurs in a National Health Service practice. The patient is female, aged about twenty.

The dentist checks that the patient understands that the treatment to be administered during the consultation will consist of fillings and one extraction ("is it erm fillings and er and a tooth to come out"), but again he offers the patient no cue to report on any developments which may have occurred since they last met.

*Technique 3*   A further technique occasionally employed by dentists to open dentist-initiated consultations is to ask the patient about the treatment

6.          Consultation 12:1
   [patient enters and sits down]
   [dentist, patient, and researcher discuss positioning of microphones, 58 seconds]
   D     (bring the) card please Vicky
   [6 seconds]
   D     thank you eh are we doing everything today Sue
{ *D     is it ( erm fillings and er ( and a tooth to come out
{  P      .  ( (I think it's) two ( fillings        yeah
   D     yeah right
   [10 seconds]
   D     have you had a tooth out with a local before
   P     yeah

administered during the most recent consultations. This is illustrated in extract 7, in which a married woman in her twenties is being treated in a National Health Service practice. The dentist involved also participates in the consultation quoted in extract 5.

7.      Consultation 4:3
D     er oh Mrs Hives     Jeanette
[patient enters]
DSA   ( )
D     hello
[patient sits down]
[dentist, patient, and researcher discuss positioning of microphones, 48 seconds]
 *D     how's that filling huh
{ *P     oh fine     it's not caused any trouble anyway
  D           alright
{ P   { (might)
  D   { right over you go
[10 seconds]
D     right
[8 seconds]
D     was it top right
P     mm
[10 seconds]
D     okay just trim that up and clean your teeth up

This type of opening is the most "generous" which patients ever experience in dentist-initiated consultations: the patient is asked a specific question about an earlier stage in the treatment program ("how's that filling huh") and is therefore constrained to make her reply relevant to that question ("oh fine . . . it's not caused any trouble anyway"). The patient is not given complete freedom to discuss wider aspects of her dental health and therefore is provided with no opportunity to draw attention to any problems which may have arisen since the previous consultation.

### The Patient: Alternatives for Reporting

What, then, is the patient to do in a dentist-initiated consultation when a new problem has arisen since the most recent consultation but no opportunity is granted for reporting it? The only courses available to the patient are the following:

1. To seize an opportunity without waiting for a cue from the dentist
2. To wait for an opportunity to confirm the treatment planned for the present consultation, respond to that opportunity in as concise a way as possible, and then immediately seize an opportunity to describe the new complaint
3. To wait for an opportunity to discuss the treatment administered in the preceding consultation, respond to that opportunity concisely, and then immediately seize an opportunity to describe the new complaint

4. To wait for a specific cue (which will never come) and therefore never succeed in reporting the complaint

The phenomenon of the seizing of opportunities to report complaints was observed above. Although seizing occurs with much greater frequency in dentist-initiated than in patient-initiated consultations, even in the former the phenomenon is not common.

*Alternative 1*    The seizing of an opportunity without any cue whatsoever from the dentist may be illustrated by the following extract. This involves an adult female patient in the orthodontics department of a dental hospital.

8.         Consultation 21:3
    [patient enters and sits down]
    D     how's Sean
    P     (   )
    D     yes I know it's ah everybody keeps telling me somebody else
    P     (under seven)
  ⎰ D    ⎰ (   ) somebody told me ⎰ (the other day)
  ⎱ P    ⎱ (   )                   ⎱ (   ) (   )        looks really (   )
    P     I said (   ) [laughs] when my turn comes round
  ⎰ D          ⎰ (   )
  ⎱ P    she ⎰ (   ) looked really (   ) (mop o' dark hair)
  ⎰ D                  ahh                    is it
  ⎱*P    just like Sean    this is very loose again    it seems
    P     to be (crushing) up all the way up all the way along
    D     is one of the bands loose
  *P·    mm and the the elastics what you give me last time
    D     yes
    P     somewhere between here and home I've lost them
  ⎰ D    ⎰ (   ) between here and ⎰ home or between home and here
  ⎱ P    ⎱ but                    ⎱ yes
    [3 seconds]
  ⎰ D    which was ⎰ (were you)
  ⎱ P              ⎱ after I left I was going home
  ⎰ D    and you didn't tell me        I could have sent
  ⎱ P                      ,          well I'd
  ⎰ D    ⎰ some (in the post)
  ⎱ P    ⎱ yeah                but but Mister (   ) promised me
  ⎰ D                         ⎰ oh              right
  ⎱ P    that he'd get some ⎱ (   ) orthodontic kit

The consultation commences with talk of Sean (the patient's child?) and of another person with whom the dentist and the patient are both acquainted. This discussion is abruptly terminated by the patient herself who, without any invitation from the dentist, introduces her first complaint: "this is very loose again . . . it seems to be (crushing) up all the way up all the way along." This complaint is almost immediately followed by the patient's report on her second problem: "and the the elastics what you give me last time . . . somewhere between here and home

I've lost them." In this way, the patient obliges the dentist to pay attention to (or at least to acknowledge) the two matters which are of immediate importance to her, before the dentist begins to pay close attention to the problem "inherited" from the preceding consultation.

The patient of extract 9, an adult female in a private practice, uses a similar seizing technique to present her complaint to the dentist.

9.       Consultation 22:3
[patient enters and sits down]

| | |
|---|---|
| D | and so you brought you brought me your weather back from Monte Carlo with you didn't you eh ( ) |
| P | mm |
| D | going off to all these foreign parts |
| P | (and) skiving off from work every afternoon [laughs] this week |
| D | (I) can think of nothing more sensible |
| P | [laughs] |
| D | very good idea    I shall put this little thing on here so's they can hear when I swear |
| P | you're not going to swear it's going to all |

{ D    it's all goin' be alright is it ⌠ I see ⌠ well I I I admire
  P    go very well             ⌡ mm  ⌡ [laughs]

{ *D    your optimism        if not your accuracy    let's find
   P                [laughs]

{ D    out what happens ⌠ er ( )
  *P                ⌡ oh I've eaten one of the crowns

| | |
|---|---|
| D | I hope you enjoyed it |
| P | I had it for me lunch on Wednesday [laughs] it's gone [laughs] |
| D | well have you had any toothache from it |

{ D    ⌠ (or have you) no                you did do well
  P    ⌡ no I haven't    so I've done very well

| | |
|---|---|
| DSA | d'you want this pin |
| D | ah yes we will have that out of the way we have erm three crowns there ( ) (in for you) and we have a wax based er that's the (three) |
| P | mm |
| D | on the side closed together |
| P | mm mm |
| D | and there's erm bit o' matching teeth the other side |
| P | mm |

{ D    but that's only on wax though as yet ⌠ 'cos we've got to get
  P                                ⌡ mm

| | |
|---|---|
| D | the teeth right and then we make the metal base for that afterwards |
| P | mm |

This consultation opens with general talk about the patient's foreign travels, the microphone used for data collecting, and the possibility of the dentist swearing during the consultation. Then the dentist indicates that he is about to begin work with his "let's find out what happens." Immediately, without any prompting from the dentist, the patient reports on a new complaint. This is done abruptly and concisely: "oh I've eaten one of the crowns." The patient in this way forces the dentist to attend to the new complaint before he becomes involved in the treatment which had already been planned for this consultation.

*Alternative 2*    Extract 10 is an instance of the second technique available to a patient who is not provided by the dentist with an overt cue to report on new symptoms; that is, an invitation to confirm the treatment planned for the present session is exploited by the patient as an opportunity to report a new complaint. This consultation, which takes place in a National Health Service general practice, involves a young adult female patient who is 8 months pregnant. The extract commences at a point 4½ minutes into the consultation after the dentist and patient have discussed an x-ray which has revealed a cyst which is making a tooth feel slack.

10.        Consultation 12:5
    D        um I'll freeze that up for you today I'll do a little bit of drilling here I'll just put you
             an ordinary composite type thing to keep the cyst from getting worse but um I
    { D      don't want to do any more than { you know the basic thing .
    { P.                                     { uhuh yeah
    { D      { okay er uh when's the baby due anyway how (    ) are you
    { P      { yeah
      P        a month
      D        a month now yeah
      P        mm
      D        oh well it's only going to make a difference of a couple of months
      P        yeah
      D        so I'll put something in just to keep it looking a bit better
      P        alright
      D        keep the tooth from getting any worse and see you afterwards
      P        mm
      D        and see what we can do with that
      P        mm
    { D      { there to get it right if you lose that there you see that
    { P      { mm
    { D      root if you feel that there you can feel { that it's loose
    { P                                               { (I know) yeah
      D        and (keep) the shape of your face
      P        yeah yeah
    { D      I don't want you to lose it { (I want) { you to keep it
    { *P                                 { k'        { wh'
      *P        can you see there is it is it going the same way
      D        there's a little discoloration    the tooth
      P        oh it
    { D      { that's usually natural don't worry on that score there Chris
    { P      { it oh that's alright
      P        every time I clean it I think my god that's
    { D      { that's going as well yes
    { P        going the same way
      D        now let me just do something for you here there's a permanent type filling but it's
             only as far as I'm concerned a temporary solution to the thing just now    could you
             wash that paste out until after you've had the baby and then we can    we can have
             a little chat my dear

    The dentist explains at some length that he intends to perform a type of treatment which will be of temporary value until the patient has given birth. He will then provide the patient with a more permanent type of treatment which will allow the patient to keep the tooth and so preserve the shape of her face. As the dentist reaches the end of this description of his treatment program, the patient tries twice to interrupt him:

```
D    I don't want you to lose it ⌠(I want) ⌠you to keep it
P                               ⌡k'       ⌡wh'
```

Eventually the patient succeeds in presenting her report on a new problem: "can you see there is it is it going the same way." Thus the patient is able to relate the complaint which concerns her with the topic which apparently is of primary concern to the dentist; besides that, the patient succeeds in getting the dentist to pay attention to this new complaint.

*Alternative 3*    In extract 11 the patient, a teenage girl, employs the third technique available for patients to report new complaints in dentist-initiated consultations by relating her report to a question concerning the treatment administered in the most recent preceding consultation.

```
11.        Consultation 7:7
           [patient enters]
  ⌠D    he ⌠llo
  ⌡P       ⌡hello
  ⌠D    d'you want to take your coat off     ⌠yeah   okay
  ⌡P                               yeah ⌡( )
           [3 seconds]
   D    (give you) a seat then
           [18 seconds]
  *D    now d'you d'you want us to make it numb again like the last time
   P    yes please ( )
   D    mm
           [6 seconds]
  *D    (now) would you like us to try and get everything finished for you today
   P    yes please
   D    yeah okay (we'll do that) you just need a couple of injections instead of one but I
        shouldn't worry about that
   P    I I'm not so scared any more
   D    good 's alright this this is not for you to bite I'm
  ⌠D    gonna just attach it to there ⌠( ) alright
  ⌡P                          ⌡oh         yeah
   D    good I'll put you down a little bit make y'a bit flatter well it's just the same as
        last time you weren't worried last time were you
   P    no
   D    no
           [3 seconds]
  *D    and these fillings have settled down up there have they
  *P    yeah you know where that tooth came out
   D    mm
   P    I've got a lump on the side now
           [3 seconds]
   P    a little hard lump
   D    does it hurt
   P    no
```

77

D     let me just see
P     not yet
[4 seconds]
D     [inhales deeply through nose] no well (there what) what you're feeling is the that's perfectly normal you're feeling the edge of the bony socket it sometimes doesn't heal in a completely rounded er shape it sometimes has a s-spikiness here or there which takes a little while to round off that will round off and disappear don't worry have you got the chart
DSA   mm
D     see what's still to do

The consultation opens with discussion of the treatment planned for the present session: "now d'you d'you want us to make it numb again like the last time" and "would you like us to try and get everything finished for you today." The patient, however, does not exploit these opportunities in the way that the patients of extracts 9 and 10 might have done. Then, just as the dentist is about to begin work, he inquires about the treatment administered during the preceding consultation: "and these fillings have settled down up there have they." The patient answers in one curt word, "yeah," and then immediately asks the dentist a question which allows her to introduce her problem: "you know where that tooth came out . . . I've got a lump on the side now."

*Alternative 4*    It has been shown that patients may make use of three techniques for reporting on new complaints which arise during a course of treatment. If they wait for an invitation to discuss the treatment most recently administered (the third alternative discussed above), they take the risk that such an invitation may never come. If they wait for an invitation to discuss the treatment planned for the present session (the second alternative described above), they also take the risk that no invitation may be presented to them. To avoid both these risks, therefore, several patients introduce their new complaints at a very early point in the consultation, before the dentist has apparently begun to think about the treatment program. (This is the first alternative illustrated above.)

But what happens if the patient waits for a cue to describe new complaints? We have shown that in dentist-initiated consultations, no such cue is ever granted. What happens, also, if the patient decides to reject alternative 1 (seizing an opportunity without any cue whatsoever) in favor of alternatives 2 or 3 (seizing an opportunity in relation to discussion of previous or planned treatment) if the dentist then fails to initiate discussion of previous treatment or planned treatment? In both these cases, patients are denied all opportunity to report on their new complaint. It has been suggested that in fact a fourth "alternative" for patients is to continue waiting patiently for a cue and therefore to fail altogether to report the complaint. It is impossible to estimate how frequently this happens. In many consultations patients play a totally passive role, are never invited to comment on the present state of their dental health, and never attempt to initiate discussion of it. It is not possible to judge whether any of these patients would have discussed new or continuing symptoms had they been given the opportunity to do so. However, it is significant that Fitton and Acheson (1979) discovered that not infrequently patients in general medical practices in the Manchester area failed to discuss with their doctors the problem which was most concerning them, because, at the last minute, embarrassment, fear of the truth, awe of the doctor, or some other factor inhibited them. Similarly, it would not be surprising to find that many patients in dentist-initiated consultations intend to report new complaints to their dentists but do not succeed in doing so, first because they are not granted an opportunity and then (for whatever reason) because they fail to seize their own opportunity. For the time being, however, this must remain hypothesis.

### Indirectness and Conciseness in Patient Reports

Up to this point, attention has been focused first on the ways in which dentists open up dentist-initiated consultations and second on the ways in which patients who have new symptoms to report react to these openings. However, it should be clear from the extracts quoted that the observations made above on the style of patient reports in patient-initiated consultations can also be made of patient reports in dentist-initiated consultations. It is characteristic that reports are indirect, but— since they are seized and not given in response to invitations—reports are concise rather than elaborated.

The patient quoted in extract 8 above declares in her first report: "this is very loose again" and then elaborates a little with: "it seems to be (crushing) up all the way up." That is, the patient describes a symptom—something is very loose— and reminds the dentist that on a previous occasion the same thing has also been very loose ("again"). Therefore, presumably, the treatment originally given to cure the problem, of which "looseness" is a symptom, has not been successful since the symptom has begun to make itself felt again. Though indirect, the patient's report is nevertheless brief and concise. The same patient's second report is also indirect: "the elastics what you give me last time . . . somewhere between here and home I've lost them." That is, the patient reports that she has lost a piece of equipment necessary for the treatment proposed by the dentist for an unspecified dental problem. It may be assumed, therefore, that the treatment is not being carried out and consequently that the problem has not been solved. But the nature of this problem is never made clear. Nonetheless, the report is made concisely.

The patient of extract 9 reports simply: "oh I've eaten one of the crowns." This is an exemplary instance of conciseness, but as the patient later claims that she has suffered no toothache as a result of this event, it must be concluded that this report is direct. If there were any evidence to suggest that the patient has experienced discomfort in consequence of losing one of her crowns, it would be reasonable to argue that the loss of the crown is presented as an indirect report on that discomfort. This, however, is not the case. Therefore, it is hypothesized that when the patient does *not* experience pain or discomfort, the necessity for indirect-ness is absent. That is to say, the patient can afford to be direct in making a report when no discomfort is felt but must employ indirectness when discomfort is experienced in order to avoid direct mention of that discomfort.

In extract 10, the patient's report is brief and concise ("can you see there is it is it going the same way"). Here, however, indirectness is manifested by the patient's asking the dentist whether what is happening to a particular tooth is the same as what has happened to another tooth on an earlier occasion. The patient, in other words, does not make a direct statement of her discomfort or symptoms but asks the dentist to make an examination and compare her present symptoms with those experienced previously.

The patient's report in extract 11 is typically brief: "you know where that tooth came out . . . I've got a lump on the side now." As with the report in extract 9 it is not immediately clear whether this is a direct report made on a symptom which is *not* proving to be a source of discomfort for the patient or whether, in fact, this is an indirect report concerning pain or distress which the patient presents through a description of a recent event (the appearance of the little hard lump). In response to the dentist's question "does it hurt, " the patient replies "no," then qualifies her answer with "not yet."

## Dismissal in Dentist Response to Patient Reports

The regularity with which dentists ignore patient reports or dismiss them as irrelevant or incorrect has been illustrated above with regard to patient-initiated consultations. It will have been observed that a similar phenomenon occurs also in dentist-initiated consultations.

The patient of extract 8 has two complaints. In response to the first of these, the dentist asks: "is one of the bands loose" but then apparently pays no further attention to the problem. In response to the second, the dentist appears to reprimand the patient: "and you didn't tell me." In extract 9 the patient reports that she has "eaten" one of her crowns. In this case the dentist does pay momentary attention to the problem and asks whether the patient has experienced any pain as a result. When the patient claims not to have had any toothaches since losing her crown, the dentist immediately begins to discuss the prearranged treatment plan for the consultation. This treatment is to include the fitting of three crowns, but it is never made clear whether one of these three is to replace the "eaten" one.

If the dentists involved in the consultations quoted in extracts 8 and 9 tend to ignore their patient's reports, the dentists of extracts 10 and 11 tend rather to dismiss them as trivial. In extract 10 the dentist admits that one of his patient's teeth is "a little" discolored, but then adds: "but that's coming from a way back before you lost the tooth . . . that's usually natural." In extract 11 the dentist dismisses the patient's report with an unusually long and detailed explanation as to why the appearance of a "little hard lump" is "perfectly normal" after an extraction.

## Summary

It has been argued that the pattern of patient complaint in dentist-initiated consultations is as regular as that in patient-initiated consultations but that there are several important differences between the two patterns.

In dentist-initiated consultations the patient is never offered an opportunity to report on any new problems which may have arisen. Some dentists, however, refer to the treatment given in the previous consultation, and others discuss the treatment to be administered in the present consultation. The patient who wishes to report new symptoms is obliged to seize an opportunity. This may be done *in vacuo* without relating the report to anything the dentist says, or by relating the report to discussion of planned or completed treatment. It is not possible to estimate how frequently patients fail to seize an opportunity to report new symptoms.

In cases where patients experience pain or discomfort, the report is made indirectly with the aid of those techniques observed in discussion of patient-initiated consultations. However, in those few cases where no pain is experienced, patients are apparently free to present a very direct and explicit report. In any case, because of the constraint of being obliged to seize an opportunity, patients make their reports as brief as possible.

Finally, dentists respond to the patient's report in a dentist-initiated consultation in the same way that they respond to a report in a patient-initiated consultation: by ignoring it or dismissing it.

## CONCLUSION

We began this paper by indicating the importance of the act of communicating complaint for an understanding of the relationship between patient and dentist. Such an understanding itself depended on an awareness of the disparity between perceived and actual behavior on the part of both participants, but especially by the patient, and subsequently on a clear analysis of the contexts and categories of communication in which dentists and patients were involved. In such an analysis it became clear that in addition to presenting characteristic patterns of consultation in terms of their stages, it was important to examine the range of techniques apparently made use of by both participants in the consultation, in respect of dentists' opening the interrogation process and patient's alternatives for response. It was significant how regularly, in both patient-initiated and dentist-initiated consultations, dentists ignored or dismissed as irrelevant patients' reports about their condition.

We would like, in this conclusion, to identify two avenues of further research arising from this paper and the research project from which the data for this paper are drawn.

The first stems from the discussion in this paper of the disparity between perception and actuality and its possible resolution by appeal to the concept of activity types and discoursal sets, in particular, the proposing of activity-type specific rules of pragmatic interpretation as a way of examining further the apparently incompatible mismatches between patients' and dentists' perceptions of each other's roles and purposes in what is for both participants a role-defining encounter.

The second area for further research is to explore a particular aspect of the dentist-patient relationship, that of the ways in which dentists control patients in terms, in particular, of determining acceptable patterns of patient response. In examining these ways of control, it is likely that the references in this paper to the distribution of talk between participants in the consultation will again be of significance, as will the rights accorded to the dentist to determine the procedures to be followed and the topics for patient-dentist talk. This matter of dentist control is examined—using the same data base as the present paper—in Coleman and Burton (1985).

# 5

# AN EMPIRICALLY BASED ANALYSIS OF COMPLIMENTING IN AMERICAN ENGLISH

Nessa Wolfson
*University of Pennsylvania*

This paper will provide a description of the role compliments play in American English as an example of one aspect of the sort of information needed by nonnative speakers if they are to interact successfully in American society. The knowledge of when and how and to whom one may (or should) offer a compliment, as well as the ability to interpret the social and cultural meanings implicit in compliments and to respond appropriately when one is on the receiving end, may seem rather obvious and even superficial to those who already possess it. Indeed, native speakers have not hesitated to depend upon their own intuitive understanding of how compliments work in American English in order to describe or to exemplify the underlying rules (as, for example, in the creation of ESL materials or in comparing the American system with those of other speech communities for the purpose of proposing an abstract sociolinguistic model; see, for example, Brown and Levinson 1978). Complimenting is, of course, not the only speech act about which descriptions and materials have been created directly from the intuitions of native speakers. The fact that this dependence on native speaker intuition for information concerning the social and cultural aspects of language use has gone largely unquestioned is due, in large part, to the dearth of empirically based analyses.

The term communicative competence has gained currency in applied linguistics. It is now the recognized goal of language instruction for students to acquire not only the lexicon, syntax, and phonology of the target language but also the rules for the appropriate use of these linguistic resources. However, the argument which the term communicative competence itself was intended to symbolize has been lost sight of. In introducing the notion of communicative competence into the sociolinguistic literature, Hymes took issue with the Chomskian emphasis on the analysis of the linguistic system of an ideal speaker-hearer whose internalized linguistic competence could be studied apart from the context in which language is actually used. Noting that "A child from whom any and all of the grammatical sentences of a language might come with equal likelihood would be of course a social monster," Hymes (1974, p. 75) argued for the necessity of describing the native speaker's internalized knowledge about how to use the resources of his language. He explicitly suggests that the system itself is not to be taken as a given but should be seen as open to empirical investigation:

The most novel and difficult contribution of sociolinguistic description must be to identify the rules, patterns, purposes, and consequences of language use, and to account for their interrelations. In doing so it will not only discover structural relations among sociolinguistic components, but disclose new relationships among features of the linguistic code itself.

(Hymes 1974, p.75)

Implicit in this discussion of the need for sociolinguistic analysis of language use is the clear recognition that no such body of knowledge presently exists. For those theorists and practitioners in the field of language teaching who have taken seriously the proposition that the aim of instruction must be the acquisition of communicative competence, the lack of information is a crucial problem. How can we apply findings which do not exist? What can we do to compensate for the absence of information which we are convinced is necessary? In dealing with this problem one can, of course, operate on the assumption that native speakers are aware of the rules which condition their own speech behavior and that they have only to use this intuitive knowledge in order to explain them. Although a good deal of teaching material has been produced based on this notion, the underlying assumption is, as I will attempt to demonstrate through my discussion of the analysis of compliments, incorrect. While I do not question that native speakers have the communicative competence to use their own language(s) appropriately, and indeed to judge whether or not language learners (be they children or adults) are breaking these rules, it is my conviction that native speaker intuitions have important limitations. The sociolinguistic literature is full of studies (e.g., Labov 1966; Blom and Gumperz 1972; Brouwer, Gerritsen, and DeHaan 1979) which demonstrate quite convincingly that the limitations on intuition have to do with the ability of native speakers to give accurate descriptions of their own speech behavior. The point has been made again and again that sociolinguistic rules are largely below the level of conscious awareness. What this means is that if we are to incorporate sociolinguistic information within an ESL curriculum, there is a great need for careful empirical studies of the communicative behavior of native speakers of English.

Such studies are, unfortunately, very scarce for any language and for English almost nonexistent. This is because linguists have generally concentrated their efforts on describing language structure outside its social context, while much sociolinguistic work has focused on correlations between phonological and grammatical features and social class background of speakers. Those scholars who take as their theoretical framework the ethnography of speaking as proposed by Hymes (1962) are, for the most part, anthropologists who work in cultures other than their own (cf. Bauman and Sherzer 1974). The result is that empirical study of the rules of speaking which obtain in speech communities where English is the dominant language has received very little attention. Yet, as Hymes (1974) has so eloquently pointed out:

There really is no way that linguistic theory can become a theory of language without encompassing social meaning, and that means becoming a part of the general study of communicative conduct and social action. . . . There is no way to analyze speech acts adequately without ethnography; no language is a perfect metalanguage for the acts that can be performed with it.

It is the job of the ethnographer to discover what one needs to know and how one needs to behave in order to function as a member of a particular culture (Goodenough 1957). The theoretical framework proposed by Hymes as a way of discovering the social rules, patterns, and meanings of language would seem to be ideally suited to uncover the information most needed by language learners.

In order to illustrate the sort of knowledge about a particular speech act which may be gained through the ethnographic approach, I will report on some aspects of the descriptive analysis of complimenting behavior which is being carried out by Joan Manes and myself. An early description of a pilot project which I carried out alone was presented at the TESOL Convention in 1978. Some of the more recent findings of the joint study have also been reported elsewhere (see Wolfson and Manes 1980, Manes and Wolfson 1980). I will begin by summarizing this information and then go on to describe further analysis in progress.

The corpus of compliments upon which our analysis rests now consists of some one thousand examples. Most of these were collected by the researchers, but because it is important in analyses of this sort to have data from as broad a range of speakers and speech situations as possible, we also enlisted the aid of some of our students at the University of Virginia and at the University of Pennsylvania. Thus the corpus includes compliments given and received by women and men of varying socioeconomic groups, levels of education, and occupation. Even more important, perhaps, the relationships of the interlocutors are equally varied, so that we have exchanges between total strangers, family members, intimate friends and colleagues, neighbors and mere acquaintances. In some cases the interlocutors were of similar age and status, and in others considerable asymmetry existed. Since factors such as the age, sex, social background, the relationship of the speaker and addressee, and the setting in which the exchange took place were all potentially important to our understanding of the structure and function of compliments in American English, we kept careful records of as much information about such features of the speech situation as was available to us.

Taking all examples of compliments together, we examined them for linguistic patterning. As native speakers, we and our students had intuitively assumed that we would find considerable variability in the way Americans give compliments. This expectation was based on the recognition that the giving of compliments is considered to be (or at least to appear to be) a spontaneous expression of admiration and/or approval. Since spontaneity is usually thought of as somehow linked with originality of expression, we had every expectation of finding this reflected in the lexical and syntactic choices made by speakers. Much to our surprise, however, we very quickly discovered that the great majority of compliments which had been uttered by a wide variety of speakers and in a great number of quite different speech situations were remarkably similar both in syntax and in lexicon. With respect to syntax, I had already reported on some rather obvious patterning discovered during my pilot study, but the amazing extent of the syntactic regularity did not become fully apparent until we had collected and analyzed the first six or seven hundred examples. It then became clear that one syntactic pattern:

NP      is/looks      (really)      ADJ

accounted for more than 50 percent of all the data. Two other syntactic patterns accounted for another 16 and 14 percent of the data, respectively:

I      (really)      like/love      NP

and

PRO      is      (really)      (a)      ADJ      NP

Together these three syntactic patterns occurred in approximately 80 percent of all the compliments in the corpus. Only six other patterns occurred with any regularity, but none came close to the frequencies of the three given above (see Manes and Wolfson 1980 for descriptions of all syntactic patterns and the frequencies with which they occurred).

It will be seen that two of the three most common compliment patterns make use of adjectives to express the positive evaluation of the speaker. Indeed, we found that by far the most frequent type of compliment belonged to the adjectival category. When we examined the lexical distribution within this category, however, we discovered that contrary to our intuitions and those of our students, more than two-thirds of the compliments using adjectives made use of only five. The two most frequent were "nice," used in 23 percent of all adjectival compliments, and "good," used in 19 percent. The fact that these two adjectives accounted for approximately 42 percent of all the data has to do with the fact that both "nice" and "good" have such weak semantic load that they can hardly be said to have any meaning more specific than positive evaluation. Thus they may be appropriately used to modify virtually any topic imaginable and are found in compliments whose topics range from new houses to babies, scholarly talks, and dance steps. The other three most frequent adjectives found in our data were "beautiful," "pretty," and "great." No other adjective appeared frequently enough to attain statistical significance, although the range of those which were used was very great.

Obviously, not all compliments make use of adjectives. As we saw in the above pattern, the verbs like and love also occur very frequently, accounting for almost 90 percent of the compliments in which a verb is used to carry the positive evaluation. In the few compliments which do not make use of an adjective or verb, the positive evaluation is carried by a noun (e.g., genius, angel) or an adverb. Of those which use an adverb, "well" is by far the most common.

As we have argued elsewhere, the fact that only five adjectives and two verbs occur in the overwhelming majority of compliments in Standard American English, combined with the very strikingly restricted set of syntactic patterns to be found, suggests that compliments in our society are formulas, like greetings, thanks, and apologies. This does not mean that all speakers always make use of precoded formulas when giving compliments, any more than all speakers make use of the other politeness formulas mentioned. Just as greetings do not always include pre-coded routines beginning with "Hello" or with some variant thereof but may instead begin with a rhetorical question (e.g., "Cold/hot enough for you?"), a joking comment, an expression of annoyance (e.g., "I've been waiting for half an hour"), the name of the addressee, followed by some completely different material (e.g., "Jane! I didn't know you were in town."), or even a compliment, so may compliments take on a variety of different forms. The point is that the great majority of compliments fall into the syntactic patterns described above.

As we have demonstrated elsewhere (Wolfson and Manes 1980) the fact that complimenting is formulaic in English has to do with the function of the speech act itself. However sincere compliments may be, they nevertheless represent a social strategy in that the speaker attempts to create or maintain rapport with the addressee by expressing admiration or approval. Since the interlocutors in such exchanges may well come from very different social backgrounds, it is important that the forms used be recognizable across social groups. As Wolfson and Manes (1980, p. 404) point out:

It is the recognition of the function of compliments in creating and maintaining solidarity which allows us to understand why it is that speakers seem to prefer conventional patterns in compliments. If anything in the compliment or the way it is worded creates social distance, the expression of solidarity may be vitiated. The use of a formula helps avoid this potential difficulty.

Thus the fact that compliments are formulaic in nature is a great advantage to speakers in that it prevents misunderstanding and minimizes the differences which might play havoc with the reason for the compliment having been given in the first place—the creation or maintenance of rapport between interlocutors.

Although it would be functionally counterproductive for speakers to use in-group expressions or lexical items when interacting with addressees who are not members, the use of just these in-group markers can have a strong positive effect when the addressee is a member of the addressee's own group. Thus Shelton (1982) in comparing the complimenting behavior among Afro-Americans with that reported by Manes and Wolfson (1980), finds that in in-group interactions, a very different set of adjectives occur: "Unlike the previous research on the compliment which revealed that the words 'nice,' 'good,' 'beautiful' and 'pretty' were used consistently, the adjectives in the compliments I heard were less traditional. They included 'serious,' 'rough,' 'sweet,' 'on time,' 'hooked,' and 'GQ'." In illustrating her findings, Shelton gives such examples as:

1.   "That outfit is serious."
2.   "Where did you cop those bad shoes?"
3.   "Man, she's rough, she's rough."
4.   "That's jive, alright."
5.   "That's on the one."

Clearly, the identity of the addressee is an important consideration in the analysis of lexical selection in complimenting, just as it has been demonstrated to be for so many other sociolinguistic choices (Beebe 1977, Wolfson 1976).

If there are important differences in the way compliments work within and between ethnic groups who speak different varieties of the same language, we must expect to find much greater differences across speech communities where totally different languages are spoken. As I have pointed out elsewhere (Wolfson 1981), compliments differ cross-culturally not only in the way they are structured but also in their distribution, their frequency of occurrence, and the functions they serve. It is not surprising, therefore, to find that nonnative speakers are often heard to remark on the frequency with which compliments occur in American English speech. Indeed, the most casual observation will reveal that compliments are not only very common in our society but occur in a wide variety of speech situations. From the point of view of the language learners, it is important to know not simply that compliments are frequent in American English but also that they perform functions which may not be at all obvious to the nonnative speaker. As Manes (this volume) points out, compliments are used to reinforce desired behavior. This may seem so obvious to a native speaker that it hardly deserves to be mentioned. If, however, we consider the fact that educational traditions and rules of classroom behavior are very different from culture to culture, we realize that the style of teaching through encouragement (and compliments) which is so common here may seem rather shocking to members of other cultures. Such examples as the following may pass unnoticed in an American context:

6. "You know something, Marc, you did a beautiful job!"
    said to an eight-year old.

7. "You handled that lesson superbly."

said to a graduate student by her supervisor. And, to another graduate student by her professor:

8. "That was outstanding. The theory was well presented and the examples were marvelous."

This sort of encouraging praise, which comes close to seeming like an offer of congratulations, occurs in many situations besides that of the classroom. The constant cries of:

9. "Good shot!"

from one teammate to another are typical background to many games. Indeed, congratulations are very much the function of compliments given after many different sorts of performance:

10. "Why did you tell me not to stay for your talk? It was one of the best talks I heard!"

An interesting aspect to the use of compliments in American speech is that they often serve to strengthen or even to replace other speech-act formulas. For example, apologies, thanks, and greetings, are often accompanied by compliments. Such co-occurrences as:

11. "Thanks for the card. We really like it."

and

12. "That was a delicious dinner. Thanks for having us."

are so commonplace that the compliment is seen as part of the expression of gratitude. On the other hand, there are some situations in which a compliment alone functions as an expression of gratitude. Indeed, there are occasions when a compliment is the only appropriate means of thanking. These usually involve a response to the performance of a service. Although a systematic study of the distribution of expressions of gratitude would be needed before we could be certain of the range of situations in which compliments actually replace thanks, it is safe to say from the existing data that role expectations are a key factor here. In most traditional American families, for example, it is expected that the wife will prepare meals and therefore it is inappropriate for the husband or children to thank her for this service. The appropriate expression of appreciation in this situation is a compliment on the tastiness of the food. (Similarly, people are frequently heard complimenting the owner of a restaurant on the food which has been served, though it would be clearly inappropriate to thank him for it.) If, on the other hand, the husband or one of the other family members not normally responsible for doing the cooking does prepare a meal, thanks and compliments are not only appropriate but expected. Although there clearly are rules concerning the expression of appreciation for the preparation of food, the thanks/compliment variation is by no means restricted to this situation. Thus a young woman who came home to find that her roommate had cleaned the apartment was heard to offer a number of compliments but not one word of thanks. Whatever the constraints on the use of thanking formulas, it is clear that compliments represent a useful substitute.

Thus, while the major function of compliments is to create or to maintain solidarity between interlocutors, there are a host of more specific functions which compliments serve. Most though perhaps not all of these fall into the category of social lubricants. A good example is the finding that when an apology, particularly of the explanation type, is called for, it often happens that a compliment (often totally unrelated to the topic of the apology) is offered. Although this sort of behavior is very typical of interactions between intimates, it is by no means confined to such relationships. Indeed, there are numerous examples of situations in which an employer who finds it necessary (or politic) to apologize to an employee tries to recreate harmony by offering a compliment.

In this connection, it should be noted that compliments are also frequently used to soften criticism, particularly when the interactants are in a relationship which is likely to continue and in which the maintenance of harmony is desirable. Thus, compliments followed by but or though, and a criticism, are very common. The following two examples are typical of those which occur in work situations:

13. "Listen, I think you're doing a good job with their classes . . . but please tell them to stay out of the office at lunch time."

and

14. "This is good. I like the way you're handling this. You might put more on the students though, and let them carry the conversation."

This combination of compliment plus criticism is not, of course, limited to the workplace. Even between close friends, a frank appraisal is often preceded by a compliment:

15. A: "Let me show you the brown skirt and what I got to go with it. How do you think it came out?"
    B: "It looks nice, but after all the time you put into making it, I think you should fix that front pleat."
    A: "Why? It doesn't bother me."
    B: "It isn't even, and it's such a nice skirt—why not make it perfect?"

Another way in which compliments serve to grease the social wheels has to do with their use in greeting routines, especially in cases where the interlocutors have not been in recent contact. Thus colleagues passing one another in the hallway of an office building or seeing one another at a meeting, and friends meeting either by chance or by design, may frequently be heard to utter compliments either as part of or in place of greeting formulas. One very striking example of the way in which compliments are combined with or serve to replace greeting routines is found in cocktail party talk. In this speech situation, the greeting plus compliment routine is so conventionalized that the greeting formula alone is seldom heard at all, a fact which language learners should be made aware of.

From the point of view of the nonnative speaker who wishes to establish social relationships with members of the target language speech community, it is useful to know that the giving of a compliment is an excellent and much used prelude to opening a conversation in American English. Here, of course, it is important to recognize that only certain types of compliments are appropriate between strangers. Since the analysis of rules of appropriateness in complimenting is still in progress, it is not yet possible to give a detailed account of the rules and patterns followed by speakers of American English. As a rule of thumb, however, it seems clear that the safest compliments to offer as conversation openers have to do with possessions (e.g., "That's a beautiful car.") or with some aspect of performance intended to be publicly observed ("I really enjoyed your talk yesterday.").

As Fishman (1965) has pointed out, a major question in sociolinguistics is who says what to whom and when. This question is relevant not only to choice of language or dialect but also to norms of usage for a particular speech act. While many types of compliments occur in an extremely wide range of speech situations, it is obvious that certain types are more or less appropriate to certain speech situations. Furthermore, as we have noted above, the specific relationship between the speaker and the addressee has a decided influence on the type of compliment considered appropriate.

With respect to topic, compliments fall into two major categories: those having to do with appearance and those which comment on ability. Typical of appearance compliments are those dealing with apparel:

16. "I like those pants on you."
17. "That outfit looks really nice."
18. "That's a very elegant dress. Did you just get it?
19. "I love that blouse."

We also find expressions of admiration on other aspects of personal appearance, as well as on homes, furniture, automobiles, and other material possessions:

20. A: "I should have had my hair cut this week."
21. B: "Oh, you! Your hair always looks beautiful. You don't know how lucky you are to have hair like that."
22. "I think your apartment is fantastic."
23. "The living room looks good. I haven't seen it this way."
24. "Boy, I really like this color. I wish I had seen this carpet when I picked out mine."
25. "Hey, that's a nice looking bike."

Favorable comments about the attractiveness of children (and occasionally other relatives and even friends) seem to fit within this category, since comments such as:

26. "Your baby is adorable."

27. "Your husband is such a nice guy."

28. "I like your friends."

appear to parallel other comments concerning possessions.

Those compliments which concern ability are of two broad types: those which are general and those which refer to a specific act well done. Examples of the more general type include categorical reference to skill, talent, personal qualities, and even taste:

29. "Jane writes extremely good papers—better than almost anyone I know." (said to a third party in Jane's presence)

30. "You have good taste."

31. "You're so honest and you explain things so beautifully. You've been a pillar of strength. We all look to you now."

32. "You do this kind of writing so well. It has just the right tone."

33. "She's eighty and she still does beautiful handiwork."

Examples of ability-related compliments which are act-specific are:

34. "You're being so nice about this. What you've suggested is so sane, so reasonable. That's very rare around here."

35. "Is that the chest you made? You really did a good job. This is really nice."

as well as the congratulatory compliments to teammates and students of the "Good shot!" or "Excellent point!" variety mentioned elsewhere in this paper.

If we consider the relationship of the status of the interlocutors to complimenting, we find that the overwhelming majority of all compliments are given to people of the same age and status as the speaker. This does not mean, however, that compliments do not occur when status is unequal. Popular wisdom has it that compliments are frequently a kind of flattery, given in an attempt to gain some advantage for the speaker. This would suggest that in cases where status is unequal, it would be more likely to be the person of lower status who would need to make use of compliments for the purpose of manipulating the addressee. What we actually find, however, is that the great majority of compliments which occur in interactions between status unequals are given by the person in the higher position. Given the fact that most interactions between people of unequal status (except in terms of age) are in some sense work-related, it is not surprising that when status is unequal, there is a disproportionate number of compliments which focus on ability, and that these are nearly always given by the person of upper status to an addressee of lower status. Indeed, the effect of status on what occurs in interaction is such that compliments from higher to lower status were found to be twice as likely to be on the subject of the addressee's ability than on appearance or possessions, although these do, of course, occur. This pattern of upper status speakers complimenting on ability or performance is in sharp contrast to that found in compliments to status equals or, for that matter, to those of higher status. The data clearly indicate that where status is equal or where the speaker is of lower status than the addressee, the topic of the compliment is most likely to fall into the appearance/possession category. It is only in compliments given by speakers of higher status that direct judgments about another's performance are common. Indeed, in unequal status relationships, the speaker of higher status is frequently expected to make judgments concerning some activity or piece of work. In these cases, the major motivation seems to be, as we have already suggested, encouragement. The use of compliments to encourage others is not, of course, limited to interactions between people of unequal status. Teammates and same-status colleagues may well use compliments in much the same way in order to encourage the addressee and to let them know that they are appreciated and that they should keep up the good work. In short, this sort of skill- or activity-related compliment may be seen as a sort of cheer.

One other way in which compliments may be used to modify the behavior of another has to do with sarcasm. Because they know the rules for the giving and interpreting of compliments, competent native speakers are capable of playing on these rules to produce stylistic effects. Thus, a comment structured in the form of a compliment may quite easily be turned into a reprimand or even an insult. This sort of play upon sociolinguistic patterns is common in many speech acts besides that of complimenting, but it is nevertheless the case that "the left-handed compliment" is a well-known device in American English. Comments like:

36.     "You play a good game of tennis—for a woman."

are usually intended as jokes. More serious are remarks like the following:

37.     "I really like the way you went through that stop sign."

which are clearly intended as reprimands.

Apart from, but not entirely unrelated to status, the attribute which would appear to have the strongest conditioning effect on frequency, type, and even syntactic and lexical choice in complimenting behavior in American English is that of sex of both speaker and addressee. Although we would need a great deal more data, especially on the ways men compliment each other, before making any sort of definitive statement on this aspect of speech conduct, several interesting indications are already noticeable. The first of these has to do with the fact that women appear both to give and receive compliments much more frequently than men do. This is, as one might expect, particularly true of compliments having to do with apparel and with appearance generally. What is more interesting is the indication that women are far more likely to be the recipients of compliments than men are and that this seems to hold true across compliment types. It is hard to avoid the implication that status is an intervening variable here. Clearly, in interactions between the sexes in our society, especially where the setting is the workplace, women are most likely to be inferior in status to the men with whom they interact. We have already noted that compliments from persons of upper or higher status to those who are in some sense their inferiors tend to be related to ability or performance more often than to appearance. When, however, appearance is the topic of the compliment, the addressee in the data so far collected seems hardly ever to be a male. It is only in cases where the male is much younger than the female that we have found this type of compliment to occur at all. Indeed there seems to be a rather strong if not categorical constraint against the giving of appearance-related compliments to higher-status males, especially in work-related settings. The same is not at all true for women, who frequently receive compliments on their appearance from both men and women of same, higher, and lower status in work settings.

Another aspect of complimenting behavior as it relates to sex has to do with the lexical choices involved. In this regard, it is interesting to recall that Lakoff (1973) hypothesized that one salient characteristic of what she called women's speech had to do with the sort of adjectives women use. That is, Lakoff claims that women use "empty adjectives" such as "divine" and "cute". These are said to be not only meaningless but also devoid of any connotation of power if contrasted with "men's adjectives" such as "great" and "terrific." Although it is not my purpose to refute Lakoff's claims here, I would like to point out that our findings clearly demonstrate that one of the five most common adjectives used by men and women alike is "great." It would also be well to mention that the adjective "cute" was found to occur in the speech of both men and women and that the adjective "divine" did not occur at all in our data. As Brouwer, Gerritsen, and DeHaan (1979) have pointed out, sex of addressee may be a more important sociolinguistic variable than sex of speaker in conditioning the choice of speech forms. In this regard, it is notable that the adjective cute, for example, though used by both men and women, was never addressed to men although often used to refer to them by women. Clearly, the effect of sex of speaker as well as addressee on the choice of adjective (and, for that matter, of verb), the topic of the compliment, and the interaction of topic, setting, and status as these condition frequency of occurrence are all important aspects of the larger study of complimenting behavior which is now in progress. The eventual findings should give some interesting insights into our understanding of differences in men's and women's speech and into the manifestation of sexism in language.

One of the most fascinating aspects of the descriptive analysis of speech acts is the insight it provides about the social structure and value system of the target speech community. In studying apologies, complaints, or expressions of disapproval, one learns what members of the speech community consider to be inappropriate behavior. The study of compliments is, in this regard, of extreme interest, since one is immediately confronted with the cultural assumptions upon which such expressions of approval are based. The underlying cultural assumptions to be inferred from the study of complimenting behavior among middle-class Americans will be taken up in detail in the following paper. I would therefore like to point out that these assumptions must always be assumed to be culture-specific and that this area more than most is fertile ground for intercultural misunderstanding or communicative breakdown. Because of the insights into the value system of the target speech community, and because of the practical applicability of knowing how a specific speech act is likely to be given and interpreted, descriptive analysis of the sort presented here can make it possible for language learners to interact more effectively with native speakers and to avoid the sort of communicative interference which too often leads to hurt feelings, negative stereotypes, and social isolation. Clearly, knowledge about appropriate speech usage can open the way for nonnative speakers to put themselves into the position to gain the very exposure to native speakers which will help them to acquire the target language. In this sense, sociolinguistic information may be seen as one of the keys to language acquisition.

Obviously, insight into a few speech acts does not add up to an understanding of what communicative competence is all about, and a great deal of empirically based research remains to be done, not only in communities where English is spoken but in speech communities all over the world. If we are to make sense of what we learn and to know how best to apply it, much more work needs to be done regarding the applications of sociolinguistic findings to language classrooms as well. In addition, the area of discourse analysis in second language acquisition research stands to profit a great deal from sociolinguistic insights.

Still another problem, and one which will become more and more important as sociolinguistic findings are applied to language teaching, is that of defining the notion of the speech community broadly enough to permit us to uncover norms and patterns of interaction which will be of use to nonnative speakers in their acquisition of communicative competence in a target language. For this reason, our concept of the group will, of necessity, be much less fine than it would be if our purpose were to investigate intergroup differences. If we agree with Hymes (1967) that a speech community is best defined as a group which shares rules for conduct and interpretation of speech, then we must also accept the fact that such groups do not necessarily share any feature external to speech which can be used as a criterion for membership. What we have is an equation between shared speech conduct and speech community. The problem is twofold. Not all native speakers of a language share the same rules of speaking, and the rules themselves are far from uniform in range. It is intuitively obvious, for example, that there are many rules which Britons and Americans do not share, and that within each of the two geographical boundaries (Great Britain and the United States) are other, much more subtle ones. At the same time, like rules of syntax, some rules of speaking apply to more speakers than do others. The rules for complimenting behavior, for example, were found to extend over a much wider area of the United States than were the rules for the use of respect forms in address (Wolfson and Manes 1980). Thus, while it is important to look for patterns of use among speakers and not to make unrealistic claims for a language as a whole, it must not be expected that we will find easily defined speech communities waiting to be studied. The boundaries of any speech community are problematic and open to empirical investigation, since they are defined precisely by the variation in the features under investigation.

Having discussed in some detail the work which Joan Manes and I have done and are still in the process of doing on the analysis of complimenting behavior in American English, I would like to point out that the analysis was made possible by the methodology. It is, in fact, my conviction that ethnographic fieldwork is the only reliable method of collecting data about the way speech acts function in interaction. Intuitions about speech usage are, as I have pointed out, notoriously unreliable, since speakers tend to be aware of the societal norms and are too often misled into believing that these norms represent the actual speech patterns of the community. For this reason, the intuitions of sociolinguistic researchers working in their own speech communities are primarily of use in the analysis of the data once they are collected. The data themselves can only be obtained through actual fieldwork. Similarly, data collected by means of tapping into the intuitions of naive native speakers, useful as they may be in pointing to some of the general outlines of differences between norms of different language groups, cannot, in themselves, provide us with the range of possible situations in which specific speech acts may occur or with the distribution of the various forms under investigation. A realistic study of speech use must involve the actual observation of speech in use.

# 6

# COMPLIMENTS: A MIRROR OF CULTURAL VALUES

Joan Manes
*University of Virginia*


The basis for the development of modern sociolinguistics has been the recognition that linguistic structure and social structure are not separate and unrelated. Within that approach to sociolinguistics known as ethnography of speaking, this has been reflected most specifically in the concept of the speech act. As Hymes defines it, "the level of speech acts mediates immediately between the usual levels of grammar and the rest of a speech event or situation in that it implicates both linguistic form and social norms" (1972, p. 57).

The social norms involved may govern specific speech acts or speech behavior in general, but in either case, as speech is one form of social behavior, so the norms governing it will be part of, and congruent with, the overall behavioral norms of the community. Looking at this from a slightly different angle, we may expect to find general cultural values and norms expressed through patterns of speech behavior. Studies by Albert (1972) on Burundi speech patterns, by Parkin (1974) on language switching in Nairobi, and by Irvine (1974) on Wolof greetings, among others, have focused attention on the expression of general cultural norms and values in speech. What I wish to do here is to examine how certain values of our own society are reflected and, further, reinforced in one particular speech act, complimenting.

Any speech act, of course, reflects a variety of cultural norms and values and in so doing serves to express and maintain those values. Compliments are of particular interest, however, in regard to the reflection and expression of cultural values because of their nature as judgments, overt expressions of approval or

96

admiration of another's work, appearance, or taste. This means, for one thing, that compliments express certain cultural values more or less explicitly, as we shall see below. In addition, the expression of approval may function as a form of positive reinforcement. Compliments represent one means whereby an individual or, more importantly, society as a whole can encourage, through such reinforcement, certain desired behaviors.

In some instances we can see very clearly how compliments are used in this way. When, as in Example 1, a police sergeant compliments a patrolman on a report or, as in Example 2, a teacher compliments a student for getting the homework assignment, it seems likely that the praise is intended to encourage similar behavior in the future on the part of the addressee or others who hear the compliment.

1. Joe, you did an excellent job on the report last night.
Situation: Police shift meeting. The speaker is a police sergeant, a white male in his mid-thirties. The addressee is a patrolman, a white male in his mid-twenties.

2. John found out what the homework was, somehow, I don't know how. But that's great, John.
Situation: Classroom. The speaker is the teacher, a white male in his mid-thirties. The addressee is a student, a white male age 12.

In cases such as these the audience is in fact also being addressed, usually indirectly, but in Example 2 directly in the sentence preceding, and explaining, the actual compliment. While compliments of this sort are most common in situations of unequal status such as an employer or supervisor speaking to an employee or a parent or teacher addressing a child, they also occur between intimates, as in the following case:

3. A: It's been fifteen weeks!
B: You're doing so well.
A: Aren't I? (self-satisfied smile)
Situation: A and B are boyfriend and girlfriend, both in their twenties. Reference is to A's giving up smoking.

It is by no means the case, of course, that all compliments are so directly manipulative. Quite the contrary, the vast majority of compliments make no reference to specific behavior and there is no reason to assume that the speaker has any intention of affecting the addressee's future actions. As Nessa Wolfson and I have indicated elsewhere, a major function of compliments is the establishment or reinforcement of solidarity between the speaker and the addressee. For this purpose the judgmental and manipulative aspects of complimenting must be played down and the elements of approval and similarity of tastes and interests brought into focus. But it is this very emphasis on similarities which results in the reinforcement of societal values.

The individual compliment must express approval of something which both parties, speaker and addressee, feel is of positive worth. Since compliments are routinely exchanged by neighbors, coworkers, and casual acquaintances, who know relatively little about one another and whose tastes and interests may not in fact be very similar, the objects or actions complimented must be ones which *any* member of the speech community will recognize as positive. For this reason, we find similar or identical compliments recurring over and over: "That's a nice dress" (or shirt, or ring, or tie); "You did a good job," "I like your hairdo," "You've lost weight. You're looking good." Thus in most instances the individual compliment is of little or no importance from the viewpoint of reinforcing societal values; it is merely a vague but easily recognizable positive comment. The social pressure comes from the fact that people compliment one another time after time on the same things: personal appearance, new acquisitions, good work. If we wish to be approved of and complimented, we must conform to the extent of doing things which others will recognize as worthy of compliments. Let us consider now what some of these are.

One of the most striking aspects of American English compliments when considered from the point of view of societal values is the overwhelming number of compliments on personal appearance, most particularly clothes and hair-dos. Also significant is the fact that such compliments typically involve women as speakers or addressees, or both. In our society it is assumed that women are concerned about appearance, both their own and others', and even more that women of all ages should try to make themselves attractive. Comments such as those in Examples 4 through 7 occur constantly in interactions between women, be they friends, colleagues, casual acquaintances or even, on occasion, total strangers.

4.  Gee, I like your skirt. I've been looking for one like it.
    Situation: Speaker and addressee are both white female college students; they have just introduced themselves, while waiting for a third party.

5.  A: I like your outfit.
    B: Thank you. I wanted to wear it while I could. Pretty soon it'll be too cold.
    Situation: A is a white female, age 20. B is a black female, same age. Both are salesclerks in a department store. Exchange takes place just after B arrives at work.

6.  A: Hi, Jane.
    B: How're you doing? Hey, you got your hair cut, didn't you?
    A: (laughs) Yeah.
    B: Looks nice.
    A: Thanks.
    Situation: A and B are friends. B has just stopped by A's apartment for a visit.

7.  A: You're looking very good. You've lost weight.
    B: No. Everyone says that. Except one person who said "Oh, you look fat." No one likes that!
    Situation: A is a white female in her thirties, B a white female in her twenties. They are good friends but have not seen each other in over a year.

Compliments of this sort are more than just a reflection of the importance of personal appearance for women in our society; they are a means of reinforcing that importance. If efforts to make oneself attractive are rewarded by overt approval, one is likely to continue those efforts. And the importance of this is highlighted by the fact that when such efforts are *not* commented upon favorably, one may feel hurt or insulted:

8. Why didn't anyone notice my new haircut?
   SILENCE
   "Doesn't anyone like it? (stomps out of room)
   Situation: Speaker is a white woman in her mid-forties. Comment is made at the end of the day, during which no one had mentioned her new hair style.

It is interesting, too, that what are complimented generally in our society are aspects of personal appearance which are the result of deliberate effort, not simply natural attractiveness. Indeed, we tend to avoid commenting on the latter. Compliments on hair style are common; compliments on having beautiful hair are not (except perhaps from hairdressers). Compliments on an attractive dress or blouse or on noticeable weight loss occur in almost any situation in which a compliment is at all appropriate; the comment, "You're beautiful," on the other hand, while certainly a compliment, is of comparatively restricted occurrence. Compliments on general attractiveness do, of course, occur, but they are typically of the form "You look nice" or "You're looking good." "Nice" and "good" are much weaker semantically than "beautiful"; more importantly, the verb "look" (as opposed to some form of the copula "be") seems to carry an implication that the state is not permanent, that it may in fact be the result of deliberate effort. This is often made explicit by the addition of "tonight" or "today" ("You're looking good today") or by following the general comment with a more specific compliment on clothing, hairdo, or weight loss, as was done in Example 7.

Certain cultural values may be reflected in and reinforced by compliments even though they are never (well, hardly ever) directly complimented. In our society, newness is undoubtedly the most important of these. While the adjective "new," unlike "nice," "beautiful," or even "thin," is not in and of itself positive, the value of newness is reflected in compliments in at least two important ways. First of all, new acquisitions regularly elicit compliments. A substantial purchase, such as a new car, will be noticed and commented on positively by almost anyone who sees it for the first time. New clothing or hair styles are, of course, more easily overlooked. A compliment can be elicited, however, by bringing the new object to the person's notice:

9. A: I'm so excited about my new clogs.
   B: Oh, you got some new ones?
   A: Yeah. (points to her feet)
   B: Oh! I really like them. They're different. You know, I've been looking for some new shoes . . .
   Situation: A and B are both white female college students. Exchange takes place as they are walking home from a football game.

Any recent acquisition, from a new house to a new hairdo, will be complimented once it is noticed or brought to one's attention. The omission of a compliment in such a case is tantamount to a statement of disapproval and, as we have seen, may be taken as an insult or rejection.

The value which members of our society attach to newness is also reflected in responses to compliments. As has been pointed out by Pomerantz (1978), the recipient of a compliment faces a conflict in that accepting the compliment and agreeing with the speaker may be seen as self-praise, while at the same time it is impolite to disagree and reject the compliment outright. Examination of our data on American English compliments indicates that there are a number of strategies which people use in responding to compliments in order to avoid or minimize this conflict. The most common is a simple "Thank you," which accepts the compliment without explicitly agreeing with its content. Another very frequent strategy, and one with which I am concerned here, is to deny or play down the worth of the thing complimented *without overtly denying the compliment*. This is done by focusing attention on some quality other than that specifically complimented, as in the following case:

10.  A: Oh, Anne, this is adorable!
     B: Well, it's really small, though.
     A: But for one person you really don't need anything larger.
     Situation: A and B are both white females age 30. A is visiting B's house for the first time.

Here A responds to the statement that her house is adorable by pointing out that it is small, in effect saying, "Yes it is adorable, *but* it's small." This is made relatively clear in this particular case by the use of "though" in the response. Of course, the quality denied must also be something valued, or the denial is meaningless. It is interesting, therefore, that the quality most frequently denied in responses to compliments on attractiveness is newness. Examples 11, 12, and 13 are typical:

11.  A: Oh! I really like that dress.
     B: It's just an old thing. I really need some new clothes.
     Situation: A and B are white females in their thirties eating in a restaurant with a number of other people.

12.  A: Oh, what pretty shoes!
     B: Oh, they're ancient. I've had them for years and years.
     Situation: A is a 26 year-old female, B a 57-year-old female. They are coworkers; the exchange takes place in their office.

13.  A: Where did you get that dress?
     B: I had it over the summer, dummy.
     A: Oh, well, it still looks great.
     B: (sarcastically) Yeah, sure.
     Situation: A is a white female, age 21. B is her boyfriend, a white male age 24. He has just picked her up at the airport; they have not seen each other in some time.

Thus while a simple comment that something is new is unlikely to be interpreted as a compliment, the value placed on newness is reflected both in the fact that new acquisitions are complimented and equally in the fact that it is possible to deny newness in responding to a compliment on attractiveness.

It is probably self-evident to most Americans that personal attractiveness is important and valuable, especially for women. We are perhaps less likely to accept, at least overtly, the proposition that something is valuable simply because it is new. Nevertheless, an analysis of compliments and responses shows that this is the case, at least for most white middle-class Americans. While one can at this point only speculate as to why this may be, it is not unreasonable to assume that it is related in some way to a consumer-oriented economy. It is not only advertising which encourages us to buy and buy, to get rid of the old and get the new. We encourage ourselves and one another by giving credit through compliments for new acquisitions.

Outside of compliments on personal appearance, by far the most frequent type of compliments are those on the quality of something produced through the addressee's skill or effort: a well-done job, a skillfully played game, a good meal. As with appearance compliments, the focus is typically not on the skill, talent, or hard work itself, although this may be referred to, but rather on the results.

An interesting paradox appears when we examine some of the responses to such compliments. Here again the recipient is faced with the problem of accepting the compliment graciously without appearing to be conceited. A common response to compliments on the result of talent or hard work is to deny that one deserves the credit. The recipient of the compliment may say, as in Example 14, that he was just lucky, or he may indicate that the credit belongs elsewhere, to the tools used, for instance, not to him, as in Example 15:

14.　A: How to go, Jack, right in the gap! (slapping hands in congratulation)
　　　B: Thanks, it was a lucky shot.
　　　Situation: A and B are white males age 24. B has just hit a home run in a softball game.

15.　A: Boy, that's nice work. I don't know how you do it.
　　　B: It's easy when you have good tools.
　　　Situation: A and B are both males in their thirties, coworkers. They are examining some refinished furniture in B's garage.

In this case, the respondent also denies credit because it was *easy;* this is a very common response, Examples 16 and 17 being typical:

16.　A: I really like this crewel-work.
　　　B: Well, you know, it comes with directions that are just about foolproof.
　　　Situation: A and B are white females in their sixties.

17.　A: Great meal!
　　　B: I just threw some things in the pot.
　　　Situation: A and B are white male college students, housemates.

The claim, of course, is that no special effort was involved; therefore, while the results may be good, the recipient of the compliment, the addressee, deserves no special credit.

On occasion, however, the recipient of a compliment responds by stating that the action or object complimented *was indeed* the result of hard work or effort of some sort. Of course, people may accept compliments outright, or they may play down a compliment by jokingly agreeing with it, but this does not seem to explain all instances. Consider Example 18.

> 18.    A: I really like the way you play banjo. I heard some licks there I'd never heard before.
> B: Well, they just come from sitting and practicing.
> Situation: A is a white male in his thirties, B a white male in his twenties. Both are musicians. Conversation takes place in a bar.

It should be noticed that what is being complimented here is not, as in Examples 16 and 17, the result of effort, but rather evidence of talent. By saying that he had to practice, the recipient of the compliment is claiming that it is hard work, *not* special talent, which is involved. On the other hand, we find no instances in which the opposite occurs, that is, in which the recipient of a compliment denies, seriously, that his good work is the result of effort and claims instead that it was just natural talent. It is difficult to imagine, for instance, speaker B in Example 15 something like, "Oh, it's easy if you've got my talent." Apparently, in our society, talent ranks above hard work; one can deny talent by claiming that effort was involved, but the opposite is not possible.

There are, of course, many other types of compliments and many societal values expressed in compliments and responses which I have not had time to discuss here. What I hope I have been able to show is that not only are certain cultural values reflected in compliments and responses but in addition compliments serve to encourage or reinforce these values, although we are not, even as givers and receivers of compliments, always aware of this. Indeed, positive reinforcement through compliments may itself be seen as valued in our society; as we all learned as children, "If you can't say something nice, don't say anything at all."

# 7

# AN ANALYSIS OF THE SURFACE STRUCTURE OF DISAPPROVAL EXCHANGES[1]

Lynne D'Amico-Reisner
*University of Pennsylvania*

A single referential meaning can be communicated through a number of different surface structures. Each structure, however, possesses stylistic meaning (Hymes 1974, p. 146) peculiar to the social context in which it occurs. As the variables making up a social situation change, so too does the stylistic meaning of a linguistic form. Verbal forms differing only in stylistic meaning differ with respect to the social information they convey about the speakers who use them. The present study explores the structural options available to middle-class American speakers who wish to *express disapproval.* It is hypothesized that the different surface structures through which speakers express disapproval convey and are constrained by the role and relative status assumed by the interlocutors within a particular social context.

As any syntactic form in American English can fulfill multiple functions, accurate interpretation of a form depends upon an examination of the conversational speech event. When expressions of disapproval[2] are considered, the specific surface signals that are acted upon by a hearer who infers disapproval from a move opening a *disapproval exchange*[3] are revealed. (Erroneous interpretation of a move as an expression of disapproval indicates that expressions of disapproval possess specific, definable characteristics.) In this study, the surface forms of moves in disapproval exchanges were examined with respect to their function within the conversational speech event (as topic openers, mid-exchange occurrences, topic closers). The distinctive syntactic categories considered in the analysis are the undressed positive/negative imperative (Imper), the dressed rhetorical question (RhQ), the dressed response-expected question (REQ), and the dressed declarative

(Dec). REQs were further defined with respect to [±wh] feature, indicating (non)occurrence of the question words *who, what, why, when,* etc., and a distinction was drawn in the Dec category among comment/explanation, criticism, opinion, advice/suggestions, and condition.

The type of syntactic structure which initially occurred in the move of the speaker who opened the disapproval exchange determined the categorization of the disapproval exchange. The analysis, however, included all of a speaker's move or subsequent moves that expressed disapproval as well as the hearer responses to those moves. The following exchange, for instance, was categorized as REQ [+wh] and analyzed as *REQ* [+wh] [4] *But-Dec (comment) REQ/*[−wh] */then-Dec (criticism)*:

> A: Hey, Xn,[5] why don't you take those things out of her hair?
> B: It'll wake her up if I do.
> A: But it's not good to leave them in all day and night, is it?
> B: They weren't in all day.
> A: Will it really wake her up if you take them out now?
> B: Yes. It will wake her up.
> A: Then, you should have taken them out before she went to bed.

Occasionally, as in the next example, only part of a speaker's move functioned as an expression of disapproval:

> A: What is this? (pause) This is a cooking implement sharp as can be, hanging around. What is it?

This move is analyzed as *REQ + Dec (explanation)* + REQ, but the final REQ functions simply as an information-seeking question.

Furthermore, lexical cues (attention-getters, terms of endearment, and the like), considered superfluous to the categorization of syntactic form, were nevertheless significant to the strength of the disapproval exchange. As semantic interpretation on the part of the hearer is the output of the lexicon, as well as the prosodic cues, aggravating and mitigating internal cues were assigned [+] or [−] values, respectively. The grammatical slots which permitted occurrence/alternation of such words or chunks were those that did not interfere with the semantic load of the expression of disapproval. Such affective lexical cues occurred in either initial or final framing positions or in medial positions, more specifically in the modifier slot of an NP or a modal auxiliary slot:

I told you coffee was no good for ya anyway.
  [+]                              [+]

Xn, you should watch her, dear.
[−]    [+]         [+]

What the hell is this you're saying? What are you going nuts? You must be some kind of a nut.
    [+]                      [+]                  [+]

The three-string speaker move immediately above is fully analyzed as *RhQ with an aggravating medial cue + REQ with an aggravating initial frame + Dec (comment with an aggravating medial cue.* Or, simply, *RhQ* (+) + [+] *REQ* + *Dec (crit* +).

Prosodic features (intonation, volume, tone of voice), recognized as important determiners of the strength of the disapproval exchange were not examined in this study. The communicative role they play, however, cannot be overlooked or under-estimated, as the strength they assign to a disapproval exchange affects the way in which the hearer interprets the expression of disapproval and, as a result, the sub-sequent design of the conversation. In some cases, prosodic features alone deliver a message of disapproval to a hearer:

> (Hearer accidentally turns off bathroom light while A is washing up)
>
> A: Xn [heavy stress on the first of the two syllables; low contrastive pitch on the second syllable]
>
> B: I'm sorry. [Turns light on again.]

By apologizing, B admits subordination in the exchange. Simultaneously, an attempt to correct the "violation" occurs when the light is turned back on. That the dis-approval implied by A has been accurately inferred by B is obvious upon a retrospec-tive examination of the exchange.

Borrowing from Goffman's (1971) discussion of offense, it can be said that expressions of disapproval cannot occur in contexts where some social or personal expectation has not been "violated" or is not in danger of being "violated" at some point in future or conditional time. In other words, an expression of disapproval is contingently relevant (Schegloff 1972) upon some "offense" (realized or potential/conditional). Clearly, not every "offense" triggers an expression of disapproval. Indeed what speakers find to be "offensive" is based upon the amount and kind of information they share, and how, when and where disapproval can be verbalized depends upon the way in which a particular speaker-hearer relationship is defined. Moreover, that relationship determines, in part, the way in which a speaker's syntactic choice of expression of disapproval and his or her use of lexical cues is interpreted by the hearer. In other words, a particular form is not equally powerful in all speaker-hearer relationships. In some relationships it can create/reaffirm solidarity; in others, it can create/reaffirm social distance. Of course, additional variables of audience, status, personality, mood, age, and the like also affect not only the occurrence of an expression of disapproval but its interpretation by the hearer as well as his or her response and therefore the subsequent design of the conversation.

Once disapproval is expressed, the hearer, who is allocated varying degrees of negotiating power by the speaker via the lexicon, syntax, and prosodic features of the speaker's expression of disapproval (which itself is the result of the interplay of contextual variables), has contextually defined response options. The hearer can either accept the expression of disapproval through acknowledgment, agreement, or apology (in the Dec, [−] disapproval form); reject it through disagreement or remediation (in the Dec, [−] disapproval form); or counter it with a [+] disapproval form.

The syntactic form that exhibited the highest frequency of occurrence in the data was the REQ. Most REQs functioned as topic openers and were characterized by [+ wh] feature, the most commonly occurring wh-Q words being *what* and *why*. In descending order of frequency, they occurred in the following forms:

What (−the hell−) $\left\{ \begin{array}{c} \text{Do} \\ \text{Be} \end{array} \right\}$ − $\left\{ \begin{array}{c} \text{Pres} \\ \text{Past} \end{array} \right\}$ − Pro − VP

What'd she pull it out?
What are you eating?

What − Be Pres ( . . . ) this ( . . . )

What's all this shit in here?

Why − $\left\{ \begin{array}{c} \text{Be} \\ \text{Do} \end{array} \right\}$ − $\left\{ \begin{array}{c} \text{Pres} \\ \text{Past} \end{array} \right\}$ − (Neg) $\left\{ \begin{array}{c} \text{NP} \\ \text{Pro} \end{array} \right\}$ −VP

Why don't you go lie on the couch?
Why are you putting more [syrup]?

Wh-Q words with the lowest frequency of occurrence were (in descending order of frequency) *where, which,* and *who* and were noted in the corpus to occur in the following forms:

Where − Be − $\left\{ \begin{array}{c} \text{Pres} \\ \text{Past} \end{array} \right\}$ − $\left\{ \begin{array}{c} \text{NP} \\ \text{Pro} \end{array} \right\}$

Where's the white out?
Where were you with the T.V. on?

Which − NP − Do Pres − You − wanna V

Which way do you wanna go, huh?

Who - VP

Who put the soap on my buff puff?

On the rare occasions when [+ wh] questions occurred in postinitial moves they contained the word *why*:

Why (−the hell−) Do Pres − (Neg) you − VP . . .

Well, why didn't you get it?

Obvious [+] internal cues included *the hell,* as in "What the hell did you do that for?" and *all* and *shit* as in "What's all this shit in here?" *What* preceding a normally inverted Q functioned as a [+] frame:

What are we throwing wings in here?
What'd [did] she pull it out?

When REQs with [− wh] feature were considered, a more diverse sampling of syntactic forms was noted. ([+] frames and internal cues have been noted in the following representative examples):

Pro − gonna − VP
X, you gonna eat that thing or what?
  [+]

Be Pres − VP
Are you coming?

Pro − Be Pres − Neg − VP − TAG
You're not putting milk in yours, are you?
  [+]

Be Pres − Neg − those . . .
Aren't those the same pjs she had on yesterday?

Do Pres − Pro − always − VP
Do you always read people's mail?
  [+]

The instances of postinitial moves with [− wh] feature are represented by these forms:

Pro − can't − VP
You can't wait until you receive your transcript?
  [+]

Would you really have the nerve to − VP
Would you really have the nerve to say that?
  [+]

Turning to an examination of the REQ within the exchange, we find that almost all of the REQs, [±wh] feature not considered, contained first moves which consisted of multiple strings. More importantly, even when the final string of the move was not a Dec, the REQ was usually followed by a Dec string. When REQs were compounded with Decs, the Decs were found to contain [+] frames and [+] internal cues such as the following:

I told you not to VP
What an insult . . .
I can't believe . . .

When second moves of disapproval exchanges characterized as REQs were examined, it was found that most of those second moves were Decs. When they were, the hearers usually responded innocently to the REQ by providing the requested information to the speaker. This [ − ] disapproval Dec was the dominant response pattern for single and final-string REQs.

REQs were not recorded as occurring either in move 1 postinitial positions or in move 2 with disapproval exchanges that were categorized as Decs. They were, however, compounded with Impers:

Wait a minute. What are ya doing?

and did occur in the first string of a speaker's second move in disapproval exchanges defined as RhQs:

What do you mean, "that's not true"? + Do you know what you just said?/
Do you know what you just said? . . .

With respect to contextual variables, REQs were found to occur between intimates or nonintimates; in situations which included intimate or nonintimate audiences; and in public or private places of occurrence. When they were used between nonintimates, however, no audience was present even where the place of occurrence was public.

The syntactic form which exhibited the next highest frequency of occurrence in the corpus was the Dec. Most Decs which functioned as topic openers were described as comments. Fulfilling that function, the dominant comment forms (in descending order of frequency) were:

Pro — VP
You look a mess.
NP — Be Pres
That bathtub is filthy.

You $\left\{ \begin{array}{l} \text{can} \\ \text{don't have to} \end{array} \right\}$ . . .

You can cut them thicker, X.

Criticisms demonstrated the next highest incidence in the data and were characterized by the following form:

You — $\left\{ \begin{array}{l} \text{didn't} \\ \text{should have} \end{array} \right\}$ — VP

You didn't iron the collar down

Noted least frequently in the data, suggestions/advice took the following form:

$\left\{ \begin{array}{l} \text{NP} \\ \text{Pro} \end{array} \right\}$ — should — VP

You should watch her
Dishes should be emptied.

The following [±] internal cues and frames were notes:

Hey honey, those socks she's got on are dirty.
    [ − ]
You can cut them thicker, X.
    [ − ]

108

Look it, I've been standing here for 10 minutes.
  [+]

Hey, she's in the closet.
   [+]

Less commonly functioning as mid-exchange occurrences, Decs were most frequently described as comments when they occurred in that position within the disapproval exchange. The syntactic pattern with the highest incidence for comments occurring in mid-exchange position varies slightly from the dominant pattern for topic openers:

$$\text{Pro} - \left\{ \begin{array}{c} \text{can} \\ \text{should} \\ \text{Do} \end{array} \right\} - \text{Neg} - \text{VP}$$

I just don't like it.
She doesn't want you to do it.
You can't get them now.

Occasionally, postinitial moves containing [+] frames and internal cues also functioned within topic-closing moves:

A: Well, I just don't like it.
B: ∅

Interestingly, when Dec expressions of disapproval were examined, it was found that in all but one instance disapproval exchanges which possessed string one Decs in the first move ended the move with a Dec. The anomaly was:

It's too loud. Turn it down, huh.

An examination of the first string of the speaker's second move of a disapproval exchange where the first move was categorized by a disapproval form that was not a Dec revealed that the second moves of such disapproval exchanges were not composed of compounded strings. To illustrate:

Speaker, move 1:  REQ:  You're not putting milk in yours, are you?
Speaker, move 2:  Dec:  You told me that under no circumstances were you to drink milk.

Furthermore, when the disapproval exchange was categorized as a REQ, almost all first-string Decs of the second move contained [+] frames:

Speakers, second moves:

   /But, you know I don't
   /You told me that . . .
   /You'd better not . . .
   /I can't believe . . .

Similarly, in the occurrences where a second-string Dec was compounded with a first-string, first-move REQ, the following [+] frames were noted:

REQ + I can't believe VP
REQ + What an insult to NP
REQ + I told you not to VP

One of two second-move, second-string Decs that were coupled with initial Imper strings was noted to use a [+] frame:

Imper + I told you . . .

Too, the one RhQ initial string that was compounded with a second-string Dec exhibited [+] internal cues:

RhQ + You <u>must</u> be <u>some kind of a nut</u>.

Considering hearer responses to Decs, those that were recorded were divided equally between two classes: [ − ] disapproval forms (remediation, thanks, agreement, REQs); and no response (i.e., hearer signals end of exchange).

With respect to context, Decs were found to occur between nonintimates as well as intimates, in private or public with both types of participants, whether the audience was intimate or not. In other words, they were noted in all contexts.

Impers, on the other hand, followed stricter occurrence rules. Found to function equally as topic openers and mid-exchange occurrences, Impers are represented by the (*Do Neg*) *VP* form. They occurred far less frequently than did REQs and Decs. [+] frames were recorded where an Imper disapproval form was a second-string that was attached to a first-string [ − ] disapproval form:

<u>So</u>, don't make yourself look as though you don't know what you're talking about.
[+]

and in final framing position where the disapproval form was a second-string that was attached to a first-string [+] disapproval Dec:

It's too loud. Turn it down, <u>huh</u>.
　　　　　　　　　　[+]

Impers were noted to occur principally as second strings in disapproval exchanges categorized as Decs and were most frequently followed by a [+] disapproval Dec string. The number of single- or final-string Impers in the data was minimal. Where they were noted, no hearer response was elicited.

Turning to context, we find no instances where Impers were used between nonintimates. In one case, a disapproval exchange between intimates which included an Imper disapproval form was overheard at a train station, but Impers did not generally occur in public settings with an audience.

The syntactic form which exhibited the lowest frequency of occurrence in the data was the RhQ. Occurring only as mid-exchange utterances, RhQs appeared most frequently in the following patterns:

What do you mean – Dec (from hearer's last move)

What do you mean, "that's not true"?

How can you – VP

How can you say that?

Most of the RhQs contained [+] frames or [+] internal cues as in:

I mean, how can you argue over such petty things?
   [+]

and only one instance was a single string. No true patterns emerged for second strings. That is to say, RhQs occurred with [±] disapproval Decs, REQs, and even a second RhQ in the string 2 position. However, only where an RhQ occurred in string 1 position was it noted to occur in string 2 position. In other words, the RhQ was found only to initiate a move.

There was only one instance of a single or final string RhQ in the data, and the hearer response was noted as acceptance. (This was the hearer's second move. Remediation for self was the hearer's response to the speaker's first-move Dec.)

In no instances were RhQs used by nonintimates or used in the presence of a nonintimate audience. In fact, the RhQ was the only form that was not noted to have occurred in a public setting. (Refer to Figures 1 and 2.)

That RhQs occurred in disapproval exchanges only where participants were intimates, where members of the audience were intimates with the speaker and

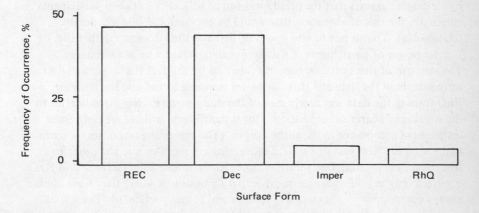

**FIGURE 1** Initiating Moves of Disapproval Exchanges

| Frequency of occurrence, % | Initiating move |
|---|---|
| 82 (27/33) | REQ |
| 12 (4/33) | REQ + Dec |
| 3 (1/33) | REQ + REQ + Dec |
| 3 (1/33) | REQ + Imper |
| | |
| 50 (3/6) | Imper + Dec* |
| 33 (2/6) | Imper |
| 17 (1/6) | Imper + REQ |
| | |
| 50 (15/30) | Dec |
| 33 (10/30) | Dec + Dec* |
| 7 (2/30) | Dec + Imper |
| 7 (2/30) | Dec + Imper + Dec* |
| 3 (1/30) | Dec + REQ + Dec* |
| | |
| 40 (2/5) | RhQ + Dec [−disapproval] |
| 20 (1/5) | RhQ + RhQ + Dec [+disapproval] |
| 20 (1/5) | RhQ + REQ + REQ |
| 20 (1/5) | RhQ |

\* = optional repetitions

**FIGURE 2** Sequencing in Initiating Moves of Disapproval Exchanges

hearer, and where the place of occurrence was private indicates that such an expression of disapproval is a strong marker of intimacy. That it was used only by intimates suggests that the presupposition of solidarity between participants eliminates the risk of alienation that would be encountered in nonintimate relationships. That is not to say, however, that the RhQ does not define the relative power of participants of a disapproval exchange who are intimates. The strength of this syntactic form is evidenced by the fact that it occurred so infrequently in the data and that the hearer response to the one single-string RhQ form in the data was acceptance of the disapproval exchange, indicative to the speaker of hearer subordination. This is significant, as there are only three instances of acceptance in the entire corpus. (The remaining responses of acceptance were to Decs: one to a second-move, single-string Dec and the other to a first move, single-string Dec.) Furthermore, RhQs, unlike Impers, Decs, and REQs, occurred only in mid-exchange, move-initiating positions where they were almost always compounded with other [±] disapproval forms, particularly Decs, that served both to buffer the impact of the RhQ and to keep the speaker in control of the exchange. In addition, although [+] frames and [+] internal cues were not needed to unambiguously convey to the hearer the function of the RhQ form as an expression of disapproval (the idiomatic Q form does that), [+] frames and internal cues were almost always included in a Dec that occurred in the string 2 position of a move that was categorized as a RhQ, making the exchange as a whole more powerful.

Interestingly, disapproval exchanges categorized as REQs or Impers were also compounded with second-string Decs that almost always included [+] lexical cues. The same held true when initial-string or final-string Decs were examined.

In short, it seems that in order for a Dec form to explicitly convey an intended message of disapproval the move must contain [+] frames or [+] internal cues (or a shift from normal of one or more prosodic features). This means that the lexicon that was noted in the Dec data to be aggravating actually functions to cue the hearer to the communicative function of the move. Such [+] frames and internal cues are not necessary to mark the function of expressions of disapproval in the other syntactic forms, although the message is strengthened by those occurrences.

Impers, which, like RhQs, exhibited a low frequency of occurrence in the data, were noted to be almost as powerful as RhQs in conveying speaker power to a hearer. Used only by intimate participants, this form occurred most often without [+] frames or [+] internal cues, indicating that it is in itself an explicit signal of disapproval. As with RhQs, compounding with Decs or REQs was commonly noted—again, buffering the impact of the form while keeping the speaker in control of the exchange. The speaker's control of the exchange is evidenced by the fact that the three single- or final-string Impers did not elicit verbal response from the hearers of the expressions of disapproval but rather succeeded in interrupting the completion of some action. As one Imper occurrence was noted in public and one where the speaker-hearer dyad did not know the members of the audience but shared societal norms with them, the Imper form, although found to mark intimacy, does not appear to do so to the same degree that the RhQ does.

That REQs occurred more frequently than Decs in nonintimate relationships and also in public settings suggests that REQs are less explicit disapproval forms than Decs. This can be explained by the fact that a Dec requires [+] frames or [+] internal cues to convey its communicative message as an expression of disapproval. If such explicit cues for criticisms, opinions, and advice are used, the disapproval form that results is unambiguous. This increases the risk factor for nonintimates. REQs, on the other hand, can communicate disapproval without [+] lexical cues because the REQ focuses on the "violation." Particularly (but not exclusively) without the use of [+] lexical cues, its function can be superficially ambiguous. This is supported by the hearer responses to REQs that simply provided the information sought by the Q, requiring the speaker to initiate a second disapproval move in the exchange that was almost always categorized as a Dec and responded to by the hearer with remediation.

It seems unlikely, however, that most hearers of REQs were unable to interpret accurately the contextual cues of the utterances which were intended by the speakers to convey disapproval. Rather, that second-move Decs were accurately interpreted by the hearers (and almost always responded to with remediation) suggests that the signaling of disapproval is sequentially arranged in discourse. The corpus on the whole supports this, as the terminating links of Dec and Imper as well as REQ disapproval exchanges (irrespective of the compounding order of the sequence) are generally Decs. (Exhibiting a low frequency of occurrence in the corpus, the RhQ did not reveal a definite pattern in its terminating link, although the [±] Dec form was favored.)

The findings in this study, demonstrating the ways in which syntactic forms of disapproval obey strict positional occurrence rules within the disapproval exchange, support signal ordering. To reiterate briefly and incompletely, REQs, for instance, functioned most frequently to open disapproval exchanges. Despite explicit lexical cues which often signaled disapproval in those utterances, first moves almost always consisted of multiple strings, ending in Decs and second moves which were characteristically Decs. Much more than coincidence, these patterns clearly indicate that disapproval exchanges obey rules for signal ordering.

This does not contradict what was initially posited in the discussion about when, by whom, and where the syntactic forms under consideration are used. Rather, it seems that the surface structure of the preliminary move in a disapproval exchange is determined by the way in which the participants of the exchange and the audience are defined, where they are, how old they are, and the like. Once the disapproval exchange is initiated, it follows syntactically predetermined moves which, in effect, signal disapproval in sequence. The number of strings composing each move and the number of moves in a disapproval exchange, however, is negotiated by the speaker-hearer dyad in light of a host of variables and cannot be predetermined. It follows that the longer a disapproval exchange remains open (in conversational time), the more likely it is that the exchange will be recognized by participants as an altercation. Altercations result when neither participant is willing to close down the exchange and are more likely to occur when some component(s) of the disapproval exchange are inappropriate to the way in which contextual variables are defined.

To sum up, the way in which a speaker-hearer relationship is defined inter-plays with contextual variables to determine the appropriate linguistic options available to a speaker who wishes to engage in a disapproval exchange. In addition, a speaker's linguistic choice of opening in a disapproval exchange and the way in which the exchange is subsequently managed reflects the relative power of a speaker and a hearer. Clearly revealing the relative status of the participants, expressions of disapproval serve to create, maintain, or change the attitudes and beliefs participants possess about themselves, about others, and about the society in which they live.

The findings presented in this study show language to be a complex interactional process which cannot be accurately understood apart from social context. While underlining the danger of intuitively enumerating speech-act rules for use as resources in the ESL classroom, they mark the need for sociolinguistic research in the development of ESL teaching materials. Only through the examination of naturally occurring speech can the rules for participating in any speech act be understood. Providing ESL students with information reflecting what we think we as native speakers do is at best a means toward the acquisition of linguistic variation. To produce linguistic forms variably without constraints, however, does not lead to the acquisition of communicative competence but rather to a grossly misrepresented picture of language. If indeed our goal is to teach ESL students how to interact as native speakers, we must be cautious of texts claiming to teach toward the goal of communicative competence by offering intuitive glimpses of linguistic variation. Instead, we must come to rely on the empirically based work of discourse analysts. Only when language learners understand linguistic variation in a nonrandom fashion will they be able to communicate accurately both an intended referential and stylistic meaning through linguistic form.

## NOTES

1. I am indebted to Nessa Wolfson not only for suggesting to me the topic of adult scolding but for providing, through her own research, the methodological model for this study. Too, I would like to thank Dell Hymes for his insights into an earlier version of this study and John Fought for his recent valuable comments.

2. Lexical alternates such as scold, reprimand, rebuke, and reproach were found to share the common function of expressing disapproval.

3. A disapproval exchange is minimally composed of one speaker move which expresses disapproval and a hearer response. (Hearer silence is considered a meaningful response.) It includes all speaker moves which express disapproval to one topic and all hearer responses to those speaker utterances from the time the topic is opened with an expression of disapproval until it is closed down. Seventy-four naturally occurring disapproval exchanges were examined in this study.

4. Signals end of speaker's move.

5. Nickname.

# 8

## HOW TO ARRANGE FOR SOCIAL COMMITMENTS IN AMERICAN ENGLISH: THE INVITATION

Nessa Wolfson, Lynne D'Amico-Reisner, and Lisa Huber
*University of Pennsylvania*

The knowledge of how to give, interpret and respond to invitations is an aspect of communicative competence (Hymes 1972) which is indispensable for those who wish to interact socially in an American English speech community. Since it is through social interaction with native speakers (which provides what Krashen 1980 calls "negotiated input") that language learners acquire the rules for using language communicatively, the ability to extend and respond appropriately to invitations is especially critical. Hatch (1978) points out that the second language learner is most likely to do best when given frequent opportunities to interact with native speakers; however, as they are often isolated from the mainstream of American social activity, adult nonnative language learners may experience difficulty in establishing social relationships which lead to regular interaction with members of native speech communities. The second language learner would do well to understand and acquire the ability to give and interpret invitations in the United States, since this aspect of communicative competence makes it possible for learners to arrange for the very opportunities that will enhance their overall acquisition of the target language.

Since it is well known that speech communities around the world vary greatly with respect to the rules which constrain speech behavior, it is obvious that nonnative speakers cannot expect to interact effectively in English if they depend on the rules of their native languages and speech communities in similar situations in the target language. Thus, if learners are to avoid misunderstandings, they must have information about the patterns of language use in the speech communities whose language they are learning.

The rules for the appropriate management of invitations are, like other aspects of communicative competence, usually well below the level of conscious awareness.

This means that although native speakers are able to recognize intuitively and respond appropriately to speech acts such as invitations, they are not in a position to describe how such interactions are patterned. Intuitions are judgments of accuracy and appropriateness, and as such they are a useful tool. However, when native speakers are asked to describe what they or others would say in a given situation, their responses do not always coincide with observed speech behavior. As Blom and Gumperz (1972) and, more recently, Borkin and Reinhart (1978) have demonstrated, native speakers are not aware of their own speech patterns and are therefore not able to explain them. Communicative competence implies the ability to assess and produce appropriate speech behavior, but not necessarily to describe it. It is important to recognize this limitation from the point of view of teachers and materials writers, and from that of researchers. Examples of speech acts which are based on introspection rather than on actual speech, and explanations of sociolinguistic rules which depend on native speaker intuitions rather than on close analysis of real data, are frequently unreliable. It follows from this that the best way in which the sociolinguistic patterns of a target language can be analyzed and made available to language learners is through empirically based descriptive analyses.

The present analysis, based upon data which were collected ethnographically through participant observation, aims at describing the behavioral patterns of invitations in American English. Not only were invitations and responses recorded for this study, but information regarding the age, gender, occupation, and relationship of the interlocutors was carefully noted.[1] As has been pointed out, social commitment is usually arrived at through what are commonly called invitations. Our operational definition of an unambiguous invitation, based on a large corpus, requires that the following properties be present: (1) reference to time and/or mention of place or activity and (2) a request for a response. In order to exemplify what we are calling unambiguous invitations, it will be helpful to consider the following:

1. Do you want (REQUEST FOR RESPONSE) to have lunch (ACTIVITY) tomorrow (TIME)?
2. . . . do you want (REQUEST FOR RESPONSE) to go to Atlantic City (ACTIVITY/ PLACE) on Thursday (TIME)?

The request for response can come before or after mention of activity/place and time:

3. Well, I'm going to Allentown (PLACE) on Saturday (TIME) to visit my cousins (ACTIVITY) and I wondered if you wanted to come along (REQUEST FOR RESPONSE)?

An unambiguous invitation does not occur without a request for response. The other components (time and/or place or activity) may appear in additional segments, as we will show. Because they are essential to the recognition of the invitation (i.e., its accurate interpretation by the hearer), we have analyzed the syntactic forms of the request for response (*kernels*). The most common patterns, each comprising 21.6 percent of the kernel data, were

$$(\text{Do you}) - \left\{ \begin{array}{c} \text{want to} \\ \text{wanna} \end{array} \right\} - \text{VP}$$

as in

4. You wanna get together for lunch?
5. Wanna go?

and

$$\text{Why} - \text{Do Neg} - \left\{ \begin{array}{c} \text{you} \\ \text{we} \end{array} \right\} - \text{VP}$$

as in

6. Why don't you join us?
7. Why don't we get together at O'Hara's . . . on Thursday?

Comprising 11 percent of the kernel data was the form:

$$\left\{ \begin{array}{c} \text{What} \\ \text{How} \end{array} \right\} \text{about} \quad - (\text{V} - \text{ing}) \quad - \text{NP}$$

as in

8. What about having a cup of coffee?
9. How about Monday?

The form

$$\text{Would you} - \left\{ \begin{array}{c} \text{be interested in} \\ \text{like to} \end{array} \right\} - \text{VP}$$

as in

10. Would you like to join us?
11. Would you be interested in seeing this singer?

was recorded in 8.1 percent of the kernel data as was

$$\text{Let's} - \text{VP}$$

as in

12. Let's go get coffee.

The only other significant pattern, occurring in 5.4 percent of the kernel data, was

$$\text{I'd} - \left\{ \begin{array}{ll} \text{like for} & \text{you to V} \\ \text{be delighted if} & \text{you Mod V} \end{array} \right\}$$

as in

13. I'd be delighted if you could come.
14. I'd like for you to come.

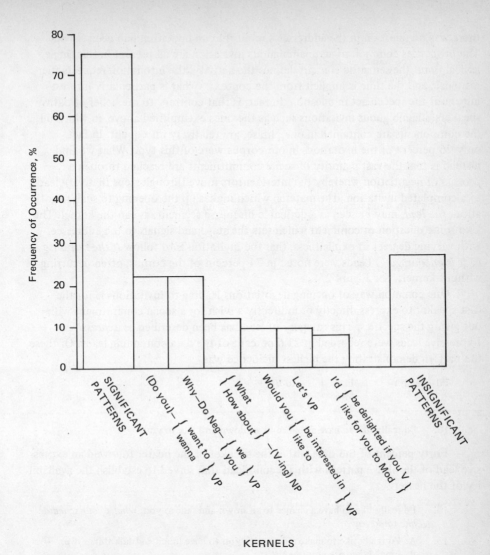

**FIGURE 1**  Kernels: Significant Syntactic Patterns

As with most conversational interaction, some of the information conveyed to the addressee is supplied by context. This, combined with the fact that a request for response may be made through intonational contour alone, can make for some interestingly terse examples which are, nevertheless, easily recognizable by native speakers of American English as unambiguous invitations. When a good friend and colleague of one of the authors opened her office door and said,

15.   Lunch?

there was no question in the addressee's mind that an invitation had been issued. The properties common to an unambiguous invitation are all present in this single lexical item: the semantic content defines the activity, the intonation requests the response, and the time is implicit from the context. What is particularly interesting about the speech act in question, in fact, is that contrary to the belief of native speakers, unambiguous invitations such as the ones exemplified above, in which all the components are contained in one phrase, are relatively infrequent. In fact, only 26 percent of the invitations in our corpus were of this type. What we find instead is that the vast majority of social commitments are reached through a process of negotiation whereby the interlocutors move through steps that *may* lead to a completed invitation. The material which makes up the opening to such negotiation, *the lead,* may be seen as a definable discourse segment, as can the kernel. The lead is the question or comment which sets the stage and signals to the addressee, with varying degrees of explicitness, that the invitation is to follow *if the response to it is encouraging.* Leads were noted in 74 percent of the corpus, often occurring without kernels. See Figure 2.

One common way of opening negotiations leading to invitations is for the first speaker to express directly or indirectly a wish for a social commitment without giving the specifics. This category of lead has been described as *expressive.* Expressive leads were recorded in 21.6 percent of the data containing leads. Of these, the pattern demonstrating the highest incidence was

$$\text{I'd}-\text{(really)}-\left\{ \begin{array}{l} \text{like} \\ \text{love} \end{array} \right\} -\text{to VP}$$

as in

16.  I'd really like to have a chance to sit down and talk to you.

Forty percent of the time, either the speaker or the hearer followed an expressive lead of the above pattern with a second lead that served to establish the availability of the hearer:

17.  I'd really like to have a chance to sit down and talk to you. *What's your schedule like tomorrow?*

18.  A: I'd really like to make a date with you to have lunch and talk things over.
     B: Fine—*When are you free?*

Serving to establish the availability of the hearer, *availability leads* were of two types, together accounting for 33.2 percent of the lead data. The first type established availability with a question or statement that elicited positive or negative response from the hearer. The utterances that occurred in this lead slot, however, exhibited varying degrees of ambiguity with respect to illocutionary point. In some, this type of availability lead revealed to the hearer that the utterance was serving to establish availability on a specific date or at a specific time for purposes of invitation negotiation. Half of these availability leads occurred in the form

$$\text{Are you (people) busy}-\left\{ \begin{array}{l} \text{this Saturday night} \\ \text{specific date} \\ \text{for dinner tonight} \end{array} \right\}$$

That this form of availability lead clearly sets the invitation negotiation into motion, its interactional goal visible to the hearer, is evidenced by the fact that in one of our examples the *hearer* delivers the kernel (i.e., she has appropriately interpreted the illocutionary intent of the speaker's utterance):

19. A: Are you busy for dinner tonight?
    B: A few of us are going to Greek town—want to come?

The illocutionary point of other availability leads of this type, however, is not so easily recognizable by the hearer. While also serving to establish the availability of the hearer, it is not always obvious why the speaker is questioning the hearer.

20. Do you have a lot of work to do tonight?

is a question that can be interpreted as, "Will you be free tonight?" as well as, "I am really wondering, 'Do you have a lot of work to do tonight'?" Looking at those occurrences where illocutionary intent is ambiguous, we find that twice as many such leads occurred without kernels as with them (67 percent vs. 33 percent) and that leads co-occurring with kernels all contained a present tense verb while those occurring alone contained either the modal auxiliary "will," marking future, or a past tense marker.

As mentioned earlier, there is a second kind of lead that serves to establish the availability of the hearer. This lead assumed the form of an information question. Like the first category of availability lead, it exhibited varying degrees of visibility with respect to illocutionary point: 25 percent of the availability leads of this second type revealed to hearers that they were clearly serving to establish their availability on a specific date or for a specific time or purpose:

21. What are you doing Saturday, May 2nd?
22. When can I be availed of your skill again?

Ambiguity was characteristic of the remaining 75 percent of availability leads of this second type:

23. What time are you going to be finished?
24. What's your schedule tomorrow?

It should be noted that availability leads of this type which occurred with kernels all demonstrated a single response pattern (the only one noted in the corpus): speakers consistently uttered the availability lead in their first move and the kernel in their second.

Whether it fell into the availability or the expressive category, the lead commonly contained at least one of the components of an unambiguous invitation. It may have been time alone, as in many of the availability leads, or it may have been a mention of place or activity:

25. Did you know Artie's is having a big sale right now?
26. What are you doing for dinner?

Closely resembling a kernel, the final category of lead distinguished in the data has been described as a *pseudo-kernel* lead. Accounting for almost 45 percent of the lead data, pseudo-kernel leads occurred most frequently without kernels—i.e., 89 percent of the time an unambiguous invitation was *not* initiated. Formulaic in nature, the features of this type of lead are immediately recognizable: time is always left indefinite, most often through the use of such vague lexical choices as "sometime," "anytime," or "soon." And not only is the verb tense in the lead often marked by the presence of a modal auxiliary or "have to," but it is most infrequent that a response is directly called for:

27. Maybe we can get together for lunch one day.

28. You know, Mary, we're going to have to get together for lunch one of these days.

29. We have to get together soon, John.

Any of the indefinite adverbial clauses beginning with "when" as in

30. Let's have lunch together when things settle down.

also function as cues that an unambiguous invitation is *unlikely* to be initiated. Other cues are the very words a learner of American English might wrongly interpret as having the most illocutionary force. Words like "definitely," for example, as in

31. Let's definitely get together.

serve as further cues to the native speaker that the lead will probably *not* be followed up.

It is suggested by the data that when a speaker delivers a pseudo-kernel lead, the hearer is not permitted to negate or reject it but can signal a desire for termination of the negotiation simply through acknowledgment of the speaker's lead:

32. A: You know, X, we're gonna have to get together for lunch one of these days.
    B: I know, I know.
    A: OK.

Expressive responses to pseudo-kernel leads are more encouraging of the initiation of an unambiguous invitation, although, as mentioned above, pseudo-kernel leads led to unambiguous invitations only in a small percentage of the data.[2] The following example is representative of that small percentage:

33. A: We should get together. Why don't we get together sometime this week?
    B: Yeah, I'd like to but I don't know . . .
    A: Why don't we get together at O'Haras . . . on Thursday night?

The function of expressive and pseudo-kernel leads in American invitations is interesting evidence of the often lamented rapid pace of life. Because time for social life is limited, it is often difficult to keep contact with old friends and acquaintances, however much one may enjoy their company. It frequently happens, however, that friends or relatives who may be well known to one another but who do not ordinarily interact are brought together through one cause or another. Chance meetings at parties, weddings, funerals, in the street, at the store, or at a restaurant may result in a desire for a closer relationship. A suggestion to "get together sometime," for instance, is not interpreted by the participants of the interaction as an invitation in itself, and neither participant will be insulted if plans are never brought to fruition. Good intentions have been expressed in the form of a lead—nothing more.

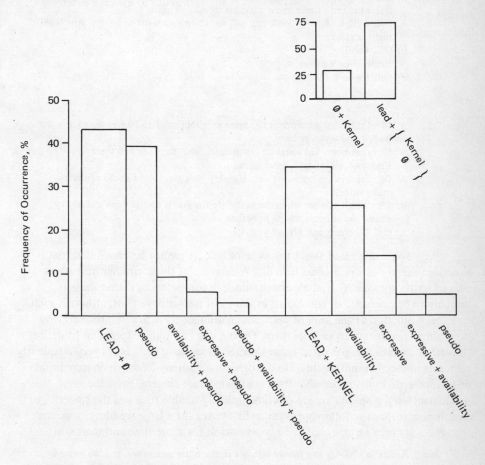

**FIGURE 2** Lead Types

Leads and the set of responses and counterresponses which follow them are linked by discourse rules such that together they form what a native speaker would unambiguously identify as an invitation. Oftentimes participants go into considerable detail in comparing their respective schedules as a preliminary to fixing an actual date without either of them ever coming to the point of suggesting a specific time. Here we come close to the negotiating which would lead to a true commitment but in the end none is made:

34.   A: It's really horrible that we never see each other.
       B: I know. We have to try to arrange something.
       A: How about dinner? Why don't we go out to dinner together?
       B: That's a good idea.
       A: What days are good for you and Joe?
       B: Weekends are best.
       A: Oh, weekends are bad for us. Don't you ever go out to dinner during the week?
       B: Well, we do, but we usually don't make plans till the last minute. Joe gets home late a lot and I never know what his schedule's going to be.
       A: OK, well, look, why don't you call me when you want to go out. Any week night is good.
       B: OK, I will.
       A: Really, don't forget.
       B: OK, I won't. I'll call you.

or

35.   A: I feel silly that we work in the same neighborhood and never see each other.
       B: Well, I know you're busy.
       A: Not that busy. Let's make a lunch date. What days are you free?
       B: Fridays—or Mondays, sometimes.
       A: Oh, Fridays are my worst day. Monday isn't great but I could probably make it then.
       B: Why don't you see when the best time for you is and give me a call? Try to call me at home the night before.
       A: OK, I'll check and I'll call you.

Whatever can be said about this type of lead, it cannot be concluded that it functions merely as a politeness formula. A measure of the sociolinguistic adroitness of native speakers (i.e., their communicative competence) is that there is unlikely to be linguistic or contextual evidence of insincerity. Thus, although such leads *may* function at the level of politeness formulas, there are two reasons why it would be inaccurate to so label them. On the one hand, the expression of desire to further a relationship is often quite sincere. As we have seen, leads very frequently do result in social commitments. On the other hand, many leads which may in fact be insincere are indistinguishable from leads which are sincere. Even the very participants in the speech act are often completely unable to assess the sincerity of an interlocutor, as the following example illustrates. At a large wedding, a woman engaged a younger female relative in conversation for some time and then said:

36.   A: There's hardly any family left. We're the older generation and we never even see each other. Look, I'm going to take the initiative. I know everyone is busy but I'm going to make the effort. I'm going to call Sally and Bill and we'll all get together for dinner at my house, OK?
       B: Sure, I think that's a great idea.

Nothing came of this promise, and it is quite clear that neither participant regards its fulfillment as a social obligation.

One interesting aspect of the findings reported here is that speakers, in choosing to *negotiate* for social engagements, are spared the necessity of exposing themselves to possible rejection. The difference in the temporal marking of verbs in leads occurring with kernels and those occurring without them and the response pattern of the second type of availability lead support this. Whether an invitation is likely to be negotiated or not, however, depends upon the social identity of the participants and their positions relative to one another. The dimensions of power and solidarity (Brown and Gilman 1960) provide some useful insights with respect to the way invitations are managed. Power, on the one hand, or inequality of status, favor direct invitations and disfavors attempts at negotiation or expressions of good intent. We have no examples at all of ambiguous invitations given to a superior and only two cases of this occurring when the addressee is the inferior. In the first instance, the speaker is a faculty member and the addressee is a student; in the second, the speaker is a faculty member and the addressee is a much younger and lower-ranking colleague:

37. A: Hi, Lyn. It's good to see you. I never see you anymore. Is everything OK?
    B: Yes, fine.
    A: I really miss seeing you.
    B: You're so busy, I don't want to bother you.
    A: It wouldn't be a bother. I'd love to see you. What we should do is arrange to have lunch together so that we can really talk.
    B: OK.

38. A: Well, it seems that we have a number of things to discuss. We'll have to try to have lunch together.
    B: That's a good idea.
    A: Yes, well right now I can hardly keep my head above water but as soon as I have things cleared away—say in 2 or 3 weeks—I'll give you a call and we'll make a date.
    B: OK, let me know when you're free.

On the other hand, some degree of solidarity must be present in order for interlocutors to attempt negotiating invitations. Even in the above invitations which were issued by a person of superior power, speakers shared commonality of both sex and profession—two solidarity-creating attributes. According to Brown and Ford (1961), interlocutors who are closest on the solidarity scale are most likely to exchange first names. Our data show that the solidarity which leads to such reciprocity is, indeed, a prerequisite to the initiation of invitation negotiations. Useful as the dimensions of power and solidarity are in any sociolinguistic analysis, it must be recognized that still another dimension—that of intimacy—is of critical importance. Intimacy implies some degree of solidarity, but the converse is clearly not true. There are cases where children of the same socioeconomic background are born and raised in the same neighborhood, go to the same schools, and even attend the same social events throughout years of their lives without ever regarding themselves as intimates. The opposite situation, where members of a dyad share almost nothing except common profession, perhaps, along with frequency of interaction may well lead to a relationship which both would acknowledge to be intimate.

As with most patterns of social interaction, the constraints on invitation negotiations vary considerably with the degree of intimacy between interlocutors. In cases where participants are intimates who share the same social status, fear of rejection is minimized (at least with respect to activities related to the social domains in which interlocutors are intimates), and as a consequence, negotiation is often unnecessary. If they wish for one another's company, they can say so:

39.  A: Want to come over this evening? We can play Scrabble.
     B: OK, I'll call you after dinner.

40.  A: Do you have anything on for Saturday evening? I thought it would be nice to get out to see a movie.
     B: I hope there's something worth seeing this week.

Indeed, intimates can even invite themselves:

41.  A: Are you busy this afternoon? I thought I'd drop over for a while.

When negotiation does occur between intimates, it is likely to involve the settling of details such as time or place of the projected arrangement:

42.  A: What's your schedule tomorrow? Are you going to be in your office?
     B: Yeah—I teach at one and I have some students to see in the morning.
     A: Will you have time for lunch?
     B: I certainly hope so. Do you want to pick me up or meet me?
     A: I'd better meet you. You'll never get out of there otherwise and if you teach at one we won't have much time.
     B: Kelly and Cohen's?
     A: OK. Or do you think we'd have time for the Middle Eastern place?
     B: Yeah, I guess so. They're pretty fast.
     A: OK, do you want to meet me then at 12?
     B: Well, it's sort of silly—if you have to walk right by my office you might as well pick me up.
     A: If you promise you'll be ready.
     B: I promise—I'll even meet you outside.
     A: OK—that's a good idea—on the side of the building near 38th?
     B: OK—I'll be there.
     A: 10 of 12?
     B: OK.

Conversely, it is with nonintimates of approximately equal social status that the type of interaction which we have labeled negotiation for invitation usually takes place. In this case, either participant may initiate the routine, but it depends on both to bring the negotiation to a successful conclusion—a social engagement:

43.  A: Did you know that Artie's is having a big sale right now?
     B: No, I didn't realize—though I guess it is that time of the year again.
     A: I'd really like to see what they have. Last time they had a sale I got 2 gorgeous skirts for $5 each.
     B: Well, do you feel like running over tomorrow? I could pick you up.
     A: Great idea—it would be fun to go together. What time is good for you?
     B: Well, I have to drive my son someplace in the morning but I'll be free by about 11. Is 11:30 OK?
     A: Perfect.

126

If either participant is hesitant about committing herself/himself to such a social arrangement, it is easy to pull back without giving offense. Since neither has openly asked for the company of the other, there is no open rejection.

One of the interesting aspects of invitation negotiations is that they provide strong evidence of the complexity of communicative competence. Interlocutors in such negotiations are keenly sensitive to the most subtle cues. In the following example, two middle-class women in their forties meet at a neighborhood tennis club on July Fourth weekend:

44.    A: You doing anything exciting this weekend?
       B: No, I'll be around the pool here.
       A: OK, I'll see you.
       B: Maybe we'll barbecue one night.
       A: OK, that's a nice idea. I'm tied up Sunday night.
       B: All right. We'll keep it loose.
       (A walks away, turns and walks back, saying:)
       A: We're supposed to do something with Helen tomorrow night. Want to do something with us?
       B: OK. Let us know.

Although not intimate friends, the interlocutors in the above example are long-time neighbors who sometimes interact socially and have some friends in common. Thus, it is not surprising that the first speaker opens negotiations for a possible social arrangement by first inquiring as to her addressee's availability. What is interesting (and not unusual) here is that by using the adjective "exciting," she protects herself in advance from possible rejection, since her question may be interpreted as a lead or simply as a friendly inquiry. The underlying cultural knowledge needed to interpret this bit of interaction is that in the United States, the weekend of July 4th is a time when barbecues and parties are traditionally given and that to have no social plans is seen as an indication of social isolation. B's response, "No, I'll be around the pool here." may have been an embarrassing admission. Although she indicates her availability, she offers no further encouragement. It is for this reason, perhaps, that her response does not lead to an immediate invitation, as so many of our examples do. A's ambiguous, "OK, I'll see you." could be interpreted as an agreement to meet again casually at the pool or as a way of holding the negotiation open. B, in an attempt to give some encouragement and arrive at a more specific engagement, uses her turn to offer a new lead of her own, specifying a social activity away from the pool. With this encouragement, A states her own time restrictions, "OK, that's a nice idea. I'm tied up Sunday night." and B, apparently taking this as a lack of interest, uses her turn to make it clear that she intends to press no further. Seeming to accept this, A walks off and then suddenly turns back and offers a completely unambiguous invitation which is accepted.

Not all invitation negotiations involve quite this much fencing, of course. Indeed, leads, even when rejected, may be followed by quite cheerful explanations and assurances of plans in the future. A good example is the following, which occurred during a telephone call between two female friends:

45.   A: Hi, are you busy?
      B: Well, reading.
      A: Oh. I just wondered—is your husband going to be home later?
      B: No, he's out of town for the whole week.
      A: That's a shame. I was going to ask you if you felt like joining us for dinner
          tonight. I don't feel like cooking. And I just thought—it's been such a long
          time since we've seen each other.
      B: I would have loved to but he's away.
      A: Well, that's all right. We'll be going out to dinner a lot all summer.
      B: Good. He'll be at home next week and we'll get together.
      A: OK. Get back to your work.

Without the understanding that leads are not invitations in themselves but can be used as steps toward the accomplishment of social commitments, foreign speakers attempting to communicate appropriately in an American English speech community often find Americans to be "insincere." Mistaking leads of the "Let's get together for lunch sometime" variety for unambiguous invitations, they misinterpret American speech behavior. They see the American as uncaring and irresponsible rather than as insecure and fearful of rejection. Conversely, an American who issues a lead to a nonnative speaker intuitively expects an appropriate response. An inappropriate response may cause the American to abandon any further attempt to negotiate for a social commitment with the nonnative speaker because she/he fears either that the nonnative speaker does not comprehend the routine or that she/he does not desire to make a social commitment with the speaker. Clearly, the abandonment of an invitation interaction means the loss of an opportunity to be included in an activity with a native speaker and, as a consequence, the loss of an opportunity which would allow for further language acquisition.

## NOTES

1. Not only were invitations and responses recorded for this study, but information regarding the age, gender, occupation, and relationship of the interlocutors was carefully noted. We would like to thank the members of Ed 534, Sociolinguistics in Education, at the University of Pennsylvania for their help in collecting the data: M. B. Carlson, M. Davenport, M. Glassman, C. R. Graizbord, Y-K. J. Kim, C-C. Liang, D. L. Mariano, F-A. Mohamed, A. S. Sesay, J. H. Smith, D. F. Weisman, M. Yorinks, and F. M. Ziezio.

2. It should be noted that suggestions or directives which are leave-taking formulas cannot lead to negotiations for social commitments. For instance, to "Y'all come on back now, y'hear?" the only proper response is "I sure will." To say "Well, how about next Friday?" is clearly inappropriate.

# II

# SOCIOLINGUISTICS AND SECOND LANGUAGE LEARNING AND TEACHING

# INTRODUCTION

## Elliot Judd
*University of Illinois at Chicago*

In the second half of this book, we turn to another aspect of sociolinguistic
research. While the papers in the first section of this anthology focused primarily
on basic sociolinguistic research, the eight papers in this section emphasize applied
sociolinguistics, especially second language learning and teaching. All the writers
share a common sociolinguistic perspective; they all view language as a social
phenomenon affected by numerous variables present in a given society. All believe
that analysis of language should extend beyond the sentence level and include
investigations of the structure of discourse. Further, all the writers are committed
to the view that sociocultural factors must be incorporated into studies of second
language teaching and learning if full understanding is to be achieved. In short,
while the articles in this section differ in terms of specific topics, methods of
research styles, and the degree of application to actual classroom use, they are all
founded on the underlying belief that second language teaching and learning occur
in natural sociocultural situations and that research must incorporate the sociolinguistic factors if any valid findings are ever to be discovered and applied.

The first paper in this section is Richard Schmidt's study of Wes, an adult
second language user living in Hawaii. Wes is a Japanese artist with close ties to
many native English speakers. According to Schumann's acculturation model, he
would appear to be a fine candidate to master English as a second language. Yet, in
the years that Schmidt observed his linguistic behavior, Wes showed little evidence
of any significant improvement in acquiring the rules and elements of native English
syntax. Nonetheless, Wes is able to engage in basic communication with native
speakers and seems content with his linguistic abilities, which fulfill social functions
in English.

Schmidt's study is important to second language acquisition research on several levels. First, it raises questions as to the validity of the acculturation model itself. Beyond that is the deeper question of how to conduct second language acquisition research. As Schmidt shows, merely focusing on syntactic elements will not present a complete picture of a learner's ability in a second language. It is only through an analysis of discourse and communicative functions that a second language learner's competence can be fully measured. In fact, as in Wes's case, analysis of syntax alone may provide a faulty picture of a learner's abilities. We are left with an even deeper and more perplexing question: What do we mean when we talk about "acquiring" a second language? The answer to this question is important to both second language acquisition researchers as well as those who create pedagogy based on research findings. Schmidt's case study of one learner incorporates sociolinguistic elements in an effort to shed light on the answers to this basic question and shows how a learner's linguistic competence can differ from his/her communicative competence.

Next, Robin Scarcella's paper offers a different perspective on the development of communicative competence in second language learners; she employs a different research framework for her investigation. Rather than focusing on one individual, Scarcella uses a group study approach. For Scarcella, one important factor in the mastery of nativelike communicative competence in a second language is the ability to participate in conversations. The author investigates two hypotheses: first, that ability to manage conversations in a second language increases with overall second language proficiency and, second, that a developmental order exists for the acquisition of conversational devices. In confirming both these hypotheses, Scarcella helps to improve understanding of the precise nature of what is often vaguely labeled "communicative competence."

Scarcella's article is a pioneer study in an effort to categorize a developmental order for the acquisition of conversational skills. It shows us that second language learners must develop these if they are to be considered fully proficient in a second language. For those in the classroom, it serves to justify the integration of conversational skills into the corpus of materials that are used to teach nonnative speakers. For the researcher, it attests to the need to accumulate data from a sociolinguistic perspective and to analyze data from the functional perspective of communication, not merely in terms of more discrete units used in more traditional forms of second language acquisition research.

The next paper is Cristin Carpenter's investigation into the modes of discourse used when university instructors address their students, both native and nonnative speakers of English. The differences that Carpenter finds are not only of a syntactic nature; in fact, most are discoursal in nature. Carpenter notes that the patterns used by native speakers when talking to nonnative speakers (commonly known as "foreigner talk") are only one part of the picture. She and others suggest that there also exists a "foreigner register," discourse styles which native speakers use when addressing nonnatives.

Again, as in the other papers, Carpenter urges us to look beyond grammatical structures. We must focus on the functions of language and on the registers and discourse patterns used by and with nonnative speakers of a language. The author also reminds us that second language learning is based on both input and output; we must look at what the learner says as well as what is said to the learner. Investigations such as this into both "foreigner talk" and "foreigner register" promise to teach us more about the second language learning process itself. In addition, they can offer exciting new directions to second language instructors when we learn what types of linguistic input aid or impede the learning process.

Leslie Beebe and Jane Zuengler's paper offers another sociolinguistic perspective on second language acquisition. Rather than conducting a new study and interpreting the results, they aim to reinterpret existing research findings within a more satisfactory framework. The authors' primary focus is on the application of accommodation theory as a model by which second language acquisition data can be better analyzed and understood. According to Beebe and Zuengler, previous explanations of second language data—such as offered in the creative construction hypothesis, the interlanguage hypothesis, the monitor model, the acculturation model, and Gardner's social-psychological model—are all inadequate because they fail to explain the variable performance data found in second language *use*. The authors argue that only Giles' accommodation theory provides an acceptable framework with the ability to account for variable performance data and also explanatory power.

Beebe and Zuengler's article is important for several reasons. First, it offers two criteria to which second language acquisition theory should conform. One is that a theory must have explanatory power to account for the data and the process of second language learning. The other is that a theory must account for variable performance data within one learner and among various learners. Second, in accordance with current beliefs in sociolinguistics, the authors stress the need to incorporate social-psychological dynamics into any linguistic analysis. Third, the recognition of variable performance data is a position that many sociolinguists have accepted in dialect and first language learning studies, but it has not received adequate attention in studies of second language acquisition. Finally, Beebe and Zuengler offer a challenge for those involved with second language acquisition research: There should be investigations to determine if Giles' work on accommodation theory is a valid construct for the analysis of language performance of second language learners in both formal and informal environments.

While the first four papers in this section focus on second language acquisition in a classical sense, the fifth offers a departure from the traditional domains of such investigations. Richard Day discusses the acquisition of three types of speech acts used by the audience in order to participate in the Rocky Horror Picture Show, a current cult movie. The style of this paper is often quite humorous and provides a pleasant change of pace for the reader. In addition, the paper offers a discussion of how nonnative speakers of a language/dialect attempt to master some of the necessary speech acts of an alien speech community. Since a novice attending a cult movie is unfamiliar with the speech events and speech acts of the veteran cultists, who have formed their own speech community, he or she is in a position similar to that of an adult entering a second language environment for the first time. That is, many of the speech events and acts are alien in nature and may even appear bizarre. Day discusses three types of speech acts, their characteristics, and the formal and informal means that a person can employ in order to master the language of "The Rocky Horror Picture Show." He further presents a hierarchy of speech events which allows an individual to obtain gradual fluency in the new language.

The type of analysis used in this paper is strongly sociolinguistic in nature and style, and we urge the reader to enjoy the tone of the paper as well as to investigate and to analyze Day's underlying hypotheses. Certainly languages are learned in a social milieu. Further, communication consists of mastery of certain speech acts, and careful sociolinguistic analysis may prove useful in detailing which speech acts are easier or more difficult to master. Finally, Day makes us aware that serious field investigations can also be fun and that putting ourselves in nontraditional speech communities not only may be pleasurable but may also provide insights into the dynamics of human communication.

The last three papers in the book discuss second language learning in more formal environments. While the first five focused on second language acquisition in natural situations, these papers provide information about second language learning in the classroom, where the environment is more controlled and more structured. As in the first five papers, the last three authors maintain a sociolinguistic perspective and assert that sociolinguistic research contributes greatly to understanding second language learning and pedagogy.

Teresa Pica's study of article use in English is the first of these pedagogical articles. Pica claims that the rules for article use provided in many ESL texts and reference grammars are often incomplete, overgeneralized, or, in fact, inaccurate. By employing sociolinguistic field methods in her investigations, Pica discovers that the descriptions of article use available in texts are contradicted by native English speakers in natural, unmonitored speech activities. Thus, ESL students may be exposed to invalid information about articles, which may hinder rather than aid the mastery process. As a result, ESL teachers may need to revise their teaching methods with regard to article instruction.

Pica's article points out the need to observe speech patterns in a natural context if we are interested in positing accurate grammatical rules for use in the ESL classroom. It further reminds us of the need to teach language in natural communicative settings if full understanding of grammatical structures is to be imparted to nonnative speakers. Finally, the methodology that Pica uses in her investigation of article use provides a research format for the investigation of other grammatical patterns in English. We are reminded that we cannot assume that all descriptions of grammar are totally accurate simply because they appear in teaching texts. Careful sociolinguistic investigations which look at natural communicative speech events are crucial if we want to devise valid instructional materials to facilitate ESL students' learning.

The article which follows focuses on another area of concern for those interested in both sociolinguistics and second language instruction. Elliot Judd discusses the problems involved in incorporating sociolinguistic findings into second language teaching materials. By focusing on male/female language differences as a particular instance of sociolinguistic inquiry, Judd describes the difficulties involved both in the accumulation of valid sociolinguistc data and in deciding which data should be included in the teaching materials. In addition, he points out some practical problems involved with teaching sociolinguistic variation within language situations where the roles and functions of English differ and/or where students' cultural values differ from those of the teacher.

Judd's overall poition is that if second language teaching materials are to be valid and of practical use to students, they must include information about female/male language differences as well as other areas of speech variation which sociolinguists recognize as part of natural human communications. On the other hand, he cautions against premature inclusion of sociolinguistic information which has not been empirically validated. Stated in another way, the author is weary of materials that claim to teach communicative competence when little is known about the specific features of linguistic behavior which make a second language user able to function with nativelike ability. Thus, we must endeavor to incorporate valid sociolinguistic data into second language textbooks while also realizing that we still have far to go in our efforts to understand both what constitutes communicative competence and how to teach it to others.

The anthology concludes with Jack Richards' paper entitled "Communicative Needs in Foreign Language Learning." This article is most appropriate as a final selection because it emphasizes the dominant theme of the anthology: that sociolinguistic knowledge contributes greatly to the understanding of second language teaching and learning. Richards considers five central aspects of verbal communication. These are that communication is (1) proposition-based, (2) conventional, (3) appropriate, (4) interactional, and (5) structured. As Richards emphasizes in this paper, each of these five statements has important pedagogical implications for second language teaching. He reminds instructors that language teaching should stress the communication of ideas through language, rather than purely grammatical structures or meaningless verbal routines.

Richards' article reminds us that those involved in second language instruction and materials development must understand how people communicate and how their communicative needs affect the discourse patterns of nonnative speakers. The more understanding we possess about the functions of language, the better our teaching and the stronger our materials will be. Through such understanding, we can be helped to better comprehend the difficulties that our students experience in acquiring a second language and we can become more appreciative of their success when mastery is achieved.

In summary, the papers presented in the second half of this book offer a variety of perspectives on the interaction between sociolinguistics and second language teaching and learning. The focus of each of the investigations differs, as do the questions asked, the research methodologies employed, and the second language users observed. The papers on second language teaching also differ in scope and emphasis. Yet all eight papers are based on shared assumptions as well. The authors believe that language is a social phenomenon and that it must be studied in its social context. They believe that investigations of second language learning must explore the function as well as the form of language. They all believe that data must be analyzed in terms of discourse and that analysis must go beyond the sentence level. All share the belief that mastery of a second language means the ability to attain communicative competence in that second language, that is, the ability to interact and communicate with native speakers in the appropriate social contexts through the use of appropriate language forms. Finally, as with the papers in the first half of the book, all the authors feel that insights from sociolinguistics have great potential for shedding light on the nature of second language acquisition and instruction. We are just beginning our work, but investigations and commentary such as those provided in this book start us on the road toward better understanding the challenges involved in mastering a second language.

# 9

## INTERACTION, ACCULTURATION, AND THE ACQUISITION OF COMMUNICATIVE COMPETENCE: A CASE STUDY OF AN ADULT

### Richard W. Schmidt
*The University of Hawaii at Manoa*

Research in second language acquisition (SLA) has to date typically concentrated on the acquisition of systems central to linguistic analysis, especially morphology and syntax. Indeed, SLA has virtually been defined (implicitly, in most cases) as the acquisition of linguistic forms, structures, and rules. Only recently has there been widespread recognition among SLA researchers that it is important to study the acquisition of other components of language ability as well, especially those interactional and social aspects of language ability that are frequently referred to under the rubric of "communicative competence" (Canale and Swain 1980, Habermas 1970, Halliday 1973, Hymes 1967, 1968, 1972, Savignon 1972).

Of course, the idea that we learn and use language for communication is hardly new. *Everyone knows* that we use language for a variety of purposes, for communication in the broadest sense: to convey to others what we have in our minds, not only information but also thoughts, feelings, desires, and intentions; to establish and maintain human relationships and gain the sympathy and support of others; to carry on conversations, both trivial and serious; to obtain goods and services and to get things done; in short, to carry on nearly all the ordinary and extraordinary business of life. Moreover, ever since Hymes pointed out forcefully that "there are rules of use without which the rules of grammar would be useless" (Hymes 1972 p. 278) and began to specify what it means to be able to use language appropriately, our technical understanding of what is involved in using language for communication and interaction has been broadened and deepened by theoretical insights and descriptive work from a great variety of language-related disciplines and subdisciplines, including (minimally) linguistic pragmatics, discourse analysis, sociolinguistics, psycholinguistics, anthropology and the ethnography of speaking, sociology and ethnomethodology, and the philosophy of language (Richards and Schmidt, forthcoming). This work has not been without impact on the language learning and teaching field but has for the most part resulted in programmatic statements of what the nonnative speaker needs to learn or be taught (e.g., Paulston 1974, Holmes and Brown 1976, Yorio 1980). What is new, in fact just beginning, is systematic study of the actual acquisition of communicative abilities by nonnative speakers (see Hatch 1978c, Larsen-Freeman 1980, and especially Larsen-Freeman 1981, for overviews of current research).

While the study of interactional and social abilities as what is learned (communicative competence as output or result) is still in its infancy, even within the relatively narrow scope of SLA as syntactic acquisition considerable attention has been devoted to social and interactional factors as variables which may foster or inhibit language acquisition, i.e., as the *why* or cause of SLA. The position that we learn a language by using it for meaningful communication rather than by studying it is shared by a great number of contemporary researchers (Rivers 1980). Indisputably true of children learning their first language, this seems to be the case as well for child SLA. Research by Hale and Budar (1970) and Fathman (1975) has indicated that for younger learners ESL instruction is less important than contact with the target language group. Fillmore (1976, 1979), in her case study of five Spanish-speaking children acquiring English as a second language in an American kindergarten, found clear evidence for a link between successful acquisition and enthusiasm for association with American children, coupled with uninhibited attempts to interact with them, focusing on communication rather than form.

For adult SLA, the relationship between interaction and acquisition is much less clear. Hatch (1978c), considering the hypothesis that syntactic structures are developed through learning to interact verbally and do conversation, concludes that the evidence is strong for children but much weaker in the case of adults. Evidence from studies contrasting exposure in informal environments with formal instruction is mixed, with studies by Upshur (1968), Mason (1971), and Carroll (1967) consistent with a hypothesis that informal interaction is as effective for adults as formal instruction, and studies by Krashen and Seliger (1976) and Krashen, Seliger, and Hartnett (1974) indicating that years of formal instruction in English is a better predictor of adult proficiency than years of natural exposure to and use of English. However, in interpreting these studies, Krashen (1976) has pointed out that years of exposure may not be an adequate indication of actual interaction, and stresses that active involvement rather than mere exposure is necessary. Krashen's monitor model distinguishes between language *acquisition*, similar to the process children use in acquiring first and second languages, and language *learning* or formal knowledge of the target language. While the monitor model recognizes that adults may be somewhat poorer acquirers than children, the fundamental claim of the model is that conscious learning is available to the performer only as a "monitor," used to alter the output of the acquired system, and that subconscious acquisition, requiring meaningful interaction in which speakers are concerned not with form but with the messages they are conveying and understanding, is far more important for adults as well as children (Krashen 1976, 1977, 1981).

Several studies in the adult SLA literature, focusing on unsuccessful acquisition, suggest that affective and social variables which lie behind and determine the amount and quality of interaction may be the root cause of adult acquisition or nonacquisition. Shapira (1978) has reported the case of Zoila, a 25-year-old Guatamalan Spanish speaker, who evidenced very little development in the acquisition of English grammar over an 18-month observation period. Shapira suggests that affect has played a decisive role. Zoila did not come to the United States out of choice, and Shapira hypothesizes that she had negative feelings toward all things American and limited instrumental motivation to learn enough English to communicate. Kessler and Idar (1979) have compared the acquisition of English by a Vietnamese mother and child. The lack of change in the mother's acquisition level, even during a 6-month period in which she was interacting daily in English at work, is hypothesized to be the result of affective variables operating negatively for the mother, who found adjustment to her new way of life difficult, and positively for the child, who needed English for peer relationships. Perhaps the best-known case of an unsuccessful adult acquirer is that of Alberto, a 33-year-old Costa Rican, the least successful language learner among six studied by Cazden, Cancino, Rosansky, and Schumann (1975). In follow-up studies by Schumann (1977, 1978a, 1978b), evidence is developed that Alberto's lack of linguistic development could be blamed largely on his social and psychological distance from speakers of the target language and the fact that his pidginized speech was adequate for his needs.

In all the above-mentioned studies and in our frequent assessments of nonnative speakers as having just enough English to communicate in limited situations, there is an assumption that if communicative needs were greater and psychological and social distance less, much greater control of the grammatical structures of the target language could have been acquired without formal instruction. This assumption is made explicit in Schumann's "acculturation model" (Schumann 1978b), which claims that two groups of variables, social and affective, cluster into a single variable of *acculturation* which is the major causal variable in SLA, i.e., that the degree to which a learner acculturates to the target language group will control the degree to which he acquires a second language. Schumann has called for the development of additional case studies in which individual patterns of acquisition can be related to factors of social and psychological distance to further explore the effects of such factors in SLA.

The present case study attempts to provide relevant evidence for the acculturation model by looking at the development of English ability of an adult with generally low social and psychological distance from target language speakers, acquiring English without formal instruction over a 3-year period characterized by steadily increasing interaction and communicative need. In addition, this study attempts to provide a broader and more global (though still partial) analysis of what is acquired than is usually the case, analyzing the learner's accomplishments in terms of a four-part framework of the components of communicative competence suggested by Michael Canale (forthcoming): grammatical competence, sociolinguistic competence, discourse competence, and strategic competence.

## SUBJECT

The subject of this study is a 33-year-old native speaker of Japanese named Wes, who first visited the United States (Hawaii) as a tourist in late 1977 and shortly afterward decided to emigrate from Tokyo to Honolulu. His initial motivations were varied, ranging from the attractions of the climate and the relaxed way of life in Hawaii to personal ties with Japanese friends who had made the same move earlier and a general attraction to the people of Hawaii. Opportunities for professional development, initially not a factor in the decision to move to the United States, soon after became an additional major consideration. Wes is an artist, very successful in Japan, with a growing international reputation, and Honolulu is a significant international art market which proved to be an ideal location for further growth and recognition. During the period of observation, Wes spent increasing amounts of time in Hawaii—3 months in 1978, 6 months in 1979, 8 months in 1980—and finally achieved permanent resident status in early 1981.

Wes has had no significant formal instruction in English, as he left school in Japan to be apprenticed to a well-known artist at age 15, just about the time when English teaching in Japan begins in earnest. He claims to remember nothing from the limited instruction he did receive except the useless sentence, "I have five pencils in my hand," and reports that he was a poor English student. He was not a complete beginner in English when he arrived in the United States for the first time, however, as he had already developed relationships with numerous American and European art collectors in Japan, beginning about 1974. It is not clear how much of this interaction took place in English and how much in Japanese, but it is clear that when Wes first arrived in the United States his ability to communicate in English was minimal. He did not need to speak much English at first, however, as Japanese is widely spoken in Hawaii and Japanese friends could translate for him when necessary and handle any problems which arose.

The past three years have been characterized by steadily increasing demands on Wes's ability to communicate in English, and he now lives in an English-speaking world. An extremely friendly and outgoing person, he has a wide circle of friends and acquaintances who are monolingual English speakers, including an American roommate. Contacts with other Japanese speakers have shrunk rather than grown, and with some Japanese he will speak English if there is a monolingual English speaker present, something which he would not do and greatly disapproved of several years ago. His professional life has also required steadily increasing interaction with English speakers in a variety of situations, for while the creation of art may be a solitary act, the promotion of an artist's career is not and in fact depends nearly as much on personal and communicative qualities as on innate talent, imagination, and developed technique. While I have no data to defend the claim,

I would estimate very roughly that something between 75 and 90 percent of all of Wes's meaningful interactions at the present time are in English.

In terms of the acculturation model for SLA, the following factors are relevant:

## Age

For those who view younger as better for SLA (e.g., Asher and Garcia 1969; Oyama 1976, 1977; Krashen, Long, and Scarcella 1979), this is a negative factor in Wes's case, whether the negative effect of age on acquisition is to be attributed to physiological, brain-related changes (Lenneberg 1967) or to age-related cognitive differences (Krashen 1975, Rosansky 1975). However, the primary issue here is whether age-related deficits can be reduced to social and psychological factors. Schumann has argued that adults don't acquire because they don't get involved in real communication, that they don't get involved in real communication because of problems of attitude, motivation, language and culture shock, and so on, and that if affective factors are favorable the adult's cognitive processes will automatically function to produce language acquisition (Schumann 1975, 1978a; see also Macnamara 1973, Taylor 1974).

## Aptitude

In the analysis which follows, some rather inconclusive evidence is presented that Wes's language aptitude, inductive ability, and grammatical sensitivity (Carroll 1973) may be low. However, the acculturation model argues against aptitude as an important variable in SLA, because it is assumed to relate to conscious learning in an instructional setting rather than to subconscious acquisition (Schumann 1978b, p. 48, Krashen 1980b).

## Length of Education

The Heidelberg study of the acquisition of German by Italian and Spanish immigrant workers (reported and discussed in Schumann 1978b) found a correlation between level of education in the native country and an index of syntactic development. Schumann hypothesizes that this might be because lack of education would lead to low socioeconomic status and social distance from target language counterparts. This does not apply in Wes's case, as he enjoys a high income and considerable social prestige in both Japan and the United States, but it is possible that the cognitive effects of suspended formal education might be relevant.

## Social Distance Factors

Wes exhibits very low social distance from native speakers of English. As a Japanese, he belongs to a group that is roughly equal (nonsubordinate, nondominant) to Americans, culturally, technologically, and economically, with the two groups having generally high respect for each other. As an individual, he expresses very favorable attitudes toward and liking for Americans. While the Japanese community in Hawaii is large and in some cases highly cohesive (e.g., Japanese university students have the reputation of sticking together), Wes exhibits very low enclosure. He does not live in a Japanese neighborhood, avoids Japanese social cliques, has notably more American than Japanese friends, and participates in American rather than Japanese social institutions. His intended length of residence in the United States is indefinite/permanent, and his social integration strategies are those of adaptation, rather than total assimilation or preservation. With respect to all these factors, the acculturation model predicts successful SLA.

Congruity or similarity of the two cultures is harder to evaluate. All observers of Japanese and American culture stress the differences, which are normally perceived by Japanese and American as great. However, in Hawaii, where nearly a third of the population is Japanese-American and mainstream United States ("haole") and Japanese cultures are merely the two most prominent strands in a multiethnic society, *perceived* cultural contrast (Acton 1979, Brown 1980) is much less than in other parts of the United States. In terms of the "high" culture in which Wes is an active participant and contributor, there is a recognition of both similarities and differences. Wes's paintings, to take a specific and relevant example, are exhibited without incongruity in the same galleries that show major American and European artists. While Wes's themes and techniques are essentially very Japanese (traditional), the presentation is contemporary and universalistic, comprehensible to those without familiarity with Japanese culture.

**Psychological Distance Factors.**

It should be pointed out that psychological factors are extremely difficult to define adequately or evaluate fairly, and that no entirely objective measures are available. For example, while motivation is generally conceived of as the inner drive or desire that is the cause of some action, we usually have no better grounds for attributing motivation than by simply seeing if such an action was taken. Thus, while Alberto gave responses indicating positive attitudes and good motivation on a questionnaire, Schumann points out that aspects of Alberto's life style which contradicted those responses should be given more weight. The judgments given here, as in most case studies, are therefore ultimately subjective, deriving their validity only from close personal friendship and familiarity with the subject, observations of his behavior, and discussions with him and others who know him well.

The variables which are easiest to assess are those related to personality. All observers agree that Wes is an extremely extroverted and socially outgoing person, with high self-esteem and self-confidence, low anxiety and inhibition. He is highly perceptive of the feelings and thoughts of others, intuitive, rather impulsive, and not at all afraid of making mistakes or appearing foolish in his use of English. All these factors have been hypothesized to be related to successful SLA, though not necessarily to classroom learning (Brown 1973, 1980; Chastain 1975; Guiora et al. 1975; Heyde 1977; Krashen 1980b, 1981; Naiman et al. 1978; Rubin 1975; Schumann 1975, 1978b; Stern 1975).

Culture shock and language shock (Stengal 1939, Clarke 1976) do not appear to have affected Wes to any significant degree, with none of the typical symptoms of disorientation, stress, anxiety, or fear reported.

Motivation is the hardest variable to assess. It is tempting to assert simply that as an immigrant by choice, Wes shows a strong integrative motivation to learn the second language in order to meet with, talk to, find out about, and at least in some respects become like valued speakers of the target language, with a healthy dose of instrumental motivation for professional success thrown in. This is correct as far as it goes, but it must be noted that Wes has shown little or no interest in studying English formally in order to achieve this end. This was true of Alberto also, and was one of the reasons Schumann felt that Alberto's professed high motivation should be questioned. In the present case, it seems necessary to recognize a distinction between the motivation, desire, or drive to communicate and motivation for studying the target language in a classroom situation or for doing certain types of self-study. The first does not necessarily imply the second.[1] Wes clearly has a strong drive to communicate for integrative purposes. Particularly striking have been his attempts to interact and make friends with all the shopkeepers, waitresses, and other workers in his urban neighborhood, quite clearly an attempt to create in Honolulu a "village within a city" community similar to the one around which his daily routine in Tokyo was centered. But in these and all interactions, his concern has consistently been with communication and not with form. Wes has been committed to learning English through natural interaction, while avoiding as much as possible any analytic study of the language code itself.

Table 1 summarizes the factors discussed above, indicating the effect on SLA predicted by the acculturation model.

Table 1   Social and Psychological Distance Factors, Evaluation of Subject Characteristics, and Predicted Effects on SLA by the Acculturation Model

| Social and psychological factors | Wes | Predicted influence on SLA |
| --- | --- | --- |
| Age | 33 | Neutral if other factors positive |
| Formal study of L2 | Insignificant | Not relevant |
| Language aptitude | Possibly low | Not relevant |
| Communicative need | High, increasing | Facilitative |
| Interaction, type and amount | Varied, increasing | Facilitative |
| Social dominance pattern | Equal | Facilitative |
| Social interaction pattern | Adaptive | Facilitative |
| Enclosure, cohesiveness | Low | Facilitative |
| Similarity of cultures | Different | Negative |
| Attitudes toward L2 group | Positive | Facilitative |
| Intended length of residence | Indefinite/permanent | Facilitative |
| Culture shock | Low | Facilitative |
| Language shock | Low | Facilitative |
| Empathy, social outreach | High | Facilitative |
| Inhibition, fear of appearing foolish | Low | Facilitative |
| Motivation type | Integrative | Facilitative |
| Motivation, drive for communication | Very high | Facilitative |
| Motivation for formal language study | Very low | Possibly negative |
| Preferred learning style | Natural acquisition | Facilitative |

## DATA AND ANALYSIS

What then has been learned in the service of the drive to communicate? On a global level, Wes appears to have learned a lot, and his ability to communicate in English has increased at a steady and impressive rate. The best evidence for this global evaluation is not comments by those who know him well and interact with him regularly (they do uniformly comment on his improved English, but have also learned to understand him better), but his successful management of difficult communication situations at the end of the observation period which he could not possibly have managed at earlier periods. For example, during the last year of this study (1980), Wes undertook a heavy schedule of promotional tours, exhibitions of paintings coupled with a daily schedule of appearances and demonstrations by the artist. The first time he did this, Wes was very worried about the inadequacy of his English, and in fact spoke hardly any English at all publicly, concentrating his attention on the handful of Japanese speakers who attended the demonstrations. By the end of the year he had become comfortable with such appearances, quite confident of his ability to paint and lecture informally at the same time, enjoying as well the constant 12- to 15-hour-a-day informal interaction with native speakers which such appearances generate. Another striking change in his overall communicative competence has been in his ability to carry on *sustained* conversations with friends, acquaintances, and strangers, without running out of discussable topics or limiting interlocutors to his topics, and without losing the thread of conversation from one topic to the next. Comprehension (not formally assessed) has clearly increased greatly. As an example, at the beginning of the observation period, Wes could really only comprehend English films with simple plots and lots of action (e.g., *Star Wars, Dirty Harry*); at the end of the observation period, he could understand, enjoy, and quite accurately summarize films which rely heavily on dialogue to advance characterization and plot development (*Elephant Man, Ordinary People*).

There are clear limits to Wes's communicative ability, however, both receptive and productive. All legal discussions (e.g., contract negotiations with all parties speaking through their lawyers) are extremely frustrating for him, and he considers himself lucky to grasp the main points through the verbiage. On one occasion he went sailing, and was completely mystified by nautical talk. An order to "slack off that line" elicited the response *Means rope take off?* a response which was neither accurate enough nor quick enough to satisfy the demands of the occasion.

Such examples, of course, represent special registers which often cause great difficulty for native speakers, and there remain much more basic and serious limitations in Wes's English communicative ability. First, he does not read or write English. At the beginning of the observation period, he could not read a menu; at the end he could read a menu but not much else. Only recently has he begun to write at all, dictating informal letters to an English speaker whom he asks to write down what he says verbatim, then painfully copying the letter over in his own handwriting. All further comments therefore have only to do with oral communication. Second, Wes's grammatical control of English has hardly improved at all during the 3-year observation period, as I will detail shortly. Grammar has been and continues to be the major problem, and very little has been acquired. Because of his inadequacies in the handling of English grammar, misunderstandings frequently arise in interaction with native speakers.

The following more detailed analysis is based primarily on 18 one-hour tape recordings concerning business and daily activities which Wes recorded in Japan and mailed to the United States on each of six trips which he made to Tokyo during the 3-year period of transition from being a Tokyo resident vacationing in Hawaii to establishing full-time permanent residence in Honolulu. The length of these visits back to Japan varied from 1 to 3 months at a time, and the amount of taped material varies from 1 to 5 hours per visit. One of the major advantages of these tapes is that they were not recorded for the purposes of linguistic analysis and consist of authentic, meaningful, and often important material, both professional and personal. A major disadvantage for the present analysis is that they are monologues. In addition, it might be suggested that Wes has a Tokyo English grammar, which emerges on each tape recorded in Japan and does not reflect changes in his developing Honolulu grammar. This does not seem to be the case, however, as Wes's grammar appears remarkably stable whether one compares early and late tapes or tapes recorded in Japan with recent, more limited recordings (3 hours total) made in Honolulu in which Wes is engaged in informal conversations with native speakers, including friends and, in one case, brand-new acquaintances. An additional source of data used in the analysis has been extensive but irregular field notes gathered by me over the entire period of observation, June 1978 to June 1981.

## Grammatical Competence

In the four-component model of communicative competence proposed by Canale, grammatical competence is concerned with mastery of vocabulary and rules of word formation, sentential grammar, linguistic semantics, pronunciation, and spelling, i.e., the elements and rules of the language code itself. Because Wes does not read or write English, spelling is not an issue, and specifying his semantic system is a formidable task which I will not attempt here.

Impressionistically, Wes's pronunciation of English is good, though clearly not native. In addition to substitutions in the segmental phonology, most final consonant clusters are reduced, far more often by consonant deletion than by vowel insertion (epenthesis). Wes articulates clearly and enjoys practicing difficult words: *banana split, patty melt, Ann Margret,* and *Cheryl Ladd* are among his favorite lexical items for such practice. Intonation is noticeably better than that of the average Japanese graduate student whom I have encountered, and no doubt contributes highly to the overall impression of fluency which native speakers often report.

Proficiency in grammar is another story, as indicated in Table 2, which shows the general lack of progress in acquiring nine commonly studied grammatical morphemes.

**Table 2** Accuracy Order for Nine Grammatical Morphemes in Obligatory Contexts

|  | *July 1978* | *November 1980* |
|---|---|---|
| 1. Copula BE | Acquired, present only | No change |
| 2. Progressive ING | Acquired (?) | No change |
| 3. Auxiliary BE | Acquired (?) | No change |
| 4. Past irregular | 25% | 55% |
| 5. Plural | 5% | 43%/33% |
| 6. 3rd singular | 0% | 21% |
| 7. Article | 0% | 19%/6% |
| 8. Possessive | 0% | 8% |
| 9. Past regular | 0% | 0% |

Source: First and last monologue tapes.

It might be noted that the rank ordering of grammatical morphemes presented in Table 2 is in most cases compatible with the invariant order hypothesis, with 16 of the 18 clear cases of pairwise ordering relations established by other studies (Krashen 1981, p. 58) holding true here. However, three grammatical morphemes—plural, article, and past regular—have lower ranks here than in most morpheme acquisition studies. These three morphemes also have lower than usual rankings in Hakuta's (1974, 1976) study of a 5-year-old Japanese girl learning English as a second language. Hakuta attributes lack of success in these areas to the nonexistence of definite-indefinite marking and plurality in Japanese and to phonological difficulties with final consonant clusters in the case of the regular past. These explanations seem reasonable in Wes's case also, but it should be noted that what is presented in Table 2 is in fact only an accuracy order, not an acquisition order. The most striking fact about Wes's performance on these morphemes is that, taking 90 percent correct in obligatory cases criterion for acquisition, nothing has moved from unacquired to acquired status. Moreover, a closer look at specific examples in the data indicates that if anything the picture presented in Table 2 may overstate Wes's actual competence with respect to these morphemes. Especially complex is the relationship between copula BE, progressive ING, and auxiliary BE.

Wes does control the English copula appropriately in most cases: *I'm a little bit confuse, if you're quite busy, he's about fifty, this is not important,* etc. There are no errors of person appearing in the data, and number errors are limited to an occasional substitution of *they is* for "they are." Deletion errors are uncommon, with over half the cases consisting of ADJ NP structures: *now so different people here,* instead of "now people are so different here"; *little hard my life,* instead of "my life is a little hard"; *almost finish this tape,* instead of "this tape is almost finished." Some of these examples are ambiguous, however (an alternative gloss for the last example might be "I've almost finished this tape"), and the source of error is not clear. Hawaii Creole English (HCE), a nonstandard variety to which Wes has frequently been exposed, allows such structures and is a possible source, although there is no other compelling evidence in Wes's grammar to suggest an HCE influence. The major source of copula errors is tense, and there are no examples at all in the data of *was/were*. This does not preclude considering copula as acquired only because the frequency of obligatory contexts for past tense in the data is low.

Progressive and AUX are most problematic. Wes has from the beginning supplied both of these in most cases when they are required, but there is still reason to question whether they are really acquired. In the case of progressive ING, the initial problem is defining, identifying, and counting obligatory contexts. While there are some cases when the progressive is clearly required, such as when a speaker is actually performing the action named at the time of speaking, or in response to an antecedent question such as "What are you doing?" determining the requirement for a progressive form usually involves trying to read the mind of the speaker. In those cases where progressive ING seems semantically required, Wes usually supplies it: *All day I'm sitting table, I don't know why people always talking me, I'm always thinking, so now I'm painting new one.* Evidence against full acquisition includes the frequent appearance of ING forms when progressive meaning was apparently not intended (*so yesterday I didn't painting*), occasional use of bare stem forms when progressive is required (*right now I'm paint new ukiyo-e*), and the fact that for most verbs Wes uses either the bare stem consistently or the ING form consistently, suggesting that the distribution may be as much lexical as syntactic or semantic. Verbs which always appear in the progressive include *joke* (*if I'm strong talk, or sometime joking*), *plan* (*before I'm planning*), *train* (*maybe today is training*, i.e., "exercise"), and *touch* (*so this one years I didn't touching my money*). There are only two verbs which Wes uses with any frequency in both bare stem and progressive form, *think* and *paint*. From the data, *paint* and *painting* appear to be in free variation (*I love paint, I love painting, today I'm start five six paint*), while *think* can often be seen as indicating opinion (*I think so*) as opposed to reflection (*today I'm thinking Honolulu*). An attempt to see whether Wes has any metalinguistic awareness of progressive vs. nonprogressive forms elicited mixed results:

RS: So what's the difference between "paint" and "painting"?
Wes: Well, if I go to exhibition, I saw "paint," but "I'm start painting" means I do it, not finish.
RS: Yeah, OK, sort of, so what's the difference between "think" and "thinking"?
Wes: "I'm think means now. "I'm thinking" means later.

(field notes, March 1981)

Auxiliary BE is an even more striking example of a grammatical morpheme which appears to have been acquired if one considers only frequency of appearance in obligatory contexts, but seems a quite different phenomenon if one considers overuse and questions of function as well as form. The obligatory environment for auxiliary BE is the presence of a progressive verb. When Wes uses a progressive form, it is almost always preceded by a form of BE, usually the correct (see examples in discussion of progressive ING). He seldom says things like "He dancing," a typical error of many nonnative speakers. However, Wes produces a great number of other utterances of BE, with a great variety of meanings, where there is no reason to use auxiliary BE:

I'm cry (meaning 'I almost cried" or "I would cry")
I'm always listen (repetitive, habitual)
Tomorrow I'm finish (future)
Before I'm finish (past)
You are sounds tired (present)
He's come to my apartment ("he used to come to my apartment")
    *has(?)*

Since utterances of these varied types are far more frequent in Wes's speech than those in which auxiliary BE is required and supplied, it would be misleading to claim that those limited cases represent acquisition of an auxiliary triggered by a syntactic environment. Again, a look at specific examples indicates some lexical influence. There are a number of verbs which are usually directly preceded by a noun or pronoun (*I think, hope, hate, love, wanna, need, said, told you so*) or by NP + *don't* or *doesn't* (*I don't like, need*, etc., *I didn't gift*). Most other verbs are regularly preceded by a form of BE: *I'm never push, this morning I'm buy,* etc.

BE thus appears not to be an auxiliary, but a generalization of the forms of the English copula to other functions. The source of this generalization is not entirely clear. Utterances such as *tomorrow I'm finish* could be related to *now I'm finish(ed),* where consonant cluster simplification accounts for the ending deletion in the sentence on which the analogy rests. Sentences like *today is a nice day* could be the source by analogy of sentences like *now is I'm work.* However, examples like the last, as well as *time is go, everything is I know,* and *now is I'm very tired* suggest a source in language transfer. Wes may be using the English copula BE simply as an equivalent to the Japanese topic marker *wa* (Hiroki Kato, personal communication). This explanation would also account for the previously mentioned cases of copula deletion in sentences like *little hard my life,* as these exhibit comment-topic rather than topic-comment order.

There is another example of overgeneralization of the copula in Wes's English which is apparently not due to transfer from Japanese but indicates that Wes does consciously or unconsciously formulate hypotheses about English structure on the basis of what he knows about English. In general, Wes has little trouble with English pronouns, other than some *she/he* confusions, but his system of possessive pronouns is incomplete. *My* and *your* are used correctly and frequently, and there are occasional occurrences in the early tapes of *their.* But no first person plural possessives appear in the data at all until early 1980, and when a form does appear it is defective: *So tonight, Tim and me we are come back here early, we are apartment.* Subsequent occurrences have made it clear that *we are,* rather than "our" is Wes's first plural form, and this has become firmly fixed in his speech. The most likely explanation seems to be that Wes has created this form by analogy with *your* (misanalyzed as "you are") and *their* (misanalyzed as "they are"). Support for this suggestion comes from the fact that the last few tapes exhibit additional possessives on the same pattern: *your friend is house* (possibly only a case of vowel insertion to break up a /ndz/ cluster), *she's name is Izumi Ukimura, she's working is beautiful.* Certainly this is evidence of creative construction, but creative construction somehow gone awry, resulting in incorrect forms that once generated have persisted without further modification.

With regard to the remaining grammatical morphemes listed in Table 2, Wes has shown some development on most, though in no case has criterion been reached to claim acquisition. In some cases, percentages figures may again give a more optimistic view than justified. The overall percentage for plural, 43 percent correct in the November 1980 tapes, is less impressive when it is noted that 7 of 17 correct occurrences (out of 40 obligatory contexts) occurred within the phrases *n years old* and *n years ago,* and that Wes also says both *one year ago* and *this one years.* If these examples are omitted, the percentage drops to 33 percent. The total score for articles is similarly inflated by high-frequency phrases, with 12 of 17 correctly supplied articles (95 obligatory contexts) occurring in the phrase *a little (bit) X.* Elimination of these cases drops the percentage correct from 19 to 6 percent.

The irregular past is perhaps the only grammatical morpheme for which real progress can be claimed. A number of irregular verb forms, including *went, sent, told, saw, said, met, bought, sold, left, made,* appear with some consistency in the later tapes, though often with accompanying copula (or topic marker), e.g., *I'm left, I'm wrote.* Perhaps coincidentally, past tense is the only aspect of Wes's grammar which I have consciously corrected or given explicit feedback about in my interactions with him over the past three years, arguing that lack of a tense system has been a major source of misunderstood messages. However, regular past tense forms, including those that are not subject to consonant cluster simplification, e.g., "started," "sounded," "wanted," do not appear at all in the recorded data, though in my field notes for March 1981 I note what may be the first appearance of a rule-governed past tense form, a correction from *he bought* to *he buyed.*

While the grammatical morphemes discussed here and in a great deal of the SLA literature represent only a small part of the grammar of English, the rather dismal picture indicated by Wes's performance on these morphemes is confirmed if other aspects of English grammar are considered. Except in routine, formulaic utterances (*do you have time? are you busy?*), Wes has no subject-verb inversion in questions (*ah, you has keys? when Tim is coming?*), no dummy or pseudo-subjects (*because here is nothing* for "because there is nothing here"), no relative clauses (*you know before people bought my painting* for "people who bought my paintings before"; *he saw before I sent painting* for "he saw the painting I sent before"), and no passives (*this is cannot help* for "this cannot be helped"). Negatives are a bright spot in the overall picture, generally well formed (*I can't do it, because she doesn't have it*), except when problems of auxiliary or other grammatical aspects of a sentence complicate matters (*I'm not complain, this is cannot*). There are no examples in the data of either Neg + S (e.g., "no more pizza") or no + Verb (e.g., "I no can see him") constructions, both of which are possible in Hawaii Creole English and appear in the data from other nonnative speakers of English, especially native Spanish speakers. However, the some-any rule has not been acquired by Wes (*you don't need something, right?*), except in formulaic utterances (*I didn't say anything*).[2]

As I have implied in passing several times, Wes has a rather rich repertoire of formulaic utterances, memorized sentences and phrases (Fillmore 1976, Peters 1977, Krashen and Scarcella 1978, Yorio 1980, Coulmas 1981, Pawley and Syder forthcoming), which increase the appearance of fluency in English. Some high-frequency formulaic items include:

Hi! How's it? So, what's new? I beg your pardon . . . what did you say your name was? You know what . . . I tell you. You know what I mean? What can I do? Whaddya want? Whaddya mean? Whaddya doing? Do you remember? I told you before. Something like that. I dunno why. That's great, terrific! Sure, I would love to. Can you imagine? Thank you VERY much. Thank you calling.

It is not always clear which of Wes's utterances are memorized wholes, except for those which clearly exceed the limits of his acquired grammatical system, but it is clear that he has chosen this as a major language strategy. He listens carefully and extracts formulaics from television commercials ("thank you *very much*" comes from a well-known tire commercial in Hawaii), from records ("what did you say your name was?), and from conversations ("you know what? . . . I'll tell you" is an expression frequently used by a particular gallery owner). He comments frequently on phrases that he finds characteristic of friends and acquaintances, and practices many of these consciously.

The importance of such memorized sentences and patterns in second language learning has been a matter of recent debate. Fillmore has argued that the strategy of acquiring formulaic speech is central to the learning of language, and reports that in the case of the children she studied routines and patterns evolved into creative language. Krashen and Scarcella maintain that routines and patterns are fundamentally different and independent from creative language, with routines and patterns playing a minor role in both language acquisition and actual speech performance. In Wes's case, I cannot find much evidence of evolution toward creative grammar from formulaics (though one interesting example is discussed in the next section), and in some cases even minor changes in formulas fail to come off (*but Shinji, what can I do?* for "but what can Shinji do?"). I do not conclude that the effort is wasted, however. Pawley and Syder claim that the importance of familiar, sentence-length expression, numbering perhaps several hundred thousand for a mature native speaker, has been underestimated in linguistic theory and in fact accounts for nativelike fluency in ordinary speech. Wes controls perhaps a hundred such memorized sentences and phrases; so he clearly has a long way to go. But it is evident that of Wes's two major language learning strategies, imitation and rule formation, imitation is more successful. While he does attempt novel utterances and hypothesis formation, his creations and hypotheses are more often than not incorrect (as in the extension of copula BE to functions such as possessive). Over a 3-year period characterized by extensive and intensive interaction with native speakers, Wes's development in terms of what is generally considered to be the heart of SLA, the acquisition of productive grammatical rules, has been minimal and almost insignificant.

## Sociolinguistic Competence

In Canale's framework, sociolinguistic competence has to do with the extent to which utterances are produced and understood appropriately in different sociolinguistic contexts, depending on contextual factors such as status of participants, purposes of the interaction, and norms or conventions of interaction. Appropriateness has two dimensions, meaning and form. Appropriateness of meaning concerns what one does in particular situations, what communicative functions or acts may be expressed. For example, in English one does not normally ask strangers their age, marital status, or salary on first meeting (excluding job interviews and other special interactions), though these may be acceptable first questions, social openers, in other cultures. Appropriateness of form concerns the extent to which a given communicative meaning is represented in an appropriate grammatical form and style.

A partial picture of Wes's command of English communicative functions and forms and his development in this respect over the 3-year observational period can be gained from looking in some detail at a sample of his directives, a major category of speech act (Searle 1976, Schmidt and Richards 1980). A directive is any utterance whose principal point is that it counts as an attempt on the part of the speaker to get the hearer to do something. The category thus includes orders, requests, pleas, hints, and suggestions, though these subtypes of directives may differ in the intensity of expression or other dimensions of the act.

The following are some of Wes's early directives, taken from my 1978 field notes:

1. shall we go?
2. ah, I have a Big Mac, n I have a french fries, small, and Coke, that's all.
3. can I have a banana spi . . lit, please?
4. NS:   you wanna go eat?
   Wes:   uh, what you ever like?
   NS:   you mean "whatever you like"?
   Wes:   yes, please.

Examples 1, 2, and 3 indicate Wes's reliance from the beginning on speech-act formulas for directives. In these examples, the formulas are both topically appropriate ("shall we go?" is thoroughly idiomatic as a suggestion) and situationally appropriate ("I'll have X" and "Can I have X?" are normal restaurant patterns). The phonological distortions (*I have* for "I'll have"; occasionally *shall* (w)*e go?*) indicate that in some cases these formulas may not be analyzed into literal meanings and parts, but other examples such as 4, in which Wes is groping for a formula which is not yet mastered, indicate that there is some analysis into constituent parts even with idiomatic expressions.

5. sitting? ("shall we sit down?" or "let's sit down")
6. nice meeting you (when being introduced)

Example 5 indicates that at this point formulas like *shall we go?* are not yet analyzed into patterns that can be used productively for a range of directives. At this stage Wes has only *shall we go?*, not *shall we sit down* or *shall we . . .* anything else. This is a case of undergeneralization of a pattern, but there are cases of overgeneralization as well, as in Example 6 (not a directive), where a speech formula sometimes used by native speakers to conclude a conversation with someone whom the speaker has just met is used here also as a direct response to the introduction (a slot more often filled by native speakers with "nice *to* meet you" or some other unrelated routine entirely).

7. Please n you taking this suitcase.
8. please, never thinking ("don't think about it")
9. maybe curtain ("maybe you should open the curtain")
10. OK n maybe betta first go to Shinji's place and I want and take back here and go to dinner, because tomorrow and Wayne he's working in the morning and seven o'clock. ("Maybe we should go to Shinji's place first and then come back here and go to dinner, because Wayne is working at seven tomorrow morning")

Examples 7 and 8 indicate several phenomena. In these early directives, Wes's usual verb form (outside of formulas) is the *-ing* form, rather than the imperative stem. *Please* occurs frequently in Wes's early directives, but not necessarily as a politeness marker. While the *please* in Example 3 does appear to be a polite tag used with unfamiliars in routine transactions, the preposed *please* of 7 and 8 more likely represents a communication strategy to make it clear that a request is in fact being made (necessary since there is no grammatical device for indicating requests), as well as establishing the sincerity of the request. Native speakers also use *please* for these functions. *Maybe,* a hedge, similarly serves as a lexical marker for suggestions, as in 9 and 10, so that the illocutionary force of the utterance is clear even if the reduced structure of 9 and the confusing suggestion + justification of 10 are ambiguous or unclear in other respects.

11.          get the light
12. Wes: Ah, Miss. (Looks at cup; waitress looks puzzled)
     NS: Could ya warm up his hot chocolate a little bit?
     Waitress: Oh, is it cold love? Sure!
     Wes: Sorry. (softly)
     Waitress: (to cook) Excuse me. This hot chocolate is not hot.

One way in which speech-act realizations differ across cultures is the degree of politeness (generally speaking, the degree of indirection) required for the performance of specific acts in particular contexts (Brown and Levinson 1978). For Wes, directives do not in general seem to require elaborate politeness devices, as in Example 11, which was issued in the context of a task orientation and is incidentally the first use of a bare stem imperative for a directive which I have recorded. But requests which also imply criticism, thereby potentially threatening or embarrassing to the "face" of the listener, are expressed very cautiously if at all, as in Example 12, which took place in a coffee shop. When Wes's hot chocolate arrived cold, he wanted a new cup but was reluctant to complain to the waitress and first tried to get a native speaker to make the complaint for him, on the grounds that his English was not adequate. When the native speaker refused, Wes first tried to convey the request for a new cup indirectly, with the barest of hints and a glance at the cup. When the waitress failed to understand his intended meaning, a second native speaker stepped in, issuing the request using the "negative" politeness strategy of minimizing the imposition, "a little bit" (see Brown and Levinson for definition of terms). When the waitress, who is polite in a friendly way to customers (but not the cook) responded, Wes was obviously embarrassed and muttered *sorry*. This extremely indirect way of conveying directives which may imply criticism is, from all reports, typically Japanese.

13.  this is all garbage ("put it out")
14.  ah, I have two shirt upstairs ("please get them while you're there")
15.  uh, you like this chair? ("please move over")
16.  you like this shirt? ("why don't you change it?")

Examples 13 to 16 are all hints, specifying neither the task to be performed nor the agent who is to perform the action (Ervin-Tripp 1976), which Wes has used extensively from the beginning. There is an important difference, however, between hints 13 and 14, which imply the request message by mentioning a reason why an action might be desired, immediately comprehended as requests by the English native speaker addressee, and hints 15 and 16 which were not understood as directives by the hearer and apparently represent transfer of a Japanese hinting pattern to English. In these cases, Wes was attempting to convey the requests not by mentioning a reason for doing an action but by questioning whether there was a reason *not* to do the action. While such hints are sometimes used in English ("Are you really going to wear that dreadful shirt again?" would work in the way in which Example 16 was intended, and "Are you busy tonight?" could convey or at least serve as a prelude for a request for a date), these are much more restricted in English than in Japanese. We might take the classic example of a speaker who is hot and wants a door opened to let some cool air in. In English, we might convey the request by a hint of the form, "It's stuffy in here." Wes's hint in precisely this circumstance was to ask *are you chilly?* which was taken by the English native speaker addressed to be simply a question about his welfare, with no uptake of Wes's intended request message.

In summary, Wes's early directives reflected a heavy reliance on a limited number of speech formulas, many of which were not available for productive use outside of the wholly fixed expressions in which they first occurred, an incorrect identification of *-ing* form with request function, a reliance on lexical clues such as *please* and *maybe,* and transfer of Japanese norms regarding both which speech acts are acceptable in particular situations (complaint example) and the linguistic strategies which are commonly used to convey such acts (hinting example).

Since I have indicated that Wes is highly motivated to engage in interaction and communication and in general has developed considerable control of the formulaic language that acts as social grease in interaction, we might expect that he would show more development over time in the area of sociolinguistic competence compared with his very limited development of grammatical competence. This is, in general, the case. By the end of the observation period, gross errors in the performance of directives had largely been eliminated: progressive forms were no longer used for directive function with any frequency, while the use of imperatives increased (*please next month send orders more quick*); "shall we?" and "let's" were used productively as patterns for a great many different requests; and in general Wes's directives showed a great deal more elaboration (*shall we maybe go out coffee now, or you want later?; Ok, if you have time please send two handbag, but if you're too busy, forget it*).

Appropriateness of meaning is one area in which Wes has shown clear evidence of acculturation. Although there are certainly still cases in which his messages are more appropriate by Japanese than by American norms for particular contexts (e.g., he tends to open many phone calls with an immediate *thank you* for some recent service rendered, while Americans tend to delay such thanks to later in the conversation), he is no longer reticent, for example, about expressing complaints to waiters (*excuse me, this milk is no good, sour I think*). He often comments on differences between the United States and Japan with respect to such norms of speaking. For example, in response to an item on a test of verbal routines designed by Scarcella (1979), he noted the following difference:

Item: Greg told his friend, Silvia, that he would see her in the cafeteria at 12:00. Greg arrives late. He feels bad. When Greg sees Silvia, he says, "Hi! . . . . . . . . . . . . . . . . . . "
Wes: "Hi! I'm sorry. Somebody call." No, this is Japan need two story. Here I'm only just say "Hi, sorry, you waiting long time?"

Moreover, when his responses are strange in American terms, this currently seems as often due to personal idiosyncratic factors as to transfer of Japanese norms to American speech situations, as in the following example from the Scarcella test:

Item: David sneezes. His friend, Sharon, politely says, ". . . . . . . . "
Wes: "Stop it! This is your habit?"

Wes's rather startling response to this test item, which I think is a good characterization of what he might actually say in the situation, is no more expected by Japanese than by Americans.

On other items on the Scarcella test, Wes's meanings are appropriate, though in some cases the form is deviant. This is at least in some cases due to experience and exposure (*excuse me, I want full* gas instead of "fill it up" can be attributed to the fact that he does not drive but relies on taxis for transportation). Overall, Wes scored 47 percent on the routines test (administered orally), better than the 38 and 30 percent mean scores which Scarcella obtained for two groups of advanced ESL learners.

While Wes's learning accomplishments appear on the whole better in the area of sociolinguistic than grammatical competence, this should not be overestimated. For example, he is able to a limited extent to provide alternate forms for a speech act appropriate to different addressees:

Item:  Robert is a waiter. He is taking an order. When he finishes taking the order, he checks
       to be sure that his customer doesn't want to order more. Robert asks his customer,
       "............"
Wes:   "Would you like something more?" But home you know I'm only just say "do you
       want." Don't need so polite.

However, this ability is limited, and Wes does not have extensive control of different registers for talking about the same things differently in different settings or with different hearers: bodily functions, sex, and other taboo topics are discussable rather crudely or not at all. The forms of speech-act realizations, though much improved, are still far from perfect also, with the mesh between productive utilization of patterns and idiomaticity still to be realized. In fact, Wes's most productive extension of a speech-act pattern, the clearest case of creative construction arising from a decomposed formula that I can find in all the data, leads to some clearly inappropriate utterances:

1.   can I getting some more coffee? (at home, intended as request)
2.   can I have a light? ("turn on the light," not "give me a match")
3.   if you back to room, can I bring cigarette? ("please bring me")
4.   uh, can I? ("would you?")

(field notes, 1980)

I believe that the source of directives 1 to 4 is the English request form which Ervin-Tripp (1976) has labeled the permission directive, utterances which have the form of asking for permission but the function of getting the hearer to perform some action. Some examples would be "may I have change for a dollar?" or "can I get some more coffee?" where it is obvious that a clerk or waiter is to make change or pour coffee. Permission directives have been frequent in Wes's English from the beginning, and it is this pattern which has emerged over time as his favored request form. However, the extension of the pattern "Can I X?" does not always work. When the resulting utterance is nonidiomatic (*can I getting?* instead of "can I get/have?") or occurs in a less role-defined situation (where Example 1 could be taken as an offer as readily as a request), the intended message fails to get through. Example 2 fails because of idiomaticity; "Can I have some light in here?" would have worked. Example 3 illustrates most clearly Wes's extension of the pattern beyond its scope in English ("can/could/will/would you?" is required), while 4, said when Wes was carrying two heavy bundles and wanted help with one, shows the degree to which native speaker listeners must rely on the nonverbal context not only to decipher the ambiguities of his grammatical system but also to discover the illocutionary force of his communicative messages.

## Discourse Competence

Both grammatical and sociolinguistic competence, as discussed so far, deal with the learner's language at the level of the single sentence or utterance. In Canale's framework of the components of communicative competence, discourse competence concerns mastery of the ways in which grammatical forms and meanings combine to achieve unified spoken or written texts. As Wes does not write English, I will be concerned in this section only with spoken discourse. Since spoken discourse other than monologue is a cooperative effort by all parties to a conversation, I will also be dealing with *conversational* competence and what we might consider *interactional* competence.

Discourse competence seems to me to be Wes's greatest strength in his use of English, compensating to an extent for his weaknesses in other aspects of language form and use. Consider the following illustrative example, once again taken from a restaurant interaction:

Waiter:    Are you ready to order?
Wes:    Yes, ah, I like teriaki steak, medium rare, rice, salad, thousand, coffee.
          (field notes, February 1980)

There is at first glance nothing special about Wes's order, which seems to be just a list, unless one realizes that its structure derives from an extended routine which is standard for the restaurant in which the interaction occurred, and many others:

Waiter:        Are you ready to order?
Customer:      Yes, I'd like teriaki steak.
Waiter:        How would you like your steak cooked?
Customer:      Medium rare.
Waiter:        Would you like rice, french fries or baked potato?
Customer:      Rice.
Waiter:        Soup or salad?
Customer:      Salad.
Waiter:        What kind of dressing do you want?
Customer:      Thousand.
Waiter:        Anything to drink?
Customer:      Coffee.

Being thoroughly familiar with the routine of ordering in that particular place, Wes placed his order not only as it is usually solicited but also in the order in which the bill is recorded. I doubt that the native-speaking waiter in that instance knew that his customer was a nonnative speaker.

Discourse competence is also the area in which the greatest improvement has been evidenced over time in Wes's use of English. The texture of the early tapes is choppy. Narratives are brief, presented without embellishment, as in the following quite typical examples:

| TRIP TO THE BEACH | I don't like boring and lazy / no / not my type / this summer you know go to beach only one time I go to pool / very crowded / and short time I'm stay and pool and coming back / = pause (monologue tape, July 1978) |
| A BURGLARY | Anyway / June twenty six I come back here many bad happening / but not my business / and someone take my jewelry / and camera / clothes / everything / anyway I'm so bad / but now is OK everything / I'm fine (monologue tape, August 1978) |

Descriptions, on the other hand, often do contain considerable detail, but these are very difficult for a listener without a great deal of background knowledge to understand:

Now I'm start and making and two album / soon I sent to you / one album / ah you know Sophia Loren? / and Dewi Sukarno / and ah you know Elsa Martinelli? / she's before movie star / but now designer / and last year my exhibition / American Club / Bangkok / Oriental Hotel my fashion show / Pattiya Beach / Cliff Hotel / ah opening Royal Cliff Hotel / in Tokyo and Gallery Seiwa / and old temple shrine / Zojoji / they have my painting / I don't remember / three four years ago / this shrine everything new / big money / and opening seven Japanese artist and they are gift paint / one artist he's very famous / but just before he's die / and one woman she's also very famous / you know Japanese and traditional calligraphy / also and sumi-e / and other artist and me / also in Tokyo TV program / camera and showing my work / one hour program . . .

(monologue tape, July 1978)

In the above passage, which is taken from a taped letter, Wes is describing to his listener a two-volume portfolio which he is compiling. One volume, not described here, is to contain photographs and reproductions of paintings. The gist of the passage cited is that the other volume will include:

1. Photos of Wes with well-known clients, e.g.:
   Sophia Loren
   Dewi Sukarno
   Elsa Martinelli
       formerly a movie star
       currently a designer
2. Clippings from five different exhibitions, i.e.:
   Tokyo American Club
   Oriental Hotel, Bangkok (a fashion show)
   Royal Cliff Hotel, Pattiya Beach, Thailand
   Seiwa Gallery, Tokyo

Zojoji Shrine, a group show with other artists, including a famous artist who died
shortly before the show, a famous woman calligrapher and sumi-e artist

3.  Still photographs from a TV documentary on Wes's work

This passage thus does have considerable coherence of ideas and is structured, but
the highly abbreviated style in which the description is presented and the lack of
transitional and other devices of cohesion make the passage extremely difficult
to comprehend. I suspect that for most readers, unfamiliar with the facts being
presented, the initial impression of the passage may have been that it was no more
than free association.

Descriptions and narratives in the later tapes are, by contrast, much easier to
comprehend. Increased redundancy and the use of structuring elements such as
*well, anyway, so,* and *then* clearly play some part in this, as in the following
excerpt:

UM / well / nothing new here / but this afternoon I went n exhibition Japanese artist / well /
quite large exhibition / New Asashi Building / very tall building / fifty something or maybe
fifty one floor / anyway / s crowded / because today is last day / very very interesting painting /
then / after / I'm always thinking my paint / so / this artist quite large piece / many large piece /
also eight or ten screen / you know his style is not Japanese / but technique is Japanese / do you
remember I paint Mount Fuji in sand? / well / very close technique / quite similar / but color
is so beautiful / beautiful / so / well / then after I went coffee shop / thinking my paint / also
his paint / well / he's not detail / he doesn't have detail / so different my paint / you know
I'm always detail / but his painting so beautiful / well also my painting is beautiful too / don't
you think so? / I think so / you know I'm so lucky / because ah my business is painting / also
my hobby is painting

(monologue tape, November 1980)

In addition to the improved comprehensibility of the last passage, I find
the expressiveness which it exhibits particularly striking. As Goffman (1974) has
pointed out, when we talk we do not just convey information or make requests,
promises, and the like. Rather, we present dramas to our audiences, relating versions
of what has happened, employing essentially theatrical means to provide evidence
for the fairness or unfairness of our current situation or other grounds for sympathy,
approval, understanding, or amusement. The fact that Wes is good at these uses of
language is clearly reflected in the later tapes, in the passage above and perhaps even
more so in the next excerpt (immediate continuation of last example):

also my hobby is painting / I can't you know stop painting / if I'm very tired / but I can't also
sleeping / now every day three four hour sleeping / well / now's a little relax / because just
now go to movie / you know / sometime / I go out after painting / very late / maybe midnight or three four o'clock / well outside is very dark / quiet / then you know I'm relax / also
natural air is good / walking / because all day I'm sitting table my studio / so my leg little bit
sleep / also little hurts / uh / but you know this is my way / this is my life / cannot stop and
paint / you know nobody push / but myself I'm always push / anyway / last night . . . . . . . .

(November 1980)

Unfortunately, I have no early data on Wes's performance in dialogue or other conversation; so no data can be offered to support my impressionistic judgment that during the early part of the observation period conversation with him was very difficult. The remainder of this section therefore deals only with his current level of competence in conversation. Consider the following narrative, from a spontaneous conversation which was unobtrusively tape-recorded:

Wes: listen / today so funny story
NS: yeah / what happened?
Wes: you know everyday I'm go to McDonald for lunch
NS: yeah
Wes: and today I saw so beautiful woman / so beautiful clothes / make-up / everything / but / so crazy!
NS: how? / what do you mean?
Wes: talking to herself / then she's listen to some person / everybody watch / but no one there / then / somebody / local woman I think say "are you OK?" / "can I help?" / but beautiful woman she doesn't want talk to local woman / she's so snobbish! / so funny!
NS: Jesus

(conversation tape, January 1981)

Wes's story contains all the elements of a well-formed narrative (Labov and Waletzky 1967, Labov 1972, Labov and Fanshel 1977). An attention getter (*listen*) is followed by an abstract, a general proposition which the narrative will exemplify (*today so funny story*), an orientation to time and place (*McDonald's*), a complicating action (*but so crazy*), a result (*then somebody . . . but she doesn't want talk to local woman*), an evaluation (*she's so snobbish!*), and a coda relating back to the original abstract (*so funny!*). Moreover, Wes introduces the complicating action in his story with a puzzle or teaser (*so crazy*), capturing and holding the interest of his listener. The story is not only well formed but cleverly formed and funny, and on those grounds it compares well with good stories told by native speakers.

Wes is a good conversationalist in many ways. The following piece of "small talk," following an ordering routine, gives an idea of Wes's ability to establish a relaxed, bantering tone with native speakers, in this case a married couple (M and G) whom he had met only a few minutes before at a hotel garden brunch:

M: I would like eggs benedict (to waitress) / that's the specialty (to Wes)
Waitress: how about you?
Wes: here eggs benedict is good?
M: { yeah
G: { it's the specialty
Wes: yeah? / OK / I have it (waitress leaves)
M: you never ate before?
Wes: no, I ate before / but not this hotel
M: it's very good over here
Wes: but only just English muffin / turkey / ham and egg / right?
G: right
Wes: so how different? / how special?

M:           because it's very good here / maybe it's the hollandaise / I don't know
G:           maybe it's just the atmosphere
Wes:         yeah / I think so / eggs benedict is eggs benedict / just your imagination is
             different / so / this restaurant is belong to hotel?
G:           no / not exactly

(conversation tape, January 1981)

{ = overlapping utterances

The good-natured, teasing type of humor of this passage (unfortunately and inevitably less obvious from a transcript than from the recording, which preserves tone of voice) is typical of Wes's conversations, as is his skill in listening to what people say and picking up topics for further development. Wes is not a passive conversationalist but nominates topics frequently. Moreover, the topics he nominates are almost always relevant to previous topics. I have never observed any instances of conversation coming to a halt because Wes has raised a topic (or commented on a topic already on the floor) in a way that indicated he had not understood what the previous speaker had said or had made an unfathomable connection to a new topic. In this respect he is quite unlike the majority of nonnative speakers of comparable linguistic level whom I have observed.

Wes is a good listener as well as a good talker. He is interested in people and what they have to say. He signals his comprehension of ongoing conversation frequently, using feedback signals such as *uh huh, I see, really?, really!, yeah, I know what you mean, my goodness,* as well as repetitions of fragments of his interlocutors' utterances. While many Japanese learners of English, even those with a high level of grammatical competence, retain the use of Japanese conversational fillers, accompanied in varying degrees by Japanese body language, Wes does not. His paralinguistic behavior is dramatically different depending on whether he is speaking English or Japanese.

Other aspects of Wes's conversational ability may well be transferred from Japanese or may simply reflect personality characteristics which are independent of language. Japanese friends report that in Japanese Wes is considered a very good conversationalist, thoughtful, witty, and refreshingly direct. Wes's own characterization of his conversational style, reporting on a Japanese conversation, is certainly in harmony with my analysis of his English conversational style:

then Sam say / people always talking me / because I'm a very warm person / then also very smart / clever talking / ah / well / I like talk to people you know / um / I'm always listen / then start talk / then listen / always thinking my head / then talk / some people you know only just talk, talk, talk, talk / similar Tom / he's only just talk, talk, talk / he's big star / but I'm not / if people ask something then nice talking / but sometime / OK / if I'm very strong talk / or sometime joking / you know if I'm talk middle age people and strong talk / but people happy / people never get angry / OK / I tell Sam / I said I think people likes you / but a little bit boring and talking / then he said ah because I'm a little old / then I said this is not important and you know talk, talk, talk / so / people always ask me / also they want something then I'm help

(monologue tape, November 1980)

## Strategic Competence

In Canale's framework, this component of communicative competence is com-posed of mastery of verbal and nonverbal communication strategies that are called into action to compensate for breakdowns in communication due to limiting factors in performance (e.g., inability to recall a word) or to insufficient compe-tence in one or more of the other areas. Typical examples would be the use of paraphrase, requests for repetition, clarification or slower speech, and the use of reference sources.

Since Wes clearly has a very limited command of the grammatical aspects of English, communication breakdowns do occur when he is talking to native speakers. Yet Wes is almost always able to repair these breakdowns, and it seems that his confidence, his willingness to communicate, and especially his *persistence* in communicating what he has in his mind and understanding what his interlocutors have in their minds go a long way toward compensating for his grammatical inaccuracies. A number of communication strategies which Wes uses have already been mentioned in the earlier parts of this paper: the transfer of Japanese gramma-tical principles and patterns when elements of English structure are not known: the use of formulaic utterances which exceed in complexity the capacities of the internalized, creative grammar: phonological practice; the practice; the use of disambiguators such as *please* to clarify illocutionary force; guessing and the extension of patterns to new contexts.

Some additional communication strategies can be identified by looking at what happens when Wes does not know an English word:

Wes:    this is what?/mo-?/ mo-? (pointing)
NS:     mole
Wes:    better take out, right?

(field notes, February 1981)

Wes:    Dick / "heroin" is English?
NS1:    yes
Wes:    OK / you know "heroin" right?
NS2:    uh huh

(field notes, February 1981)

In the first example, Wes had forgotten a word which he had heard the day before; so he simply asked a native speaker to supply it. The second example is a bit more complicated. The context is that Wes wanted to tell NS2 a story about the rising incidence of heroin addiction in Japan. However, although he knew the word "heroin," he was not sure if it was an English word. Wes knew the word not from hearing it in English conversation but from Japanese, which has borrowed the word from English, and specifically from written Japanese, which marks foreign borrow-ings by spelling them in the katakana syllabary. However, Wes has learned from experience that the fact that a word is written in katakana does not guarantee that it is an English borrowing, e.g., the word "arbeit," which Wes is aware from previous attempts at use is not only a German rather than an English loan but has

161

also acquired a particularly Japanese meaning. He therefore asks for confirmation from NS1 before using the word with NS2.

If Wes does not know a borrowed word for what he wants to communicate, he will paraphrase. Paraphrases may be brief word coinages, e.g. *money-girl* for "prostitute" (possibly from Japanese English, although Japanese informants I have asked are unfamiliar with the expression), or extended, as in the following example:

Wes:    well / also / I go to movie and / you know movie / always in Japan / titles / you know everything is writing Japanese, right?
G:        { oh!
M:        { uh huh
Wes:    if somebody speaking English / { so
M:                              { subtitles

(conversation tape, January 1981)

Paraphrase may involve associations to context and to real-word knowledge, which are sometimes unsuccessful if his interlocutors do not share the same knowledge or cannot make the association rapidly. The following example is an attempt to identify the actress Meryl Streep on the basis of her appearance in a movie with actor Dustin Hoffman:

Wes:    no / I know her / you know her / you remember girl in movie with big nose guy?/ what's name?
NS:    no
Wes:    you know (annoyed tone) / OK / little guy movie / he loves his father / also mother
NS:    oh / you mean "Kramer versus Kramer"?
Wes:    yeah / Kramer Kramer
NS:    no / that's not her

(conversation tape, February 1981)

It is interesting to observe as well some common communication strategies which Wes does *not* use. He does not use a Japanese-English dictionary to look up words. Although he owns such a dictionary, he reports that he has never used it. I have never heard him ask a native speaker to explain the difference between two words. I have never heard him ask whether a particular word is appropriate or idiomatic. Whereas other nonnative speakers have asked me questions such as whether the word "dishwasher" could be applied to people as well as machines, Wes seems content if the basic idea is communicated. For example, although I have pointed out to him several times that *money-girl* is not idiomatic English, and have supplied several lexical substitutes, *money-girl* remains his only active lexical entry for that meaning (he comprehends other terms but does not use them). He does not often ask for information on the semantic range or precise meaning of a word. In fact, I have noted only one such instance, when a client commissioned a painting and later rejected it without paying: Wes wanted to know if the meaning of "order" was different in Japanese and English. Finally, I would note that when native speakers supply lexical items, Wes seldom does what I have observed students to do often, repeat the word just supplied by native speakers, one in the "heroin" sequence quoted above, when Wes turned to a new addressee, and "subtitles" in the following example:

Wes: well / also / I go to movie and / you know movie / always in Japan / titles / you know everything is writing Japanese, right?
G:    oh!
M:    uh huh
Wes: if somebody speaking English /    so
M:    subtitles
M: subtitles
Wes: subtitles?
M:    subtitles
G:    subtitles / right
Wes: then I'm never looking Japanese / only just listen / then sometime I don't understand / but I'm enjoy

(conversation tape, January 1981)

It is interesting that although Wes did repeat the word "subtitles," perhaps as acknowledgment of the insistence of his interlocutors, he did not use the word in his last utterance, although the intended meaning was "then I never looked at the subtitles."

On the grammatical level, Wes also has a number of communication strategies that partially compensate for inadequate knowledge of English structures. He relies to a great extent on reasonable associations among semantic elements to compensate for the lack of surface structure markings [*this afternoon I went n exhibition Japanese artist* for "this afternoon I went to an exhibition (of paintings) by a Japanese artist"] or non-English word order (*maybe ten paint I'm one month sometime* for "sometimes I can finish ten paintings in one month"). To compensate for an almost total lack of a tense system in English, Wes uses time adverbials, a communication strategy that is certainly frequent and perhaps universal among second language learners. *All day, always, right now, today, yesterday, tomorrow, before, last year, tonight, this morning, etc.* are high-frequency items in Wes's English.

With regard to the discourse component of communicative competence, I find Wes's development of topics particularly impressive. Especially in the later monologue and conversational tapes, he is usually quite concerned with establishing the sequence of information necessary to understand a story or the main point to be drawn from it. In some cases, this means doing a lot of topic preparation (Hatch 1978c), initially establishing background information that will be drawn upon in the narrative or description which follows:

Wes: well / OK / this is new guy / he's about fifty / I think last time you met him / he's also own company / small company / he's go to Canada / quite old guy / his nickname is I think Sam / so / every morning nine thirty or ten I went Max Coffee Shop / also this guy's coming . . .

(November 1980)

| Wes: | well / I'm start painting six o'clock / then / OK / my good friend / his name is Ken / before I'm teaching him / so sometime he's come to my apartment before / then he try paint / well / quite good / but he's not strong / he's always tired and complain / but he loves paint / so / anyway / today he's come my studio / then he said . . . |
| --- | --- |

(November 1980)

In both of the above examples, Wes is making sure that the listener has some information about a person mentioned, before beginning the story in which that person will figure as a character. Native speakers use this technique too, of course, and I have no baseline native speaker data for comparison, but Wes may be more conscientious than native speakers usually are in establishing such reference points for development of narrative. Note also that in both of the above examples, and in many others, background information is prefaced by *OK* and concluded by *so* or *anyway*.

    Communication strategies are particularly evident in conversational material, since native speakers may signal the fact that a message has not been received, although it may not be clear whether phonological, syntactic, or other problems have caused the mistransmission. The simplest repair strategy is repetition:

| Wes: | you have stereo? |
| --- | --- |
| NS: | huh? |
| Wes: | you have stereo? |
| NS: | yeah |

(conversation tape, February 1981)

| M: | so you can speak Arabic? (to R, native speaker) |
| --- | --- |
| Wes: | Arabic sounds like Germany (softly) |
| R: | you like the sound of German? |
| Wes: | right? |
| R: | I hate the sound of German |
| Wes: | no / means Arabic sounds like . . |
| R: | oh / Arabic sounds like German |
| Wes: | yeah |

(conversation tape, January 1981)

In the first example above, the native speaker clearly signaled his failure to receive the message; so Wes simply tried again, successfully. In the second example, native speaker R thought that he heard Wes accurately but wasn't sure, so tried to check his comprehension by repeating what he thought was Wes's message. Wes missed this, and his *right?* is a tag on his original utterance; apparently not related to R's move. R's next comment, however, indicated that he had not heard Wes correctly the first time; so Wes repeated the message.

    Repetition is the favored strategy if an interlocutor seems not to have heard a message. This is true also if Wes has not clearly heard a message directed at him by native speakers:

| Wes: | what time is it now? |
| --- | --- |
| NS: | ten after nine |
| Wes: | ten to nine? |

NS:        ten after nine
Wes:       uh huh / so tired!

(field notes, December 1980)

If it seems that an interlocutor has heard the words but has not understood the message, then paraphrase and expansion of content are Wes's favored strategies:

Wes:       Doug / you have dream after your life?
NS:        whaddya mean?
Wes:       OK / everybody have some dream / what doing / what you want / after your life / you have it?
NS:        you mean after I die?
Wes:       no no / means next couple years or long time / OK / before I have big dream / I move to States / now I have it / this kind you have it?
NS:        security I suppose / not necessarily financial / although that looms large at the present time

(conversation tape, April 1981)

In attempting to ask the native speaker whether he has a goal or purpose for his future, Wes's nonidiomatic vocabulary triggers a miscommunication, which he repairs first by explaining what he means by *dream* (*what doing, what you want*) and *after your life* (*means next couple of years or long time*) and second by giving a specific example, his realized goal of moving to the United States.

Wes clearly pays a great deal of attention to feedback from native speakers, whether this is explicitly provided (*huh?, whaddya mean?*) or only identifiable from subsequent discourse (*Arabic sounds like Germany* example). Wes also reports that he makes a point of watching the face of interlocutors carefully, not only to enhance receipt of native speaker message—he claims to be an expert lip reader in Japanese and has several times surprised me by accurately reporting English conversations observed across a crowded and noisy room—but also to detect facial expressions indicating that native speakers are not understanding him.

The fact that Wes pays attention to and is alert for signals of miscommunication and energetically repairs messages that are not received the first time raises the question of why this has not had a salutary effect on his grammatical competence. Vigil and Oller (1976) have argued that feedback is the primary factor controlling the development of learner grammars. They argue that positive affective feedback ("let's increase the intensity of this relationship") and positive cognitive feedback ("I understand what you are saying") will be apt to produce fossilization of errors, while positive affective feedback and negative cognitive feedback ("I want to understand, but don't understand") create a desired instability in incorrect utterances and prod the learner to make appropriate modifications. Hence, whatever grammatical rules were used in the attempt that failed will tend to destabilize are are not apt to be fossilized without modification (Vigil and Oller 1976, p. 291).

Wes receives many affectively positive and cognitively negative responses from native speakers, yet the result has not been destabilization of his interlanguage grammar. There may be several reasons for this. First, as Selinker and

Lamendella (1979) have observed, feedback may take place separately for communicative competence versus grammatical correctness. This means that deviant utterances such as *this morning I'm finish new paint* are understood and get positive reinforcement more often than not. Second, in real-world interaction native speakers seldom provide explicit focused corrective feedback for grammar in conversation with nonnative speakers. I have observed Wes in interaction with many native speakers, including at least a dozen language-teaching professionals, and have not noted a single instance of feedback explicitly focused on grammatical form other than my own inconsistent attempts to prod Wes into an awareness of tense. Native speakers do, however, provide some corrective feedback for vocabulary and pronunciation (e.g., *subtitles* examples above) and usually do let nonnative speakers know if they have not understood them. Third, even if native speaker feedback is intended as corrective and at least partially focused on form, the nonnative speaker may not respond by modifying the form but may attempt a nongrammatical solution to repair the message. This is the case in the form:

Wes:     I'm go to airport eleven thirty
RS:      do you mean you have to leave here at 11:30 or you have to arrive there at 11:30?
Wes:     means 11:30 I'm airport / not here

(field notes, October 1980)

In the next exchange, Wes's repair does involve a grammatical distinction, which perhaps unfortunately clarified the message sufficiently for understanding:

Wes:     today I'm buy cigarettes
RS:      do you mean this morning or now?
Wes:     not I'm bought / I'm buy! (annoyed tone)

(field notes, December 1980)

An additional reason why feedback from native speakers may not affect the learner's grammar is that, although miscommunication may be caused by inadequate grammar, the conversational management strategies such as requests for clarification or paraphrase of message to check understanding which native speakers use to signal the need for repair are no different in essence (they may be in frequency) from what native speakers do with native speakers and, indeed, what nonnative speakers do to uphold their side of the conversational interaction with natives. In the "goal of life" dialogue presented above, the native speaker several times asked Wes for clarification or expansion of his messages. In the continuation of that dialogue, the roles are reversed, with Wes demanding the same kinds of clarification and confirmations from the native speaker:

NS:      security I suppose / not necessarily financial / although that looms large at the present time
Wes:     but not only just money, right?
NS:      right

Wes:    so what dreaming?
NS:     well / I guess first you worry about the basics / then if you have that / then maybe
        prestige / ultimately peace of mind and enlightenment
Wes:    so means you want famous and happy?
NS:     shit / I'm not interested in being famous / no / you know we're still trying to find our
        place in the community / we're displaced
Wes:    where from? / you're from mainland right?

                                                            (conversation tape, January 1981)

In native/nonnative conversations, the interlocutors face essentially the same
task: to understand and be understood by someone who is speaking a radically
different version of "the same" language. Each party must therefore make an
attempt to bridge the gap. The native speaker has far superior knowledge and
power, and the nonnative is expected to do most of the work. But it seems clear
that many nonnative speakers, Wes included, do not expect to have to do all the
work or to reach perfection. This may be because the nonnative perceives his level
of proficiency to be adequate for most needs, or—as I believe is true in Wes's case—
because the nonnative may simply not accept the fairness of greatly disparate levels
of effort by conversational partners. A final communication strategy which I
believe Wes has quite consistently relied upon, no doubt valuable in the short term
but probably detrimental in the long run, is to expect native speakers to learn his
interlanguage, both to understand him and to speak in a way that is comprehensible
to him, and to consider it the native speaker's problem as much as his own if this
does not happen. From the point of view of the learner, this is perhaps not as
irrational a position as it might seem at first, since in the individual learner's
experience his own effort may be maintained at a more or less constant level, and
interactive success on particular occasions may depend largely on what the native
speaker does. Some native speakers are simply better at carrying on conversation
with nonnatives than others. Some are better at modifying their input to nonnative
speakers, including vocabulary, or at modifying their discourse structure. Some
are adept at understanding nonnatives of a particular language background or
nonnatives in general (a talent which many teachers develop). Other native speakers
may mumble or act as though everyone knows their experience. Some are deaf or
don't listen closely. On numerous occasions I have heard Wes express displeasure
at native speakers who are not able to understand him.

A by-product of Wes's expectancy that native speakers can learn to understand him if they try has been a degree of dependency on those who have demonstrated that they can, who therefore can serve (if present) as interpreters and
general caretakers. Native speakers also rely on other native speakers to assist in
communication:

Wes:    what kind of song you like it?
NS1:    what's he saying?
Wes:    this is grea(t) song
NS1:    gray?

| Wes: | this is grea(t) song / listen / you know this music? / what's name? / oh / American Gigolo |
|---|---|
| NS1: | what's he saying / gray? |
| NS2: | no / great |

(conversation tape, January 1981)

## DISCUSSION

Wes: I know I'm speaking funny English / because I'm never learning / I'm only just listen / then talk / but people understand / well / some people confuse / before OK / but now is little bit difficult / because many people I'm meeting only just one time / you know demonstrations everybody's first time / sometime so difficult / you know what I mean? / well / I really need English more / I really want speak more polite English / before I'm always I hate school / but I need studying / maybe school / I don't have time / but maybe better / whaddya think? / I need it, right?

(monologue tape, November 1980)

Whether one considers Wes to be a good language learner or a poor language learner depends very much on one's definition of language and of the content of SLA. If language is seen as a means of initiating, maintaining, and regulating relationships and carrying on the business of living, then perhaps Wes is a good learner. If one views language as a system of elements and rules, with syntax playing a major role, then Wes is clearly a very poor learner. Friends and acquaintances who are not in the language or language teaching business generally evaluate Wes's English favorably, pointing out, for example, that "I understand him a lot better than X, who's been here over twenty years." Several sociolinguists with whom I have discussed his case have given similar evaluations, sometimes proclaiming him a superior language learner who just doesn't care about grammatical do-dads, most of which are eliminated in normal speech anyway. Grammar teachers, on the other hand, generally consider him a disaster, possibly beyond rescue. Wes's own evaluation of his English ability is mixed, recognizing both strengths and weaknesses. He is quite clearly proud of what he has accomplished and knows that he can communicate much better in English than many nonnative speakers with much greater linguistic knowledge. On one occasion Wes introduced me to some Japanese friends honeymooning in Hawaii, for whom he was acting as guide and interpreter, friends who by all appearances knew no English. Yet in subsequent encounters, with Wes not present, it turned out that the husband at least knew English quite well, had a large vocabulary, and spoke very grammatically, but was simply too shy to attempt much conversation and had some difficulty comprehending what native speakers said to him. On several different occasions I have heard Wes give impromptu English lessons to other Japanese, explaining what to say in a particular circumstance, supplying forms which were almost always wrong but which had worked for him. At the same time, Wes knows that he speaks *funny English*, that there are many things he wants to say that he can communicate only with great difficulty, that people do sometimes have a difficult time understanding him, and that his command of English is not adequate to his needs.

Wes is a different type of learner from many others with the same language background, for example, the Japanese graduate student at an American university who has studied English for many years and can write well, perhaps even at the scholarly level, but who is barely comprehensible in conversation. However, the major point of this paper is that Wes is also unlike Alberto, who lived in an Hispanic/Portuguese ghetto, Zoila, who never wanted to come to the United States, and the Vietnamese mother suffering from intense culture shock. It seems to me quite clear that Wes's failure to learn much of the grammatical component of his second language cannot be attributed to social distance factors, to lack of need for or interest in meaningful communication and interaction, to personality factors such as self-consciousness, or to poor attitudes toward target language speakers. Low social distance, positive attitudes toward the second language community, and high integrative motivation to use the second language for communication have led to a considerable increase in overall *communicative* competence but have had little effect on improved *grammatical* competence. I conclude, therefore, that the hypothesis that "the degree of acculturation toward the 'model' language group seems to be the primary consideration in attempting to account for the varied levels of *linguistic* achievement reached by second language learners" (Stauble 1978, p. 46, emphasis mine) is false.[3]

There are, of course, a number of ways in which one might attempt to explain away or modify this conclusion. It is possible that the period of observation reported here might not be the relevant time span in which to observe the effect of social and psychological variables on SLA. The acculturation model might be relevant to explaining Wes's acquisition of a limited form of English in Tokyo, but perhaps once such a system has developed and has been perceived as adequate for a period of time it fossilizes, so that changes will not be effected simply by changes in social and psychological distance factors. Such a rationalization would explain not only Wes's case but also the case of Angela, an Italian immigrant reported on by Bruzzese (1977). Angela came to the United States when she was 37 and initially lived in an Italian neighborhood in New York. Twenty-three years later, she moved to California and integrated into an English-speaking community, but this did not result in defossilization of her very limited linguistic system. If this kind of explanation is accepted, however, it restricts the importance of the acculturation model to a very limited time span.

Conversely, the most relevant period in which to observe the effects of social and affective factors on SLA might be still in the future in Wes's case. Perhaps eventually his rudimentary grammatical system for English, maintained so far through compensatory strength in the area of discourse competence and the extraordinary use of communication strategies, will "crack" and syntactic development will resume. While I certainly hope that this happens, and expect some progress in the future, I doubt that Wes will change his basic approach to language learning, and assume that he will continue to emphasize message content over message form.

A third possibility is that in my description of Wes I may have unfairly deemphasized negative affective factors. For example, Wes is indeed extroverted and uninhibited, but under the bravado one can find, if one looks hard enough, some insecurity, even shyness. Perhaps it is detrimental that Wes has a strong personality and a strong sense of identity, as a person and as a Japanese. This suggests that he may lack ego-permeability (Guiora's term), although this is expressed not in lack of empathy or in self-consciousness but rather in sensitivity to criticism and a degree of stubbornness. Identification as a Japanese also puts limits on the level of integrative motivation which I have attributed to Wes, though Schumann is clear that the acculturation model does not require adoption of the life style and values of the target group for successful acquisition; social and psychological contact are enough.

The concept of field dependence/independence might be relevant. These concepts attempt to combine perceptual, personality, and learning characteristics. The field-independent person is one who is good at finding the trees in the forest or identifying monkeys hidden in pictures. The field-independent person is competitive self-confident, independent, and possibly good at classroom learning. The field-dependent person is concerned with the overall picture, ignoring the trees in the forest and the monkeys in the pictures, is affectively empathetic, with social outreach, is concerned with communication and thought to be good at acquisition. The problem with applying these concepts to Wes is that he has characteristics of both types. He is self-confident and competitive but also shows social outreach. He is concerned with communication but is not good at acquisition, if by acquisition we mean the acquisition of grammar. However, the main reason the dichotomy does not hold up is that there is a clear task-specific difference (Brown 1980 p. 93). Perhaps because he is an artist, Wes has no difficulty finding monkeys hidden in pictures. In his work he is a perfectionist, and his paintings rely to a great extent on detail for their impact. In language learning he is not a perfectionist, and appears to care little or nothing for the details.

The factors which appear to best explain Wes's failure to acquire much grammar are therefore partly psychological, but these have less to do with social or psychological distance from target language speakers than with cognitive style, personality characteristics, and attitudes which are specifically relevant to learning the grammatical code. While the acculturation model predicts that such factors will interact with acculturation but will not dominate it (Schumann 1978b, p. 48), this appears to have happened in Wes's case.

The following factors remain candidates for identification as causal variables operating negatively for Wes's acquisition of grammar:

## Age

It remains to be demonstrated whether any mature adult can actually *acquire* impressive control of the grammar of a second language (see below).

## Aptitude

Wes's hypotheses about English grammar are more often than not incorrect, suggesting that aptitude may be important in acquisition as well as in classroom learning. However, Wes's failure to correctly induce the grammatical rules of English may be due less to innate analytical ability than to his basic lack of interest in this aspect of language and/or his failure to test and revise preliminary hypotheses.

## Hemispheric Dominance

No direct evidence is available, and this factor is only suggested by Wes's gestalt approach to learning, his strengths in intonation and comprehension as compared with syntax, and current theorizing that there is greater left hemispheric involvement in second language processing among early bilinguals and relatively greater right hemispheric involvement among late bilinguals. However, the hypothesis that left hemispheric processing is associated with formal learning environments and relatively more right hemispheric processing is associated with informal acquisition (Genesee 1981) suggests that this factor, if relevant, may be as much effect as cause.

## Cognitive Style

Expressive/gestalt rather than analytic, with consistent focus on message content over form; monitoring of communication rather than grammar; use of communication strategies which resolve immediate problems but do not also serve as long-term learning strategies.

## Exposure

Lack of formal instruction in English; lack of experience with the written code of English, which might make grammatical features more salient; lack of developed metalinguistic awareness for either first or second language.

## Sociolinguistic

The multidimensional demands of conversation and interaction, with feedback focused on content and message transmission; the redundancy of grammar in communication; requirements and expectations for nonnative speaker proficiency.

## Personality/Attitudes/Interests

Dominant personality, sensitivity to criticism and dislike of the subordinate learner role; dislike of formal study and defeatist attitude toward classroom abilities; great curiosity about people but no interest in linguistic analysis; unwillingness to expend time and energy studying English outside the actual context of use.

Talent, temperament and experience are all involved, and Wes has shown improvement in just those aspects of English which he enjoys and has devoted the most attention to, using strategies that have been facilitative. However, the relationships among age, lack of instruction, and failure to acquire grammar—features which Wes shares with the other unsuccessful learners in the SLA literature with whom I have compared him—remain the most provocative and significant for an adequate theory of SLA. The question which remains unanswered is whether or not adults really can acquire much grammar through interaction alone. If by acquisition we mean to include only wholly unconscious learning, I believe the answer is no, they cannot. Adults do seem to have lost the still mysterious ability of children to acquire the grammatical forms of language while apparently not paying attention to them.[4]

At least, there is no evidence presently available to argue convincingly that this ability is retained. The studies by Carroll (1967), Upshur (1968) and Mason (1971) which showed increased proficiency without formal study all involved subjects who already had a substantial base of formal instruction, implying both a body of knowledge to build upon and at least some developed sensitivity to form. The SLA literature does not yet contain any well-documented studies of adults who have successfully learned the grammar of a second language solely through interaction, without any formal instruction at all, regardless of their purported social and psychological attitudes toward target language speakers. There might well be some such individuals, however, and I do not wish to argue that instruction is a necessary condition for adult SLA, but only conscious attention to form, which could be accomplished through self-study, using conscious learning strategies such as some of those identified by Rubin (1981) which Wes does not make use of: asking questions of native speakers, consulting available sources and actively using deductive reasoning to look for general rules and exceptions.

A good deal of current theorizing in SLA is built on the principle that a watched pot never boils. This approach, with its stress on interaction and meaningful communication, responds well to the problems of the overly conscious "monitor over-user" (Krashen 1978), whose rules get in the way of fluent communication, and is in harmony with research findings that grammatical competence derived through formal training is not a good predictor of communicative skills (Canale and Swain 1980, Savignon 1972, Tucker 1974, Upshur and Palmer 1974). However, the partial independence of grammatical competence from the other components of communicative competence is also reflected in the ability of second language learners like Wes to communicate well without much grammatical control. For such learners, interaction, which they are already good at, is no panacea. The "watched pot" analogy begins to fall apart, because learning a second language is not as simple as boiling water but has at least as many aspects and dimensions as preparing a meal. First, one must turn on the heat and assemble the ingredients. Social and affective factors have a lot to do with providing the heat, and the interaction which they engender provides manageable data for the learner (Long, forthcoming), but surely that is not the end of the endeavor. The learner must cook the complementary courses of the meal, and in the case of grammar that means processing data received through interaction: analyzing them, formulating hypotheses (which may not be expressible as formal rules but may nevertheless be conscious at some stage of the process, at least through the ability to recognize nativelike linguistic strings), and testing those hypotheses against native speaker speech and native speaker reactions. These are of course psychological processes, but the idea that if affective factors are positive then cognitive processes will function automatically, effortlessly, and unconsciously to put together conclusions about grammar is overly optimistic. Interest and attention are additional minimum requirements if the sauce is to come out as well as the main course, and most language learners would agree that hard work is involved as well.

## NOTES

1. Schumann (1978a) has argued that adults with high social and psychological distance from target language speakers will not avail themselves of instruction even if available. However, unwillingness to take classes may have other sources, such as previous school failure or the realistic demands of a busy life. It is important not to automatically consider lack of formal study as prima facie evidence of high social and psychological distance and low motivation, since this makes separation of the variables of instruction and affective factors impossible and trivializes the affective argument. The claim that acculturation and affective factors are the major causal variable in SLA, with instruction playing only a minor role, can only be empirically justified if the model recognizes the possibility of individuals with positive affect but no instruction.

2. In general, Japanese speakers do not have the same degree of difficulty with English negation as do native speakers of many other languages. This makes an index of development based on stages of negation documented for Spanish learners of English (Cazden et al. 1975, Schumann 1978a/b, Stauble 1978) inappropriate for Japanese learners, and accounts for Agnello's (1977) inability to demonstrate that the English of his Japanese subject Masa was "pidginized" to the same extent as Spanish, Italian, and Greek subjects in the same study.

3. While it can be argued that case studies cannot be used as proof or disproof of theoretical models which have to do essentially with group tendencies, the acculturation model makes sufficiently explicit claims about the way in which diverse factors interact in the individual to make all case study material relevant for its evaluation. Particular case studies will support or detract from the model to the extent that they represent common types of learners rather than idiosyncratic exceptions. I believe that many readers will recognize similarities between Wes and other nonnative speakers they have known, not in all details of course, but certainly in broad outline.

Moreover, the major case studies used to develop the acculturation model do not provide thoroughly convincing evidence and support for it either. Alberto, the poorest language learner of six in the Cazden et. al. study was not only the most socially and psychologically distant from target language speakers but also the oldest. The only other adult in the study is reported to have had significant prior instruction and knowledge of English. Stauble's study involves the comparison of 40- and 50-year-old learners on a developmental continuum for negation observed in the acquisition of English by 10- and 12-year-olds. Based on a questionnaire concerning social and psychological distance factors, Stauble concludes that there is a hierarchy of importance of factors, with psychological variables outranking social variables and motivation outranking other psychological factors. However, she could have equally concluded that social distance does not matter at all or even detracts from acquisition, since the most socially distant subject acquired the most and the least socially distant subject acquired the least control over English negation. The argument that psychological factors are differentially important is not particularly convincing, as Stauble's best and middling subjects had identical psychological distance scores, differing only in the responses to two questions on a 14-item questionnaire. Finally, it should be noted that once again the poorest learner in the group was the oldest.

4. I do not intend to raise the issue here of whether conscious attention to form may also be important in child first and second language acquisition, but confine the argument to adult SLA. However, there is some evidence in Fillmore's (1976) study that this was an important factor with 5- and 6-year-olds learning English as a second language. Wes is rather like Nora, Fillmore's best subject, in his use of social skills which encourage exposure and interaction. However, in his lack of attention to the structural possibilities of language, he is much more like Jesus, another much less successful subject in Fillmore's subject group.

# 10

## DEVELOPMENTAL TRENDS IN THE ACQUISITION OF CONVERSATIONAL COMPETENCE BY ADULT SECOND LANGUAGE LEARNERS[1]

### Robin C. Scarcella
*University of California, Santa Barbara*

This paper focuses on an important task of the adult second language (L2) learner, acquiring "conversational competence," that is, the ability to participate in conversations. Underlying this competence are the rules and mechanisms which allow conversations to flow smoothly. These enable conversations to be opened and closed and ensure that attention and understanding are established. Conversational competence in English includes, for example, such subtle knowledge as knowing that "well," "yeah," and "okay" may indicate that a conversation is coming to an end (Schegloff and Sacks 1973), as in Example 1.

1. A: *Well* I gotta get goin'
   B: *Okay* Talk to you later
   A: *Yeah*
   B: *Okay*
   A: Bye

and that "by the way" is a misplacement marker used to introduce information which is "out of order" in a conversation (Jefferson 1972), as in Example 2.

2. A: So you're a business major
   B: Yeah

   (10 minutes later)

   A: *By the way,* my name's Mark.

During the last decade, several breakthroughs have been made in the field of conversational analysis. For example, in a now classic paper, Sacks, Schegloff, and Jefferson (1974) proposed rules for the American English turn-taking system.

Edelsky (1981) demonstrated that occurrences of simultaneous talk are not necessarily perceived as degenerate or inappropriate. Another major advance was the characterization of the English "repair" system (Sacks, Schegloff, and Jefferson 1977). This system enables speakers to fix or "repair" trouble sources in conversation. Such findings cannot be ignored by language teachers. As many scholars have pointed out (Applegate 1975, Hymes 1972, Paulston 1974, Rivers 1973, Taylor and Wolfson 1978, Wilkins 1976), it is no longer enough for the language teacher to teach grammar and pronunciation; language students must also acquire the rules and norms which govern conversation.

Thus researchers and teachers have long recognized the importance of developing the language student's conversational competence, but only quite recently have researchers begun to study how this ability is acquired. (For a review of some current research, refer to Larsen-Freeman 1980.)

A central question when examining the development of conversational competence is to what extent knowledge of conversational rules and norms is universal. Assuming that adults do not approach L2 acquisition entirely naively but have already acquired a great deal of conversational competence in their first language (and possibly other languages), what aspects do they need to acquire in order to achieve nativelike proficiency in the L2?

In answering this question, it will be helpful to discuss briefly some current research. Several investigators have proposed that certain aspects of conversational competence are universal (see Ervin-Tripp 1981, Grice 1975). For example, it is often claimed that all cultures have procedures for entering into and sustaining a mutual state of involvement. Yet the conventions underlying these procedures may vary greatly from one society to another. For instance, each society may employ a different range of linguistic devices. In addition, the co-occurrence restrictions and distributional rules and norms governing the environment and extent of use of these forms may be highly culture-specific (see Blum-Kulka, this volume).

Recent studies suggest that while universal tendencies undoubtedly exist for many aspects of conversation (for example, most languages are said to have greetings and leave takings, turn-taking systems, and repair systems), and while such tendencies help learners converse in the L2, learners do not begin the task of acquiring an L2 fully equipped with knowledge of the target language conversational rules and norms. In fact, they often have difficulty conversing with native speakers. For instance, among other things, they may lack knowledge of the appropriate greetings and address terms. (Refer to Examples 3 and 4.)

| *Second Language Speaker* | *Content* |
| --- | --- |
| (first language is Arabic) | |
| 3. Hello my teacher (Scarcella 1978) | greeting teacher |
| 4. Hi sir (Scarcella and Brunak 1981) | greeting boss |

Adult L2 learners have also been reported to have difficulty using the rules of the English turn-taking system. While in most cultures interlocutors take turns speaking, there are considerable differences in the amount of time speakers are permitted to overlap (Reisman 1974). Thus, in some societies a large number of overlaps are tolerated. In such societies interruptions may not be considered offensive. Rather, they might be considered cooperative, indications of attentive listening.[2] The following exchange typified interaction between Farsi L2 learners and native English speaker instructors.

5. *Context*

English instructor:

Abdulla, what { did you say?  University classroom, teacher is talking
                               to a student, Abdullah
Mahmood: { My teacher
I need your help.
(Scarcella 1978)

Here it appears that the L2 learner is using the conversational rules of his L1 when conversing in the L2. In Newmark's (1976) terms, since the learner may not yet have acquired the English turn-taking rules, he may be "falling back" on his first language (L1).

In recent times, similar conversational problems have been reported (see, for instance, Graham 1980, Richards 1980, Scarcella in press, Sato 1981.) While these reports identify the conversational difficulties of specific adult L2 learners (thus providing further evidence that all aspects of conversation are not universal), they do not reveal much about developmental trends in the acquisition of conversational competence.

The primary concern of this paper is therefore developmental trends. Knowledge of these trends can provide researchers with further knowledge concerning *when* specific conversational features are acquired and teachers with information which may aid in the establishment of realistic teaching goals, instructional materials, and language assessment instruments.

I argue here that conversational competence is not "built in." Although learners are accomplished conversationalists in their L1, they must also acquire additional conversational skills if they are to be conversationally competent in the L2. To provide evidence for this position, a study was undertaken which investigated the following hypotheses:

1. That the ability to manage conversations in an L2 increases with overall language proficiency
2. That a developmental order exists for the acquisition of the forms of conversational devices (such that greetings and closings are acquired before introductions and responses to introductions which in turn are acquired before pre-closing and requests for clarification)

## SUBJECTS

The subjects of this study consist of 63 adult university students studying English as a second language (ESL) at the American Language Institute at the University of Southern California. Of these students, 20 were in beginning ESL classes, 20 in intermediate classes, and 23 in advanced classes. Proficiency level was determined by placement on the International Student Exam, oral interview scores, and teacher evaluation. First languages represented were, for the beginning students, Arabic (9), Farsi (6), Japanese (5); for the intermediate students, Arabic (3), Chinese (4), Farsi (8), Urdu (1), Japanese (4); and for the advanced students, Arabic (6), Farsi (7), Chinese (3), Japanese (4), Hebrew (2), and Spanish (1). Six ESL instructors also participated in the study.

In addition, a control group, consisting of six native English speakers (university students) provided baseline data.

## TASK

The ESL students were interviewed by two ESL instructors as part of the placement procedure of the American Language Institute. In the course of the interview, one of the instructors elicited seven specific conversational devices from the students: greetings, responses to introductions ("Nice to meet you"), introductions ("My name is _____"), requests for clarification ("what?" "huh?"), responses to pre-closings (such as "well" and "It's been nice talking to you") which prepare the conversationalists for the conversational ending (Schegloff and Sacks 1973) and closings ("bye"). Verbal cues were used to elicit these devices (refer to the interview format below).

### INTERVIEW FORMAT

| Conversational skills elicited | Verbal cue (given by the interviewer to elicit conversational skills) |
| --- | --- |
| 1. Response to greeting | Hello (pause) |
| 2. Response to introduction | My name is _____ (long pause) |
| 3. Introduction | (long pause following the interviewer's introduction) |
| 4. Request for clarification | When you first came here, were you overwhelmed by Los Angeles? (long pause, mumbled and spoken quickly) |
| 5. Response to 1st pre-closing | Well, I don't have any other questions (long pause) |
| 6. Response to 2nd pre-closing | It's been nice talking to you (long pause) |
| 7. Closings | Bye |

The feasibility of using these cues to elicit conversational devices was tested with the native English speaker control group. In all cases, the native English speakers responded with expected conversational forms when these were elicited by the investigator in an interview situation.[3]

## DATA ANALYSIS

While one instructor interviewed the students, the other recorded the students' responses to the verbal cues on a specially provided form. Students received a 1 for a response given by the native English speaker control group and a 0 for a different, inappropriate response. Ambiguous responses were recorded separately.

Examples 6 and 7 illustrate the types of responses considered inappropriate.

6.  Interviewer:                 Well, I don't have any more questions.
                                        (long pause)

     Student: (beginning) (Inappro-     No response
        priate response to first
        pre-closing)

     Interviewer:               It's been nice talking to you. (long pause)
     Student:                   No response
     (Inappropriate response to
        second pre-closing)

     Interviewer:               Thanks very much. Good luck.
     Student:                   No response.
     Interviewer:               (Stands up, walks to door and opens it) Bye.
     Student:                   Bye.

     Interviewer:               When you first came here were you over-
                                        whelmed by Los Angeles?

     Student (advanced): (Inappro-   My husband from Spain too.
        priate; expected response =
        request for clarification)

All interviews were audio-tape-recorded, thus allowing the investigator to review each of the interviews. Interrater reliability, determined by comparing the instructors' evaluations of the students' responses with that of the investigator's evaluation of the recorded responses, was considered adequate (.95 or 369/388 of the responses).

## FINDINGS

As seen in Tables 1 and 2, the first hypothesis was confirmed. There was a significant difference in the use of the seven conversational devices by the three groups of L2 learners. The more advanced the learner, the more conversational skills she or he used (see also Figure 1).

Table 1   Percentage of Accuracy for 63 Adult ESL Learners of 3 Proficiency Levels in 7 Conversational Skills*

|  | Beginning (n = 20) | Intermediate (n = 20) | Advanced (n = 23) |
|---|---|---|---|
| Greetings | 1.00 (20/20) | .90 (18/20) | 1.00 (23/23) |
| Responding to introductions | .55 (4/13) | .55 (11/20) | .86 (19/23) |
| Introducing oneself | .55 (11/20) | .80 (16/20) | .86 (19/22) |
| Getting the speaker to clarify | .30 (4/13) | .62 (8/13) | .63 (14/22) |
| Response to first pre-closing | .30 (4/13) | .69 (11/16) | .68 (15/22) |
| Response to second pre-closing | .64 (11/17) | .85 (17/20) | .90 (20/22) |
| Closing | .71 (5/7) | 1.00 (20/20) | 1.00 (22/22) |
| Totals: | .58 (59/103) | .77 (101/129) | .84 (132/156) |

*Note that the number of subject responses on each conversational skill varies, since only clear, unambiguous responses were recorded. The number of accurate responses over the number of total responses is given in parentheses.

**Table 2** Summary of One-way ANOVA of Conversational Skills Experiment

| Source of variation | SS | df | MS | F | p |
|---|---|---|---|---|---|
| Between groups | 2693 | 2 | 1346 | 3.82* | .05 |
| Within groups | 6348 | 18 | 353 | | |

*$F$ test for ANOVA is significant at $\ell$ = .05, indicating that there is a significant difference in the use of the 6 conversational skills examined by the 3 groups of L2 learners (beginning, intermediate, and advanced). The MODLSD procedure indicated significant differences between beginning and advanced learners (LSD = 2.13, $p$ < .05, df = 4, one-tailed).

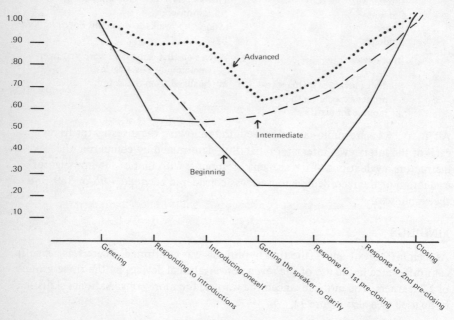

**FIGURE 1** Comparison of Beginning, Intermediate, and Advanced Adult ESL Students; Mean Accuracies for 7 Conversational Skills

    The data also indicate developmental patterns in the acquisition of the conversational management devices examined. More specifically, greetings and closings are acquired before introductions, which are acquired before pre-closings and requests for clarification. Group accuracy orders (based on mean group scores on the seven conversational devices) were obtained for each of the three groups of ESL students (beginning, intermediate, and advanced). Group orders were compared using Kendall coefficient of concordance $W$. There was a significant correlation between accuracy orders ($W$ = .96, $p$ < .01, one-tailed, rho = .99, $p$ < .01, one-tailed). The group accuracy orders of the intermediate and advanced learners also correlated significantly ($r$ = .74, $p$ < .05, one-tailed, rho = .98 $p$ < .01,

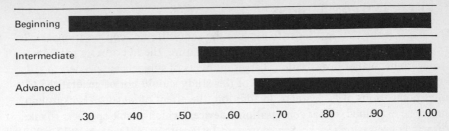

**FIGURE 2**    Range of Percentages of Accuracy on 7 Conversational Skills Used by Beginning, Intermediate, and Advanced Adult ESL Learners (Based on Group Means)

one-tailed). Correlations between beginning and intermediate groups, though not reaching statistical significance with Pearson (4 = .68, ns), only slightly missed significance with Spearman rho (rho = .71, $p$ < .10, one-tailed). These results make it reasonable to posit a developmental sequence for the acquisition of the forms of conversational management devices by adult L2 learners (refer to Table 3).[4]

Thus, just as developmental patterns exist in the acquisition of conversational skills by first language (L1) learners (see, for example, Keenan 1974, Ervin-Tripp and Mitchell-Kernan 1977), there are also developmental trends in the acquisition of these skills by adult L2 learners. For instance, as in L1 acquisition, greetings and closings are among the first conversational skills to be acquired (refer to Ferguson 1976). Pre-closings are acquired later (Weeks 1979).

**Table 3**    Percentages and Rank Orders of Conversational Skills Accurately Used by Adult ESL Students of 3 Proficiency Levels During an Oral Interview

|  | Beginning | Intermediate | Advanced | Developmental order* |
|---|---|---|---|---|
| Greeting | 1.00 | .90 | 1.00 | Greetings |
| Closing | .71 | 1.00 | 1.00 | Closing |
| Response to 2nd pre-closing | .64 | .85 | .90 | Response to 2nd pre-closing |
| Introducing oneself | .55 | .55 | .86 | Introducing oneself |
| Introductions | .55 | .80 | .86 | Introductions |
| Response to 1st pre-closing | .30 | .69 | .68 | Response to 1st pre-closing |
| Getting the speaker to clarify | .30 | .62 | .63 | Getting the speaker to clarify |

*The developmental order suggested here reflects trends in the acquisition of conversational skills rather than a fixed, invariant sequence.

## CAVEATS AND CONCLUSIONS

This paper is the first in a series to explore the acquisition of conversational skills by adult L2 learners. Because of its pioneering nature, the hypotheses presented here warrant further investigation. Larger numbers of subjects are needed to confirm the findings. Also, the results of this study should not be generalized to other populations of L2 learners. In addition, the effect of language background should be examined. Other conversational devices, which enable speakers to take turns in conversation (Sacks, Schegloff, and Jefferson 1974; Duncan 1972, 1973), establish and maintain attention (Keenan and Schieffelin 1976), and handle digressions (Jefferson 1972) also merit examination. Finally, and most important, the acquisition of conversational strategies should be investigated in a variety of naturally occurring situations (Wolfson 1976). The formal interview context, combined with the interviewer's use of verbal cues, obviously affected the students' responses.[5] By investigating natural conversation, researchers will gain valuable insight concerning the acquisition of the functions, sequencing, and co-occurrence restrictions which underlie the use of conversational devices. Individual variation in the acquisition of these devices can be tapped through longitudinal study.

This study, though a first effort, opens the door to a rich, untapped area of L2 research: that of sequential patterns in the acquisition of conversational devices. While recent studies of L2 discourse have made advances in determining how conversational skills are used by L2 learners (see, for example, Hatch 1978, Gaskill 1980, and Peck 1978) and some investigations have examined the acquisition of specific conversational skills (refer for instance, to Schwartz 1980), this is the first study to investigate the possibility that the forms of conversational devices are acquired in a specifiable sequence.

Clearly, adult L2 learners do not begin the task of learning conversational skills with a blank slate. Yet this study provides strong evidence that adult L2 learners must acquire additional skills if they are to be considered fully competent speakers in the L2. (Recall that even the most advanced L2 learners in the study had difficulty responding to preclosings and using requests for clarification.) Moreover, the developmental patterns in the use of conversational skills indicate that universal processes in language learning affect the acquisition of these skills by adult L2 learners. This is of significant consequence for L2 teaching: it provides empirical evidence justifying the need to develop the conversational skills of adult L2 learners while, simultaneously, indicating that the learner's proficiency level is correlated to the acquisition of these skills.

## NOTES

1. I thank Elaine Anderson, Michael Long, and Nessa Wolfson for helpful suggestions on an earlier version of this paper. Errors in content are my own.

2. See Tannen (1981) for a discussion of different patterns of interrupting within American English (ed.).

3. These forms were:

| | |
|---|---|
| 1. Response to greeting | Hello, Hi, How are you? |
| 2. Response to introduction | Nice to meet you |
| | Pleased |
| 3. Request for clarification | huh? What? hm? |
| 4. Response to 1st pre-closing | okay, alright, yeah, whah (It's been) nice talking to you |
| 5. Response to 2nd pre-closing | Well, I don't have any other questions |
| 6. Closing | (Good)bye, see you (later) |

4. To confirm these findings, percentages were converted to raw scores and reanalyzed in the following manner. 1 was given to incorrect responses, 2 to ambiguous responses, and 3 to correct responses. Mean accuracies for each of the seven strategies and combined totals were obtained for the three groups. One-way analysis of variance (ANOVA) revealed significant differences between groups ($F = 6.7$, $p < .002$, one-tailed). MODLSD procedure indicated significant differences between the beginning and intermediate groups and beginning and advanced groups (LSD = 3.48, $p < .05$, one-tailed). To confirm the results of the MODLSD procedure, the Scheffe procedure was also performed. In all cases, the Scheffe results corroborated the findings.

5. As McCurdy (1980) points out, in situations in which the participants feel threatened (such as that of an oral interview), requests for clarification are often avoided.

# 11

## "FOREIGNER TALK" IN UNIVERSITY OFFICE-HOUR APPOINTMENTS

### Cristin Carpenter
*University of Michigan*

This paper presents an overview of a project investigating language used in academic settings, specifically in higher education. This work grows out of the conversational analysis framework developed by Sacks, Schegloff, and Jefferson (1974) and also relies on the more recent approaches to the analysis of spoken discourse developed by Labov and Fanshel (1977) and by Linde (1981).

The data consist of 53 tape-recorded office-hour appointments between university professors and their graduate students at the School of Education of the University of Michigan. All participants had given their consent to being recorded prior to their appointments, which ranged in length from 20 to 50 minutes. To learn as much as possible about the participants' reasons for holding these appointments, I asked the professors and students after each appointment to fill out short questionnaires in which they were given a list of possible purposes and asked to check which one or ones were most important to them, whether or not they felt these purposes had been successfully accomplished, and who had initiated the appointments. Because it has been suggested that purpose plays an important part in determining the direction of conversation (Hymes 1972), two groups of conversations were chosen for study, one of 24 native speakers of English and one of 4 nonnative speakers, consisting of all the native and nonnative graduate students who had indicated a common goal: that one of their purposes or the major purpose for the office-hour appointment was to get their professors' approval on the choice of a topic for a term paper. Students in other appointments not investigated here indicated other purposes for holding them, such as getting to know their professors or choosing the next semester's coursework. The foreign students whose conversations are investigated here had attained an advanced level of English language proficiency, as defined by the requirements for full-time graduate study at the School of Education: a minimum score of 520 on the Test of English as a Foreign Language (TOEFL) or of 80 on the Michigan Test of English Language Proficiency (MTELP). All professors and other graduate students were white native speakers of American English.

The major focus of the study is how participants exert conversational control, such as in topic selection, topic initiation and closure, and question-answer exchange sequences, as well as through other indicators of how professors and students create and signal their roles and relative status. My purpose in this paper, however, is to relate my initial impressions of the foreign students' appointments, in order to begin to test the hypothesis that there can be significant differences between professors' interactions with American students and those with foreign students. The findings here are in no way conclusive, but they suggest that there may indeed be important differences which have yet to be characterized fully.

In what follows, I will give a brief description of the office-hour appointments with American students, and then of the appointments with the foreign students. I will then look more closely at the professors' question patterns in the foreign students' appointments, and discuss how they fit into the concept of foreigner talk.

## BACKGROUND: OVERALL IMPRESSIONS

In the appointments between American professors and students, doing the actual academic planning begins with the student's explanation, with or without a written outline to accompany it, of what has been planned for the term paper. Subsequent discussion with the professor seems to rely heavily on participants' knowing what knowledge they share and on the subtle process of guessing what knowledge they share, in order to determine what information needs to be imparted: for example, a professor's suggesting bibliographic references which he or she thinks the student hasn't seen or a student asking for bibliographic references which he or she assumes the professor can provide.

Like some of the content information exchanged in the conversation, the social information through which the professors' and students' roles are created is also transmitted in subtle ways. These include such sophisticated conversational activities as jokes, split-second timing in showing deference in turn taking, and metaphor: one professor encouraged a student to initiate the discussion of his term paper topic by using a metaphor that refers to making a call from a pay telephone: "It's your nickel, so, okay?" Participants also make oblique references to what they seem to assume are shared academic values and traditions, such as this familiar saying: "Write as much as you need to, to say what you have to say." (paraphrased example).

In contrast, the appointments with foreign students showed a lack of coordination in turn taking and in topic flow. They seemed to include more backtracking and attempts at clarification, moving forward choppily, chiefly through the professors' initiation, in question-answer sequences or in professors' explicit instructions. In the following example, the student is proposing to write a term paper about programs to re-enroll people who have dropped out of community colleges (P= professor, S= student):

P: Is there any literature on it?
S: UM—what?
P: Li: te: ra: ture: Any references?
S: Yes, we have, I have been using all of these the different community college. In each community college they use different name. You know. They call the program returning student or they call re-entering student, they call drop-in or reach-out or ⎧ (         )
P:     ⎩ And you're going to call it drop-in?
S: Yes . . . and I have been reading all of the material, the lich- how you call it?
P: Literature.
S: Okay

The appointments between professors and foreign students seemed to contain comparatively little discussion of extended topics and few of the comments, digressions, negotiations, and references to shared beliefs which tended to characterize the native speaker interactions. This indicates that part of what it may mean to "play the academic game" in English may depend on social, cultural, and linguistic resources which many foreign students probably do not have. With this possibility in mind, I will turn now to foreigner talk and to some of the question patterns used in the appointments with the nonnative students.

## USES OF QUESTIONS IN APPOINTMENTS WITH NONNATIVE STUDENTS

Literature on foreigner talk, as in Henzl (1973); Ferguson (1971, 1975, 1977); Hatch, Shapira, and Gough (1978); Arthur, Weiner, Culver, Lee, and Thomas (1980); and Long (1981), isolates techniques used by native speakers of English, German, and Czech to adjust their language for the purposes of communicating with nonnative speakers. These techniques include phonological, morphological, lexical, and syntactic adjustments, other strategies to facilitate communication such as speaking loudly, repetition, restatement, changing the topic, or checking the listener's comprehension, as in asking "Do you understand?" or "Okay?" and still other patterns which may be used more or less often in foreigner talk as contrasted with native-speaker interaction.

In this paper, I have used the term "foreigner talk" as a very general cover term, but it is relevant here to refer to an important terminological distinction noted in Ferguson (1977) and Arthur et al. (1980). The term "foreigner talk" in its strictest use refers only to the group of sentence-level grammatical rules, such as the deletion of the copula (Ferguson 1971), which constitute in some sense a system of their own, outside of what is thought of as ordinary competence in the language as it is used among native speakers. "Foreigner register," on the other hand, refers to the sociolinguistic options which the native speaker *may* draw on in certain interactional settings in order to facilitate communication. In this study,

I looked for instances of foreigner talk and foreigner register in four office-hour conversations between dyads of male American professors and nonnative graduate students, two male and two female. My analysis of these conversations focused primarily on the kinds of questions professors used to try to clarify for themselves what the students were planning to write their term papers about.

The questions in each conversation's transcript were divided first into two categories, on the basis of my interpretation of their functions in the discourse. The two categories were (1) information-seeking questions, in which professors asked for information on topics or subtopics which had not come up in the conversation before, and (2) clarification questions, referring back to something that was part of the preceding discourse. I included noninterrogative, indirect question forms such as those beginning with "I assume" when they appeared to function as questions, that is, seeking a verbal response, as indicated by the presence of a pause following the utterance, in which the listener was expected to respond.

In turn, the clarification questions were classified into two major types, serving either to confirm or to repair something a student had said earlier. Examples of these question types are given in Table 1; they are the same *kinds* of questions that could easily be found in native/native conversations.

Table 1   Clarification Question Types

Type 1. Requests for confirmation
  a. Summary/repetition, falling intonation:
  (15–2)
      P:  Do you think you'll be able to find . . . * or do you have to make just an inference?
      S:  No, I have that.
      P:  You *do* have some.
      S:  Yeah.
  b. Repetition/paraphrase, rising intonation:
  (15–2)
      S:  (has talked at length about a community college program she is organizing as a course project)
  → P:  Is it gonna be advertised in the newspaper, like you said?
      S:  Yes.
  c. Idea the professor has deduced:
  (4–1)
      P:  (on males and females teaching in the student's home country) Would—okay but would they—remember we discussed earlier that they (females)† went to less prestigious institutions and um—not so?
      S:  No, not so.
  → P:  They go to the same places?
      S:  No, they go to different schools, but uh . . .
Type 2. Requests for repair, asking for an explanation or interpretation of what the student has said:
  (15–2)
      P:  (referring to the student's written outline of the term paper) Now when you talk about films, speakers, group discussions, conferences, seminars and workshops, you've got quite a mouthful. What's that mean?

*The symbol ". . ." indicates material omitted from the excerpt.
†Parenthesized material added.

These functions of questions, as mentioned above, are commonly found in native speakers' conversations as well; so it is important to show just how they can relate to the concept of foreigner talk. I would like to suggest in this paper that such a relationship may be found in the relative frequency with which these forms appear in equivalent types of discourse with native and nonnative speakers.

First of all, although no firm conclusions can be drawn since the group of nonnative speakers was so small, it was noted that in general, professors tended to use more questions with nonnative speakers, particularly questions of clarification, than with native speakers. This is shown in Table 2.

Table 2   Information and Clarification Questions

| | Mean total number of information and clarification questions | Mean number of information questions | Mean number of clarification questions | Clarification questions: overall percentage of total questions |
|---|---|---|---|---|
| American students (N = 24) | 9.75 | 7.54 | 2.21 | 22.7 |
| Foreign students (N = 4) | 20.25 | 9.0 | 11.25 | 55.6 |

As indicated above, in the conversations with nonnative speakers, the occurrences of information questions and clarification questions were reasonably similar, averaging 9.0 and 11.25 instances respectively in each conversation. In contrast, there appeared to be more information questions than clarification questions in the conversations with native speakers: on the average, 7.54 and 2.21 instances respectively. Clarification questions averaged less than one-fourth of the total number of questions asked of the native speakers (22.7 percent) but slightly over half the questions posed to the nonnative students, 55.6 percent on the average.

This discrepancy was highlighted by one particular type of clarification question, type 1a in Table 1, the noninterrogative summary/repeat pattern with falling intonation. That pattern was used several times in all four nonnative conversations, six, three, six, and four times, averaging 4.8 instances. However, this pattern occurred rarely in native-speaker office-hour appointments, and in fact, many of the appointments in this study contained no instances of it: eleven conversations did not include it, ten conversations included it once, one conversations did not include it, ten conversations included it once, one conversation included two instances, and two conversations used it three times each, averaging .75 instances, or less than one occurrence per conversation.

Apparently, then, professors in these appointments seek clarification of what their nonnative students say more frequently than they seek to clarify what their native speaker students say. At least three factors may be contributing to the discrepancy. One, it may be that in native/native conversations, little confirmation is solicited, since everything is rightly or wrongly felt to be already understood.

Two, the pattern may have been intentionally avoided, since a request for confirmation of this sort can have negative illocutionary force (Searle 1969): it can be used to belittle someone or to express disbelief; alternatively, this "declarative" question type is used coercively in legal settings (Danet, Kermish, Rafn, and Stayman 1976). The confirmation question adds no new information to the discourse; a third way it might be used is in performing two functions at one time: checking understanding of what someone has said, and pragmatically stalling for time, in order to plan what to say next.

Although any or all of these factors may have been present in one or more of the conversations with nonnative students, together they add up to the suggestion that professors may have been somewhat uncertain about what to expect from interactions of this nature. Compelling reasons for feeling uncertain in native/nonnative interactions are complex but have been drawn together in a concept developed by Gumperz (1978) which he termed "contextualization cues."

This refers to the selection and combination of verbal, paralinguistic, and nonverbal elements in interlocutors' speech styles which enable them to make accurate interpretations of each other's intended meaning as they converse. As Gumperz has shown, misunderstandings occur when interlocutors' contextualization cues do not match or when they mean different things to different speakers. It is possible that some native speakers assume that their contextualization cues will *not* match those of nonnative speakers; the expectation of unfamiliar or unrecognizable responses may, I would argue here, give rise to a higher incidence of checks on interpretation as conversation proceeds, whether or not those checks actually facilitate comprehension.

In the case of professors' using confirmation questions, then, they may have been reacting to their *expectations* that confirmation as a type of clarification would be useful in helping to interpret what nonnative students say. If that is the case, then it can be said that a higher incidence of this pattern in native/nonnative interaction may be a feature of foreigner talk. As such, it arises from native speakers' expectations that contextualization cues will not match, rather than from the actual, localized demands of the interaction as it unfolds.

Another unusual feature of the type 1 summary/repeat question with falling intonation was observed in two of the nonnative speaker appointments. This pattern appeared in groups of three questions in sequence, of which the first was an information question and the second and third were summary/repeat requests for confirmation. I have called groups like this "triplets":

→ P: Do you um um are you able to follow me and the class
      { with ease?
→ S: { Yes.     Yes.
→ P: No communication  { problems.
                  { No.     No problems.
→ P: None at all.
   S: No.

No instances of these triplets appear in the 24 native-native conversations. As in the use of confirmation questions discussed above, there are a number of functions which may be served by the triplet sequence: as well as being a possible feature of foreigner talk, this may give the professor time to decide what to say next. However, this strategy could potentially be interpreted as doubting or insulting in a case where the respondent has no reason to think his/her answer to the first question of the three might not have been understood.

Examples of triplets of a different sort were noted in two of the nonnative conversations, in which professors attempted three times in a row to get an answer to one question. No instances of this pattern occurred in the native/native conversations:

On the subject of women getting teaching jobs in the student's home country:
→ P: (1)   Do you think the females will adopt male expectations?
→ P: (2)   No, I understand that, but I mean as teachers, do you think the females who are now looking for teaching jobs will take on the kind of expectations that a male would have?
→ P: (3)   But don't you think that the females will—will expect the students to be more polite or quieter?

After the third question in the above question group, the student answers, "Yes, to some extent," and the professor does not try again. In all the examples of these type 2 request-for-repair triplets, questions either appear in consecutive speaking turns or with *one* Wh-question related to the topic intervening after the first or second try. In the information-confirmation triplets, however, no intervening material was present.

The two types of question triplets I have seen in these conversations lead me to suspect not that there are certain question *types* but that certain discourse *conventions* are associated with the use of questions in foreigner talk, which might prove to be a very fruitful area for research. In addition to the features I have discussed, I have noted another possible aspect of the uses of questions in foreigner talk; rather than being a feature which is noted in the foreign students' appointments and not in the native/native conversations, it is a feature which is present in some of the native speakers' appointments and not present in others. Some of the professors make use of certain questions both to gain information and to instruct students at the same time. I call these "instruction questions." One type is a question that mentions an aspect of the student's plans that the professor expects *will* be covered but that the student hasn't brought up yet in conversation. This is the "teaching question" (Borkin and Carpenter 1979). It can serve as a reminder to a student who has already taken that notion into account, or as a new instruction to a student who never considered the notion before. On the surface it appears to be merely a request for information. A good example of this is the professor who asked, "How do you get away from bias?"

The other kind of instruction question is the "modeling question," in which the professor asks questions not to get information or to test the student but only as *examples* of the degree of generality or type of content that the student should use in a term paper:

> P: To find out—understand what's going on in an urban high
>    school today might mean that you would find out, let's
> → say, what percentage of the kids attend classes. What
> → percentage of the kids attend—get to classes on time.
> → What uh percentage of the kids go on to college or some
>    other form of higher education. Now these are all kind
>    of facts, I would think, or ideas you could work up that
>    would help you quote understand, right?

It is important to note that a great deal of individual variation affects the use of instruction questions, as some professors do not use this kind of "teacher talk" at all. However, if further investigation reveals that professors who *do* use these questions with American students *avoid* using them with foreign students, I would attribute the distinction to the process of adjustment which characterizes foreigner talk, motivated perhaps by the fact that instruction questions can be syntactically and rhetorically complex and can operate on several interactional levels at once. In these data I have noted no instances of instruction questions used in appointments with nonnative speakers.

## OTHER FEATURES OF APPOINTMENTS WITH NONNATIVE STUDENTS

Two other aspects of the foreign student appointments appeared to arise from foreigner talk. The first has to do with professors' explicit instructions to students, which were more prominent in the conversations with foreign students than in those with Americans. In three of the four conversations, professors gave explicit instructions to students about how to proceed with their papers. Although strict imperatives were not used to give these directions, they were couched in firm language, such as the following: "What you wanna do now is you wanna develop this, and you're gonna write an extensive paper on it as to all these different points." As Ferguson suggested, both questions *and* commands tend to increase in foreigner talk (1977, p. 31), and that tendency may account for the use of rather explicit directions in these interactions.

Ferguson has pointed out that there are certain social settings such as among American university students where foreigner talk is considered inappropriate (1977, p. 32). This appears to be true for professors in this university setting as well, whose contributions to these conversations contained only occasional instances of these phenomena reported in previous literature: restatement, repetition, loudness, drawing out words syllable by syllable for repair when a student didn't understand, and nonnative use of "no?" as a question tag. However, phenomena of that sort are found on the level of the individual utterance; I believe that these conversations contain enough divergence from native-native conversations *at the discourse level* to warrant further exploration of possible features of foreigner talk embedded in the structure of discourse. The second and last area I will touch on here is the discourse-level phenomenon of topic selection, which can play a part in foreigner talk in the following way.

Topic selection as a discourse function can be influential in determining how close the participants feel to each other during a conversation. If they share knowledge of or experience with certain topics, they will be able to relate on a more equal basis than when they are discussing topics that only one of them knows about. It stands to reason, then, that emphasizing participants' cultural differences can be akin to focusing on a person's age; Ferguson (1971) has documented this at the level of the utterance, showing similarities between baby talk and foreigner talk.

On the discourse level of topic, several topics were noted in the foreign students' office-hour appointments which could be considered "foreigner-talk topics," initiated by the professors during the interactions:

1. References to speaking other languages
2. References to educational procedures in the students' home countries
3. Comparisons between the United States and the home countries
4. Inquiries about the students' success in understanding coursework
5. Comments on the students' ability to use English
6. Discussions of travel

Because these are topics about which participants potentially do *not* share knowledge, selection of these topics can contribute to the creation of psychological distance between participants. This can lessen the chances for what Lakoff and Tannen have called "camaraderie" or "open communication and rapport" (1979, p. 583), which is an essential ingredient in a friendly conversation in English. Scarcella (forthcoming) has also noted the use of foreigner-talk topics in a study of interethnic communication and has suggested that this feature was in some way connected to prejudice. Prejudice is difficult to identify, but it is essential to be aware of its potential influence on the data in this kind of study. At this point, although much individual variation is present, it is safe to say that some Americans' foreigner talk contains both utterance-level and discourse features, and that systematic research into native speakers' expectations of and attitudes toward interaction with nonnative speakers should be included in an investigation of the total picture of what foreigner talk consists of.

With respect to topic selection, I will make one final observation which relates to both the native-speaker and the nonnative speaker conversations. One of the most salient topics in the native-speaker appointments is the professor's evaluation of the student's work. If the evaluation is positive, it takes the form of a verbal statement of the student's progress; for example, a professor may say, "Well, that sounds like you're doing fine" or "Well, that's a good choice." This statement can appear at the end of the section on paper planning, at the very end of the appointment, or in both places.

On the other hand, if the professor's evaluation is not positive, a correspondingly overt statement of a negative nature is "noticeably" absent. In this case the possibility of negative evaluation can be inferred from the professor's failure to initiate the topic at all. In those few native-speaker appointments in which professors had reservations about the students' choices of term paper topics, they indicated this by withholding statements of evaluation in the sequential positions in which they would ordinarily be found, and offering instead specific suggestions as to how the students should proceed. These cues combined into a subtle, indirect statement of evaluation, perhaps due to a general constraint in American culture against giving direct criticism which might be interpreted as impolite or overly authoritarian. What is interesting to note in the native/native conversations is that whether the apparently negative cues were understood as such or not, the students did *not* ask any questions about how they were doing. However, in two of the four nonnative conversations, statements of evaluation were lacking, but both students asked their professors at the end of the appointments whether their work was acceptable or not. Although not dealing specifically with foreigner talk, this occurrence illustrates the subtlety of contextualization cues and the possibility that misunderstandings can have serious consequences in educational settings.

## SUMMARY

What I have tried to do in this short exploratory study is to note some of the features of four office-hour appointments between American professors and foreign graduate students, and to show how those features are compatible with the concept of foreigner talk modifications. What I have found in the office-hour conversations suggests that the university setting all but prohibits the use of utterance-level foreigner talk features. On the other hand, this setting does allow participants to exercise linguistic options from the wider set of choices included in foreigner register, particularly at the level of discourse.

## SUGGESTED FUTURE DIRECTIONS

Research seems to be needed in two areas in particular: in native/nonnative interactions in other specific situations, according to gender and language background, and also in psychological, sociological, and sociolinguistic aspects of foreigner register, and in what situations it is found. Large data bases are needed, since individual variation is so typical in this kind of data. Many theoretical questions in this area need to be explored, such as what is the relationship between the system of foreigner talk rules which is built into our language or into all languages, the sociolinguistic options associated with foreigner register, and the locally managed processes of clarification and other modifications which we use when we are having trouble in specific communicative situations? In academic situations an important question which has not been addressed here relates to a fourth kind of modification, that is, "teacher talk," such as may be found at the level of higher education. Long's (1981) study of foreigner talk with elementary ESL students suggests that native speakers' tendency to rely on questions is *not* a function of teacher talk. To what degree, then, do teacher talk and foreigner talk overlap, and how do they relate to normal processes of negotiated clarification? Which processes are governed by linguistic universals, which are language-specific, and which are governed by individual style and mood? These are good examples of modeling questions, mentioned earlier in this paper, and hopefully will be addressed in later studies.

I have not attempted in this study to prove the hypothesis that there are qualitative differences between native/native and native/nonnative conversations but merely to suggest where some of these differences might be found within the context of the university setting. To be of practical value to foreign students who will study in American universities, classroom and office-hour interactions in representative academic departments might be video-taped, analyzed, and assembled into an orientation package for newly enrolled foreign students or for preuniversity ESL students. Particular attention should be given to the indirect nature of language used to give guidance, instructions, and evaluation, in light of the possibility that our academic experiences as native speakers may be quite different from the experiences foreign students have in our universities.

# 12

## ACCOMMODATION THEORY: AN EXPLANATION FOR STYLE SHIFTING IN SECOND LANGUAGE DIALECTS[1]

### Leslie M. Beebe and Jane Zuengler
*Teachers College, Columbia University*

For years the myth persisted that the sole cause of variation in a second language (L2) was interference from the speaker's first language (L1). Although no one denies that native language (NL) interference exists, many types of second language variation have now been identified, and there is a growing realization that one of the most important is socially conditioned variation. It is claimed that second languages are natural languages (Adjemian 1976). L2 speakers have social dialects in their second language, just as L1 speakers do (Beebe 1977, 1980, 1981; Tarone 1979). But the problem for researchers of sociolinguistic variation in second languages is that there is no readily available theoretical basis with which to account for the variation. Within the field of second language acquisition (SLA), a lot of work is being done on model building, but as we shall discuss later, the models are primarily developmental and therefore not oriented toward variation in L2 performance at a given time. Sociolinguistic research findings (which are largely L1-focused) do not automatically apply to L2 data. With L2 data, one has to account for the distinction between intermittent L1 interference in L2 and dialect switching among various, native, but socially conditioned, forms of the target language (TL).

In addition, sociolinguistic research is currently being challenged in a fast-growing body of literature within social psychology (e.g., Smith, Giles, and Hewstone 1980; Giles, Hewstone, and St. Clair in press; Giles 1979b). The social psychologists argue that sociolinguistics should not limit itself to viewing speech as simply a reflection of large-scale sociological categories (Smith, Giles, and Hewstone 1980, p. 287). They suggest that we build a more expensive, integrated model which will combine sociolinguistic variables with social psychological variables (see, for example, Giles, Hewstone, and St. Clair in press, Fig. 3, and Smith, Giles, and Hewstone 1980, p. 297 for proposed schematizations). They argue that we must consider such social psychological aspects as the interlocutors' motives, feelings, and values, as well as their perceptions of each other, and of the interaction in general, in order to fully understand how and why people use and respond to language the way they do.[2]

In the social psychology field, much of the theoretical work on language has been conducted within the framework of Accommodation Theory. Developed primarily by Howard Giles, this theory attempts to explain interactional socio-linguistic variation (Giles 1977, Giles and Powesland 1975, Giles and Smith 1979). As such, Accommodation Theory is potentially valuable and applicable to social variation data in second languages. It seems to have an explanatory power for sociolinguistic phenomena such as style shifting in L2 dialects, which is not to date found in SLA models.

In this paper, we will apply Accommodation Theory to L2 data to test out what it has to offer in the analysis of second language dialects. Our goals are (1) to introduce Accommodation Theory to SLA researchers who are not familiar with it, (2) to review the empirical studies of accommodation, (3) to test out Accommodation Theory on our data, and (4) to demonstrate the value of applying it to second language dialect data. An outline and discussion of SLA models will be given first in order to point up the need for expanding SLA schemas to account for sociolinguistic variation.

## MODELS OF SECOND LANGUAGE ACQUISITION

In this section we shall review five hypotheses or models of second language acquisition and attempt to show that although each one is a major contribution to the field of SLA, none explains performance that varies according to social and psychological factors. It should be emphasized that such was not the purpose of those who developed the models. It is not our intention to criticize what has been done but rather to point up the need for expansion and suggest a possible avenue for it. Sociolinguistic variation should not be ignored as researchers work toward building a theory of SLA.

The creative construction hypothesis (Dulay and Burt 1974, 1975, 1978) applies to first or second language acquisition. Creative construction refers to:

the process by which learners gradually reconstruct rules for speech they hear, guided by innate mechanisms which cause them to formulate certain types of hypotheses about the language system being acquired, until the mismatch between what they are exposed to and what they produce is resolved

(Dulay and Burt 1978, p.57).

Burt and Dulay see SLA as a gradual cognitive reformulation of linguistic hypotheses evidenced by a gradual shift in the speech learners produce. Their notion of creativity is as valid for L2 data as Chomsky (1965) claimed it to be for L1. Beebe (1980) demonstrated that Thai subjects used ten different phonetic variants for the English initial /r/, six of which were creations that did not exist in those same environments in Thai, English, or any other language they could speak. Flege (1980), Dickerson and Dickerson (1977), Johansson (1973), and Nemser (1971) have also provided data indicating L2 creativity. Thus, second language learners (like first language learners) say things they have never heard before. But a problem arises in applying the notion of hypothesis formulation and revision to social variation in speech. Aside from the fact (which Burt and Dulay acknowledge) that adult second language learners seldom achieve a perfect match between their output and the TL they hear, we find that we can infer conflicting hypotheses when looking at the systematic variation in a learner's output. Of course, some of the variation is due to slips of the tongue (performance errors), and conflicting forms occur when speakers "appeal to authority," using two forms alternatively in hopes of eliciting a native speaker judgment on which is correct (Tarone 1977). Still, there is a great deal of variation that is systematic if one looks at a whole pattern of speech. For example, Beebe (1980) demonstrated systematic style shifting in the choice of pronunciation of initial /r/ in the L2 English of Thais. One could claim that different L2 speakers had different hypotheses about which variant was appropriate to which style. But such an explanation is inadequate, because a given speaker, in several identical circumstances, appears to have judged more than one variant appropriate. We cannot attribute the variation simply to lack of motor control because it is a much too systematic variation. On the other hand, if we attribute all forms that are not performance errors to learner hypotheses, we emerge with a view of the learner as terribly confused—full of conflicting hypotheses.

The model Dulay and Burt propose for SLA suggests that L2 speech is a result of the learner's personality and native language in conjunction with three cognitive processes (the socioaffective filter, the cognitive organizer, and the Monitor) working on linguistic input. Personality and native language are self-explanatory. The cognitive organizer is the "internal data processing mechanism" used in constructing grammar. It is responsible for the types of systematic errors made and the order of acquisition of structures (Dulay and Burt 1978, p. 69). The Monitor is the conscious editing of one's speech on the basis of a formally learned rule. The socioaffective filter is of major concern here because it would be the mechanism responsible for sociolinguistic variation. Yet Dulay and Burt define the socioaffective filter as the:

conscious or unconscious motives or needs, attitudes or emotional states of the learner. As the term suggests, these filter the input and affect the rate and quality of language acquisition. Among other things, the socioaffective filter contributes to (a) individual preferences for certain input models over others; (b) prioritizing aspects of language to be learned; and (c) determining when language acquisition efforts should cease

(1978, p. 68).

The concept of the socioaffective filter is an appealing one, and it accounts for a great deal of research (e.g., Gardner and Lambert 1972; Gardner 1979; Taylor, Meynard, and Rheault 1977) which demonstrates the central role that attitudes and motivation play in determining the success of one's attempt at second language acquisition. It seems, however, that the socioaffective concept should be extended to include a filter determining the variable choice of *output*. To date, we understand it primarily as a filter limiting the linguistic input that will become intake (i.e., the input that can be used for acquisition). Since there is a large amount of social variation and dialect code switching in second language speech, there must also be a mechanism for allowing the learner to take in alternative (socially marked) forms of the same sound or structure and for socioaffectively filtering the one that seems appropriate as output in a given social situation. Thus the notion of the filter would be useful in accounting for L2 social dialect data if it were extended to output.

The interlanguage hypothesis (Selinker 1972) is consistent with the creative construction hypothesis. Basically, Selinker sees SLA as a gradual move from the native language toward the target language by means of a series of "interlanguages," variously called "transitional dialects" (Corder 1971) and "approximative systems" (Nemser 1971). Corder (1971) emphasizes that an interlanguage (IL) is an idiosyncratic dialect which is systematic (has its own rules), unstable (changing), and creative (has newly created variants, not just borrowings from other languages or dialects). While Corder acknowledges that a speaker's repertoire is subject to sociolinguistic variation, he argues that the interlanguage continuum is largely *developmental,* "characterized by increasing complexity toward some particular target in the case of a language learner" (1977, p. 16). We do not question the developmental aspects of interlanguage but would argue that both types of variation (i.e., sociolinguistic and developmental) occur simultaneously in L2 speech, and to call the interlanguage continuum a *developmental* continuum is to ignore a second very important source of L2 variation. In addition, these phenomena merit attention: (1) the variable nature of both the NL and the TL, and (2) the systematic variability *across* learners in the IL. Furthermore, much of the apparent instability *within* learners' speech can be attributed to systematic, but socially conditioned, choice of forms from a multitude of social dialects, not just one target language or target social dialect. We are arguing that the sources (NL and TL) are both varied; thus we cannot explain our data on social dialect shifting in terms of "*the* target dialect" (Corder 1971 in Richards 1974, p. 165; emphasis ours). The interlanguage continuum that Corder (1977, p. 16) describes as basically developmental is, we would argue, simultaneously both developmental *and* sociolectal. And in addition, the interlanguage continuum might be more appropriately schematized as *multiple* continua spanning NL social dialects and TL social dialects.

The interlanguage hypothesis must also be expanded to predict relative influence of NL and TL. From a developmental perspective, Taylor (1975) demonstrated that NL has more influence in early stages of SLA than in later ones. But there are important sociolinguistic factors influencing the process as well. For example, Beebe (1980) showed that there is systematic, socially determined fluctuation in the extent to which the NL versus the TL is adopted as the superordinate rule system. The interlanguage diagram (Corder 1971, p. 103) in Figure 1 might be expanded to reflect this as well as the already-mentioned variation within NL and TL. Another point regarding the diagram is that it says that IL does not belong to either NL or TL. Although it is not native speech, even an elementary ESL learner's interlanguage is clearly a variety of English, not a variety of the NL. The problem, as Corder (1971) acknowledges, is that there is not always a clear division between an interlanguage and a social dialect of a TL. Examples frequently cited in the literature are Puerto Rican English (e.g., Wolfram 1974, Anisman 1975) or Chinese-American English. Assigning IL to its own position equidistant between NL and TL seems more arbitrary than realistic.

The Monitor Model (Krashen 1977) is one of the most prominent models of SLA. Fundamental to this model is the distinction between natural, subconscious language "acquisition" that occurs primarily in informal settings and formal, conscious "learning" of explicit linguistic rules that occurs primarily in classroom settings. It is an important empirical question whether the kind of adaptive language behavior reported later in this paper can be "learned" rather than "acquired." In the studies we shall discuss, the linguistic switching behavior is assumed to have been acquired because we know that it was never formally taught. But regardless of whether we consider it learning or acquisition, the Monitor Model does not, as conceptualized, predict socially determined variation in an L2 speaker's performance. This model is basically a model of the *internalization* of L2 by the learner, rather than the learner's output process. Not surprisingly, there has been very little research to date which specifically applies the Monitor Model to sociolinguistic data. Several researchers, though, refer to monitoring as one possible factor in variation. Tarone (1979), for example, discussed monitoring (i.e., attention paid to speech) as a factor in sociolinguistic variation in second language speech, and Beebe (1980) showed that monitoring (i.e., editing with a formal, consciously learned rule) from the NL produced a style shift among Asian adult ESL speakers in English, the target language. But the Monitor Model does not attempt to explain (1) a speaker's variable performance with different interlocu-

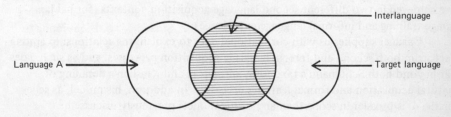

**FIGURE 1**    A Schematization of Interlanguage*

*Corder 1971, p. 103.

199

tors when the settings and tasks are controlled, as our data will show, and (2) the aspects of L2 speech which are most subject to sociolinguistic variation. In short, the model in its current form is not designed to explain socially variable output.

The Acculturation Model of SLA (Schumann 1978a, 1978b) more closely approximates a sociolinguistic model than other models of SLA because it discusses social factors that affect language acquisition. The model asserts that there is one primary causal variable in second language acquisition and that that variable is composed of social factors and affective factors. Schumann calls the variable "acculturation," which, applied to L2 learners, refers to their psychological and social relationship to the target language group. The greater the learner's integration with the TL group, the more successful her/his acquisition of the TL (Schumann 1978, p. 29). While Schumann acknowledges that there are other factors (e.g., personality, cognitive, biological, aptitude, input, and instructional) which also affect acquisition, he claims that acculturation is the major causal variable in second language acquisition.

Despite the importance of socioaffective factors in the Acculturation Model, it is not a sociolinguistic model in the traditional sense of being primarily directed at explaining dialect switching, choice of social dialect, or variation within a second language learner's dialect. It is aimed, rather, at accounting for differential levels of success, across learners, in acquiring a standard version of the target language. The relationship central to the model is that between the L2 learner and the TL group; while this relationship, and the social and psychological factors affecting it, are obviously important, confining the model to the L2 learner's distance/ proximity vis-à-vis the TL group only enables us to predict the learner's eventual, general level of L2 success. It does not help us in explaining the dynamics of an individual's second language speech within each interactional situation. It accounts for differential levels of success ( i.e., variation across learners) in second language acquisition but does not explain any type of variation within each learner's speech.

Gardner (1979) proposes a social psychological model of second language acquisition which is derived, in part, from his and Lambert's earlier work (Lambert 1963; Gardner and Lambert 1972) (see Figure 2). He claims that social milieu (i.e., cultural beliefs) determines the relative importance of individual differences [intelligence, language aptitude, motivation, and situational (e.g., classroom anxiety)] , which in turn influence the degree to which possible outcomes in SLA are achieved in two different second language acquisition contexts (formal language training and informal language experience).

Gardner supplies us with correlational data to explain the relationship among factors in both second and foreign language acquisition processes, and as such, goes far beyond both Schumann's taxonomy of factors and Krashen's detailing of natural acquisition and formal learning processes. In addition, his model, as schematized, is broader in scope than any of the models previously discussed.[3]

Gardner's social psychological model, however, posits outcomes which are static in the same sense as Schumann's. That is, the outcomes in his model represent the ultimate level of competence that learners reach in their second language

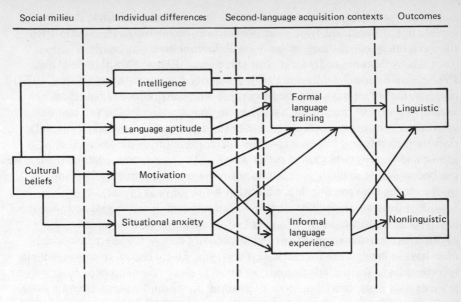

| Social milieu | Individual differences | Second-language acquisition contexts | Outcomes |

**FIGURE 2**   Gardner's Model of Second Language Acquisition*

*Gardner 1979, p. 196.

acquisition. The model does not attend to factors affecting the dynamics of an individual's variable performance at any one point in time. In sum, this model, as well as the others discussed in this section, is aimed at accounting for factors affecting L2 *acquisition,* rather than use.

## ACCOMMODATION THEORY

According to Accommodation Theory, people adjust their speech in order to express their values and intentions to their interlocutors (Giles, Bourhis, and Taylor 1977, p. 322). If speaker X, for example, wants to win speaker Y's approval, speaker X will sample Y's speech, and from it infer Y's personality characteristics and values. Assuming that Y approves of these characteristics, X (largely unconsciously) chooses from her/his repertoire aspects of speech to project Y's characteristics (Giles and Powesland 1975, p. 158). The alteration is labeled a style shift. Shifts occur in both multilingual and monolingual settings; person x can shift from one language to another, or x can, within one language, make changes with regard to accent, speech rate and amount, pauses, etc. The general adjustment of a speaker's speech style in reaction to an interlocutor's speech style is called "accommodation." Accommodation represents a psychological phenomenon. A speaker's style shifting toward the interlocutor is termed "convergence," while a shift away (to maintain or assert distinctiveness) is called "divergence." "Convergence" and "divergence," as employed by the theory, are descriptive sociolinguistic labels for the style shifts (Giles and Smith 1979, p. 53).

Accommodation Theory encompasses four social psychological theories as explanations for style shifts: similarity-attraction, social exchange, causal attribution, and intergroup distinctiveness. We will describe each one briefly. They are discussed by Giles in greater length elsewhere (e.g., Giles and Smith 1979; Giles 1977; Giles, Bourhis, and Taylor 1977). Similarity-attraction theory (Bishop 1979) suggests that we are more attracted to people whose attitudes and beliefs are similar to ours. For example, in a study asking middle-class subjects to rate the speech and personality of perceived middle- and lower-class speakers, the middle-class subjects rated middle-class speakers higher overall than the lower-class speakers (Ryan and Sebastian in press). Relating this to Accommodation Theory, we can become more similar to our interlocutors (in our desire to gain their approval) by converging our speech style toward what we perceive as theirs.

But there are trade-offs which are often involved in convergent acts. According to social exchange theory (Homans 1961), we weigh both rewards and costs of different alternatives prior to acting. We usually choose the alternative which promises the greatest reward and lowest cost. If speakers choose to converge their speech styles to their interlocutors, they do so because of anticipated higher rewards than costs. In a job interview situation, for example, prospective employees could be expected to converge their speech toward that of their interviewers, rather than vice versa.

The third theory subsumed under Accommodation Theory is causal attribution (Kelly 1967, Jones and Davis 1965). According to causal attribution, we perceive and evaluate other people's behavior in terms of what we think their motives are, or what we know about the causes of their behavior. We don't automatically conclude, for example, that a man who stays in his office until midnight every night is hard-working. We first attempt to attribute a motive for his behavior. Once we think we know the motive, we evaluate him as reclusive, ambitious, unhappily married, or alcoholic.

The fourth theory, intergroup distinctiveness, was formulated by Tajfel (1974, 1978). This theory says that when people interact who are members of different groups, they make social comparisons across groups. Their social identity as a group member, for example, is maintained insofar as they are able to retain a distinctiveness from their ethnically different interlocutor. This can be expressed via mode of dress, type of hairstyle, and food preference as well as through language divergence away from the interlocutor.

Theoretically, any number of these four can be operating simultaneously to cause variation in a speaker's language and to provide explanations for the occurrence of speech convergence or divergence. The majority of research studies conducted to empirically test Accommodation Theory have been undertaken by Giles himself, and date from the mid 1970s; his most frequent collaborator is Richard Bourhis, another social psychologist. A review of some of the empirical studies will provide the reader with an idea of the nature and scope of the authors' interests.

## REVIEW OF SOME SOCIAL PSYCHOLOGICAL
## STUDIES ON SPEECH ACCOMMODATION

There are two basic types of empirical studies on accommodation. One entails having subjects evaluate taped speech samples, usually by means of a written questionnaire. In the other type of study, subjects actually become participants in the interaction, and it is their speech as interlocutors which is analyzed.

In the first type, the communicative context of the taped speech samples is explained to the subjects. The tapes contain diverging and/or converging speech, occurring within a single language, or through a choice of languages. Doise, Sinclair, and Bourhis (1976) hypothesized that cooperative behavior would likely lead to convergence in accent. On the other hand, competitive situations in which we would expect divergence of behavior might lead to accentual divergence. Consequently, the researchers hypothesized that both of these behavior and accent combinations would be viewed by subjects as the norm. Testing this by asking subjects to evaluate taped conversations between ethnolinguistically different interlocutors, they found support for their hypotheses. Where the nonlinguistic behavior (i.e., either competitive or cooperative) matched the hypothesized linguistic behavior (i.e., either accentual divergence or convergence), subjects evaluated the conversation as natural.

Bourhis and Genesee (1980) asked English and French Canadian subject groups to evaluate a recorded conversation between a French Canadian salesman and English Canadian customer. In each tape version, they varied the languages used by the interlocutors. The evaluations, they discovered, were not always the most favorable when one interlocutor was heard to converge toward the other. The subjects rated the French Canadian salesman lower when he maintained French (i.e., failed to converge). But, they *didn't* rate the English Canadian customer higher when he converged to the salesman's French. The authors suggest that the use of English, at least in the role of store customer, may be more acceptable even to French Canadian subjects, regardless of whether it reflects divergence or convergence. This is possibly why the customer's convergence to the salesman's language didn't enhance subjects' evaluation of him. The explanation corresponds to what Lambert et al. (1960) reported earlier—both English and French Canadian subjects evaluated a French guise less favorably, on most traits, than an English guise. Scotton (1980, p. 364), in referring to a 1980 replication of the Bourhis and Genesee study, offers an additional explanation: in this particular type of interaction, the salesman is aware that his customer is English Canadian. It is important for him to please the customer in order to make a sale. Because of what Scotton terms the "gains maxim" (reminiscent of social exchange theory discussed earlier), it is in the salesman's best interest to converge toward the customer's speech. Hence, the salesman would be expected to switch to English, and therefore carry out the anticipated sale in the customer's language. Giles (personal communication) indicates that the results of Bourhis and Genesee's studies do in fact support accommodation principles.

Convergence and divergence can be both "upward" and "downward" when interlocutors represent two different statuses. A speaker of a lower-status dialect or language converging to a higher-status listener would be exhibiting upward convergence. If, on the other hand, the higher-status interlocutor converges linguistically toward the lower-status speaker, that would exemplify downward convergence. Downward divergence occurs, theoretically, when the lower-status interlocutor maintains or emphasizes his/her speech style; if the higher-status interlocutor linguistically emphasizes his/her speech style, that would be upward divergence. Bourhis, Giles, and Lambert (1975) tested subjects' reactions to both downward and upward convergence and divergence. The results indicated that the subjects were particularly successful in perceiving upward convergence, and evaluated the upward converger as being higher in perceived intelligence. This is not surprising, inasmuch as we normally converge our speech styles to our interlocutors as a means of gaining their social approval. Downward divergence was perceived less accurately, however. The authors suggest that this could be because their subjects weren't used to this type of shift within the particular taped conversational setting used. Or perhaps people in general are not used to experiencing downward divergence.

As previously mentioned, there are several studies specifically testing Accommodation Theory which have the subjects participate in the interaction. Instead of asking the subjects what their reactions are, the subjects' actual verbal behavior is analyzed. Simard, Taylor, and Giles (1976) hypothesized that accommodation (convergence) would not always be favorably received, nor would it necessarily lead to reciprocal accommodation. The hypothesis is similar to that in Bourhis and Genesee (1980), but the subjects in the 1976 study became interlocutors. What appeared from the results was that the French Canadian subjects frequently spoke English (i.e., accommodated) to an English Canadian interlocutor when they knew he had volunteered previously to accommodate in French; when he did not accommodate to them, the subjects made a distinction between nonaccommodation due to a lack of effort and nonaccommodation due to a lack of language ability. They responded more favorably to the latter.

Flemish subjects in a study by Bourhis, Giles, Leyens, and Tajfel (1979) were asked to respond in English to a Francophone speaker. It was hypothesized that when a member of an ethnolinguistic group was addressed in a threatening way by an outgroup speaker, linguistic divergence would occur. The results showed that the implicitness or explicitness of intergroup categorization made a difference. That is, when intergroup distinctions were implicit (i.e., not specifically mentioned), the subjects did not diverge into their own language (Flemish). When the categorization was explicit, however, and when it was clear that the Francophone speaker considered Flemish ethnolinguistic aims illegitimate, 50 percent of the subjects diverged from English into Flemish.

Bourhis and Giles (1977) also asked subjects to interact with speakers of a different ethnolinguistic group. The ethnically Welsh subjects responded to an RP-accented Englishman. All subjects were L1 English speakers and were learning Welsh as L2. It was hypothesized that the type of motivation the subjects had for learning Welsh (integrative or instrumental) would affect their linguistic response to the RP speaker. The results bore this out; the instrumentally motivated group tended to reduce the <u>accent</u> differences between themselves and the speaker (i.e., converged), while the integratively motivated group emphasized group differences and diverged accentually by increasing the Welsh <u>accent</u> in their English. However, as in Bourhis, Giles, Leyens, and Tajfel (1979), divergence tended to occur only if intergroup categorization was explicit and the subjects' group identity was being threatened. When intergroup distinctions were only implicit, divergence did not occur. As this and the previous studies show, convergence and divergence have complex causes and responses.

An interesting set of studies recently conducted focused on status differences between interlocutors. Thakerar, Giles, and Cheshire (in press) taped conversations between British nurses of unequal status (similar to LPN's versus RN's in the United States). Asking linguistically native raters to judge the speech samples, they found that the high-status (HS) interlocutor was judged to *decrease her* speech rate as well as become *less* standard in accent, while the low-status (LS) interlocutor *increased* her speech rate and became *more* standard in accent. In addition, a phonological analysis (not normally found in other social psychology studies of language) was conducted by the researchers (on /ʔ/ versus /t/). The results confirmed the raters' subjective judgments of variation in standard features. That is, the HS interlocutor produced a higher proportion of the nonstandard variant /ʔ/, while the LS interlocutor's speech contained more /t/ (i.e., standard) variants.

The interlocutors' speech diverged linguistically, yet Thakerar, Giles, and Cheshire concluded, through further investigation of the interactions, that the interlocutors were psychologically *converging*. To resolve this apparent contradiction, the researchers suggest that the interlocutors

> may not only have been converging psychologically towards their partners but may also have been attempting to converge linguistically to what they *believed* the speech of the other to be. That is, the lower status speaker increased her speech rate and standardized her accent to comply with the speech stereotype associated with a higher status speaker whereas the higher status speaker decreased her speech rate and became less standard accented so as to comply with the speech stereotype associated with the lower status partner
>
> (Thakerar, Giles, and Cheshire in press, pp. 37-38).

It is therefore theoretically possible for apparent divergence on a linguistic level of analysis to actually represent convergence (on a psychological level).

The empirical evidence collected thus far suggests that convergence and divergence can occur through a variety of linguistic means. Language choice can represent convergence or divergence, as can accent, speech rate, choice of dialect, etc., within the same language. More evidence needs to be gathered on the various linguistic means which are used to express convergence and divergence in general. In addition, Accommodation Theory must be tested out not only in L1 and fluent L2 settings but specifically on SLA data if we are to be certain of its applicability to the acquisition process. What follows is an attempt in this direction.

# THE APPLICATION OF ACCOMMODATION THEORY TO L2 VARIATION

Some of the data to be analyzed in this paper come from a study of third grade Puerto Rican children who were enrolled in either the bilingual program or the monolingual program of an elementary school on the edge of New York City. The subjects were equally divided between the two programs. All were from blue collar and welfare families. Each subject was interviewed in English three times, each time by a different interviewer. The interviewers, close in age, were all middle-class women born in the United States, and had the same amount of education. One interviewer was a monolingual, native English-speaking Anglo (MI); one was an English-dominant Hispanic (EDI); the third was a Spanish-dominant Hispanic (SDI). MI spoke Standard English, and so did EDI. EDI's English contained no noticeable Spanish characteristics, whereas SDI's did. The interviews were conducted in a constant setting (the school), and the topics on which the subjects were questioned were carefully controlled across interviews for close similarity in number, order, and content, without exact repetition.

Table 1 contains data representing the relative amounts of talk between subjects and interviewers. Amount of talk was measured in "T-units," using

**Table 1** Accommodation in Amount of Talk, Number of T-Units with Control for Number of Questions, Number of Units, and Content of Questions

| | Interviewer | | | | | |
| | MI | | EDI | | SDI | |
| Subjects | Subj. | Int. | Subj. | Int. | Subj. | Int. |
|---|---|---|---|---|---|---|
| Monolingual program | | | | | | |
|   Girls | 509 | 535 | 331 | 387 | 385 | 461 |
|   Boys | 608 | 678 | 346 | 314 | 249 | 283 |
|   Total | 1,117 | 1,213 | 677 | 701 | 634 | 744 |
| Bilingual program | | | | | | |
|   Girls | 505 | 581 | 388 | 407 | 168 | 148 |
|   Boys | 457 | 512 | 294 | 311 | 388 | 402 |
|   Total | 962 | 1,093 | 682 | 718 | 556 | 550 |
| All subjects | | | | | | |
|   Total | 2,079 | 2,036 | 1,359 | 1,419 | 1,190 | 1,294 |
| | $r = .76$ | | $r = .37$ | | $r = .63$ | |
| | $(n = 17)$* | | $(n = 19)$ | | $(n = 13)$† | |

*Two subjects were eliminated because they talked a great deal more than any of the other subjects or interviewers. What seemed to occur, especially with one of the subjects, is that the talk became a monologue rather than a conversation. When $n = 19$ (the full sample), $r = .315$. We feel that the enormous correlational difference justifies making $n = 17$. (For a discussion of the advisability of removing extreme scores, see Blalock 1960, p. 289.) As the scores with EDI for the two subjects eliminated with MI were closer to those of the other subjects, we did not remove them from the EDI column. They were among those not destroyed with SDI (see below).

†Unfortunately, because of an accident, some of the data were destroyed, and we were left with complete data for only 13 subjects with SDI.

Loban's (1976) definition of the oral "communication unit." Subjects are shown by program and sex, and as a whole group, with each interviewer. The correlations between amount of subject talk and interviewer talk are positive for each interview column, and are particularly high (.76 and .63) with the monolingual interviewer (MI) and the Spanish-dominant interviewer (SDI). We see, then, that despite interview controls, the amount of actual talk by subjects approximated that of the interviewers, and vice versa. This was true of both monolingual and bilingual program subjects. The more the interviewer talked, the more the subject talked; the less the subject spoke, the less the interviewer spoke. It represents convergence in speech quantity. Evidently, speech quantity reflects the degree to which one interlocutor accommodated to the other.

It is impossible to determine from these data why the subject-EDI correlation is weaker than the others (.37). But we might speculate that there was less convergence toward the English-dominant interviewer because the subjects do not identify with her to the same extent as they identify with MI and SDI. At first we might think that EDI would seem the perfect role model for children living in a bilingual community. After all, EDI is an educated Spanish speaker who has acquired the necessary tool (Standard English) for easy acculturation and the psychological and material benefits it often brings. But it may be quite wrong to assume that the children would identify most with her. Their linguistic convergence toward MI and SDI would certainly suggest that EDI is not the role model one might expect. And this, upon deeper reflection, makes perfect sense. SDI, rather than EDI, is most like the children in this sample. She lives in a Hispanic neighborhood (as they do) and travels back and forth between the United States and Puerto Rico (as they do). According to her own statement, she would go to Puerto Rico any chance she got. The children expressed the same preference in postinterview conversations. When asked where they would go if they had the money to travel anywhere in the world, they answered (almost to the last individual) that they, too, would go to Puerto Rico. Of all three interviewers, SDI seems subjectively to be most like the children's parents and the adults they know in their communities in terms of feelings of ethnic identity and language. The children's teacher in the bilingual program, also on subjective impression, is between SDI and EDI in terms of acculturation, but it is important to note that her English is accented like SDI's and she, like SDI, seems more comfortable in Spanish than in English. The children may have identified SDI with her. In sum, the children are very familiar with people like SDI, but EDI is not typical of the people they know. It is impossible to say, based on the data here, whether the children would aspire to being like EDI. In fact, if they wish to completely assimilate into the target culture, they will have to take the path EDI has taken. But that does not mean that they will necessarily use her as a role model or aspire to be like her. The children may view EDI as a "cultural traitor," and look instead to MI as a model for their linguistic (and possibly cultural) aspirations, because MI represents no ethnic threat (Giles, personal communication). The part of them that wants to assert their distinctive *ethnicity* would probably look to SDI (not

EDI) as a model. SDI has a noticeable Hispanic accent in her L2 English, while EDI has none. There is evidence that people prefer their own ethnic group members to maintain a distinctive accent in L2; they are viewed *less* positively if they speak L2 without a discernible accent (Segalowitz and Gatbonton 1977). If this reasoning is sound, it is not surprising that we can interpret high levels of solidarity, and therefore convergence, toward MI and SDI, but with EDI there may be no such feelings of identification, and the level of convergence is consequently much lower. Their conflict between acculturation, on the one hand, and maintenance of their ethnic identity, on the other, may show up in their speech, causing them to be most Hispanic with SDI, and least Hispanic with MI.

A second list of evidence from the Puerto Rican data is still incomplete, but it is so closely related that findings to date are reported. We found when we looked at the data that the subjects as a whole used a higher absolute number of dependent clauses with MI than with EDI. They used 333 with MI, but only 187 with EDI. Here again, they seemed to be converging more clearly toward MI than EDI, insofar as the greater use of dependent clauses may indicate attempted accommodation to an expected or perceived level of syntactic complexity. Since work for this part of the project is still in progress, we do not yet know whether MI herself actually used more dependent clauses than EDI. And, as Thakerar, Giles, and Cheshire (in press) point out, the interviewers' actual speech might not be the crucial variable here. The subjects may instead be converging toward the *expected* speech of their interviewer. A great amount of additional analysis is needed to determine the import of these data. First, further study of interviewer speech will be needed to show whether this accommodation was technically (i.e., linguistically) convergence or divergence. If the interviewers did not differ in their use of dependent clauses, for example, yet the subjects used many more with MI than with EDI, we might say that the subjects were converging toward MI but diverging away from EDI. Second, the cause of these shifts must be analyzed. It would be of interest to know whether the large difference in number of dependent clauses used by subjects with MI is a function of sustained effort toward this type of complexity with MI, or whether it might be attributed to lack of effort with EDI. It could be a function of "foreigner talk discourse" (see, for example, Long 1981). MI, as a monolingual native speaker of English, might be exhibiting more characteristics of foreigner talk discourse in her speech than EDI does. To her, the subjects she interviews are (at least ethnically) foreign. This is not the case with EDI. EDI's interviews are not clearly native speaker–nonnative speaker interactions. The speech input would then differ within the interaction, giving us cause to expect differential output from the subjects. Other studies of these same subjects have shown additional differences in speech behavior between interviewers. Though Beebe (in press 1980) has found that the accuracy (i.e., number of correct T-units) of these subjects was significantly higher with EDI than with MI, risk taking and syntactic complexity were significantly higher with MI, which may explain the lower accuracy scores with MI. Only a complete analysis of the interviewers' speech (forthcoming) can give us a definite answer as to whether this apparent accommodation to MI (i.e., the known shifting) is attempted convergence or divergence. Preliminary evidence suggests that it is convergence.

The next set of data that we will discuss were elicited in a study of 61 Chinese-Thai children in Thailand. The subjects were 9 to 10 years old and were fluent in Teochiu Chinese (called Swatow), which was their first language, as well as in Thai, their second language. Each subject was interviewed twice in Thai—once by an ethnic Thai interviewer and once by an ethnic Chinese interviewer. The contrast and similarities between the interviewers in this study were like that of MI and EDI in the study we have just discussed: (1) both were middle-class women of the same age, (2) the ethnic Chinese looked recognizably Chinese and was bilingual in Swatow and Thai but spoke Standard Bangkok Thai with no Swatow characteristics, and (3) the Thai interviewer looked ethnically Thai and spoke only a native, standard dialect of Thai. As in the Puerto Rican study, the interviews were conducted in school and were controlled for topic, order and number of questions, and content. Analysis of these data has focused on phonological variables,[4] which are listed in Table 2.

The data shown in this table indicate that the Chinese-Thai subjects used a Thai variant for each of six phonological variables a higher percentage of the time when they were interviewed by the monolingual ethnic Thai than when they were interviewed by the ethnic Chinese. The differences were statistically significant in the case of /a/, which is the only variable with a Thai variant corresponding directly to the same sound in Swatow . With the five other variables, there is no exact correspondence between Thai and Swatow. They were acquired by the subjects as part of their acquisition of Thai as a second language. We cannot ascribe the statis-

**Table 2**   Percentage of Thai Variants* Used by 61 Bilingual Chinese-Thai Subjects with Thai and Chinese Interviewers

| | Interviewer | | Statistical |
| Variant | Thai | Chinese | significance |
| --- | --- | --- | --- |
| [uu]† for /uu/‡ | 47 | 35 | $p < .01$ |
| [ɛɛ] for /ɛɛ/ | 42 | 31 | $p < .001$ |
| [ɔɔ] for /ɔɔ/ | 30 | 23 | $p < .01$ |
| [o] for /o/ | 61 | 48 | $p < .001$ |
| [aa] for /aa/ | 65 | 61 | $p < .02$ |
| [a] for /a/ | 92 | 91 | $ns$ |

*"Thai variant" refers to the vowel quality considered correct in Standard Bangkok Thai.

†[ ] denotes the actual phonetic variant heard on tape.

‡/ / denotes the phonological variable.

[uu]:  $t_{60} = 3.16$ (SD = .295)
[ɛɛ]:  $t_{60} = 3.84$ (SD = .246)
[ɔɔ]:  $t_{60} = 3.04$ (SD = .194)
[o]:  $t_{60} = 3.91$ (SD = .265)
[aa]:  $t_{60} = 2.56$ (SD = .139)

tically significant differences between interviewers to linguistic difficulty, since they are equally difficult when speaking to each interviewer. Nor can we argue that they were due to topic, interview length, or content differences, because these variables were controlled in the interviews. We would suggest instead that the Chinese-Thai subject increased the use of five variants with the Thai interviewer in an (unconscious) attempt "to modify or disguise his persona in order to make it more acceptable to the person addressed" (Giles and Powesland 1975, p. 158). For the Chinese-Thais, a kind of dual identity is common; most see themselves as both Chinese and Thai. The Chinese-Thai subjects projected themselves as Thai when speaking to the Thai interviewer. The five variants studied are part of the phonology of standard native Thai, and these variants became a linguistic means of accommodating to the Thai interviewer.

At the same time, the subjects' Thai contained some Chinese variants, particularly in speaking to the Chinese interviewer. Table 3 provides data on the percentage of two Chinese variants for final consonant variables. The two variants were acquired by the subjects as they acquired their first language (Swatow). The variants do exist in Thai as well, but not in the words that the subjects used them in. Thus, they are clear Chinese markers in Thai which, as the data indicate, were used significantly more often with the Chinese interviewer than with the Thai. It has been suggested that people who identify with a particular ethnic group exhibit at least minimal characteristics (linguistic and nonlinguistic) which they use to express their ethnic affiliations (Giles 1979a). The subjects are ethnically Chinese. Even though they spoke Thai (their L2) with the Chinese interviewer (and the interviewer herself didn't use the variants), they introduced Chinese phonological variants into their speech. The variants became ethnic markers of Chinese identity for the Chinese-Thai subjects. They were accommodating ethnically to the interviewer by adjusting their speech to sound more Chinese.

Table 3  Percentage of Chinese Variants for Final Consonant Variables Used by 61 Bilingual Chinese-Thai Subjects with Thai and Chinese Interviewers

|  | Interviewer | |
| --- | --- | --- |
| Variant | Thai | Chinese |
| [__ŋ] for /__n/* | 9.5 | 16.1 |
| [__k] for /__t/† | 5.8 | 10.7 |

$*t_{60} = 3.88; p < .001$ (SD = .129)

$†t_{60} = 3.77; p < .001$ (SD = .10)

## CONCLUSION

As discussed earlier, none of the present SLA models is aimed at accounting for sociolinguistic variation in second language data. The field of SLA does not have models which explain the convergence in Table 3, where amount of subject talk is positively correlated with amount of interviewer talk. The SLA models do not have a descriptive terminology, let alone an explanatory theory, for these performance data. A model such as Schumann's Acculturation Model would help us to understand why two groups of Chinese-Thais with equal opportunity to learn the Thai language might be differentially successful in doing so. But none of the models, including Schumann's, explains why Chinese-Thais are significantly more successful in approximating Standard Thai vocalic norms in the presence of a Thai interlocutor than in the presence of a Chinese interlocutor, and none of the models explains why different numbers of dependent clauses are used by the same speakers with different interlocutors. We are not dealing here with the social and psychological distance of an individual (or group) from the target culture, but with the social and psychological distance of an individual from an interlocutor at a particular situation. We are not focusing on the correlation of an indivudual's L2 proficiency to social and psychological distance from the *target culture* but on the dynamics of social and psychological distance between individual and *interlocutor*. We agree with Schumann that social and psychological distance from the target culture are the critical factors in second language acquisition, but we believe that in order to fully understand this, we must also study the ebb and flow of feelings of distance/proximity in one controlled situation. Thus, we examine variable performance data.

More than any other existing theory we are familiar with, Giles' Accommodation Theory could be used to analyze and account for the variable performance data we have gathered. As we see it, this theory could be used to extend Schumann's concept of a relatively fixed social and psychological distance/proximity between an individual and a target culture (at one point in time) to include the idea of fluctuating feelings of social and psychological distance/proximity between one individual and another (at one point in time). But whether or not the reader is convinced that Accommodation Theory is a natural and needed extension of Schumann's Acculturation Model, the fact is undeniable that Giles' theory is the only one discussed here that focuses on the factors affecting variable performance data. Accommodation Theory does account for the positive correlations between subject and interviewer talk. It accounts as well for the significantly different proportions of vowel and consonant variants in the speech of Chinese-Thais. The notion that Chinese-Thais might be unconciously trying to win approval by their chameleon-like behavior makes sense.

As discussed earlier, we found that the Chinese-Thai children used a greater proportion of Chinese-influenced variants when speaking Thai to the ethnic Chinese interviewer. The interviewer herself, as we pointed out, *didn't* use the variants in her speech. At first glance, it appears that the children are *diverging* away from the interviewer's speech. But Thakerar, Giles, and Cheshire (in press), in providing empirical evidence for distinguishing between psychological and linguistic levels of convergence and divergence, enable us to account theoretically for this seeming divergence. The Chinese-Thai children, while appearing to linguistically diverge away from their interviewer's actual speech characteristics, may in fact be *psychologically* converging toward their ethnic Chinese interviewer. As with

211

Thakerar et al.'s subjects, the speech might represent attempted convergence toward a *stereotype* of their interviewer's speech, rather than toward her actual speech. Thus, though the linguistic behavior is technically divergence, the psychological force underlying it may actually be convergence. The children may be asserting a sense of ethnic solidarity. Most likely their feelings of Chinese ethnic identity are heightened in the presence of an ethnic Chinese who looks Chinese no matter how perfectly Thai she sounds.

We would suggest a further elaboration of Accommodation Theory to account for different levels of linguistic analysis. Linguistic divergence may arise as a function of attempted convergence on some other deeper linguistic level. For example, Beebe (in press) demonstrates that the Puerto Rican children have somewhat lower accuracy on WH questions with MI than with SDI, but significantly higher syntactic complexity attempted in this situation. If we look at accuracy as a measure of convergence, knowing that MI's speech is accurate in WH structure, we have to say that the children diverged from MI. That is perfectly possible, but the finding is suspect in this case since the accuracy rates are most probably a function of the syntactic complexity attempted. We do not have an overall measure of syntactic complexity for either the interviewers or the subjects, but it is likely that subjects would unconsciously expect that, in terms of syntactic complexity, MI > EDI > SDI. It is surely true that both MI and EDI used greater syntactic complexity than SDI, who was not fully bilingual. It is quite possible that MI used syntactically more complex discourse than EDI; this is an empirical question that is as yet unanswered. Still, the hypothesis that children's perceptions (regarding syntactic complexity) were that MI > EDI > SDI is a good one. In addition, Beebe (in press) found that subjects had significantly lower accuracy but significantly higher rates of risk taking with MI than EDI. The lower accuracy is again technically divergence, but there clearly seems to be the motivation of convergence. If Accommodation Theory is elaborated to handle analyses of different linguistic levels of behavior, we feel it could better account for the data we have just discussed.

We conclude, nevertheless, that Accommodation Theory is at present the most effective theory available. It is directed at variable performance data, and it has explanatory power. Although the previous work of SLA model builders is a tremendous contribution to the field, it so far does not encompass sociolinguistically variable performance data. Sociolinguists such as Labov and ethnographers such as Hymes have made extremely impressive contributions, but their work, too, can be enhanced by the social psychological theory Giles proposes. Although sociolinguistic labels are good predictors of behavior, they have limitations as static categories which do not explain why we do what we do. Giles is justified in emphasizing that we need a dynamic model with a psychological dimension that provides explanatory power. When searching to explain our second language variation data, we see the need for SLA researchers to broaden their horizons. In the future, SLA researchers will have to extend their models to incorporate social psychological dynamics, or they will have to work on revising what Giles has already done if they are to account for variable performance data. We suggest both.

# NOTES

1. The authors are grateful to Howard Giles and Jitendra Thakerar for valuable comments on an earlier draft of this paper; in addition, the authors wish to thank Herbert Seliger, Miriam Eisenstein, Nathalie Bailey, Diana Berkowitz, and the other members of the Second Language Acquisition Circle of New York for their helpful suggestions. The research assistance of Maturot Ketsomboon, Porntip Ittatirut, Celsa Renta, Liz Rios, Irene Antipa, and Moira Chimombo is also greatfully acknowledged. This research assistance was sponsored first by the Ford Foundation in Bangkok, Thailand, and second by Teachers College, Columbia University, under a grant from the Spencer Foundation.

2. In the Giles et al. discussions, the contributions of sociolinguistic research are perhaps too rapidly brushed aside in favor of social psychology's contributions to language study (see Beebe and Zuengler 1981 for comments regarding this). This may, not surprisingly, reflect their disciplinary bias. Nevertheless, these social psychologist present a very cogent argument for the building of a more expansive model of language behavior in both L1 and L2. In fact, some attention has already been paid specifically to second language acquisition (see Giles and Byrne 1980, Hildebrandt and Giles 1980).

3. Gardner's model, while more comprehensive than the other SLA models, has nonetheless been criticized for not including the concept of ethnic identification. For a detailing of the criticism, see Giles and Byrne (1980, pp. 16-21).

4. The term "phonological variable" is borrowed from Labov (1966) to name a continuum itself, not any one phonetic realization. It has been adapted for describing continua in second language speech. For example, in this study, /ʉ/ may be represented by a continuum of sounds with varying degrees of sociolinguistic influence from native Swatow patterns, accepted Chinese-Thai norms, and recognized Standard Thai conventions.

# 13

## ROCKY HORROR PICTURE SHOW: A SPEECH EVENT IN THREE ACTS[1]

### Richard R. Day
*Department of English as a Second Language*
*University of Hawaii at Manoa*

Since reports of research into the social uses of language began to appear in the literature in the 1970s, there have been descriptions of conversational sequencing, joke telling, greetings, leave takings, directives, turn taking, and so on. These reports have been useful in expanding our knowledge of what language is and how it functions. Some investigations into speech events have also proved useful in teaching English to speakers of other languages (e.g., Sullivan 1979).

This paper seeks to extend our knowledge of language and its functions by examining a speech event which I call *audience participation at cult movies.*[2] This is a unique speech event in two respects. First, the audience is generally made up of adults who are fluent—know the rules governing the speech event—and those who are not. Second, most members of the audience share the same first language. Thus audience participation at cult movies is a speech event in which adult native speakers are placed in a situation which requires them to learn new rules if they are to attain fluency in the new speech event. Of interest is how similar this process is to adult second language learning. I attempt to show how the three speech acts which characterize this speech event make use of learning strategies which are used in adult second language learning: immediate mimicry and chanting, memorization and choral repetition, and creativity. Finally I demonstrate how formulaic expressions play a major role in this speech event, much as they do in other speech events. Before I examine these issues, it is necessary to discuss the concept of cult movies.

# CULT MOVIES

In American society there is a genre of movies often referred to as cult. There are many differences between cult movies and regular movies. A cult movie is not generally shown in the major movie theaters during regular movie hours but may be screened late at night, perhaps at midnight or later. Film societies on college campuses show cult movies. While some may be X-rated, pornography is not a necessary ingredient—compare *Pink Flamingo* with *Casablanca.*

Cult movies are often box office flops initially, and only when they achieve cult status do they begin to turn a profit. One general characteristic of many cult movies is that they have what the audience sees as antiestablishment themes (e.g., a young man in love with an older woman in *Harold and Maude*). It is difficult to predict if a certain movie will acquire cult status. That is, not all movies which are box office flops and which have antiestablishment themes become cult movies.

Another noticeable difference between a cult movie and a regular movie is the audience. The audience which attends a regular movie may be seen as a group of individuals—individuals who happen to find themselves together for the purpose of watching a movie. Generally the members of the audience at regular movies pay scant attention to each other, and they often show their displeasure at those who talk to each other during the movie by "shushing" or staring. They normally are seeing the movie for the first, and only, time.

The members of the audience at cult movies, on the other hand, form a community. They have come together to experience, to share, and to participate in an event. The cult movie is an event, an activity which is similar to a religious rite and other solidarity displays in which the basic goal is the establishment, maintenance, and celebration of a community. An in-group is formed which is exclusionary.

Attendance at a particular cult movie is not a one-time thing. Cult movies attract faithful followers who come time and time again. There is a report of an individual who claimed to have seen a particular cult movie over 100 times. Seeing a movie over and over again obviously implies that the members of the audience are not there for the plot. Most become familiar with the characters, the dialogue, the action, and so on. Before the movie begins there may be a great deal of activity and noise—laughing, singing, dancing, sharing of favorite lines and scenes. On college campuses, the small lecture halls in which the movies are screened help to create an atmosphere of intimacy, of a gathering of friends to experience and share a sacred event. Newcomers may be identified, and veterans often explain to them the intricacies of the movie, its values and its symbols. For some cult movies, the members of the audience dress up in costumes resembling their favorite characters, and parade around the theater, encouraged by the cheers and shouts of the other members of the audience. The most famous movie in this regard, and the focus of this paper, is *The Rocky Horror Picture Show*.

Another major difference between audiences at regular movies and at cult movies is the use of language. As noted above, the audience at regular movies dislikes and discourages talking by patrons during the movie. However, at cult movies, the audience does not remain silent during the movie. At *Rocky,* for example, the members of the audience speak the characters' lines along with them, shout and sing, and make comments and jokes about the characters and the action. The actions of the audience may be seen as a speech event where certain appropriate speech acts are used. Malinowski's notion of phatic communion is appropriate, since one of the primary functions of this speech event is to claim and display in-group membership and common ground. The use of language and the possible ways in which newcomers acquire competency in its use at *Rocky* form the remainder of this paper.

## THE SPEECH EVENT: THE ROCKY HORROR PICTURE SHOW

Using the audience at *Rocky* as a source of the corpus, the most noticeable first use of language is, to the newcomer, an apparently spontaneous shouting from the audience of "lips." This has no meaning whatsoever to the novitiate, but she is encouraged by the cult member acting as caretaker to go ahead and just shout "lips." This proves rather easy, and soon the novitiate is able to scream "lips." with the best of them. However, it still lacks meaning.

As the houselights dim and the movie begins, the shouting reaches the threshold of pain: "Lips, lips, lips!" This word is on everyone's lips. Then, a tiny image appears on the screen; as it gradually comes into focus and becomes larger and larger, the image acquires meaning—a gigantic pair of red lips! "Lips, lips, lips!" The sound and its meaning are merged. Understanding is reached. "Lips, lips, lips!"

However, as soon as this understanding is grasped, the novitiate discovers that the cult members have moved on, and are now shouting "Cheese, cheese, cheese!" This doesn't last long, for the novitiate quickly realizes that the lips appear to be speaking. It doesn't matter that the din in the theater is so loud that no one can hear the lips, for at this point, the cult members have begun to sing along with those gigantic red lips. The newcomer is unable to participate in this, unlike the first two situations, for she does not know the words. It is clear that this is a different situation. The first two involved immediate mimicry and chanting, utterances which we might label *imitation*—a subcategory of Searle's term, *representative* (1976). They are rather easy to perform, for all the learner has to do is pay attention and repeat (imitate) what the cult member/caretaker prompts.

Life at cult movies, as life elsewhere, is more than it appears to be. What looks like on the surface as a single speech act, imitation, as the cultists shout "lips" may also be viewed as another speech act, a *directive*. Shouting "lips" is the audience's way of directing the film projectionist to begin the movie. Of course there is no way for the novitiate to know this until she has been thoroughly indoctrinated into the speech event. The mouthing of "lips" may be construed, then, as two speech acts. The learner, however, is only aware of one of them at first, and learns the second by being immersed in the speech community.

Learning the lines sung by the gigantic pair of red lips takes somewhat more time and effort than learning to say "lips." There are several ways this could be accomplished. A novitiate could purchase a paperback which contains the dialogue (Henkin 1979), or she could buy the *Rocky* record and rehearse the lines by listening and repeating. Another way is to attend a *Rocky* party, usually held immediately before a screening. There the sound track is played numerous times, allowing everyone to speak the lines, sing the songs, and do the "Time Warp" dance. A fourth way to learn the dialogue would be to go to the movie over and over again, listening to a cult member, imitating the caretaker. The good language learner, of course, will undertake all four methods. Gradually, the newcomer can begin to mouth the words or hum the tune, and then later will reach the stage where she can proudly sing along with the lips and the other cult members. The learning strategy for this speech act of imitation, then, is memorization and choral repetition. I should note the similarity to community language learning, in particular, aside from the obvious parallels in this experience to classroom second language learning. In addition, the use of techniques similar to those in using drama in foreign language learning is apparent.

Meaning generally presents few problems, because the verbal behavior by the audience anticipates the action on the screen, allowing the meaning to become clear in short order. For example, shouts of "asshole" greet the appearance of one of the main characters, Brad. The newcomer joins in, shouting "asshole, asshole" and as Brad's character becomes immediately apparent, the label acquires meaning.

Note that a third type of speech act is involved in hollering "asshole," namely *comment* [or, in Searle's terminology, *expressive* (1976)]. As with the other two speech acts, imitation and directive, the learning strategy involved is immediate mimicry and chanting.

If the novitiate has a particularly understanding and protective caretaker, she can be guided through her first showing of *Rocky* with no traumatic experiences, allowing her to participate verbally to a great extent. The newcomer has to accept on faith that she must shout out the appropriate word or phrase when nudged and that it will be acceptable to do so. Meaning, as mentioned above, usually comes soon after, which further encourages the novitiate.

I have been able to identify only three types of speech acts—imitation (or representative), comment (or expressive), and directive. The speech event tightly constrains the type of speech acts which can occur within it. This event also demonstrates the applicability of Grice's four maxims of conversation: be relevant, informative, brief, and truthful. An irrelevant remark would be ignored, as would one which was not informative. A remark which was not brief would not be completed, as the action moves rapidly. The maxim to be truthful is also appropriate. For example, following a remark by Rocky Horror, the creature created by the movie's leading character, Frank N Furter (a sweet transvestite from Transexual Transylvania), that he is just seven hours old, a cultist may shout, "And can't dance!" This is true. If Rocky were a good dancer, like Frank N Furter, then that line would not be appropriate or funny. This notion of humor leads me to suggest that a fifth maxim be added to this speech event: Be witty. As I describe later in the paper, creative speech acts have to be witty or they will not be appreciated or recognized. This maxim is not only applicable to this speech event but may apply to other speech events such as jokes and conversation at cocktail parties and similar settings.

A great deal of the speech in these three acts involves one-word utterances (e.g., lips, asshole). In addition to one-word utterances, the neophyte can participate in the verbal action through the use of what may be termed *formulaic speech*— expressions which are standardized or fixed. For example, before the first appearance of the narrator, the newcomer is coaxed to shout, "Where's your neck?" While any speaker of English can recognize this as a wh-question, its significance may not be apparent to the neophyte. She rehearses it silently and gets prepared to shout it out when told to do so. The appropriate moment arrives, the narrator makes his first appearance on the screen to shouts of "Where's your neck?" and, of course, he has a rather small neck. Note that this is a speech act of comment, while superficially a question, but an unusual one in that it occurs before the act or state commented upon. A speech act which is a directive using formulaic speech occurs when Janet, another main character, enters a bedroom in the castle (where Frank N Furter is attempting to create Rocky). As Janet enters the bedroom, shouts from the audience of "Look out for the stand!" or "Why don't you bump into the vase?" are heard. And, as one can readily imagine, she bumps into the vase which is on a stand, much to the delight of the audience.

Like the line, "Where's your neck?" these shouts of "Why don't you bump into the vase?" are also formulaic speech. In addition, we see that there is variation in the speech behavior of the audience. The cultists are not restricted to shouting only "Why don't you bump into the vase?". There is a choice. But the choice is restricted to a limited set of appropriate comments or questions. By way of contrast, the speech acts which are labeled as imitation allow no variation. The cultists, if they are going to participate in this type of verbal behavior, must say or repeat certain words or phrases at precise moments. An individual member of the audience cannot simply shout out anything she wishes.

Just as novel utterances are an integral part of other speech events, they are also a factor in the language of audience participation at *Rocky*. A creative utterance involves an original remark, and may comment on a speech act by the audience, when a predictable phrase has been shouted out, or it may comment on an action or a remark which a character on the screen is about to perform or is performing. To illustrate this type of creativity, let me describe an event. Off camera, Frank N Furter murders Eddie, a marginal character, one-half of whose brain had been previously removed and placed in Rocky's head. As Furter returns, bloody pickax in hand, a voice from the audience is heard to shout, "Now it's Miller time!"—referring to the television commercial for Miller beer which shows men heading for a bar after a hard day at work or play.

Another fine example involves Riff-Raff, one of Furter's servants, and Rocky. Rocky is sleeping, face down, with his head away from Riff-Raff. As Riff-Raff approaches him from behind, a cult member shouts, "Servants use the rear entrance!" A third example of creativity occurred when the audience had just finished shouting "Bitch! Bitch!" at one of the female characters, Magenta, after she had just made a nasty remark. A female voice shouted, "Everyone is entitled to their own opinion!" The audience went wild, cheering and clapping for the clever and appropriate remark.

Indeed, this is one of the pleasures that the cult members enjoy in their countless viewings of *Rocky,* for it is obviously not the plot or the character development that bring the members back time and time again. They look forward with high anticipation to clever and funny remarks by their fellow cultists and reward them with appreciative cheers and applause. I have noticed two types of creative remarks: spontaneous and rehearsed. The former involves one person who apparently is inspired to create an original and novel utterance on the spot. Rehearsed utterances are usually group remarks which seem to have been the result of group practice.

Creative utterances of both types are subject to the rules of conversational turn taking described by Sacks, Schegloff, and Jefferson (1974), in that self-selection is used at transitional-relevance places. And once a would-be creative speaker self-selects, she must start fast, to avoid being overlapped. This minimizes the likelihood of gap.

Creative utterances cannot occur randomly throughout the movie; rather, there are certain places and scenes which are appropriate for novel utterances. These transition points are characterized by a break in the dialogue. Then, suddenly, there may be a fleeting pause, which can be filled by a novel utterance. Or the utterance can accompany an action on the screen, as described above. Note that the creative speaker must be quick, must know the movie sequence well, and must pay close attention, or the time is lost, so rapidly does the action move. This parallels verbal behavior in other speech events. The major difference, of course, is that in other settings such as a lecture or a conversation there is time to repair misunderstandings. In audience participation at cult movies, a would-have-been speaker can only go to another screening and try again. Not only must the speaker be prepared, what she says must not take a great deal of time to say—it must be brief—and it must be something which is clearly and quickly recognizable to all—it must be relevant. Obscure remarks are ignored, as they should be. But, as I noted above, clever remarks are appreciated and rewarded—be witty.

Indeed, the ultimate reward for an exceptionally clever creative utterance is to be institutionalized into the lore of *Rocky.* Such utterances may become formulaic speech and are available to any member of the cult. A good example of this is Janet's bumping into the vase, described above. Although I have no evidence of the origin of this remark, I am confident that it began as a clever remark by a cultist and then spread, gradually over time, to the point where it became institutionalized and was shouted out by cult members who probably were not aware of its origin.

I should point out that I have noticed that a nifty line has been coined to follow shouts of "Don't bump into the vase!" It is, "She does it every time!" When I first heard this, it was said only by one person. Subsequently, however, I have observed it being said by a number of different persons scattered throughout the audience. Perhaps this is an example of a speech change in progress.

All these speech acts are rule-governed. The strategies used to learn them are similar to those used in second language learning situations by adults. What is unique is that this speech event is being learned by adult native speakers. What makes a good second language learner also is characteristic of an adult native speaker who is a good learner in this event: She puts herself in situations in which the target language is used; she learns outside of the theater/classroom (goes to *Rocky* parties, plays the sound track, etc.), does extra work (buys the books about the movie), and is not afraid to make mistakes or look or sound foolish.

## PARASPEECH ACTS

I would like to mention briefly another characteristic of audience participation at *Rocky* which I have labeled *paraspeech acts,* by which I refer to nonverbal behavior which occurs above the hollering and shouting and singing which mark the three speech acts described in this paper. Four choice examples should serve to illustrate.

During a rainstorm, Janet and Brad have a minor car accident and leave their car to seek help in a nearby castle. They have no raingear or umbrellas to protect them from the rain; so they put newspaper over their heads. At this point in the action, cultists produce squirtguns and liberally douse each other. And, in order to protect themselves from the "rain," the cultists put newspapers over their heads.

At a wedding ceremony, as the bride and groom leave the church, the cultists pelt each other with rice. During dinner at the castle, at which Eddie, in the form of meatloaf, is reportedly served, glasses are produced and filled with liquid. As the characters raise their glasses and toast one another, the audience throws pieces of toast at the screen. When Frank N Furter is accused of being a hot dog, cultists throw hot dogs at the screen.

These paraspeech acts are imitation and rather easy for the neophyte to perform. Of interest is how such acts originated. We might try to determine if they preceded speech acts, and the origins of new paraspeech acts.

## CONCLUSION

I have attempted to show how audience participation in a particular cult movie may be seen as a speech event featuring three speech acts—imitation, comment, and directive. The strategies involved in learning these three speech acts include immediate mimicry and chanting, memorization and choral repetition, and creativity. I have also described the role which formulaic speech plays in this speech event, and how some formulaic expressions may have originated.

With this brief excursion into a world which is not familiar to most of us, I hope to have demonstrated how insights into language, language use, and language learning can come from the most unlikely places. It is obvious that more research is needed. Future studies might be concerned with the origins of creative expressions and their subsequent incorporation into formulaic expressions. We might study different audiences in different parts of the country to see if dialect areas exist. In addition to such comparative studies, longitudinal studies might be undertaken to investigate linguistic change. We might be able to determine how certain linguistic phenomena such as language death occur. Pidginization and creolization are obvious targets of investigation, along with the acquisition of *Rocky* speech acts by nonnative speakers. We should also look at caretaking styles and the relative success of the linguistic performances of neophytes. Finally, future researchers might concentrate on other cult movies to determine if the speech acts described here represent universals of audience behavior at cult movies.[3]

I should point out to future investigators that this line of fieldwork is not without its dangers. This researcher has a pair of dress pants ruined by the "rain" and was picking the rice out of his hair for days after seeing *The Rocky Horror Picture Show.*

## NOTES

1. I would like to thank Robert Gardner, East-West Center, Honolulu, for his translation and interpretations of *The Rocky Horror Picture Show.* Any errors of fact are Gardner's responsibility. I should also like to thank him for supplying me with numerous props, some of which are mentioned in this paper.

Sincere appreciation is extended to Richard Schmidt, University of Hawaii, for his invaluable aid in helping me conceptualize my thinking, and to Charlene Sato, UCLA, for her insightful observations on earlier drafts of this paper.

Thanks should also be extended to Roger Ebert and Gene Siskel, film critics, whose television program, *Sneak Previews/Take II,* WTTW, Chicago, first introduced me to the concept of cult movies.

2. The term *speech act* as used in this paper is part of a *speech event* which we may call *audience participation at cult movies.* I use *speech event* as defined by Hymes (1974, p. 52): "The term speech event will be restricted to activities, or aspects of activities, that are directly governed by rules or norms for the use of speech. An event may consist of a single speech act, but will often comprise several."

3. Lise Winer (personal communication) pointed out to me some parallels between audience behavior at *Rocky* and *The Harder They Come* and *Rockers.* She also suggested examining speech acts at other events such as baseball games to determine the universality of the findings presented in this paper.

Perhaps we should not confine ourselves to cult movies and sporting events. As Peter Tanaka (personal communication) informed me, the ancient Japanese drama, Kabuki, utilizes audience participation at appropriate moments as an integral part of a performance.

# 14

## THE ARTICLE IN AMERICAN ENGLISH: WHAT THE TEXTBOOKS DON'T TELL US

Teresa Pica
*University of Pennsylvania*

Using English articles is often a frustrating experience for students of English as a second language. Even students at advanced proficiency levels, after years of exposure to usage rules through grammars, textbooks, and classroom instruction, seldom attain mastery of the article system. Although difficulties in article use have been attributed to native language interference (Duskova 1969), evidence from the following study has suggested that there may be another source for these difficulties: Because the linguistic information the student needs to use and interpret articles is often discourse-related, the system is impossible to master through textbook study and classroom practice alone.

The latter position is based on evidence from a threefold investigation of article rules which consisted of (1) review of ESL instructional material (textbooks and grammars) which exposed limitations in the presentation of article rules to the learner; (2) analysis of article use by native speakers in the speech events of requesting and giving directions and ordering food at restaurants which identified complexities in article rule application, particularly at the discourse level; and (3) comparison of the rules presented in the teaching materials with those demonstrated in the empirical data of the speech events which revealed discrepancies between the two. Details of this investigation of article rules, its findings, and their pedagogical implications will be discussed in this chapter.

### REVIEW OF INSTRUCTIONAL MATERIALS

There is no dearth of material for teaching the articles *a* and *the*. Rules for article usage appear in ESL grammars and textbooks for all levels of language proficiency, from elementary through advanced. Some materials present these rules in itemized lists; others include sentence-level realizations or practice exercises. Despite these differences in skill-level suitability and instructional format, the following popular ESL textbooks and reference grammars display striking similarities in the article rules on which they focus.

Rule 1. Most grammars and textbooks point out the distinction between *a* for introductory usage of an item, followed by *the* for second mention of the item:

His car struck a tree; you can still see the mark on the tree

(Thomson and Martinet 1980, p. 3).

Rule 2. Nearly all materials explain the relationship between *the* and uniqueness:

The sun and the planets remain a mystery

(Danielson and Hayden 1973, p. 118).

Rule 3. Many materials indicate the use of *a* for typicality or representativeness:

A man and a boy are on a bus

(Lado 1978, p. 46).

Rule 4. Many teaching materials point out that *the* is used with nouns preceded by ordinals and superlatives:

Which country of the world has the most famous art collection?

(Praninskas 1975, p. 320).

Rule 5. Most indicate that *the* can be used with a first mention item if the item is familiar or identifiable to both speaker and listener:

Where did you park the car?

(Danielson and Hayden 1973, p. 117).

Mr. Allen: I'm going to leave the car at the garage on my way to the office.
Mrs. Allen: Be sure to tell the mechanic that the radio isn't working and the wiper needs to be adjusted.

(Crowell 1964, p. 41).

Have you read the paper this morning?

(Rutherford 1977, p. 109).

The book on Mr. Allen's desk is yellow.

(Krohn 1971, p. 54).

These rules and examples pose two problems for ESL students when they try to use articles in their own speech and writing. First, because demonstrated at the sentence level, the rules lend themselves to grammatically correct counter-examples such as the following:

Counterexample to rule 1 (second mention):   His car struck a tree. He was surprised to see how much damage a car could do to a tree.

Counterexample to rule 2 (uniqueness): A sun and some planets were sighted by a group of astronauts during a recent space probe.

Counterexample to rule 3 (typicality): A man named Higgenbottom and a boy with seven fingers are on a bus.

Counterexample to rule 4 (superlative): Our university library has a most famous art collection.

Counterexample to rule 5 (familiarity/identifiability): A book on Mr. Allen's desk is yellow.

Second, students may have difficulty in applying rule 5 because they cannot decide if an item is mutually identifiable or familiar to their listeners. The question, "Where did you park the car?" asked by a speaker who has a particular car in mind may be confusing if addressed to a group of roommates with whom the speaker shares several cars; yet the question, "Where did you park a car?" would be even more confusing to the roommates. Even though Mrs. Allen and her husband know which wiper she is speaking about, should Mr. Allen refer to "the wiper" when addressing his mechanic, the mechanic may not be able to identify the referent. Native speakers respond without request for clarification to the question, "Have you read the paper this morning?" even in cities which publish more than one newspaper. Rule 5 appears to operate even in situations where it should not apply.

## ANALYSIS OF ARTICLE USE IN TWO SPEECH EVENTS AND COMPARISON WITH ARTICLE USAGE RULES IN ESL INSTRUCTIONAL MATERIALS

In an effort to examine the pedagogical rules presented above in terms of their validity for real-life article use, an investigation of the use of *a* and *the* in two speech events—requesting and giving directions, and ordering food at restaurants—was undertaken. Both events were chosen in the expectation that they would provide many examples of the rules cited most frequently in ESL instructional materials: For example, referents might be given first or second mention. (A location would be requested or a food ordered, then further discussed.) Perceptions of uniqueness or typicality might be prevalent. (The speaker might ask for a special destination or food, or make a more general request.) In addition, it was believed that these two speech events would provide a good test for the concepts of familiarity and identifiability associated with use of *the*. Since the participants in 108 out of 110 of the speech events were strangers, their use of *the* might signal a sense of familiarity which could then be examined in terms of features in the linguistic or situational context.

**Speech Event Study 1: Requesting and Giving Directions:**

*Design:*    Events involving requesting and giving directions took place in communities in the Philadelphia area: on three college campuses and in shopping districts of four sections of the city and one suburb. One event occurred in the researcher's home; four events during telephone conversations. In all, 62 speech events formed the corpus of this study. All participants in the study appeared to be native speakers, based on assessment by two independent judges.

The procedure for data collection was as follows: The researcher approached a stranger on the street and asked how to get to an unfamiliar location. Exceptions involved asking directions from two people who were not strangers, and requesting directions over the telephone on four occasions. A hidden tape recorder was used to record each speech event (with the exception of the phone calls, which were written down). Participants' permission was then requested to use the recorded data for research purposes.

The data were transcribed and analyzed for patterns of article use. These patterns were then compared with usage rules presented in ESL instructional materials.

*Finding 1. Article Use for Introduction and Second Mention of Items:*
Although introductory use of *a* and second mention of *the* is a pattern often reported in teaching and reference material, this pattern was seldom demonstrated in actual discourse. On the 23 occasions in which the researcher asked for directions to a place, introducing it with *a*, e.g., "Can you tell me where I can find a drugstore?" participants never referred to that place again using anaphoric *the*, but instead used proforms such as *it* and *one*, repeated the name of the place using introductory *a*, or used synonyms or proper nouns related to the place name. On the 14 occasions in which participants other than the researcher introduced an item using *a*, only twice did they refer to it anaphorically with *the*; in 11 instances, they used a proform and on one occasion simply repeated the place name with introductory *a*. Examples of such article use are as follows:

| Request | Directions |
|---|---|
| . . . a newspaper? | There's a restaurant up ahead. They probably have it. |
| . . . your theater? | . . . We're in a small shopping with a large supermarket. It's very obvious. |

Participants in this speech event category often used *the* rather than *a* to introduce any item, place name or otherwise. In all, there were 74 introductions with *the* vs. 50 introduction with *a*.

*Finding 2: Article Use in Situational Contexts:*    Analysis of the natural data revealed explicit details of the situational context which either had not been noted or had been lumped together in the instructional materials under the headings of mutual identity or familiarity to participants. Article use appeared to be related to participants' familiarity with an item referred to but was a complex of each participant's interpretation of (1) each other's previous experience, (2) immediacy and visibility of the referent, and (3) scope of a given setting. These interpretational factors will be dealt with separately:

*Finding 2A: Previous Experience:* When a speaker introduced an item with *the* which was part of the previous experience of the listener in a given setting, successful communication occurred. For example, when the researcher was told to "go past the bridge" and "the toll booth" on the way to visiting a speaker's new home, the researcher knew exactly which items were being referred to, based on previous excursions to the city of the new home. Similarly, speakers directed the researcher to locations in terms of landmarks such as "the parkway," "the museum," "the student center," and "the river." Even though the researcher was acquainted with more than one "parkway," "museum," etc., with regard to life experiences, only one such item was known to the researcher within the setting in which the directions had been requested. On the other hand, when a speaker used *the* with a first-mention item not in the previous experience of the researcher for a given setting, confusion occurred. That a speaker's introduction of an item with *the* was based on perceptions of the researcher's previous experience is supported by the following examples:

Upon arriving in an unfamiliar community, the researcher asked a young woman for directions:

| Request | Directions |
|---|---|
| . . . a drugstore | Oh. That's right inside the terminal. |
| Terminal? | Yeah. You don't know the terminal? |
| No. | Oh. You're not from around here? |

Another example, this from a telephone conversation:

| Request | Directions |
|---|---|
| How do I get to your store? | Are you familiar with Passayunk? |
| A little. | Do you know where the junkyards are? |
| You mean the Yellow Cab Depot? | No. How about the bridge? Do you know where the drawbridge is? |
| No . . . | |

In the first example, the woman giving directions apparently assumed the researcher was from the city in which the speech event occurred; hence her response, "Oh. You're not from around here?" In the second example, the researcher gave an indication of familiarity by responding "A little." to the participant's question "Are you familiar with Passayunk?" This led to the participant's references to items in familiar terms.

*Finding 2B. Visibility/Immediacy:* *The* was frequently used with an item which was in both participants' view. However, when the visible item was sighted by only one of the participants, confusion resulted. This happened, for example, when a building was described in features similar to the buildings surrounding it:

| Request | Directions |
| --- | --- |
| ... the School of Education? | It's on the other side. The big red building. You can see it. |
| You mean the one with the TV antenna. | |

Much confusion resulted when one participant perceived the scope of the setting differently from the other participant. While the setting was often narrowed by the researcher because it was new or strange, the person giving directions tended to base from a wider setting. For example, in eight visits to college campuses, the researcher, apparently using the uniqueness rule, requested "the library," "the bookstore," or "the gym," with the assumption that there would be only one such place on a given campus. Based on their responses, some participants seemed to perceive these items in terms of the neighborhood including and surrounding the campus which in all instances contained several bookstores, libraries, and gymnasiums; hence the participants appeared to apply the typicality rule of article usage in response to what the researcher interpreted as a unique item. Examples of this pattern are as follows:

| Request | Directions |
| --- | --- |
| ... the bookstore? | Uh, the university bookstore? |
| ... the bookstore? | Zavelle's? Which bookstore? I can tell you where you can find *a* bookstore, and they can help you. |
| ... either the bookstore or the library. | If you want to go to the library? Paley? |
| ... the library? | ... the Drexel University library? |
| ... the gym? | ... the Drexel University gym? |

On four occasions, participants seemed to attempt to narrow the setting by providing a specific context for an item they had introduced with *the:*

| Request | Directions |
| --- | --- |
| How do I get to your sister's house? | ... under the tunnel (pause) that goes under Thirtieth Street ... you're gonna go under the bridge (pause) the Benjamin Franklin Bridge. |
| How do I get to your store? | Do you know where the junkyards are? Around Sixty-third and Passayunk? |
| ... a public library? | ... You know the area? You know where the police station used to be? Down on Garrett Road? |

On three occasions, the setting was automatically narrowed because the speech events took place within a building. At these times, no confusion resulted when items were introduced by *the:*

| Request | Directions |
|---------|-----------|
| . . . the luggage department? | . . . on the ninth floor, behind the gifts. |
| . . . the periodicals room? | . . . There's a door. You can come down the stairs. |
| . . . the restroom? | . . . probably the basement. |

*Finding 3:Article use in Linguistic Contexts:*    Association, Synonymy, Entailment: Use of *the* with first-mention items in relations of association, synonymy, and entailment with their linguistic context was a pattern of article use found in abundance in the natural data but was not made explicit in the teaching material. Analysis of the natural data revealed that for successful communication to occur, participants had to have considerable cultural knowledge of the referent in its linguistic context in order to make associations, note synonymy, and recognize entailment. For example, buses were referred to as "the 7 or 48" or "the number 2." The researcher was told to "give the driver the transfer," to ". . . ask the busman what bus to take," to ". . . ask the driver for a transfer. It'll save you the fifty cents." When giving directions via roads and highways, participants advised: " . . . When you get to the end of the exit ramp, you go through the light . . . " or "Take Vine Street. You have to turn with the traffic . . . " Also, "Take Vine Street to Eighth . . . you'll see the exit." and "Make a left on Germantown Avenue, . . . When you get to the top, the road splits into a fork." When giving directions to buildings, participants referred to "the stairs," "the first floor," "the lobby," "the front door," "the complex," and "the desk," even though these items were not in sight.

Summarizing, patterns of article use revealed in the natural data could not be correctly or completely described by the rules of article usage presented in the instructional materials. Specifically, patterns in the natural data did not often follow rules for introduction and second mention of items presented in the ESL materials. In addition, the natural data revealed a complex interplay of factors which included participants' interpretations of each other's previous experience, of the immediacy and visibility of a referent, and of the scope of a setting, tended to be lumped together in the materials under the single heading of mutual familiarity or identifiability to participants. Lastly, the nature of the linguistic context accompanying use of introductory *the* was made explicit in the analysis of the natural data and included a strong cultural component not identified in the instructional materials.

## Speech Event Study 2: Ordering Food at Restaurants

*Design:*    Data for study of this speech event were obtained from 52 customers of 11 restaurants in Philadelphia and New Haven, Connecticut. Two collection techniques were employed:

1. The researcher recorded consenting strangers and friends who were told that their conversation during the meal was needed as a sample of "anonymous, authentic speech" for ESL students. This procedure was followed at restaurants in EXP and MOD L and MOD D categories (described below). In addition, these customers were interviewed immediately following data collection regarding how often they had eaten at the restaurant.

2. The researcher recorded people ordering food at restaurants of categories TS and FF (described below). These orders went so quickly that it was impossible to interview customers after each data collection.

All participants appeared to be native English speakers, based on the assessment of two independent judges.

The 10 restaurants observed represented four categories:

1. Three expensive restaurants (EXP).

2. Four moderately priced restaurants. Data were collected during both lunch- and dinnertime. In analyzing the data, the two dinnertime observations presented article use distinct from that of the lunchtime observations. Therefore, this restaurant category was classified as MOD D and MOD L (for dinner and lunch).

3. Two "fast food" truck stands on the University of Pennsylvania campus (TS).

4. Two "fast food" chain restaurants, serving modestly priced food (FF).

The data for food orders were transcribed and analyzed for patterns of article use.[1] These patterns were then compared with usage rules presented in ESL instructional material.

*Finding 4.*   Food items analyzed were introduced with *the* only in EXP and MOD D restaurant categories, and by *a* in all restaurant categories; Zero article occurred only in restaurants of MOD L, TS, and FF categories. For example, in the three EXP restaurants, requests were made for "the stuffed game hen," "the prime ribs," "the stuffed shrimp," "the lobster Fra D'Avalo," "the veal scallopine," "the Reuben sirloin burger," and "the corned beef sandwich." Even "the garden vegetables," "the onion soup," "the tossed salad," and "the cheese omelette" were requested. However, in the FF, MOD L, and TS restaurants, orders included "a fish and salad combo," "a cheese omelette," "a chicken salad platter," and "a snack julienne."

Use of *the* in higher-priced restaurants may have indicated customers' perceptions of their orders as unique; i.e., the food items did not exist until the listeners (waiters and waitresses) placed the order with the cook, or the items were specialties of the restaurant. Use of *a* preceding names of main dishes at modestly priced fast food and truck stand restaurants as well as during the rather hectic paced lunchtime in a moderately priced restaurant may have indicated speakers' perceptions (or acceptance) of typicality: The items ordered would not be specially prepared; restaurant service would take the food from a counter or oven and bring it to customers.

In the MOD L, TS, and FF restaurant settings, *a* and ∅ appeared in free variation, but there was a tendency for *a* to precede orders in types MOD L and FF restaurants (10 out of 15 orders and 8 out of 9 orders respectively) and for ∅ to precede 14 out of 16 TS orders. Also apparent was an alternation of *a* and ∅ for the same item ordered in similar settings:

| Category | Order |
|---|---|
| MOD L | I want a tuna melt |
| MOD L | I'd like a tuna melt with chips |
| MOD L | I'd like a grilled cheese |
| MOD L | . . . a grilled cheese with bacon on rye bread |
| FF | I'd like a fries |
| FF | Give me fries . . . |
| | |
| TS | Strawberry yogurt |
| TS | A coffee yogurt |

Furthermore, in different eating establishments, a similar food item was often ordered separately:

| Category | Order |
|---|---|
| FF | I'll have a cheese steak with onions . . |
| TS | Cheese steak with onions |
| | |
| MOD L | I'd like a tuna salad on toast |
| TS | May I have tuna salad on rye? |
| | |
| FF | . . . a quarter pounder |
| TS | Hamburger on a kaiser |
| MOD D | . . . and the Reuben sirloin burger |

The absence of preceding article for food items ordered at truck stands may have been related to the speakers' desire for clarity and economy of language in the midst of confusion and noise usually created by the gathering of customers simultaneously ordering, waiting for, or obtaining their orders. This may also have been why orders in the somewhat hectic lunchtime atmosphere of the category MOD L restaurant often had ∅ before food items.

Although ESL materials might not be expected to indicate such a level of detail or postulate so many motives with regard to article selection as was rendered in analysis of this speech event, these materials do overlook an important fact—the possibility for free variation in article choice. Usage rules in the instructional materials implied that *a* and *the* always signal meaning differences and that article choice was fixed once linguistic and situational context were identified. Yet many of the restaurant data revealed that article choice could vary without regard to these contextual factors and without interfering with communication.

This finding leads to another pattern of article use not indicated in the instructional materials—the relationship between article use and speech event: In the speech event of requesting and giving directions, there was little free variation in article use. In fact, asking for *the* place rather than *a* place often led to listener confusion. Yet in the speech event of restaurant ordering, free variation was a successful pattern of article use.

The restaurant data also suggest a hierarchy of article rule application: In the MOD L restaurant, food items ordered were both typical (not specially prepared) and familiar (customers reported that they had eaten there at least ten times previously and had interacted with restaurant personnel). Hence both *a* and *the* could have been used to introduce food items ordered. The fact that most orders were introduced with *a* suggests that the typicality rule is more dominant given the situational context of this speech event.

## SUMMARY OF FINDINGS AND PEDAGOGICAL IMPLICATIONS OF THIS INVESTIGATION OF ARTICLE RULES

The findings of this study suggest that a key to ESL students' attaining proficiency in article use lies not in the study of grammatical rules and the practice of sentence or even paragraph exercises but through developing awareness of variations of article use within communicative contexts. Because the linguistic information the student needs to use and interpret articles is often discourse-related, it is not easily accessible through the sentence-level examples provided in grammars and textbooks.

Findings have revealed that rules in the article system appear to be based on a complex interplay of features and communication components. Change in even one such feature or component may prevent application of a rule in one speaking situation but allow its application in another. Acquisition of this complicated article system may take a lifetime of communication experiences unavailable to most students of English as a second language.

Comparison of article use in the natural data and usage rules in the instructional materials has indicated that article use may have more to do with communication and communicative competence than with grammar and linguistic competence. In the sentence-level examples of grammars and textbooks, *a* and *the* could be interchanged without resulting in a loss of grammaticality; on the other hand, in the natural data of requesting and giving directions, even though participants spoke in grammatically correct utterances, communication broke down when articles were used in reference to items in one participant's experience but not in another's.

Comparison with the natural data of speech events has also shown that the instructional materials used by ESL students (and their teachers) present a seemingly complete but actually partial description of the article system. Findings of the comparison study thus suggest that ESL students might use article rules correctly according to the dictates of a grammar or textbook, but inappropriately according to the demands of a communicative context. It is in light of these findings for article use that the following recommendations for instruction are given:

1. Communicative effectiveness in ordering food did not seem contingent upon article choice. Speakers achieved a cooperative response regardless of whether

231

they used *a, the,* or no article at all. This is probably one of the few events in which ESL students cannot err in their use of articles. Practice in ordering food should therefore be presented in the early stages of instruction as a nonfrustrating lesson for beginning students. No matter which article they used, in this activity, all students would be correct.

2. Use of *a* and *the* for introduction and second mention of an item was not as common a pattern as ESL materials lead students to believe. When giving directions, speakers mainly used proforms to refer to items previously introduced. By teaching article rules for first and second mention, teachers may be compounding students' difficulties with article use. In spoken discourse, use of proforms is preferred. Students should be made aware of this.

3. *The* had an introductory use in requesting and giving directions when the speaker believed a word's referent mutually identifiable because previously experienced by the listener or within a shared interpretation of setting. Determining what is mutually identifiable is not an easy matter. Thus confusions were frequent even among the native speakers in this study. Since speakers cannot be sure of their listeners' sense of setting, students should be told that unless contained in a building or certain of their addressees' previous experiences with the location requested, *the* should be used with a qualifying description, e.g., the nearest post office, the university bookstore. Students should also be reminded, and may be relieved to know, that when requesting and giving directions, even native speakers err in their article use.

4. Since many ESL materials focus on speech events such as the two analyzed in this study (Carver and Fotinos 1977, Dubin 1977, Finocchiaro 1970, Harris and Hube 1975, Keltner and Bitterlin 1981, Kettering 1975, Taylor 1967), ESL instructors can use dialogues and key expressions offered in these existing materials to provide students with meaningful and relevant examples of article use. Instructors can also record their own samples of people requesting or giving directions or ordering food in restaurants, or have their students collect these samples to provide empirical data of how speakers use articles. During class time, these data can then be analyzed for article patterns and rules. Additional materials can be provided by teacher- and, eventually, student-composed dialogues indicating, for example, how communication breaks down when *the* is used under falsely presumed familiarity or in nonassociative contexts, or how in some contexts, communication continues despite alternation of *a* and *the* for the same lexical item. Students may thus begin to appreciate how, when, and why to use *a* and *the* and the options open for appropriate use.

Finally, the classroom, by its very nature, cannot provide the multitude of language experiences necessary for exposing the vastness and complexity of the article system. The ESL teacher must therefore encourage students who have difficulty with articles (probably a majority in many classrooms) to interact with English speakers in numerous, diverse, and frequent communicative experiences, both in and outside the classroom. Engaging in such experiences may be ESL students' optimal means of gaining access to the complex article system. Providing opportunities for such experiences may be ESL instructors' most meaningful contribution toward making this access possible.

## NOTES

1. Analysis was conducted primarily on the data involving requests for main dishes and sandwiches. Orders for beverages and desserts were excluded from the analysis. Requests for side orders (salads, potatoes) were included in the analysis only if they were the only item ordered in a given speech event. In all orders analyzed, customers had access to a menu (hand-held or painted on a wall) but did not read from it while ordering.

# 15

## THE PROBLEM OF APPLYING SOCIOLINGUISTIC FINDINGS TO TESOL: THE CASE OF MALE/FEMALE LANGUAGE

### Elliot L. Judd
*University of Illinois at Chicago*

One of the major contributions of sociolinguistics, either as a theoretical construct or as a body of empirical studies, is its position on the nature of language itself. Language, as viewed by the sociolinguist, is not a giant monolith with fixed, all-encompassing rules which are uniformly applied by the idealized speaker/listener in all circumstances and under all conditions. Instead, the sociolinguist views language as more than a complex series of utterances which are affected by human differences and natural environmental situations. Thus language is seen as an aspect of social behavior, with rules which are strongly conditioned by context. Generalized rules and formulas which ignore human variables are seen as unrealistic and therefore lacking in important insights. For the sociolinguist, a description of a speech event should specify the particular conditions under which the patterns have occurred including such factors as who the speaker and listener were, the place where the utterance has occurred, the desired goals of the speaker, the mood of the speaker, and the underlying norms of the general society, to mention just a few of the relevant conditions (Hymes 1974).

One specific area of recent sociolinguistic research has been concerned with language and sex. Although not a totally new area of study (see Jesperson 1922 and a review of anthropological studies in Swacker 1975), it is only recently that scholars have begun to systematically investigate linguistic differences which have been linked with gender both in the literature and as a part of folk wisdom. (For examples see Thorne and Henley 1975; Lakoff 1973; Kramarae 1981; McConnell-Ginet, Borker, and Furman 1980; Nilsen et al. 1977; Spender 1980; and Key 1975). It is important to note that such investigations are in their infancy and thus far from complete. In fact, entire aspects of male/female speech remain virtually unstudied. Furthermore, as in all new research domains, theories and explanations are still being formulated and studies are being conducted to confirm or refute the validity of hypotheses. Therefore, care must be taken in assuming that we have precise, unchallengeable data.

For the purposes of generalization, the studies on female/male speech can be organized into two major categories: how language is used to describe women and men, and how men and women use language. The former types of study focus on how language itself portrays males and females in a given society (for examples see Kingston and Lovelace 1978; Kramarae 1981; Nilsen et al. 1977; and Thorne and Henley 1975a, b). Some investigations focus on which words (for example, adjectives or verbs) are used to describe the activities or physical and mental characteristics of women and men in society. Others seek to study the amount of sex-linked speech or the number of male/female characters in a piece of writing, for example, in elementary school textbooks, and the roles and activities which are assigned to members of each sex. Still others look at differences in the ways women and men interpret the same piece of language. The goal of all these studies is not simply to describe and quantify language use. They also seek to postulate how society's basic behavioral values are reflected in language and the effect that such attitudes have on all of us. As a corollary, these studies often discuss the question of "sexism" in language and alternatives that may be employed to alleviate forms of linguistic inequalities.

Investigations of the second general category aim at identifying the similarities and differences in male/female speech. These studies look at language—verbal and nonverbal, written and oral—on all levels (phonological, morphological, syntactic, and discourse) to determine which features can be classified as belonging to either women or men. (For example, see Thorne and Henley 1975a, b; Kramarae 1981; Lakoff 1973; and Key 1975). Those engaging in such research are interested in both the actual features of language which constitute male and female speech of one sex (for example, the myth that women talk more than men when, in fact, studies have shown the reverse to be true— see Zimmerman and West 1975). As in the first type of research, efforts are made to go beyond mere identification of features. Hypotheses are often provided by the researchers to explain why certain linguistic characteristics occur and what the connection is between the various sex-linked speech patterns and overall societal roles for men and women.

For applied linguists, especially those interested in the creation of second-language learning materials, sociolinguistic research has become crucial. It is now a widely accepted principle that language materials should be based on models that represent valid linguistic data. Artificial models, while perhaps useful to create linguistic security or to explain a specific grammatical point, fail to provide learners with the information needed to function successfully in an uncontrolled, nonclassroom environment. Failure to use natural language not only will cause the learners to fail in the communicative process but will also cause them to experience frustration and even rejection when they leave the classroom. Thus the trend in TESOL has been toward the teaching of "communicative competence" or the mastery of the sociolinguistic rules of speaking. Obviously, the works of sociolinguists help the applied linguist in the attainment of this goal, for such investigations provide useful data on which materials can be based.

However, the task is not as simple as it may first appear. Although the terms "communicative competence" and "natural language materials" have become common phrases in the vernacular of second language teachers and researchers, they are often ill-defined in terms of their application to specific ESOL materials. In fact, developing communicative abilities and teaching natural language are very difficult goals to accomplish. The aim of this paper is to offer some discussion of the problems involved in applying sociolinguistic data to the creation of ESOL materials. Since this is an extremely large topic, the paper will specifically focus on research dealing with female/male language patterns (for a discussion of sexism in ESOL materials, see Hartman and Judd 1978). It is hoped that the ensuing discussion will shed light on the particular issue of applying male/female language as well as serve as a guide for all those desiring to apply sociolinguistic findings to the creation of second language materials in general.

## WHY INCLUDE MALE/FEMALE LANGUAGE PATTERNS?

Some may accuse those who insist on the inclusion of female/male language differences of being faddists who are simply reacting to the latest societal trend. No doubt texts which portray inaccurate male/female language use are offensive to many and therefore need to be revised or avoided, especially in cases where changes that do not endanger the linguistic and pedagogical quality of the materials can be made or in cases where alternative books of equal quality can be found. However, most in the profession would not choose a text solely on the criterion of the accuracy of its portrayal of female/male language. Other strengths would also have to exist in order for a book to acquire a following.

For many, the demand for the inclusion of male/female language patterns is part of a much wider issue. As stated earlier, it is now felt that language materials must provide students with accurate linguistic models. If a given set of materials only provides the speech patterns of one sex, then a complete picture of language usage is not provided to the student. Thus the demand for language models for both sexes is not an idle concern but a plea for linguistic accuracy in language materials.

## HOW TO ACCUMULATE THE DATA

In order to succeed at the desired goal of including male/female language data in teaching materials, a writer can employ three strategies in obtaining the necessary linguistic information. Each of these approaches has some inherent value, yet each also has some obvious limitations.

One strategy is for the materials creator to turn to published studies whose focus is on women's and men's speech behavior. This approach saves time, since others have already done the investigations, leaving the materials developer free to concentrate on applications to teaching materials. However, there are certain pitfalls in this decision. One of these is the fact that, as previously mentioned, there are many areas of male/female language use which have yet to be studied, and thus there are no such findings to read. This leaves the writer of materials with the question of why there are no data. Is it that there are no differences in certain areas or merely that the differences have yet to be identified? Another problem is that even when studies are available, how can it be proved that they are accurate? Some writers have made claims which have been refuted by later investigations (for example, see Dubois and Crouch's 1975 comments on Lakoff's 1973 claim regarding the use of tag questions). For the applied linguist, who desires to create accurate language materials, this poses a dilemma. Should materials be based on existing studies even though the data may later prove questionable, or should materials not include information on language variations and run the risk of being criticized for ignoring existing research?

A second tactic that can be employed is for language materials developers to embark on their own field investigations. This strategy permits those who strive for linguistic accuracy to check for themselves the validity of existing research findings and then incorporate the significant findings into classroom materials. It also may prove effective in cases where no prior studies exist. Although field investigations have some benefits, there are also several factors which may limit the effectiveness and usefulness of this technique: One of these is that many who design materials lack the necessary training and knowledge to conduct accurate field investigations. Therefore, the data which are accumulated may be inaccurate and be unsuitable for language materials. Other related limitations are those of time and money. In order to conduct a valid experiment, the field investigator must devote a good deal of time in formulating, executing, and evaluating the study. Often this process entails expenditures which may be beyond the economical and temporal abilities of a material developer. Finally, it should be realized that even if a person can conduct a valid field investigation, there is no guarantee that such a researcher has the knowledge and ability to devise valid language materials suitable for classroom instruction. In fact, it is rare to find people who possess expertise in both areas. Thus the use of field investigations, while solving some problems, does not provide a viable solution in most cases.

A third strategy is for the material developer to rely on intuitive judgments about women's and men's language (as was done in Lakoff 1973). Such an approach may yield some valuable insights, but it may also lead to incorrect or overgeneralized statements about male/female speech. Since personal observations may or may not be accurate, they provide a questionable source for valid linguistic models.

Since all these approaches have both strengths and weaknesses, the logical solution is to combine all three strategies. The existing literature should be checked; limited field investigations can then be used to reevaluate existing studies or to explore new areas, and intuitive judgments should be used as a monitoring device to double-check the first two methods or to raise questions for field investigations or to embark on reviews of the existing literature. Ideally, data which are accumulated through the use of all three methods should be incorporated into classroom texts. In reality, the more techniques that are employed, the better the chances are for sociolinguistic accuracy in language teaching materials.

## HOW TO INCORPORATE THE DATA INTO LANGUAGE MATERIALS

Once the desired information on female/male language patterns has been accumulated, the next step is that of integrating the findings into the teaching materials. While each set of language materials is different, some general principles can be suggested to aid writers.

The primary area to explore is whether or not the males and females in the materials are using those features which have been linked to their respective sex. In other words, do the women speak like women and do the men sound like men? If not, alterations are needed to make the speech patterns conform to the research findings. Attention must be given not only to particular linguistic features (choice of words, the use of hedges, etc.) but also to the discourse styles and topics which identify male and female speech usage. For example, it is obvious that some topics may characterize the speech of one sex but not the other. Also, all-female conversations have different discourse styles than all-male ones in terms of how speakers build on or ignore the comments of the previous speakers. Thus the creators of language materials must simultaneously focus on several levels of language use.

The other crucial factor which must be incorporated into language materials when they are designed to include male/female variations is that of the status relationships between the participants. Many of the differences between female and male language use have been attributed to an unequal power relationship between women and men in our society (Spender 1980; Kramarae 1981; and McConnell-Ginet, Borker, and Furman 1980). In fact, some have argued that most gender differences in English occur because of status inequalities rather than sex alone. Of course, since women are generally in lower-status positions, linguistic differences caused by lower status are more apparent in most women's speech than in men's (O'Barr and Atkins 1980). Thus this factor must necessarily be reflected if valid language models for men and women are desired.

Beyond this general level of analysis, specific attention must be devoted to certain domains in order to come near to the goal of incorporating valid male/female language patterns into language teaching materials. One of these areas is that of mixed-sex conversations. Conversations among all-male or all-female groups are quite different from those of mixed-sex groups. Research has pointed to the fact that males often tend to dominate females in such situations, both in the amount of speaking time and in interruption patterns (Zimmerman and West

1975). Therefore, a writer must be cognizant of the fact that language patterns will vary not only at the individual level but also at the group level depending on the sexual makeup of the group in question.

Other things to check for in incorporating female and male usage into language materials are factors such as the age of the speakers in the materials, their socioeconomic levels, the situations where the conversations occur, and the status relationships among the speakers (Thorne and Henley 1975a). It is obvious that boys and girls speak differently from grown men and women. Nonetheless, female/male language differences appear early in life, and materials developers should not assume that the speech patterns of little girls are identical to those of little boys. Similarly, on an individual level, the language of women and men will vary with their socioeconomic status, educational background, and particularly by occupation. However, it may again be assumed that even among these varied groups, there are still differences in male/female speech. On the other hand, care must be taken not to have all the speakers of either sex speak in uniform patterns. Women's speech on all levels is just as varied as men's speech, and care must be taken to show a great variety of speech patterns for both sexes.

The writer of language materials must also be conscious of the situational context of discourse and the effect it has on female/male language use. Depending on where a conversation takes place and who is present, people change their speech patterns. Nonetheless, the writer should be careful to include sex differences in language within these varied sociolinguistic contexts.

In short, a writer of language materials who desires to include sex differences in language has to be sure to focus on many factors which affect male/female language. Failure to do so will result in stereotypical portrayals that defeat the ultimate goal of accurate language models.

## SOME POTENTIAL PROBLEMS

Throughout this paper it has been argued that ESOL materials creators should endeavor to include patterns of female/male language usage in their materials. However, there still exists a question of whether or not such a generalization is applicable in all situations where English is taught to nonnative speakers. This section will explore some of these situations in an effort to determine if there may be some exceptions to this general recommendation.

It is now accepted by most in TESOL that there is a need to recognize that English is taught in a variety of circumstances throughout the world. It can no longer be assumed that American and British English are the only acceptable varieties of the language (Strevens 1980 and Kachru 1976), for many regional varieties of English are the accepted language models and form the basis for teaching materials. It can be asked whether or not it is advisable to include male/female language variations in these situations.

The answer should be based on sociolinguistic reality. It would be inappropriate to assume, without testing, that findings on female/male language are valid in places where a different English language variety is the accepted norm. If materials from one variety were applied to another without empirical validation, unrealistic models would be applied to language materials and would defeat the entire goal of creating accurate language models. This would not only be true in the case of female/male language but also for all language use. On the other hand, there probably exist male/female language variations in the indigenous variety of English, and efforts should be made to identify these differences and incorporate them into the teaching materials. Thus the same general rule of incorporating male/female language patterns applies, but the specific context will differ from one language variety to another.

A second possible point of discussion is whether or not students will object to using male/female language variations in their classroom. In other words, will the use of such variations prove offensive to students who come from cultures where female and male societal roles differ from those of English-speaking cultures? The answers to this problem are complex. First, it should be made clear to students that they are not expected to change their own cultural beliefs. To insist on their doing so would represent a form of linguistic and cultural imperialism which all professionals should avoid. However, in language study students must also be taught that other cultures and languages have different systems and that to become truly fluent in a language, these systems must also be mastered. Furthermore, for certain students, failure to learn male/female differences might cause them greater embarrassment in the future. If a female student has only learned the language of men or vice versa, the student may encounter awkwardness or even rejection when dealing with native speakers of English. This type of situation may lead to as much, or even more, cultural resentment than the initial teaching of male/female language patterns themselves. Therefore, there is indeed a real need to teach nonnative speakers the rules governing female/male language to enable them to achieve full communicative language ability. This process should also include statements explaining the societal norms behind language usage, with reminders that each language has its own rules.

Finally, there is the question of when to introduce male/female language differences into the teaching materials. Should differences in English language use be introduced immediately or should there be a gradual introduction of sociolinguistic differences in second language materials? The answer to this question will vary according to the students for whom the materials are intended. It would seem that at the earliest stage of second language learning we need to teach the basic grammatical and communicative structures of English, for without them any communication at all would be impossible. Yet we often underestimate our students' capacities for dealing with sociolinguistic information. The delay in presenting sociolinguistic variations, including male/female language patterns, only leads to the inefficient process of students' having to unlearn material before mastering new material. Consequently, it seems prudent to introduce variations in speech at the earliest possible point when mastery can be assured. Of course, choice of the exact spot is best left to the individual classroom instructor who has the particular knowledge which all materials developers lack. It should be further noted that, when such variations are added, language becomes a living, functioning entity which most students find both enjoyable and interesting. Therefore, there is psychological as well as pedagogical value in introducing sociolinguistic data as early as possible.

# *16*

## *COMMUNICATIVE NEEDS IN FOREIGN LANGUAGE LEARNING*

### Jack C. Richards
*Department of English as a Second Language*
*University of Hawaii at Manoa*

The theme of language and the learner's communicative needs is a familiar one in language teaching. In recent years applied linguistics has been revitalized by attempts to describe how language reflects its communicative uses, and by demonstrations of how syllabus design and methodology can respond to the need for communicative uses of language in classrooms and teaching materials. This paper attempts to contribute to our general understanding of how language use reflects underlying communicative needs by considering some central aspects of communication. Five assumptions about the nature of verbal communication will be discussed, namely, that communication is meaning-based, conventional, appropriate, interactional, and structured. These will be discussed in relation to the communicative needs of second or foreign language learners.

### COMMUNICATION IS MEANING-BASED

Let us begin by examining basic survival language needs, those, for example, of a learner who has an active vocabulary of perhaps two hundred words and a minimal knowledge of the syntax of English, but who is in a situation where English is required for simple basic communicative purposes. The most immediate need of the speaker is to be able to refer to a core of basic "referents," or things in the real world, that is, to be able to name things, states, events, and attributes, using the words he or she knows. In addition the learner must be able to link words together to make predications, i.e., to express propositions. A proposition is the linking together of words to form predications about things, people, and events. For example, the words *book* and *red* constitute a proposition when we understand the meaning of *The book is red.*

Propositions are the building blocks of communication, and the first task in learning to communicate in a language is to learn how to create propositions. Language is comprehensible to the degree that hearers are able to reconstruct propositions from a speaker's utterances. When the child says "hungry" to its mother, the mother understands "I am hungry"; from "no hungry" the mother understands the child's message as being "I don't want to eat" (Wells 1981). From these examples we see that sentences do not have to be complete or grammatical for their propositional meaning to be understood. We often make good sense of a speaker who uses very broken syntax, just as we can understand a message written in telegraphese; *no money send draft.*

Sentences may refer to more than one proposition. *The girl picked the red flower* contains the propositions *the girl picked the flower, the flower is red.* Sentences may refer to the same proposition but differ in what they say about it. The following sentences refer to the proposition *John married Mary* but differ in what they say about it:

When did John marry Mary?
Why did John and Mary get married?
Mary and John have been married for ages.

"Survival-level" communication in a foreign language, however, consists of more than the construction of propositions. Speakers use propositions in utterances in a variety of ways. They may wish to ask a question about a proposition, affirm a proposition, deny or negate a proposition, or express an attitude toward a proposition. They may use propositions to communicate meanings indirectly, as when the speaker says *I'm thirsty* but means *I'd like a glass of water,* the latter being the illocutionary effect the speaker intends (see Austin 1962). Now while the adult native speaker of English can use the resources of adult syntax to code propositions in the appropriate grammatical form and to communicate a wide range of illocutionary meanings, the beginning foreign language learner finds that the demands of communication often exceed his or her knowledge of the grammar of English. The learner's immediate priority is to construct a way of performing such operations as stating, affirming, denying, or questioning propositions, in the most economical way, using a partial knowledge of the vocabulary and syntax of the target language. Here the learner has similar needs to the child learning its mother tongue. Child language is characterized by its ability to express complex meanings within the limits of a restricted grammatical system. Mother talk—that variety of speech which mothers use when talking to young children—is coded to make propositions and illocutionary intentions more readily identifiable (Goody 1978b). Mothers' questions to children, for example, contain far more yes-no questions that WH questions, because propositions are more readily identifiable with yes-no questions.

How do foreign language learners communicate meaning when they lack the fully elaborated grammatical and discourse system of the target language? To answer this question, let us consider how a learner might try to express the meanings contained in the following sentences:

John ought to have come on time.
I regret I wasn't able to get to your class on time.
I can't afford to buy that dress.

One strategy learners adopt in communicating complex meanings is to "bring propositions to the surface" by expressing meanings and intentions directly rather than indirectly and by expressing lexically aspects of meaning that are coded in the auxiliary system, in complex clauses, and by grammatical devices in the target language (Richards 1981, Dittmar 1981). The first sentence, for example, implies the proposition *John came late* and communicates the speaker's attitude toward the proposition. The meaning is roughly *Speaker disapprove that John came late.* This could be communicated by saying:

Why John late? (said with nonapproving intonation) or John late. That bad.

(The distinction between propositions which are expressed and those which are presupposed is an important one but will not be pursued further here.) The second sentence contains the proposition *I am late* together with the speaker's expression of regret. It might be communicated by saying:

I late, So sorry.

*I can't afford to buy that dress* contains the propositions:

*The dress is expensive. I don't have enough money to buy the dress.*

It could be restated:

The dress expensive. Cannot buy.
Can't buy the dress. No money.

This type of "restructuring" is seen in the following examples in which utterances in simplified learner syntax are compared with standard adult grammar.

| L2 utterances | Equivalent in standard adult syntax |
|---|---|
| 1. Mary lazy. No work hard. | 1. Mary can work hard if she wants to. |
| 2. Tomorrow I give money. | 2. You will have your money tomorrow, I promise you. |
| 3. You no money. I lend you. | 3. I will lend you some money if you need any. |

4. This way. See the map.

4. According to the map, this ought to be the way.

5. One day I go England.

5. I would like to go to England some day.

(De Silva 1981)

Teachers too often resort to this type of language in communicating with speakers of limited language proficiency. The following examples were produced by teachers who are native speakers of English.

1. A teacher is explaining the meaning of *wash*. "In your house, you . . . a tub . . . you (gestures) wash."

2. Here is a teacher explaining how to take telephone messages. "I want to speak other person. He not here. What good thing for say now?"

3. A teacher explaining an interview procedure produced: "Not other student listen. I no want. Necessary you speak. Maybe I say what is your name. The writing not important."

4. And here is a teacher reminding her students to bring their books to class. "The book . . . we have . . . (hold up book) . . . book is necessary for class. Right . . . necessary for school. You have book."

(Examples from Evelyn Hatch, personal communication)

The examples above illustrate a linguistic system which can be used for communicating basic propositional meanings. Such a system is known as *child language* when it is produced by infants learning their mother tongue, *interlanguage* when it is produced by foreign language learners, *teacher talk* when it is used by teachers, and *foreigner talk* when it is produced by native speakers communicating with foreigners. The linguistic system of syntactic, lexical, and semantic organization behind this type of communication is one which uses a basic "notional-functional" core of vocabulary items, a syntax which depends on simple word order rules (such as the formation of negation by placing the negative word in front of the proposition) and in which the communication of meaning is not dependent on grammatical systems of tense or aspect, auxiliaries, function words, or plural morphemes, at the initial stages of communication.

The ability to use such a communicative system is crucial in the first stages of foreign language learning. We should consequently be tolerant of grammatical "errors" from learners who are at this stage of the learning process. Learners should not attempt active communication too soon, however. Before the learner is ready to begin speaking a foreign language, he or she should have a vocabulary of at least 200 words and a feel for the basic word order rules of the target language. The learner needs to develop a feel for the system of basic word order (in English, subject predicate sentence order, adverb and adjectival positions, negation, question formation, etc.). When speaking is taught, the initial goal should be the production of comprehensible utterances through expressing basic propositional meanings and illocutionary intentions.

## COMMUNICATION IS CONVENTIONAL

While much of the learner's efforts in speaking a foreign language center on developing the vocabulary and syntax needed to express propositional meanings, it is native speaker syntax and usage that is ultimately the learner's goal. As language acquisition proceeds, the learner revises his or her ideas about how propositions are expressed in English. The learner's syntax complexifies as knowledge of negation, the auxiliary system, questions, words order, embedding, conjoining, etc., expand. In short, the learner begins to develop grammatical competence.

Both linguists and applied linguists in recent years have emphasized the creative properties of human grammatical systems. Language users were said to possess as part of their grammatical competence the ability to produce an infinite number of sentences, most of which are novel utterances. The learner's task was said to be the internalization of the rules needed to generate any and all of the possible grammatical sentences of English. The primary focus of language teaching was to create opportunities for these grammatical abilities to develop in language learners.

The fact is, however, that only a fraction of the sentences which could be generated by our grammatical competence are actually ever used in communication. Communication largely consists of the use of sentences in conventional ways. Strict constraints are imposed on the creative-constructive capacities of speakers, and these serve to limit how speakers are entitled to code propositional meanings. In telling the time, for example, we can say, *It's two forty*, or *it's twenty to three*, but not *it's three minus twenty, it's ten after two thirty*, or *it's eight fives after 20*. If I want you to post a letter for me I may say, *Please post this letter for me*, or *Would you mind posting this letter for me*, but I am unlikely to say, *I request you to post this letter*, or *It is my desire that this letter be posted by you*. Although these sentences have been constructed according to the rules of English grammar, they are not conventional ways of using English. Though they are grammatically correct "sentences," they have no status as "utterances" within discourse, since they would never be used by native speakers of English.

This fact considerably complicates the task of foreign language learning. Once learners have progressed to the stage where they are beginning to generate novel utterances, they find that a considerable percentage of their utterances fail to conform to patterns of conventional usage, although they are undoubtedly English sentences. Constraints which require speakers to use only those utterances which are conventional affect both the lexical and grammatical structure of discourse. Constraints on lexical usage manifest themselves in idiosyncrasies and irregularities of usage which affect particularly verb, noun, preposition, and article usage and are usually rationalized as "exceptions" or collocational restrictions in teachers' explanations.

Thus teachers must explain that *a pair of trousers,* refers to one item but *a pair of shirts* to two, that we can speak of *a toothache* or *a headache* but not *a fingerache,* that someone may be *in church* but not *in library*. Conventionalized language is seen in many other dimensions of discourse. For example:

1. *Conversational openers. How are you?* may be used to open a conversation in English, but not *Are you well?* or *Are you in good health?*

2. *Routine formulas.* Some conventional forms are expressions whose use is limited to particular settings, such as *Check please* said when a bill is requested in a restaurant.

3. *Ceremonial formulas.* These are conventional phrases used in ritualized interactions, such as *after you,* said as a way of asking someone to go before you when entering a room, and *how nice to see you,* said on encountering a friend after an absence of some time (Yorio 1980).

4. *Memorized clauses* (Pawley and Syder in press). The concept of conventionalized language usage may be applied to a broader class of utterances. These are clauses which do not appear to be uniquely generated or created anew each time they are required in discourse but which are produced and stored as complete units. Pawley and Syder cite the following examples:
   Did you have a good trip?
   Is everything ok?
   Pardon me?
   Please sit down.
   Call me later.
   I see what you mean.

They argue that speakers of a language regularly use thousands of utterances like these. Unlike "novel" utterances (those which speakers put together from individual lexical items), these are preprogrammed and run off almost automatically in speech production. Researchers in second language acquisition have likewise observed that language learners often use conventional formulas and memorized clauses as crutches which make communication easier. There is often a high frequency of such forms in their speech in the early stages of conversational competence (Schmidt 1981).

The observation that language is conventional has important implications for language teaching. First, it suggests that there is reason to be skeptical of the suggestion that language cannot be taught but only "acquired." Many of the conventionalized aspects of language usage are amenable to teaching through various pedagogic formats. Second, applied linguistic effort is needed to gather fuller data on such forms, through discourse analysis and frequency counts, with a view to obtaining information of use to teachers, textbook writers, and syllabus designers.

## COMMUNICATION IS APPROPRIATE

Mastery of a foreign language requires more than the use of utterances which express propositional meanings and are conventional forms of expression. The form of utterances must also take into account the relationship between speaker and hearer and the constraints imposed by the setting and circumstances in which the act of communication is taking place. *What's your name?* is a conventional utterance, for example, but it is not an appropriate way of asking the identity of a telephone caller, for which purpose *May I know who is calling?* is considered a more appropriate way of requesting.

Communicative competence (Hymes 1972) includes knowledge of different types of communicative strategies or communicative styles according to the situation, the task, and the roles of the participants. For example, if a speaker wanted to get a match from another person in order to light a cigarette, he or she might make use of one of the following utterances, according to the speaker's judgment of its appropriateness:

1. Make a statement about his need. "I need a match."
2. Use an imperative: "Give me a match."
3. Use an embedded imperative: "Could you give me a match."
4. Use a permission directive: "May I have a match?"
5. Use a question directive: "Do you have a match?"
6. Make a hint: "The matches are all gone I see."

(Ervin-Tripp 1976)

Young children learning their mother tongue soon become skilled at using communicative strategies which they judge to be appropriate to different types of situations. Thus a child who wants something done for her may bargain, beg, name call, or threaten violence in talking to other children, reason, beg, or make promises in requesting to parents, or repeat the request several times or beg in talking to grandparents.

The choice of an appropriate strategy for performing a communicative task or speech act is dependent on such factors as the age, sex, familiarity, and role of speaker and hearer, which will determine whether a speaker adopts conversational strategies which mark *affiliation* or *dominance.* In the former case, "got a match" may be considered an appropriate way of requesting a match, and in the latter, "I wonder if I could bother you for a match" (Brown and Levinson 1978). Foreign language learners typically have less choice available to them for performing speech acts appropriately. They may use what they think of as a polite or formal style, for all situations, in which case they may be judged as being overformal, or they may create novel ways of coding particular speech acts, such as the use of *please + imperative* as a way of performing requests, regardless of who the speaker is talking to. For example, "Please, you carry this suitcase" said by a nonnative speaker to a friend, where "How about carrying this suitcase for me" would be a more appropriate form, or "Please. Bring me more coffee," said to a waitress, where a more appropriate form would be "Could I have another cup of coffee, please?" (Schmidt 1981).

Canadian researchers investigated the problem nonnative speakers have when they are put in a situation where they feel they lack the means of speaking appropriately, such as when a person who has been taught to use a formal type of French needs a style of speaking suitable for communication in informal situations. It was hypothesized that speakers would show considerable discomfort in using a casual style of speech and that they would handle this discomfort by downgrading the personality of the interlocutor and by judging that the interlocutor had formed a bad impression of them. It was argued that subjects would have some awareness that they were not speaking in a suitably friendly and casual manner and would conclude that they really did not like the person they were speaking to anyway. The results of the study supported this prediction. "These findings have certain implications for second language learners who have only mastered basic vocabulary and syntax in their new language but have not developed skills in the domain of linguistic variability. Such people may find social interaction with native-speakers in their new language to be a relatively negative experience and may become discouraged from pursuing language practice with native speakers" (Segalowitz and Gatbonton 1977, 86). Language learning texts have only recently begun to focus on the strategies learners need to use to express various types of speech acts appropriately. The emphasis is not simply on teaching functions and their exponents but on performing functions or speech acts appropriately in different types of communicative situations. Textbooks thus need to give practice in using particular speech acts with interlocutors of different ages, rank, and social status and practice in varying the form of speech acts according to these social variables.

## COMMUNICATION IS INTERACTIONAL

The use of utterances which are appropriate manifestations of speaker-hearer roles reflects the fact that conversation is often just as much a form of social encounter as it is a way of communicating meanings or ideas. This may be described as the interactional function of conversation. It is the use of language to keep the channels of communication open between conversationists and to establish a suitable atmosphere of rapport. Goffman has argued that "in any action, each actor provides a field of action for the other actors, and the reciprocity thus established allows the participants to exercise their interpersonal skills in formulating the situation, presenting and enacting a self or identity, and using strategies to accomplish other interactional ends" (cited by Watson 1974, p. 58). We see evidence of this at many levels within conversation. In the initial stages of conversation with a stranger, for example, conversationists introduce uncontroversial topics into the conversation, such as small talk about the weather or the transport system. These topics are carefully chosen so that there is a strong likelihood of mutual agreement between speaker and hearer. "The raising of safe topics allows the speaker the right to stress his agreement with the hearer's desire to be right or to be corroborated in his opinions . . . . The weather is a safe topic for virtually everyone, as is the beauty of gardens, the incompetence of bureaucracies, etc." (Brown and Levinson 1978, p. 117). These are examples of what has been called "phatic communion." "Much of what passes for communication is rather the equivalent of a handclasp, or an embrace; its purpose is sociability" (Bolinger 1975, p. 524).

The mechanisms of phatic communion include (1) the speaker's repertoire of verbal and visual gestures which signal interest in what our conversational partner is saying, such as the use of *mmm, uh uh, yeah, really,* etc.; (2) the speaker's stock of "canned topics" and formulaic utterances which are produced at relevant points in discourse, such as the small talk which is required to make brief encounters with acquaintances comfortable and positive; (3) knowledge of when to talk and when not to talk, that is, appropriate use of turn-taking conventions.

Adequate management of these dimensions of conversation is essential to create a sense of naturalness in conversational encounters. Nonnative speakers who lack the ability to use small talk and to manipulate the interactional aspects of communication may find many encounters awkward and may avoid talk where talk is appropriate. A foreign couple with a good command of English but lacking the ability to provide an ongoing output of conversational small talk was judged as cold, standoffish, and reserved by their American relatives (personal observation).

Communication as interaction is thus directed largely to the face needs of speaker and hearer, which require that we feel valued and approved of. If our conversational teaching materials emphasize primarily transactional skills, such as how to ask directions and how to order a meal, learners may not have the chance to acquire the interactional skills which are also an important component of communicative competence.

## COMMUNICATION IS STRUCTURED

The last aspect of communication I wish to consider is the ongoing organization of discourse. This can be considered from two perspectives, a "macro" perspective which looks at differences in rhetorical organization which reflect different discourse "genres" or tasks, and a "micro" perspective which considers how speech reflects some of the processes by which discourse is constructed out of individual utterances.

### Task Structure

Communication consists of different genres of discourse, such as conversations, discussions, debates, descriptions, narratives, and instructions. These different rhetorical tasks require the speaker to organize utterances in ways which are appropriate to that task. When we tell a story, for example, we follow certain conventions as to how stories proceed and develop. Stories consist of a setting, followed by episodes. The setting consists of states in which time, place, and characters are identified. Episodes consist of chains of events and conclude with reactions to events. Most stories can be described as having a structure of this type, and it is this structure which gives coherence to stories or narratives. Just as a sentence is grammatical to the extent that it follows the norms of English word order and structure, so a story is coherent to the extent that it follows the norms of semantic organization which are used in English.

Other types of rhetorical acts derive coherence from norms of structural organization. When we describe something, for example, coherence in our description is determined by how appropriately we deal with such elements as the level of the description, the content, the order in which items are described, and the relations between items mentioned in the description (Clark and Clark 1977).

In describing a landscape, for example, the writer must decide on the appropriate level of the description and decide whether to focus on the general impressions of the scene or focus on every detail, as, for example, in a police report. The writer must also make decisions concerning content, which will determine which elements of the scene to include or exclude. Then the elements must be arranged in an appropriate order and the relations between the things mentioned must be decided. Some objects may be highlighted in the description, for example, and other items related to them. The result will be a description that is coherent, that is, organized according to appropriate norms for that type of discourse. Similar decisions must be made when we describe people, rooms, states, or events. If we adopt solutions that are conventional, we create rhetorical acts that are coherent.

Other types of rhetorical acts develop in ways which are also organized and structured. Conversations, for example, begin with greetings and progress through various ordered moves in which speaker and hearer roles are ascertained, topics introduced, rights to talk assumed, new topics introduced, and at an appropriate time, the conversation terminated in a suitable manner. The development of communicative competence in a foreign language is crucially dependent on the speaker's ability to create discourse that is coherent. Schmidt (1981), in his study of the development of communicative competence in a Japanese adult, studied how the subject developed in his ability to perform coherent narratives and descriptions. At an early stage in his language development, the subject's attempts to narrate events suffered through the inclusion of excessive details presented in a random order, which made comprehension difficult.

## Process Structure

When we talk, much of our verbal output is made up of words and phrases which indicate how what we are going to say relates to what had been said. For example, our reaction to an idea or opinion may be to expand it, to add something to it, to disagree with it, to substantiate it, to give a reason for it, or to explain it. The following are examples of phrases or lexical items which may serve these or related functions:

When it comes to that, and another thing, all the same, consequently, in my case, all the same, to give you an idea, yes but, well maybe, actually, anyway, as a matter of fact, to begin with.

These have been termed conversational gambits (Keller 1981), and they signal directions and relations within discourse. Evidence suggests that these contribute significantly to the effect of fluency in conversation. Course materials are now available which focus just on these aspects of conversational competence. They can be used inappropriately, however, if used too often or in the wrong places, as in the following example:

To my mind I'll have another cup of coffee.

## CONCLUSIONS

Theories of how we teach a foreign language reflect our view of what the nature of language is. While it is no innovation to define language as a system of communication, the way the dynamics of the communicative process influence the form of verbal communication is often less fully appreciated. ESL materials have too often focused only on the finished *products* of communication rather than on the *processes* by which people communicate. A deeper understanding of the effects of communicative needs on nonnative speaker discourse should make us more understanding of our students' difficulties in using English and more tolerant of their partial successes.

# REFERENCES

Acton, W. 1979. "Second language learning and perception of differences in attitude." Unpublished Ph.D. dissertation, University of Michigan.

Adjemian, C. 1976. "On the nature of interlanguage systems." *Language Learning* 26(2):297-320.

Agnello, F. 1977. "Exploring the pidginization hypothesis: a study of three fossilized negation systems." In C. A. Henning (ed.). *Proceedings of the Los Angeles Second Language Research Forum.* Los Angeles: UCLA.

Albert, E. 1972. "Cultural patterning of speech behavior in Burundi." In J. J. Gumperz and D. Hymes (eds.). *Directions in Sociolinguistics.* New York: Holt, Rinehart and Winston.

Anisman, P. H. 1975. "Some aspects of code-switching in New York Puerto Rican English." *Bilingual Review* 2(1, 2):56-85.

Applegate, R. B. 1975. "The language teacher and the rules of speaking." *TESOL Quarterly* 9(3):271-281.

Aronson, E. 1965. *The Social Animal.* 2d ed. San Francisco: Freeman.

Arthur, B., R. Weiner, M. Culver, Y. J. Lee, and D. Thomas. 1980. "The register of impersonal discourse to foreigners: verbal adjustment in foreign accent." In D. Larsen-Freeman (ed.). *Discourse Analysis in Second Language Acquisition.* Rowley, Mass.: Newbury House.

Asher, J., and R. Garcia. 1969. "The optimal age to learn a foreign language." *Modern Language Journal* 8:334-341.

Austin, J. L. 1962. *How to Do Things with Words.* Cambridge, Mass. and Oxford: Harvard and Oxford University Presses.

Basso, K. H. 1972. "To give up on words: silence in Western Apache culture." In P. P. Giglioli (ed.). *Language and Social Context.* Baltimore: Penguin.

Bauman, R., and J. Sherzer. 1974. *Explorations in the Ethnography of Speaking.* London: Cambridge University Press.

Beebe, L. M. 1977. "The influence of the listener on code-switching." *Language Learning* 27(2):331-339.

Beebe, L. M. 1980. "Sociolinguistic variation and style shifting in second language acquisition." *Language Learning* 30(2).

Beebe, L. M. 1981. "Social and situational factors affecting the communicative strategy of dialect code-switching." *International Journal of the Sociology of Language* 32:139-149.

Beebe, L. M. 1983. "Risk-taking and the language learner." In H. Seliger and M. Long (eds.). *Classroom Oriented Research in Second Language Acquisition.* Rowley, Mass.: Newbury House.

Beebe, L. M., and J. Zuengler. 1981. "A word before the final vows." Review of H. Giles and R. N. St. Clair (eds.). *Language and Social Psychology. Contemporary Psychology* 26(4):279-280.

Bishop, G. D. 1979. "Perceived similarity in interracial attitudes and behaviors: the effects of belief and dialect style." *Journal of Applied Social Psychology* 9(5):446-465.

Blalock, H. M. 1960. *Social Statistics.* New York: McGraw-Hill.

Blom, J-P., and J. J. Gumperz. 1972. "Social meaning in linguistic structures: code switching in Norway." In J. J. Gumperz and D. Hymes (eds.). *Directions in Sociolinguistics: The Ethnography of Communication.* New York: Holt, Rinehart and Winston.

Blum-Kulka, S. 1980. "The study of translation in view of new developments in discourse analysis: the problem of indirect speech acts." In I. Even Zohar and G. Toury (eds.). *Theory of Translation and Intercultural Relationships.* The Porter Institute for Poetics and Semantics.

Blum-Kulka, S. 1982. "Learning to say what you mean in a second language: a study of the speech act performance of learners of Hebrew as a second language." *Applied Linguistics* 3(1).

Bolinger, D. 1975. *Aspects of Language.* 2d ed. New York: Harcourt Brace Jovanovich.

Borkin, A., and C. Carpenter. 1979. "Academic guidance in professor-student consultations." Presented at the Thirteenth Annual TESOL Conference, Boston.

Borkin, A., and S. M. Reinhart. 1978. "Excuse me and I'm sorry." *TESOL Quarterly* 12(1): 57-70.

Bourhis, R. Y., and F. Genesee. 1980. "Evaluative reactions to code-switching strategies in Montreal." Presented at the International Conference on Social Psychology and Language University of Bristol, July 16-20, 1979. In H. Giles, W. P. Robinson, and P. Smith (eds.). *Language: Social Psychological Perspectives.* Oxford: Pergamon Press.

Bourhis, R. Y., and H. Giles. 1977. "The language of intergroup distinctiveness." In H. Giles (ed.). *Language, Ethnicity, and Intergroup Relations.* London: Academic Press.

Bourhis, R. Y., H. Giles, and W. E. Lambert. 1975. "Some consequences of accommodating one's style of speech: a cross-national investigation." *International Journal of the Sociology of Language* 6:55-72.

Bourhis, R. Y., H. Giles, J. P. Leyens, and H. Tajfel. 1979. "Psycho-linguistic distinctiveness: language divergence in Belgium." In H. Giles and R. N. St. Clair (eds.). *Language and Social Psychology.* Baltimore: University Park Press.

Brouwer, D., M. Gerritsen, and D. DeHaan. 1979. "Speech differences between women and men: on the wrong track?" *Language in Society* 8(1):33-50.

Brown, H. D. 1973. "Affective variables in second language acquisition." *Language Learning* 23(2):231-244.

Brown, H. D. 1979. "The seventies:learning to ask the right questions." (editorial) *Language Learning* 29(1):v-vi.

Brown, H. D. 1980. *Principles of Language Learning and Teaching.* Englewood Cliffs, N.J.: Prentice-Hall.

Brown, P., and A. Gilman. 1960. "The pronouns of power and solidarity." In T. Sebeok (ed.). *Style in Language.* Cambridge, Mass.: MIT Press. Reprinted in P. Giglioli (ed.). *Language and Social Context.* New York: Penguin Books, 1972.

Brown, P., and S. Levinson. 1978. "Universals in language usage: politeness phenomena." In E. N. Goody (ed.). *Questions and Politeness: Strategies in Social Interaction.* Cambridge: Cambridge University Press.

Brown, R. L., Jr. 1980. "The pragmatics of verbal irony." In R. W. Shuy and A. Schnukal (eds.). *Language Use and the Uses of Language.* Washington, D.C.: Georgetown University Press.

Brown, R. W., and M. Ford. 1961. "Address in American English." *Journal of Abnormal and Social Psychology* 62:375-385. Reprinted in D. Hymes (ed.). *Language in Culture and Society.* New York: Harper and Row, 1967.

Brown, T. H., and K. C. Sandberg. 1969. *Conversational English.* New York: Wiley.

Bruzzese, G. 1977. "English-Italian secondary hybridization: a case study of the pidginization of a second language learner's speech." In C. A. Henning (ed.). *Proceedings of the Los Angeles Second Language Research Forum.* Los Angeles: UCLA.

Campbell, R., W. Rutherford, M. Finocchiaro, and H. Widdowson. 1978. "Notional-functional syllabuses: 1978." In C. Blatchford and J. Schachter (eds.). *On TESOL '78.* Washington, D.C.: TESOL.

Canale, M. 1981. "On some dimensions of language proficiency." In J. W. Oller, Jr. (ed.). *Current Issues in Language Testing Research.* Rowley, Mass.: Newbury House.

Canale, M. In press. "From communicative competence to communicative language pedagogy." In J. Richards and R. Schmidt (eds.). *Language and Communication.* London: Longman.

Canale, M., and M. Swain. 1980. "Theoretical bases of communicative approaches to second language teaching and testing." *Applied Linguistics* 1(1):1-47.

Cancino, H., E. J. Rosansky, and J. H. Schumann. 1978. "The acquisition of English negatives and interrogatives by native Spanish speakers." In E. M. Hatch (ed.). *Second Language Acquisition: A Book of Readings.* Rowley, Mass.: Newbury House.

Candlin, C. N., C. J. Bruton, and J. H. Leather. 1974. *Doctor-Patient Communication Skills: Working Papers 1-4.* Lancaster: University of Lancaster Department of Linguistics and Modern English Language.

Candlin, C. N., C. J. Bruton, and J. H. Leather. 1976. "Doctor speech functions in casualty consultations: some quantified characteristics of discourse in a regulated setting." In G. Nickel (ed.). *Proceedings of the III AILA Congress.* Stuttgart: Hochschulverlag.

Candlin, C. N., C. J. Bruton, and J. H. Leather. 1978. *Doctor-Patient Communication Skills.* Chelmsford: Graves Audio-Visual Medical Library.

Candlin, C. N., J. Burton, and H. Coleman. 1980. *Dentist-Patient Communication: A Report to the General Dental Council.* Lancaster: University of Lancaster Department of Linguistics and Modern English Language.

Candlin, C. N., J. H. Leather, and C. J. Bruton. 1976. "Applying communicative competence to components of specialist course design." *I.R.A.L.* 14 (3).

Carroll, J. 1967. "Foreign language proficiency levels attained by language majors near graduation from college." *Foreign Language Annals* 1:131-151.

Carroll, J. 1973. "Implications of aptitude test research and psycholinguistic theory for foreign language teaching." *Linguistics* 112:5-13.

Carver, T. K., and S. D. Fotinos. 1977. *A Conversation Book: English in Everyday Life,* Book 1. Englewood Cliffs, N.J.: Prentice-Hall.

Castello, K. 1981. "Contrastive analysis: speech acts: apologies." Los Angeles: ESL Section, Department of English, UCLA.

Cazden, C., H. Cancino, E. J. Rosansky, and J. H. Schumann. 1975. *Second Language Acquisition Sequences in Children, Adolescents and Adults.* Final report, U. S. Department of Health, Education and Welfare.

Chafe, W. 1968. "English questions." *ERIC/Pegs Paper* 26 for the Center for Applied Linguistics.

Chambers, J. K., and P. Trudgill. 1980. *Dialectology.* Cambridge: Cambridge University Press.

Chastain, K. 1975. "Affective and ability factors in second language learning." 25:153-161.

Chomsky, N. 1965. *Aspects of the Theory of Syntax.* Cambridge: MIT Press.

Churchill, L. 1978. *Questioning Strategies in Sociolinguistics.* Rowley, Mass.: Newbury House.

Clark, H. H., and E. V. Clark. 1977 *Psychology and Language.* New York: Harcourt Brace Jovanovich.

Clarke, M. 1976. "Second language acquisition as a clash of consciousness." *Language Learning* 26:377-390.

Cohen, A. D., and E. Olshtain. 1981. "Developing a measure of sociocultural competence: the case of apology." *Language Learning* 31(1).

Cole, P., and J. Morgan (eds.). 1975. *Speech Acts.* Volume 3 of *Syntax and Semantics.* New York: Academic Press.

Coleman, H. 1984. "Perceptions of language use in a bilingual industrial community." *International Journal of the Sociology of Language* 49:51-72.

Coleman, H., and J. Burton. 1985. "Aspects of control in the dentist-patient relationship." *International Journal of the Sociology of Language* 51:75-104.

Cook, V. 1981a. "Some uses for second language acquisition research." Presented at New York Academy of Sciences Conference on Native Language and Foreign Language Acquisition, New York.

Cook, V. 1981b. "Language functions in second language learning and teaching." Presented at AILA, Lund, Sweden.

Corder, S. P. 1971. "Idiosyncratic dialects and error analysis." *IRAL* 9(2):147-160.

Corder, S. P. 1977. "Language continua and the interlanguage hypothesis." In S. P. Corder and E. Roulet (eds.). *The Notions of Simplification, Interlanguages and Pidgins and Their Relation to Second Language Pedagogy.* Neuchatel: Faculte des Lettres.

Coulmas, F. (ed.). 1981. *Conversational Routine: Explorations in Standardized Communication Situations and Prepatterned Speech.* The Hague: Mouton.

Crandall, J., and A. Grognet. 1979. "The notional-functional syllabus in adult ESL: promises and problems." In R. di Pietro, W. Frawley, and A. Wedel (eds.). *First Delaware Symposium on Language Studies.* Newark: University of Delaware Press.

Crowell, T. L., Jr. 1964. *Index to Modern English.* New York: McGraw-Hill.

Danet, B., N. Kermish, H. J. Rafn, and D. Stayman. 1976. "Language and the construction of reality in the courtroom II: toward an ethnography of questioning." Working Paper 5 on the role of language in the legal process. Boston: Boston University.

Danielson, D., and R. Hayden. 1973. *Using English.* Englewood Cliffs, N.J.: Prentice-Hall.

Dickerson, L., and W. Dickerson. 1977. "Interlanguage phonology: current research and future directions." In S. P. Corder and E. Roulet (eds.). *The Notions of Simplification, Interlanguages and Pidgins and Their Relation to Second Language Pedagogy.* Neuchâtel: Faculté des Lettres.

Dittmar, N. 1981. "On the verbal organization of L2 tense marking in an elicited translation task by Spanish immigrants in Germany." *Studies in Second Language Acquisition* 3(2): 136-164.

Doise, W., A. Sinclair, and R. Y. Bourhis. 1976. "Evaluation of accent convergence and divergence in cooperative and competitive intergroup situations." *British Journal of Social and Clinical Psychology* 15:247-252.

Dubin, F. 1977. *It's Time to Talk.* Englewood Cliffs, N.J.: Prentice-Hall.

Dubois, B. L., and I. Crouch. 1975. "The question of tag questions in women's speech: they don't really use more of them, do they?" *Language in Society* 4:289-294.

Dulay, H., and M. Burt. 1974. "A new perspective on the creative construction process in child second language acquisition." *Language Learning* 24(2):253-278.

Dulay, H., and M. Burt. 1975. "Creative construction in second language learning and teaching." In M. Burt and H. Dulay (eds.). *New Directions in Second Language Learning, Teaching and Bilingual Education.* Washington, D.C.:TESOL.

Dulay, H., and M. Burt. 1978. "Some remarks on creativity in language acquisition." In W. C. Ritchie (ed.). *Second Language Acquisition Research: Issues and Implications.* New York: Academic Press.

Duncan, S. 1972. "Some signals and rules for taking speaking turns in conversation." *Journal of Personality and Social Psychology* 23:283-292.

Duncan, S. 1973. "Toward a grammar for dyadic conversation." *Semiotica* 9:29-46.

Duskova, Libuse. 1969. "On sources of errors in foreign language learning." *IRAL* 7:11-36.

Edelsky, C. 1981. "Who's got the floor?" *Language in Society* 10:383-421.

Ervin-Tripp, S. 1972. "On sociolinguistics rules: alternation and co-occurrence." In J. J. Gumperz and D. Hymes (eds.). *Directions in Sociolinguistics.* New York: Holt, Rinehart and Winston.

Ervin-Tripp, S. 1976. "Is Sybil there? The structure of American English directives." *Language in Society* 5(1):25-66.

Ervin-Tripp, S. 1977. "Wait for me, roller skate!" In S. Ervin-Tripp and C. Mitchell-Kernan (eds.). *Child Discourse*. New York: Academic Press.

Ervin-Tripp, S. 1981. "Social process in first- and second-language learning." In H. Winitz (ed.). *Native Language and Foreign Language Acquisition*. New York: New York Academy of Sciences.

Ervin-Tripp, S., and C. Mitchell-Kernan. 1977. *Child Discourse*. New York: Academic Press.

Fathman, A. 1975. "The relationship between age and second language productive ability." *Language Learning* 25:245-266.

Ferguson, C. A. 1971. "Absence of copula and the notion of simplicity: a study of normal speech, baby talk, foreigner talk and pidgins." In D. Hymes (ed.). *Pidginization and Creolization in Language*. New York: Cambridge University Press.

Ferguson, C. A. 1975. "Toward a characterization of English foreigner talk." *Anthropological Linguistics* 17(1).

Ferguson, C. A. 1976. "The structure and use of politeness formulas." *Language in Society* 5(2):137-151.

Ferguson, C. A. 1977. "Simplified registers, broken language and Gastarbeiterdeutsch." In C. Molony, H. Zobl, and W. Stolting (eds.). *Deutsch im Kontakt mit Anderen Sprachen*. Kronberg: Scripto Verlag.

Fillmore, L. W. 1976. "The second time around: cognitive and social strategies in language acquisition. Ph.D. dissertation. Stanford University.

Fillmore, L. W. 1979. "Individual differences in second language acquisition." In C. J. Fillmore, D. Kempler, and W. S-Y. Wang (eds.). *Individual Differences in Language Ability*. New York: Academic Press.

Finocchiaro, M. 1970. *Let's Talk*. New York: Regents.

Fishman, J. A. 1965. "Who speaks what language to whom and when?" *La Linguistique* 2:67-88. Also in J. B. Pride and J. Holmes (eds.). *Sociolinguistics*. Harmondsworth, England: Penguin Books, 1972.

Fitton, F., and A. W. K. Acheson. 1979. *The Doctor-Patient Relationship: A Study in General Practice*. London H. M. S. O. for D. H. S. S.

Flege, J. E. 1980. "Phonetic approximation in second language acquisition." *Language Learning* 30(1):117-134.

Ford, C. 1981. "Areas of mastery and difficulty in the English apology performance of three native Spanish speakers." 18247 Ludlow St., Northridge, Calif.

Fraser, B. 1977. "Conversational mitigation." Ditto. Boston: Boston University.

Fraser, B. 1978. "Acquiring social competence in a second language." *RELC Journal* 9(2):1-26.

Fraser, B. 1980. "On apologizing." In F. Coulmas (ed.). *Conversational Routine*. The Hague: Mouton.

Gardner, R. C. 1979. "Social psychological aspects of second language acquisition." In H. Giles and R. N. St. Clair (eds.). *Language and Social Psychology*. Baltimore: University Park Press.

Gardner, R. C., and W. E. Lambert. 1972. *Attitudes and Motivation in Second Language Learning*. Rowley, Mass.: Newbury House.

Garvey, C. 1979. "Contingent queries." In M. Lewis and L. Rosenbaum (eds.), *Interaction, Conversation and the Development of Language*. New York: Wiley.

Gaskill, W. 1980. "Correction in native speaker-nonnative speaker conversation." In D. Larsen-Freeman (ed.). *Discourse Analysis in Second Language Research*. Rowley, Mass.: Newbury House.

Genesse, R. 1981. "The state of the art of neurolinguistics and second language learning and teaching." Presented at the Fifteenth Annual TESOL Conference, Detroit.

Giddens, D. 1981. "An analysis of the syntax and discourse of oral complaints in Spanish." M.A. thesis. UCLA.

Giles, H. 1977. "Social psychology and applied linguistics: towards an integrative approach." *ITL: Review of Applied Linguistics* 33:27-42.

Giles, H. 1979a. "Ethnicity markers in speech." In K. Scherer and H. Giles (eds.). *Social Markers in Speech.* Cambridge: Cambridge University Press.

Giles, H. 1979b. "Sociolinguistics and social psychology: an introductory essay." In H. Giles and R. N. St. Clair (eds.). *Language and Social Psychology.* Baltimore: University Park Press.

Giles, H., R. H. Bourhis, and D. M. Taylor. 1977. "Towards a theory of language in ethnic group relations." In H. Giles (ed.). *Language, Ethnicity and Intergroup Relations.* London: Academic Press.

Giles, H., and J. L. Byrne. 1980. "An intergroup approach to second language acquisition." *Revista de educacion.* Special issue 265 on bilingual education.

Giles, H., M. Hewstone, and R. N. St. Clair. In press. "Cognitive structures and a social psychology of communication: new integrative models and an introductory overview." In H. Giles and R. N. St. Clair (eds.). *The Social Psychological Significance of Communication.* Hillsdale, N.J.: Lawrence Erlbaum Associates.

Giles, H., and P. F. Powesland. 1975. *Speech Style and Social Evaluation.* London: Academic Press.

Giles, H., and R. N. St. Clair (eds.). 1979. *Language and Social Psychology.* Baltimore: University Park Press.

Giles, H., and P. M. Smith. 1979. "Accommodation theory: optimal levels of convergence." In H. Giles and R. N. St. Clair (eds.). *Language and Social Psychology.* Baltimore: University Park Press.

Goffman, E. 1971. *Relations in Public.* New York: Harper Colophon Books.

Goffman, E. 1974. *Frame Analysis: An Essay on the Organization of Experience.* Cambridge, Mass.: Harvard University Press.

Goodenough, W. H. 1957. "Cultural anthropology and linguistics." In P. L. Garvin (ed.). *Report of the Seventh Annual Roundtable Meeting on Linguistics and Language Study.* Washington, D.C., pp. 167-173.

Goody, E. N. (ed.). 1978a. *Questions and Politeness: Strategies in Social Interaction.* Cambridge: Cambridge University Press.

Goody, E. N. 1978b. "Toward a theory of questions." In E. N. Goody (ed.). *Questions and Politeness: Strategies in Social Interaction.* Cambridge: Cambridge University Press.

Gordon, D., and G. Lakoff. 1975. "Conversational postulates." In P. Cole and J. Morgan (eds.) *Speech Acts.* Volume 3 of *Syntax and Semantics.* New York: Academic Press.

Graham, J. 1980. "Cross-cultural negotiation." Unpublished Ph.D. dissertation. University of California, Berkeley.

Green, M. G. 1975. "How to get people to do things with words: the wh imperative question." In P. Cole and J. Morgan (eds.). *Speech Acts.* Volume 3 of *Syntax and Semantics.* New York: Academic Press.

Greene, J. 1980. "Which." In R. Shuy and A. Shnukal (eds.). *Language Use and the Uses of Language.* Washington, D.C.: Georgetown University Press.

Grice, H. P. 1975. "Logic and conversation." In P. Cole and J. Morgan (eds.). *Speech Acts.* Volume 3 of *Syntax and Semantics.* New York: Academic Press.

Guiora, A., M. Paluszny, G. Beit-Hallahmi, J. Catford, R. Cooley, and C. Dull. 1975. "Language and person: studies in language behavior." *Language Learning* 25:43-61.

Gumperz, J. J., and D. Hymes (eds.). 1972. *Directions in Sociolinguistics.* New York: Holt, Rinehart and Winston.

Gumperz, J. J. 1978a. "Language, social knowledge and personal relations." Manuscript.

Gumperz, J. J. 1978b. "The conversational analysis of interethnic communication." In E. L. Ross (ed.). *Interethnic Communication: Proceedings of the Southern Anthropological Society* 12. Athens, Ga.: University of Georgia Press.

Habermas, J. 1970. "Introductory remarks to a theory of communicative competence." *Inquiry* 13(3). Reprinted in H. P. Dreitsel (ed.). *Recent Sociology.* London: Macmillan.

Hakuta, K. 1974. "A preliminary report on the development of grammatical morphemes in a Japanese girl learning English as a second language." *Working Papers on Bilingualism* 3:18-43.

Hakuta, K. 1976. "A case study of a Japanese child learning English as a second language." *Language Learning* 26:321-351.

Hale, T., and E. Budar. 1970. "Are TESOL classes the only answer?" *Modern Language Journal* 54:487-492.

Halliday, M. A. K. 1970. "Language structure and language function." In J. Lyons (ed.). *New Horizons in Linguistics.* London: Penguin Books.

Halliday, M. A. K. 1973. *Explorations in the Functions of Language.* London: Edward Arnold.

Halliday, M. A. K. 1975. "Explorations in the functions of language." In P. Doughty and G. Thornton (eds.). *Explorations in Language Study.* London: Edward Arnold.

Harris, J. G., and R. Hube. 1975. *On Speaking Terms.* New York: Collier Macmillan.

Hartman, P. L., and E. L. Judd. 1978. "Sexism and TESOL materials." *TESOL Quarterly* 12:383-393.

Hatch, E. M. 1978a. "Acquisition of syntax in a second language." In J. C. Richards (ed.). *Understanding Second and Foreign Language Learning.* Rowley, Mass.: Newbury House.

Hatch, E. M. 1978b. *Second Language Acquisition: A Book of Readings.* Rowley, Mass.: Newbury House.

Hatch, E. M. 1978c. "Discourse analysis and second language acquisition." In E. M. Hatch (ed.). *Second Language Acquisition: A Book of Readings.* Rowley, Mass.: Newbury House.

Hatch, E. M., R. Shapira, and J. Gough. 1978. "Foreigner talk discourse." *ITL: Review of Applied Linguistics* 39/40.

Henkin, B. 1979. *The Rocky Horror Picture Show.* Hawthorn Books.

Henzl, V. 1973. "Linguistic register of foreign language instruction." *Language Learning* 23(2):207-222.

Heyde, A. 1977. "The relationship between self-esteem and the oral production of a second language." In H. D. Brown, C. Yorio, and R. Crymes (eds.). *On TESOL '77, Teaching and Learning English as a Second Language: Trends in Research and Practice.* Washington, D.C.: TESOL.

Higa, M. 1971. "Toward contrastive sociolinguistics." *PCCLV Papers* 3(4):211-219.

Hildebrandt, N., and H. Giles. 1980. "The English language in Japan: a social psychological perspective." *JALT Journal* 2:63-87.

Holmes, J., and D. F. Brown, 1976. "Developing sociolinguistic competence in a second language." *TESOL Quarterly* 10(4):423-431.

Homans, G. D. 1961. *Social Behavior: Its Elementary Forms.* New York: Harcourt, Brace and World.

Hudson, R. A. 1980. *Sociolinguistics.* Cambridge: Cambridge University Press.

Hymes, D. 1962. "The ethnography of speaking." In T. Gladwin and W. Sturtevant (eds.). *Anthropology and Human Behavior.* Washington, D.C.: Anthropological Society of Washington. Reprinted in J. Fishman (ed.). *Readings in the Sociology of Language.* The Hague: Mouton, 1968.

Hymes, D. 1964. "Directions in (ethno)linguistic theory." *American Anthropologist* 6, 3 (part 2):6-56.

Hymes, D. 1967. "Models of the interaction of language and social setting." *Journal of Social Issues* 23(2):8-28.

Hymes, D. 1972a. "Models of the interaction of language and social life." In J. J. Gumperz and D. Hymes (eds.). *Directions in Sociolinguistics: The Ethnography of Communication.* New York: Holt, Rinehart and Winston.

Hymes, D. 1972b. "On communicative competence." In J. B. Pride and J. Holmes (eds.). *Sociolinguistics.* Harmondsworth, England: Penguin Books.

Hymes, D. 1974. *Foundations in Sociolinguistics: An Ethnographic Approach.* Philadelphia: University of Pennsylvania Press.

Hymes, V. 1975. "The ethnography of linguistic intuitions at Warm Springs." *Proceedings of the 1975 LACUS Forum.* Columbia, S.C.: Hornbeam Press.

Inoue, J. 1982. "A discourse analysis of complaints made by Japanese students. M.A. thesis. UCLA.

International Student Exam. American Language Institute Placement Test. Los Angeles: University of Southern California.

Irvine, J. 1974. "Strategies of status manipulation in the Wolof greeting." In R. Bauman and J. Sherzer (eds.). *Explorations in the Ethnography of Speaking.* Cambridge: Cambridge University Press.

Jakobovits, L. A., and B. Y. Gordon. 1975. *Community Cataloguing Practices, Series III: Standardization patterns.* Honolulu: Department of Psychology, University of Hawaii.

Jakobson, R. 1972. "Motor signs for 'yes' and 'no'." *Language in Society* 1(1):91-96.

Jefferson, G. 1972. "Side sequences." In D. Sudnow (ed.). *Studies in Social Interaction.* New York: Free Press.

Jefferson, G. 1973. "A case of precision timing in ordinary conversation: overlapped tag-positioned address terms in closing sequences." *Semiotica* 9(1).

Jespersen, O. 1922. *Language: Its Nature, Development and Origin.* London: Allen and Unwin.

Johansson, F. A. 1973. *Immigrant Swedish Phonology: A Study in Multiple Contact Analysis.* Lund, Sweden: CWK Gleerup.

Johnston, M. V. 1973. "Observations on learning French by immersion." Psycholinguistics Paper, UCLA. Abstracted in E. M. Hatch (ed.). *Second Language Acquisition: A Book of Readings.* Rowley, Mass.: Newbury House, 1978.

Jones, E. E., and K. E. Davis. 1965. "From acts to dispositions: The attribution process in perception." In L. Berkowitz (ed.). *Advances in Social Psychology II.* New York and London: Academic Press.

Jordens, P., and E. Kellerman. 1981. "Investigations into the 'transfer strategy' in second language learning." In J. Savard and L. La forge (eds.). *Proceedings of the Fifth Congress of l'Association Internationale de Linguistique Appliquée.* Quebec: Laval University Press.

Kachru, B. B. 1976. "Models of English for the Third World: white man's linguistic burden or language pragmatics?" *TESOL Quarterly* 10:221-239.

Keenan, E. O. 1974. "Conversational competence in children." *Journal of Child Language* 1:163-183.

Keenan, E. O. 1976. "On the universality of conversational implications." *Language in Society* 5(1):67-80.

Keenan, E. O., and B. B. Schieffelin. 1976. "Topic as a discourse notion: a study of topic in the conversations of children and adults. In C. Li (ed.). *Subject and Topic.* New York: Academic Press.

Keller, E. 1981. "Gambits: conversational strategy signals." In F. Coulmas (ed.). *Conversational Routine.* The Hague: Mouton.

Kelly, H. H. 1967. "Attribution theory in social psychology." *Nebraska Symposium on Motivation* 14:192-241.

Keltner, A., and G. Bitterlin. 1981. *English for Adult Competency.* Englewood Cliffs, N.J.: Prentice-Hall.

Kessler, C., and I. Idar. 1979. "Acquisition of English by a Vietnamese mother and child." *Working Papers on Bilingualism* 18:65-80.

Kettering, J. C. 1975. *Developing Communicative Competence.* Pittsburgh: The University Center for International Studies, University of Pittsburgh.

Key, M. R. 1975. *Male/Female Language.* Metuchen, N.J.: Scarecrow Press.

Kim, S. B. 1981. "A contrastive analysis of sociocultural competence between a native English speaker and a native Korean speaker in the case of apology." Los Angeles: ESL Section, Department of English, UCLA.

Kingston, A., and T. Lovelace. 1978. "Sexism and reading: a critical review of the literature." *Reading Research Quarterly* 13:133-161.

Kramarae, C. 1981. *Women and Men Speaking*. Rowley, Mass.: Newbury House.

Kramer, C. 1974. "Folklinguistics." *Psychology Today 8(1):82-85.*

Krashen, S. D. 1975. "The critical period hypothesis and its possible bases." In D. R. Aaronson and R. W. Reiber (eds.). *Developmental Psycholinguistics and Communication Disorders*. New York: The New York Academy of Sciences.

Krashen, S. D. 1976. "Formal and informal linguistic environments in language learning and language acquisition." *TESOL Quarterly* 10:157-168.

Krashen, S. D. 1977. "The Monitor Model for adult second language performance." In M. Burt, H. Dulay, and M. Finocchiaro (eds.). *Viewpoints on English as a Second Language*. New York: Regents.

Krashen, S. D. 1978a. "The Monitor Model for second-language acquisition." In R. C. Gingras (ed.). *Second Language Acquisition and Foreign Language Teaching*. Arlington, Va.: Center for Applied Linguistics.

Krashen, S. D. 1978b. "Individual variation in the use of the Monitor." In W. Ritchie (ed.). *Principles of Second Language Learning*. New York: Academic Press.

Krashen, S. D. 1980a. "The theoretical and practical relevance of simple codes in second language acquisition." In R. Scarcella and S. D. Krashen (eds.). *Research in Second Language Acquisition*. Rowley, Mass.: Newbury House.

Krashen, S. D. 1980b. "Attitude and aptitude in relation to second language acquisition and learning." In K. Diller (ed.). *Individual Differences in Language Learning Aptitude*. Rowley, Mass.: Newbury House.

Krashen, S. D. 1980c. "The input hypothesis." In J. E. Alatis (ed.). *Current Issues in Bilingual Education*. Washington, D.C.: Georgetown University Press.

Krashen, S. D. 1981. *Second Language Acquisition and Second Language Learning*. Oxford: Pergamon Press.

Krashen, S. D., M. H. Long, and R. C. Scarcella. 1979. "Age, rate and eventual attainment in second language acquisition." *TESOL Quarterly* 13(4):573-582.

Krashen, S. D., and R. Scarcella. 1978. "On routines and patterns in language acquisition and performance." *Language Learning* 28:283-300.

Krashen, S. D., and H. Seliger. 1976. "The role of formal and informal linguistic environments in adult second language learning." *International Journal of Psycholinguistics* 3:15-21.

Krashen, S. D., H. Seliger, and D. Hartnett. 1974. "Two studies in adult second language learning." *Kritikon Litterarum* 2/3:220-228.

Krohn, R. 1971. *English Sentence Structure*. Ann Arbor: The University of Michigan Press.

Labov, W. 1966. *The Social Stratification of English in New York City*. Washington, D.C.: Center for Applied Linguistics.

Labov, W. 1972a. *Sociolinguistic Patterns*. Philadelphia: University of Pennsylvania Press.

Labov, W. 1972b. *Language in the Inner City: Studies in the Black English Vernacular*. Philadelphia: University of Pennsylvania Press.

Labov, W., and D. Fanshel. 1977. *Therapeutic Discourse: Psychotherapy as Conversation*. New York: Academic Press.

Labov, W., and J. Waletzky. 1967. "Narrative analysis." In *Essays on the Verbal and Visual Arts*. Seattle: University of Washington Press.

Lado, R. 1978. *Lado English Series*, Book I. New York: Regents.

Lakoff, R. 1973. "Language and women's place." *Language in Society* 2:45-80.

Lakoff, R., and D. Tannen. 1979. "Communicative strategies in conversation: the case of 'Scenes from a marriage'." *Proceedings of the Fifth Annual Meeting of the Berkeley Linguistics Society*. Berkeley: University of California.

Lambert, W. E. 1963. "Psychological approaches to the study of language. Part two—On second language learning and bilingualism." *Modern Language Journal* 14:114-121.

Lambert, W. E., R. C. Hodgson, R. C. Gardner, and S. Fillenbaum. 1960. "Evaluational reactions to spoken languages." *Journal of Abnormal Social Psychology* 60:44-51.

Lambert, W. E., R. C. Hodgson, R. C. Gardner, and S. Fillenbaum. 1972. "Evaluational reactions to spoken languages." In A. S. Dil (ed.). *Language, Psychology and Culture.* Stanford: Stanford University Press.

Larsen-Freeman, D. (ed.). 1980. *Discourse Analysis in Second Language Research.* Rowley, Mass.: Newbury House.

Larsen-Freeman, D. 1981. "The WHAT of second language acquisition." Plenary session, Fifteenth Annual TESOL Conference, Detroit.

Lenneberg, E. H. 1967. *Biological Foundations of Language.* New York: John Wiley & Sons.

Levenston, E. 1970. *English for Israelis.* Jerusalem: Israel Universities Press.

Levenston, E. 1971. "Some thoughts on contrastive analysis and translation equivalence." *PCCLV Papers* 3(4):275-283.

Levinson, S. 1979. "Activity types and language." *Linguistics* 17.

Linde, C. 1981. "The organization of discourse." In T. Shopen, A. Zwicky, and P. Griffin (eds.). *The English Language: English in Its Social and Historical Context.* Cambridge, Mass.: Winthrop Press.

Loban, W. 1976. *Language Development: Kindergarten through Grade Twelve.* NCTE Research Report 18. Urbana, Ill.: National Council of Teachers of English.

Long, M. 1981. "Questions in foreigner-talk discourse." *Language Learning* 31(1):135-157.

Long, M. In press. "Input, interaction and second language acquisition." Presented at the New York Academy of Sciences Conference on Native Language and Foreign Language Acquisition, New York, January 15-16, 1981. To appear in *Annals of the New York Academy of Sciences.*

Macnamara, J. 1973. "The cognitive strategies of language learning." In J. W. Oller and J. C. Richards (eds.), *Focus on the Learner.* Rowley, Mass.: Newbury House.

Manes, J., and N. Wolfson. 1980. "The compliment formula." In F. Coulmas (ed.). *Conversational Routine.* The Hague: Mouton.

Marlos, E., and S. Gass. 1981. "The effect of grammaticality on judgments of nonnative pronunciation." Presented at the Fifteenth Annual TESOL Conference, Detroit.

Mason, C. 1971. "The relevance of intensive training in English as a foreign language for university students." *Language Learning* 21:197-204.

McConnell-Ginet, S., R. Borker, and N. Furman. 1980. *Women and Language in Literature and Society.* New York: Praeger.

McCurdy, P. 1980. "Talking to foreigners: the role of rapport." Unpublished Ph.D. dissertation. University of California, Berkeley.

McTear, M. 1978. "Hey, I've got something to tell you: a study of the initiation of conversation exchanges by preschool children." Presented at the AILA Conference, Montreal.

Morrow, K. 1977. *Techniques of Evaluation for a Notional Syllabus.* London: The Royal Society of Arts.

Munby, J. 1978. *Communicative Syllabus Design.* Cambridge: Cambridge University Press.

Naiman, N., M. Frohlich, D. Stern, and A. Todesco. 1978. *The Good Language Learner.* Toronto: Ontario Institute for Studies in Education.

Nemser, W. 1971. "Approximative systems of foreign language learners." *IRAL* 9(2):115-123.

Newmark, L. 1976. "How not to interfere with language learning." *International Journal of American Linguistics* 40.

Nilsen, A. P., H. Bosmajian, H. L. Gershuny, and J. P. Stanley. 1977. *Sexism and Language.* Urbana, Ill.: National Council of Teachers of English.

O'Barr, W., and B. Atkins. 1980. "Women's language or powerless language?" In S. McConnell-Ginet, R. Borker, and N. Furman (eds). *Women and Language in Literature and Society.* New York: Praeger.

Oller, J. W., and K. Perkins. 1978. "Intelligence and language proficiency as sources of variance in self-reported affective variables." *Language Learning* 28(1):85-97.

Olshtain, E. 1983. "Sociocultural competence and language transfer: the case of apology." In

S. Gass and L. Selinker (eds.), *Language Transfer in Language Learning*. Rowley, Mass.: Newbury House.

Oyama, S. 1976. "A sensitive period for the acquisition of a non-native phonological system." *Journal of Psycholinguistic Research* 5:261-285.

Oyama, S. 1978. "The sensitive period and comprehension of speech." *Working Papers on Bilingualism* 16:1-17.

Parkin, D. J. 1974. "Language switching in Nairobi." In W. Whitely (ed.). *Language in Kenya*. Nairobi: Oxford University Press.

Patkowski, M. S. 1980. "The sensitive period for the acquisition of syntax in a second language." *Language Learning* 30(2):449-472.

Paulston, C. B. 1974. "Linguistic and communicative competence." *TESOL Quarterly* 8(4): 347-362.

Pawley, A., and F. H. Syder. In press. "Two puzzles for linguistic theory: nativelike selection and nativelike fluency." In J. C. Richards and R. W. Schmidt (eds.). *Language and Communication*. London: Longman.

Peck, S. 1978. "Child-child discourse in second language acquisition." In E. M. Hatch (ed.). *Second Language Acquisition: A Book of Readings*. Rowley, Mass.: Newbury House.

Peters, A. 1977. "Language learning strategies: does the whole equal the sum of its parts?" *Language* 53:560-573.

Peters, A. 1980. "The units of language acquisition." *University of Hawaii Working Papers in Linguistics* 12(1):1-72.

Pomerantz, A. 1978. "Compliment responses: notes on the co-operation of multiple constraints." In J. Schenkein (ed.). *Studies in the Organization of Conversational Interaction*. New York: Academic Press.

Praninskas, J. 1975. *Rapid Review of English Grammar*. Englewood Cliffs, N.J.: Prentice-Hall.

Reisman, K. 1974. "Contrapuntal conversation in an Antiguan village." In R. Bauman and J. Sherzer (eds.). *Explorations in the Ethnography of Speaking*. Cambridge: Cambridge University Press.

Richards, J. C. (ed.). 1974. *Error Analysis: Perspectives on Second Language Acquisition*. London: Longman.

Richards, J. C. 1980. "Conversation." *TESOL Quarterly* 14(4):1-31.

Richards, J. C. 1981. "Form and function in second language learning: an example from Singapore." In R. Anderson (ed.). *New Dimensions in Second Language Acquisition Research*. Rowley, Mass.: Newbury House.

Richards, J. C., and R. W. Schmidt (eds.). In press. *Language and Communication*. London: Longman.

Ritchie, W. C. 1978. "Introduction: theory and practice in second language research and teaching." In W. C. Ritchie (ed.). *Second Language Acquisition Research: Issues and Implications*. New York: Academic Press.

Rivers, W. M. 1973. "From linguistic competence to communicative competence." *TESOL Quarterly* 7(1):25-34.

Rivers, W. M. 1980. "Foreign language acquisition: where the real problems lie." *Applied Linguistics* 1(1):48-59.

Rosansky, E. J. 1975. "The critical period for the acquisition of language: some cognitive developmental consideration." *Working Papers on Bilingualism* 6:92-102.

Rubin, J. 1975. "What the good language learner can teach us." *TESOL Quarterly* 9(1):41-51.

Rubin, J. 1981. "Study of cognitive processes in second language learning." *Applied Linguistics* 2(2):117-131.

Rubio, O. 1982. "An attempted cross-cultural investigation of a speech act: the compliment." Unpublished manuscript, University of Pennsylvania.

Rutherford, W. E. 1975, 1977. *Modern English*. 2d ed. 2 vols. New York: Harcourt Brace Jovanovich.

Ryan, E. B., and R. J. Sebastian. In press. "The effects of speech style and social class background on social judgments of speakers." *British Journal of Social and Clinical Psychology*.

Sacks, H., E. Schegloff, and G. Jefferson. 1974. "A simplest systematics for the organization of turn-taking for conversation." *Language* 50:696-735.

Sacks, H., E. Schegloff, and G. Jefferson. 1977. "The preference for self-repair in conversation." *Language* 53:361-382.

Sato, C. J. 1981. "Ethnic styles in classroom discourse." In M. Himes and W. Rutherford (eds.). *On TESOL '81*. Washington, D.C.: TESOL.

Savignon, S. J. 1972. *Communicative Competence: An Experiment in Foreign Language Teaching*. Philadelphia: Center for Curriculum Development.

Scarcella, R. 1978. "Developing discourse competence through role-play." Presented at the 1978 CATESOL Convention, San Francisco.

Scarcella, R. 1979a. "Watch up!: prefabricated routines in adult second language performance." *Working Papers on Bilingualism*. Toronto, OISE 19:79-88.

Scarcella, R. 1979b. "On speaking politely in a second language." In C. Yorio, K. Perkins, and J. Schachter (eds.). *On TESOL '79*. Washington, D.C.: TESOL.

Scarcella, R. In press. "Discourse accent in adult second language performance." Presented at the Ninth Conference on Applied Linguistics: Language Transfer in Language Learning. Ann Arbor, Mich., 1981. To appear in S. Gass and L. Selinker (eds.). *Language Transfer in Language Learning*. Rowley, Mass.: Newbury House.

Scarcella, R., and J. Brunak. 1981. "On speaking politely in a second language." *International Journal of the Sociology of Language* 30.

Schaefer, E. 1982. "An analysis of the discourse and syntax of oral complaints in English." M.A. thesis, UCLA.

Schegloff, E. 1972. "Sequencing in conversational openings." In J. J. Gumperz and D. Hymes (eds.). *Directions in Sociolinguistics*. New York: Holt, Rinehart and Winston.

Schegloff, E., and H. Sacks. 1973. "Opening up closings." *Semiotica* 8:289-327.

Schmidt, R. W., and J. C. Richards. 1980. "Speech acts and second language learning." *Applied Linguistics* 1(2):129-157.

Schumann, J. H. 1975. "Affective factors and the problem of age in second language acquisition." *Language Learning* 25:209-235.

Schumann, J. H. 1977. "Second language acquisition: the pidginization hypothesis." *Language Learning* 26:391-408. Reprinted in E. M. Hatch (ed.). *Second Language Acquisition: A Book of Readings*. Rowley, Mass.: Newbury House.

Schumann, J. H. 1978a. *The Pidginization Process: A Model for Second Language Acquisition*. Rowley, Mass.: Newbury House.

Schumann, J. H. 1978b. "The acculturation model for second language acquisition." In R. C. Gingras (ed.). *Second Language Acquisition and Foreign Language Teaching*. Arlington, Va.: Center for Applied Linguistics.

Schwartz, J. 1980. "The negotiation for meaning: repair in conversations between second language learners of English." In D. Larsen-Freeman (ed.). *Discourse Analysis in Second Language Research*. Rowley, Mass.: Newbury House.

Scollon, R., and S. Scollon. 1980. "Athabaskan-English interethnic communication." Manuscript.

Scotton, C. M. 1980. "Explaining linguistic choices as identity negotiations." In H. Giles, W. P. Robinson, and P. M. Smith (eds.). *Language: Social Psychological Perspectives*. Oxford: Pergamon Press.

Searle, J. R. 1965. "What is a speech act?" In M. Black (ed.). *Philosophy in America*. Ithaca, N.Y.: Cornell University Press.

Searle, J. R. 1969. *Speech Acts: An Essay in the Philosophy of Language*. Cambridge: Cambridge University Press.

Searle, J. R. 1975. "Indirect speech acts." In P. Cole and J. Morgan (eds.). *Speech Acts*. Volume 3 of *Syntax and Semantics*. New York: Academic Press.

Searle, J. R. 1976. "The classification of illocutionary acts." *Language in Society* 5(1):1-14.

Searle, J. R. 1979. *Expression and Meaning.* Cambridge: Cambridge University Press.

Segalowitz, N., and E. Gatbonton. 1977. "Studies of the nonfluent bilingual." In P. A. Hornby (ed.). *Bilingualism: Psychological, Social and Educational Implications.* New York: Academic Press.

Selinker, L. 1972. "Interlanguage." In J. C. Richards (ed.). *Error Analysis: Perspectives on Second Language Acquisition.* London: Longman. Also in J. H. Schumann and N. Stenson (eds.). 1974. *New Frontiers in Second Language Learning.* Rowley, Mass.: Newbury House.

Selinker, L., and J. T. Lamendella. 1979. "The role of extrinsic feedback in interlanguage fossilization." *Language Learning* 29(2):363-376.

Shapira, R. G. 1978. "The non-learning of English: a case study of an adult." In E. M. Hatch (ed.). *Second Language Acquisition: A Book of Readings.* Rowley, Mass.: Newbury House.

Shaver, K. G. 1977. *Principles of Social Psychology.* Cambridge, Mass.: Winthrop.

Shelton, E. 1982. "The compliment: an Afro-American perspective." Unpublished manuscript, University of Pennsylvania.

Shuy, R. W. 1973. "What is the study of variation useful for?" In R. Fasold and R. Shuy (eds.). *Analyzing Variation in Language.* Washington, D.C.: Georgetown University Press.

Simard, L., D. M. Taylor, and H. Giles. 1976. "Attribution processes and interpersonal accommodation in a bilingual setting." *Language and Speech* 19:374-387.

Sinclair, J., and M. Coulthard. 1975. *Towards an Analysis of Discourse.* London: Oxford University Press.

Smith, P. M., H. Giles, and M. Hewstone. 1980. "Sociolinguistics: a social psychological perspective." In H. Giles and R. N. St. Clair (eds.). *The Social and Psychological Contexts of Language.* Hillsdale, N.J.: Lawrence Erlbaum Associates.

Spender, D. 1980. *Man-Made Language.* London: Rutledge and Kegan.

Stauble, A-M. E. 1978. "The process of decreolization: a model for second language development." *Language Learning* 28(1):29-54.

Stauble, A-M. E. 1981. "A comparison of a Spanish-English and Japanese-English second language continuum: verb phrase morphology." Presented to the European North American Workshop on Cross-Linguistic Second Language Research.

Stengal, E. 1939. "On learning a new language." *International Journal of Psychoanalysis* 2:471-479.

Stern, H. H. 1975. "What can we learn from the good language learner?" *Canadian Modern Language Journal* 31(4):304-318.

Strevens, P. 1980. *Teaching English as an International Language: From Practice to Principle.* London: Pergamon Press.

Sullivan, P. 1979. "Conversation: saying hello and goodbye." *TESOL Newsletter* 12(1):29.

Swacker, M. 1975. "The sex of the speaker as a sociolinguistic variable." In B. Thorne and N. Henley (eds.). *Language and Sex: Difference and Dominance.* Rowley, Mass.: Newbury House.

Tajfel, H. 1974. "Social identity and intergroup behavior." *Social Science Information* 13:65-93.

Tajfel, H. (ed.). 1978. *Differentiation between Social Groups: Studies in Intergroup Behavior.* London: Academic Press.

Tannen, D. 1978. "Ethnicity as conversational style." Presented at American Anthropological Association, Los Angeles.

Tannen, D. 1981. "New York Jewish conversational style." *International Journal of the Sociology of Language* 30:133-149.

Tarone, E. 1977. "Conscious communication strategies in interlanguage: a progress report." In H. D. Brown, C. Yorio, and R. Crymes (eds.). *On TESOL '77:* 194-203. Washington, D.C.: TESOL.

Tarone, E. 1979. "Interlanguage as chameleon." *Language Learning* 29(1):181-192.

Taylor, B. P. 1974. "Toward a theory of language acquisition." *Language Learning* 24(1):23-35.

Taylor, B. P. 1975. "Adult language learning strategies and their pedagogical implications." *TESOL Quarterly* 9(4):391-400.

Taylor, B. P., and N. Wolfson. 1978. "Breaking down the free conversation myth." *TESOL Quarterly* 12:31-39.

Taylor, D. M., R. Meynard, and E. Rheault. 1977. "Threat to ethnic identity and second-language learning." In H. Giles (ed.). *Language, Ethnicity and Intergroup Relations.* London: Academic Press.

Taylor, G. 1967. *English Conversational Practice.* New York: McGraw-Hill.

Thakerar, J. N., H. Giles, and J. Cheshire. In press. "Psychological and linguistic parameters of speech accommodation theory." In C. Fraser and K. R. Scherer (eds.). *Social Psychological Dimensions of Language Behavior* (provisional title). Cambridge: Cambridge University Press.

Thomson, A. J., and A. V. Martinet. 1980. *A Practical English Grammar. New Edition.* London: Oxford University Press.

Thorne, B., and N. Henley (eds.). 1975a. *Language and Sex: Difference and Dominance.* Rowley, Mass.: Newbury House.

Thorne, B., and N. Henley. 1975b. "Difference and dominance: an overview of language, gender and society." In B. Thorne and N. Henley (eds.). *Language and Sex: Difference and Dominance.* Rowley, Mass.: Newbury House.

Treffner, C. 1982. "Compliments among Spanish-speaking people." Unpublished manuscript, University of Pennsylvania.

Tucker, G. R. 1974. "The assessment of bilingual and bicultural factors of communication." In S. T. Carey (ed.). *Bilingualism, Biculturalism, and Education.* Edmonton: University of Alberta Press.

Ueda, K. 1974. "Sixteen ways to avoid saying 'no' in Japan." In J. C. Condon and M. Saito (eds.). *Intercultural Encounters with Japan: Communication, Contact and Conflict.* Tokyo: Simui Press.

Updike, J. 1960. *Rabbit Run.* New York: Fawcett Crest.

Upshur, J. 1968. "Four experiments on the relation between foreign language teaching and learning." *Language Learning* 18:111-124.

Upshur, J. A., and A. Palmer. 1974. "Measures of accuracy, communicativity, and social judgments for two classes of foreign language speakers." In A. Verdoodt (ed.). AILA Proceedings, Copenhagen 1972, Volume III: *Applied Sociolinguistics.* Heidelberg: Julius Groos Verlag.

Van Ek, J. 1976. *The Threshold Level for Modern Language Teaching in Schools.* London: Longman.

Vigil, N. A., and J. W. Oller. 1976. "Rule fossilization: A tentative model." *Language Learning* 26(2):281-296.

Watson, K. A. 1974. "Understanding human interaction: the study of everyday life and everyday talk." *Topics in Culture Learning* 2:57-66.

Weeks, T. 1979. *Born to Talk.* Rowley, Mass.: Newbury House.

Weiser, A. 1975. "How to answer a question: purposive devices in conversational strategies." Presented at the Chicago Linguistic Meetings.

Wells, G. 1981. "Becoming a communicator." In G. Wells (ed.). *Learning through Interaction: The Study of Language Development.* Cambridge: Cambridge University Press.

Widdowson, H. 1978. "The significance of simplification." *Studies in Second Language Acquisition* 1(1):11-20.

Wilkins, D. A. 1976. *Notional Syllabuses.* London: Oxford University Press.

Wolfram, W. A. 1974. *Sociolinguistic Aspects of Assimilation.* Urban Language Series 9. Washington, D.C.: Center for Applied Linguistics.

Wolfson, N. 1976. "Speech events and natural speech: some implications for sociolinguistic methodology." *Language in Society* 5:189-209.

Wolfson, N. 1979. "Let's have lunch together sometime: perceptions of insecurity." Presented at the Thirteenth Annual TESOL Conference, Boston.

Wolfson, N. 1981a. "Compliments in cross-cultural perspective." *TESOL Quarterly* 15(2): 117-124.

Wolfson, N. 1981b. "Invitations, compliments and the competence of the native speaker." *International Journal of Psycholinguistics* 24.

Wolfson, N., and J. Manes. 1980. "The compliment as a social strategy." *Papers in Linguistics* 13(3):391-410. Reprinted in *International Journal of Human Communication* 13(3).

Wu, Z. 1981. "Speech act—apology." Los Angeles: ESL Section, Department of English, UCLA.

Yorio, C. A. 1980. "Conventionalized language forms and the development of communicative competence." *TESOL Quarterly* 14(4):433-442.

Zimmerman, D. H., and C. West. 1975. "Sex role, interruptions and silences in communication." In B. Thorne and N. Henley (eds.). *Language and Sex: Difference and Dominance.* Rowley, Mass.: Newbury House.

# SUBJECT INDEX

# AUTHOR INDEX

Vigil, N. A., 165

Waletzky, J., 159
Watson, K. A., 249
Weiner, R., 186
Weiser, A., 13
Wells, G., 243
West, C., 235, 238
Widdowson, Henry G., 33
Wilkins, D., 33, 176

Wolfram, W. A., 199
Wolfson, Nessa, 7, 11, 24, 33, 82, 84, 86, 87,
    94, 115n., 116, 176, 182, 182n.
Wu, Z., 29–30, 31

Yaacov, Ilana, 26
Yorio, C. A., 138, 150, 247

Zimmerman, D. H., 235, 238
Zuengler, Jane, 133, 195, 213n.